IT Security Governance Innovations:

Theory and Research

Daniel Mellado
Spanish Tax Agency, Spain

Luis Enrique Sánchez
University of Castilla – La Mancha, Spain

Eduardo Fernández-Medina
University of Castilla – La Mancha, Spain

Mario Piattini
University of Castilla – La Mancha, Spain

A volume in the Advances in Information Security, Privacy, and Ethics (AISPE) Book Series

Managing Director:	Lindsay Johnston
Senior Editorial Director:	Heather A. Probst
Book Production Manager:	Sean Woznicki
Development Manager:	Joel Gamon
Development Editor:	Myla Merkel
Assistant Acquisitions Editor:	Kayla Wolfe
Typesetter:	Travis Gundrum
Cover Design:	Nick Newcomer

Published in the United States of America by
Information Science Reference (an imprint of IGI Global)
701 E. Chocolate Avenue
Hershey PA 17033
Tel: 717-533-8845
Fax: 717-533-8661
E-mail: cust@igi-global.com
Web site: http://www.igi-global.com

Library of Congress Cataloging-in-Publication Data

IT security governance innovations : theory and research / Daniel Mellado ... [et al.], editors.
    p. cm.
  Includes bibliographical references and index.
  Summary: "This book provides extraordinary research that highlights the main contributions and characteristics of existing approaches, standards, best practices and new trends in IT Security Governance"--Provided by publisher.
  ISBN 978-1-4666-2083-4 (hardcover) -- ISBN 978-1-4666-2084-1 (ebook) -- ISBN 978-1-4666-2085-8 (print & perpetual access) 1. Computer security--Management. 2. Information technology--Security measures. 3. Business enterprises--Security measures. 4. Data protection. I. Mellado, Daniel, 1980-
  QA76.9.A25I894 2013
  005.8--dc23
                                    2012014224

This book is published in the IGI Global book series Advances in Information Security, Privacy, and Ethics (AISPE) Book Series (ISSN: 1948-9730; eISSN: 1948-9749)

British Cataloguing in Publication Data
A Cataloguing in Publication record for this book is available from the British Library.

Advances in Information Security, Privacy, and Ethics (AISPE) Book Series

ISSN: 1948-9730
EISSN: 1948-9749

MISSION

In the digital age, when everything from municipal power grids to individual mobile telephone locations is all available in electronic form, the implications and protection of this data has never been more important and controversial. As digital technologies become more pervasive in everyday life and the Internet is utilized in ever increasing ways by both private and public entities, the need for more research on securing, regulating, and understanding these areas is growing.

The **Advances in Information Security, Privacy, & Ethics (AISPE) Book Series** is the source for this research, as the series provides only the most cutting-edge research on how information is utilized in the digital age.

COVERAGE

- Access Control
- Device Fingerprinting
- Global Privacy Concerns
- Information Security Standards
- Network Security Services
- Privacy-Enhancing Technologies
- Risk Management
- Security Information Management
- Technoethics
- Tracking Cookies

IGI Global is currently accepting manuscripts for publication within this series. To submit a proposal for a volume in this series, please contact our Acquisition Editors at Acquisitions@igi-global.com or visit: http://www.igi-global.com/publish/.

Titles in this Series

For a list of additional titles in this series, please visit: www.igi-global.com

Theory and Practice of Cryptography Solutions for Secure Information Systems
Atilla Elçi (Aksaray University, Turkey) Josef Pieprzyk (Macquarie University, Australia) Alexander G. Chefranov (Eastern Mediterranean University, North Cyprus) Mehmet A. Orgun (Macquarie University, Australia) Huaxiong Wang (Nanyang Technological University, Singapore) and Rajan Shankaran (Macquarie University, Australia)
Information Science Reference • copyright 2013 • 351pp • H/C (ISBN: 9781466640306) • US $195.00 (our price)

IT Security Governance Innovations Theory and Research
Daniel Mellado (Spanish Tax Agency, Spain) Luis Enrique Sánchez (University of Castilla-La Mancha, Spain) Eduardo Fernández-Medina (University of Castilla – La Mancha, Spain) and Mario Piattini (University of Castilla - La Mancha, Spain)
Information Science Reference • copyright 2013 • 390pp • H/C (ISBN: 9781466620834) • US $195.00 (our price)

Threats, Countermeasures, and Advances in Applied Information Security
Manish Gupta (State University of New York at Buffalo, USA) John Walp (M&T Bank Corporation, USA) and Raj Sharman (State University of New York, USA)
Information Science Reference • copyright 2012 • 319pp • H/C (ISBN: 9781466609785) • US $195.00 (our price)

Investigating Cyber Law and Cyber Ethics Issues, Impacts and Practices
Alfreda Dudley (Towson University, USA) James Braman (Towson University, USA) and Giovanni Vincenti (Towson University, USA)
Information Science Reference • copyright 2012 • 342pp • H/C (ISBN: 9781613501320) • US $195.00 (our price)

Information Assurance and Security Ethics in Complex Systems Interdisciplinary Perspectives
Melissa Jane Dark (Purdue University, USA)
Information Science Reference • copyright 2011 • 306pp • H/C (ISBN: 9781616922450) • US $180.00 (our price)

Chaos Synchronization and Cryptography for Secure Communications Applications for Encryption
Santo Banerjee (Politecnico di Torino, Italy)
Information Science Reference • copyright 2011 • 596pp • H/C (ISBN: 9781615207374) • US $180.00 (our price)

Technoethics and the Evolving Knowledge Society Ethical Issues in Technological Design, Research, Development, and Innovation
Rocci Luppicini (University of Ottawa, Canada)
Information Science Reference • copyright 2010 • 322pp • H/C (ISBN: 9781605669526) • US $180.00 (our price)

www.igi-global.com

701 E. Chocolate Ave., Hershey, PA 17033
Order online at www.igi-global.com or call 717-533-8845 x100
To place a standing order for titles released in this series, contact: cust@igi-global.com
Mon-Fri 8:00 am - 5:00 pm (est) or fax 24 hours a day 717-533-8661

Nandan Parameswaran, *University of New South Wales, Australia*

Pradeep Ray, *University of New South Wales, Australia*

B.B.Chakrabarti, *Indian Institute of Management Calcutta, India*

Ambuj Mahanti, *Indian Institute of Management Calcutta, India*

Olav Skjelkvåle Ligaarden, *SINTEF ICT & University of Oslo, Norway*

Atle Refsdal, *SINTEF ICT, Norway*

Ketil Stølen, *SINTEF ICT & University of Oslo, Norway*

Mamoun Alazab, *Australian National University, Australia*

Sitalakshmi Venkatraman, *University of Ballarat, Australia*

Paul Watters, *University of Ballarat, Australia*

Moutaz Alazab, *Deakin University, Australia*

Table of Contents

Section 1
IT Security Governance Landscape

Chapter 1

Oscar Rebollo, Ministry of Labour and Immigration, Spain

Chapter 2

Theodosios Tsiakis, Alexandrian Technological Educational Institute of Thessaloniki, Greece
Theodoros Kargidis, Alexandrian Technological Educational Institute of Thessaloniki, Greece
Aristeidis Chatzipoulidis, University of Macedonia, Greece

Chapter 3

Gemma María Minero Alejandre, University Autónoma of Madrid, Spain

Section 2
Security Standards and Guidelines in the IT Security Governance

Chapter 4

Magdalena Arcilla, Universidad Nacional de Educación a Distancia, Spain
Jose A. Calvo-Manzano, Universidad Politécnica de Madrid, Spain
Mercedes de la Cámara, Universidad Politécnica de Madrid, Spain
Javier Sáenz, Universidad Politécnica de Madrid, Spain
Luis Sánchez, Universidad Politécnica de Madrid, Spain

Section 3
IT Security Governance Innovations

Detailed Table of Contents

Section 1
IT Security Governance Landscape

Chapter 1
    Oscar Rebollo, Ministry of Labour and Immigration, Spain

Security awareness has spread inside many organizations leading them to tackle information security not just as a technical matter, but from a corporate point of view. Information Security Governance (ISG) provides enterprises with means of dealing with the security of their information assets in a comprehensive manner, involving every stakeholder through the whole governance and management processes. Boards of Public and Private Entities cannot remain unaware of this development and should make efforts to include ISG into their business processes. Realizing of this relevant role, scientific literature contains a variety of proposals which define different frameworks to foster ISG inside any corporation. In order to facilitate the adoption of any of them by the public sector, this chapter compiles existing approaches, highlighting the main contributions and characteristics of each one. Senior executives and security managers may need support on their decisions about adopting one of these frameworks, so a comparative analysis is performed. This chapter tries to provide an overview of state of the art of the most current relevant security governance frameworks by means of a comparison through a set of comparative criteria that have been defined and applied to every proposal, so that strengths and weaknesses of each one can be pointed out. These criteria have been selected from a deep analysis of existing ISG papers, including both governance and management aspects.

Chapter 2
    Theodosios Tsiakis, Alexandrian Technological Educational Institute of Thessaloniki, Greece
    Theodoros Kargidis, Alexandrian Technological Educational Institute of Thessaloniki, Greece
    Aristeidis Chatzipoulidis, University of Macedonia, Greece

Most industries have been influenced in different ways by e-commerce, and the banking industry is no exception. Particularly, banks are embracing electronic banking (e-banking) as a service to reach a wider market share, increase customer satisfaction and lower operational costs. This increased supply and demand in e-banking services has caused not only opportunities but also risks. The need to manage and regulate those risks calls for a sound Information Technology Security Governance (ITSG) program as means to deliver value business and mitigate Information Technology (IT) risks. In this regard, the chapter's objectives are to explore, evaluate, and compare the current status and characteristics of Information Security Governance (ISG) approaches for e-banking. Therefore, the authors focus on an analysis of reputed best standards, guidelines on governance, risk management methods, and internal controls currently used for e-banking as means to research which satisfies best ISG objectives. Results show that banks should not be restricted to currently used approaches to ISG for e-banking but should take into consideration benefits and shortcomings other approaches possess. In this regard, the authors propose an ITSG framework for e-banking as a continuous process for assuring ISG objectives. They also highlight the importance of consistent measurement of metrics of ITSG performance with the aid of security content automation protocol.

The protection of the investment and creativity made in producing computer programs and databases by intellectual property rights is still not harmonised internationally. Taking into account that IT is used not only to produce these goods, but also to infringe their intellectual property rights, national laws nowadays also protect the so-called technological protection measures, such as passwords, encryption or copy-protection software, created to protect the intellectual property rights. Besides, IT must fulfill the privacy protection regulations currently in force and the companies using it must carry out the international auditing standards. But intellectual property rights cannot protect simple data and information, apart from the substantial investment made in either obtaining, verification, or presentation of data, by sui generis right over databases (or database right). This chapter examines and compares the current legislations of developed countries in order to find the characteristics -and the criticism- in common.

Section 2
Security Standards and Guidelines in the IT Security Governance

Nowadays, there is an increasing dependence on information and on the systems that provide such information. So, for many organizations, the information and technology that supports them represent the most valuable assets of the company. Research on Information Technology (IT) management practices in many organizations around the world has revealed that most of them are not optimizing their investment on IT. The differentiating factor between those who succeed and those who failed is the participation of management in key IT decisions that must be aligned with the strategic and operational business plans and a proper corporate governance of IT. Corporate governance evaluates and directs the use of IT to support the organization, monitoring its use to achieve plans, and provides guidance to advising, informing or assisting directors, and assuring the compliance with laws and regulations. Some frameworks and models have been developed related to the governance and service management of IT. ITIL® (Information Technology Infrastructure Library) is the most used and extended model related to IT service management. The purpose of this chapter is to describe briefly the main phases and processes related to the ITIL® service lifecycle, detailed information related to the information security management process, and the qualifying system for IT Service Management with ITIL®.

Chapter 5

Hisham M. Abdelsalam, Cairo University, Egypt

Ahmed M Marzouk, IBM Egypt, Egypt

Haitham S. Hamza, Cairo University, Egypt

Banking sector in Egypt is one of the largest business sectors in terms of contributing to country economic growth and in terms of investing in information technology (IT). Thus, implementing a good Information Technology (IT) governance framework inside Egyptian banks is a rather critical issue. The purpose of this chapter is to assess the importance and the implementation of Control Objectives for Information and Related Technology (COBIT) high level processes in the Egyptian banking sector. A total of 25 working banks in Egypt which are registered in the Central Bank of Egypt (CBE) from (public sector, private and joint venture and foreign) banks were interviewed in a series of one-to-one interviews. The results of this study showed that although the majority of interviewed Chief Information Officer (CIO), IT Managers, IT Auditors and others perceived the importance of COBIT high level processes in their organizations, the majority of the Egyptian banks have a below average maturity level for most of the COBIT processes.

Chapter 6

Ioanna Dionysiou, University of Nicosia, Cyprus

Angelika Kokkinaki, University of Nicosia, Cyprus

Skevi Magirou, University of Nicosia, Cyprus

Theodosios Iacovou, University of Nicosia, Cyprus

The purpose of this paper is to propose an IS security governance model to enhance the security of information systems in an organisation by viewing security from a holistic perspective of encompassing information security, information assurance, audit, governance, and compliance. This is achieved through the strategic integration of appropriate frameworks, models, and concepts in information governance, IS service management, and information security. This involves analysing the relevant frameworks, models, and concepts used in the above domains, extracting the best practices for implementing them from the literature and mapping these into an integrated standard. The frameworks identified are Control Objectives for Information and related Technology (COBIT), Information Technology Infrastructure Library (ITIL), ISO 27002, Risk IT, and Payment Card Industry Data Security Standard (PCI DSS). While it is evident that each of these five frameworks serve different purpose of information systems, such as information auditing and governance, facilitating the delivery of high-quality IT services, providing a model managing an Information Security Management System, providing a risk focus, and protection of cardholder data, all of these frameworks have the common objective to secure the IS assets in an organisation. Hence, extraction of the best practices in each of these framework can provide effective security of organisational IS assets rather than adequate security.

Chapter 7

Matthew Nicho, University of Dubai, UAE

The purpose of this paper is to propose an IS security governance model to enhance the security of information systems in an organisation by viewing security from a holistic perspective of encompassing information security, information assurance, audit, governance, and compliance. This is achieved through the strategic integration of appropriate frameworks, models, and concepts in information governance, IS service management, and information security. This involves analysing the relevant frameworks, models, and concepts used in the above domains, extracting the best practices for implementing them from the literature and mapping these into an integrated standard. The frameworks identified are Control Objectives for Information and related Technology (COBIT), Information Technology Infrastructure Library (ITIL), ISO 27002, Risk IT, and Payment Card Industry Data Security Standard (PCI DSS). While it is evident that each of these five frameworks serve different purpose of information systems, such as information auditing and governance, facilitating the delivery of high-quality IT services, providing a model managing an Information Security Management System, providing a risk focus, and protection of cardholder data, all of these frameworks have the common objective to secure the IS assets in an organisation. Hence, extraction of the best practices in each of these framework can provide effective security of organisational IS assets rather than adequate security.

Section 3
IT Security Governance Innovations

Chapter 8

Shrikant Tiwari, IT-Banaras Hindu University, India
Sanjay Kumar Singh, IT-Banaras Hindu University, India

To establish the identity of an individual is very critical with the advancement of technology in networked society. Thus, there is need for reliable user authentication technique to solve the growing demand for high level of Information Security Governance (ISG) depending on the requirement. Biometrics can be explained as the method to recognize an individual based on physical (face, fingerprint, ear, iris, etc.) or behavioral (voice, signature, gait, etc.) features to identify an individual person. Nowadays, biometric systems are being used for different purposes for information security like commercial, defense, government, and forensic applications as a means of establishing identity and to mitigate the risk which is one of the important objectives of Information Security Governance. In this chapter, an attempt has been made to explain the use and proper selection of biometric trait to help in Information Security Governance.

Chapter 9

Partha Saha, Indian Institute of Management Calcutta, India
Ambuj Mahanti, Indian Institute of Management Calcutta, India

IT security governance bridges the gap between corporate governance and information security which is defined as the protection of information and other valuable assets in the organization from a wide range of threats in order to maximize ROI (Return On Investment) and minimize risk. These risks emanate from multiple sources like espionage, sabotage, malicious code, computer hacking, sophisticated denial of service attacks, vandalism, fire, flood, and other natural or manmade calamities. Information security in an organization is achieved by implementing suitable sets of safeguards or controls, including policies, processes, procedures etc. These controls need to be established, monitored, and suitably implemented across organization to ensure smooth functioning of business. There are existing sets of internationally recognized standards like CobiT, ISO17799, and others available, which are country and industry specific. These standards include a set of specific controls. Organizations operating in a particular country should be compliant of these standards, and as often these are legal obligations. Stakeholders and auditors are concerned with discrepancies that accrue in the implementation phases of implementation of these standards in any organization. Compliance Auditing (CA) is the process that identifies and analyses any misalignment of the organization's rules and policies with respect to government regulations/industry best practices, which they are supposed to implement. A distinct challenge in compliance auditing is the measurement of discrepancies between company policies, controls, and industry standards vis-a-vis actual organizational practices.

Chapter 10

Olav Skjelkvåle Ligaarden, SINTEF ICT & University of Oslo, Norway

Atle Refsdal, SINTEF ICT, Norway

Ketil Stølen, SINTEF ICT & University of Oslo, Norway

Systems of systems are collections of systems interconnected through the exchange of services. Their often complex service dependencies and very dynamic nature make them hard to analyze and predict with respect to quality in general, and security in particular. In this chapter, the authors put forward a method for the capture and monitoring of impact of service dependencies on the security of provided services. The method is divided into four main steps focusing on documenting the system of systems and IT service dependencies, establishing the impact of service dependencies on risk to security of provided services, identifying measureable indicators for dynamic monitoring, and specifying their design and deployment, respectively. The authors illustrate the method in an example-driven fashion based on a case within power supply.

Chapter 11

Mamoun Alazab, Australian National University, Australia

Sitalakshmi Venkatraman, University of Ballarat, Australia

Paul Watters, University of Ballarat, Australia

Moutaz Alazab, Deakin University, Australia

Detecting malicious software or malware is one of the major concerns in information security governance as malware authors pose a major challenge to digital forensics by using a variety of highly sophisticated stealth techniques to hide malicious code in computing systems, including smartphones. The current detection techniques are futile, as forensic analysis of infected devices is unable to identify all the hidden malware, thereby resulting in zero day attacks. This chapter takes a key step forward to address this issue and lays foundation for deeper investigations in digital forensics. The goal of this chapter is, firstly, to unearth the recent obfuscation strategies employed to hide malware. Secondly, this chapter proposes innovative techniques that are implemented as a fully-automated tool, and experimentally tested to exhaustively detect hidden malware that leverage on system vulnerabilities. Based on these research investigations, the chapter also arrives at an information security governance plan that would aid in addressing the current and future cybercrime situations.

Foreword

The French statesman Georges Clemenceau once said that "warfare is too serious a matter to entrust to military men." Today, the same thing could be said about information warfare, which is fought every day over the Internet and on corporate networks. Indeed the permanent and global nature of security threats and the increasing complexity of IT infrastructures are leading organizations worldwide to revise their approach to information security. Hiring and entrusting the ICT equivalent of military men, i.e. security technologists and white-hat hackers, is no longer enough.

Most organizations fully recognize that they need to continuously improve their internal security culture, establishing and maintaining proper security governance processes. However, this is easier said than done. Some European companies still rely on obsolete security standards like the 17799, which were developed when current ICT threats and complexities were still unheard of. The more recent ISO/ IEC 270001 standard has finally introduced a notion of security policy life-cycle; but in today's dynamic ICT environments, emerging threats and sudden technology changes may require much more agile decision-making procedures. For all these reasons, establishing a security governance process tailored to an organization's needs is still considered more an art than a science in most domains.

This book, written by internationally recognized leaders in this field, takes a significant step toward a scientifically sound, repeatable approach to information security governance. Its initial section takes a fresh look at existing security governance frameworks, challenging conventional wisdom on what information security actually is. Also, this section provides some sound advice on how to choose the right security governance framework and processes for a specific organization in critical domains like banking and healthcare. Another important contribution is providing a clear outline of the legal issues underlying corporate security governance, including the (law-mandated or contractual) responsibilities of the different organizational roles.

The second section of the book deals with enterprise-level security governance processes. It covers most standards for security governance at the enterprise level, highlighting their different models for decision-making, including risk-based ones. Describing some interesting case studies, this section leads the reader toward a dynamic, flexible security governance based on decentralized decision making, where security objectives and strategies are the main focus – without forgetting traditional security risks and controls.

The third section of the book looks at a number of open frontier issues that are likely to accompany information security and security governance into the 21st century. This fascinating set of research essays, each suitable for supporting a Ph.D. level short course, goes from the increasingly important role of biometrics to malware, risk monitoring, and ontology-based models.

As a whole, this book is a "must read" for both advanced practitioners and researchers working on security governance issues. From a researcher's point of view, the book chapters and their rich bibliography are ideal starting points for young scientists looking for a new topic, or for experienced researchers wishing to gain a good understanding of the state of the art in this field. However, this book will be even more useful to practitioners working toward establishing a sound security governance process in their organization. In order to improve security, organizations have to understand the different assumptions underlying the standards and the distinctive features of different decision-making procedures. The techniques discussed in the book are a key prerequisite to implement the "right" security governance practices, ensuring that crucial decisions about information security are taken in the best possible way.

Ernesto Damiani
University of Milan, Italy

Ernesto Damiani *is involved in several projects at different institutions. He is a Professor at the Dept. of Computer Technology, University of Milan, Italy. Since Jan 2008, he has been the Head of the University of Milan's Ph.D. School in Computer Science. He holds visiting positions at several other places, including: UTS: University of Technology, Sydney, Australia; eBMS, University of Lecce, Italy; Computer Science Dept, LaTrobe University, Melbourne, Australia; and Computer Science Dept, Free University of Bozen, Italy. He is a Senior Member of the IEEE, and a Distinguished Scientist/ Member of ACM.*

Preface

IT security can no longer be considered as a technical issue, but it is a process that involves the whole company. It is widely accepted that security needs to reach the governance level so that senior directors understand the risks and the opportunities, and have assurance that these are being properly and continuously managed.

This relevant role assumption has caused the development of a lot of initiatives (frameworks, standards, etc.) in the last few years to foster IT Governance inside any corporation, such as CobiT or ISO/IEC standards (ISO/IEC 27000, ISO/IEC 38500…). From a global perspective, this diversity, also found in the context of security technical issues, has made us consider its application as a very complex and hard process to understand with a very difficult implantation curve.

In order to facilitate the adoption of IT Security Governance by the different types of organizations, the objective of this book is to compile existing approaches, standards, best practices, and new trends in IT Security Governance. The book will highlight the main contributions and characteristics of each one. From the theoretical and practical perspectives, this book is intended to address security during the whole IT Security Governance implantation lifecycle. From IT risk-based security goals and policies up to IT security governance tools and metrics implemented by most sound IT security standards or guidelines for each specific scenario. This book can also help managers to be aware of limitations of current approaches and the gaps which need to be covered in order to achieve a complete integration of the security governance within the global governance.

This book aims to provide a theoretical and academic description of IT security governance issues, and practical and innovative guidelines, standards, models, and frameworks for implementing IT security governance in organizations.

The proposed book could serve as a reference for CEOs and CIOs, security managers, systems specialists, systems architects, security developers, information security professionals, software engineers, project managers, and computer science students.

Finally, this book will allow the knowledge and experience of renowned ICT Governance professionals to be shared, and thus supposes an important reference with which to assist companies to obtain their strategic goals.

GENERAL PICTURE OF INFORMATION TECHNOLOGY GOVERNANCE

Information Technology (IT) Governance is the component of Corporate Governance focused on the management of new technologies inside any organization. As any governance area, it does not only include the lower levels operational aspects, but also the higher tactical and strategical ones, guaranteeing an alignment of the company's utilization of technologies and IT investment with the global objectives. Its origin arises with the necessity to apply to the company's IT the same procedures that have been developed over other governance areas to foster its competitive advantage, making it essential in today's economy that the board of directors of any organization are responsible of its IT usage. In this book's way to define ISG, it is also important to understand previously IT Governance because, under some perspectives, ISG can be considered a sub-component of IT Governance. As a result, ISG inherits its core characteristics from both Corporate Governance and IT Governance.

What is IT Governance?

A first general approach to IT Governance may be to state that it is the decision rights and accountability framework for encouraging desirable behaviors in the use of IT (Weill and Ross 2004). It is important to highlight from this definition that the responsibility of IT Governance, as any other governance subject, belongs to the board of directors and high executives. Usually this responsibility is delegated on the IT department, but the accountability of the use of IT remains still in the board.

Offering more detail, the ITGI defines IT Governance as *the responsibility of the board of directors and executive management. It is an integral part of enterprise governance and consists of the leadership and organizational structures and processes that ensure that the organization's IT sustains and extends the organization's strategies and objectives* (ITGI 2003). The responsibility of the board is again mentioned, and positions IT governance as part of the Corporate Governance. As a result, it cannot be considered as an isolated discipline, but in coordination with other governance structures. IT is linked to other organizational key assets (like financial, human, or physical) so it must be included in the same decision making processes.

Other definitions can be found on literature, but most of them focus on the same highlighted aspects. Summarizing, in (Webb, Pollard, et al., 2006) twelve other definitions are analyzed to suggest the following one that unifies the main concepts: *IT Governance is the strategic alignment of IT with the business such that maximum business value is achieved through the development and maintenance of effective IT control and accountability, performance management and risk management.* In developing this definition, authors realize that IT Governance shares many similarities with Corporate Governance and with Strategic Information Systems Planning. This analysis shows that IT Governance is built upon five elements, which are:

- Strategic Alignment.
- Delivery of business value through IT.
- Performance Management.
- Risk Management.
- Control and Accountability.

These five elements are aligned with the ITGI statement which indicates that IT Governance's purpose is to direct IT endeavours, to ensure that IT's performance meets the following objectives:

- Alignment of IT with the enterprise and realisation of the promised benefits.
- Use of IT to enable the enterprise by exploiting opportunities and maximising benefits.
- Responsible use of IT resources.
- Appropriate management of IT-related risks.

The same as Corporate Governance is conformed by multiple sub-governance areas, one of which is IT Governance; IT Governance itself can be subdivided in multiple governance components. Some examples of these areas are: Performance and Capacity Governance, IT Services Governance, IT Resources Governance, and Information Security Governance (ISG).

Why is IT Governance Important?

Information Technologies have become an essential element of every business, showing the potential of offering new opportunities to obtain competitive advantages and increase productivity. These new technologies have burst into traditional procedures transforming them so that more efficient results are obtained and more value is created with the same resources. Even more, the widespread use of IT has allowed the creation and delivering of new market services based fundamentally on intangible assets such as information, knowledge trust or reputation. Therefore, it is of paramount importance an effective governance of IT to achieve enterprise goals.

Although these new technologies are fundamental to sustain many business operations, they also generate new risks. A sight on how strongly enterprises rely on IT is enough to understand the dependence generated by most companies on the new networked economy. With IT so intrinsically imbricate within enterprises, boards of directors need to analyze it specifically to determine how it can contribute to the execution of the business strategy. Therefore, IT reaches the strategic decision level because of its contribution to the company's growth and innovation, and its support to the organization's objectives.

Despite the importance of the IT risks generated and the high volume of investments associated with IT, traditionally it has not been an issue tackled by the board of directors. In doing so, the governance body cannot expect to deliver quality IT solutions on time and budget, and business losses may appear in the form of higher costs, damaged reputations, or less efficient core processes. IT has been usually derived to technical departments and treated separately of the business as an independent area, which has proven a poor governance strategy.

Best Practices on IT Governance

To finish the discussion on IT Governance, the authors introduce existing proposals of best practices on this subject. Although several guidelines and recommendations exist in literature over IT Governance, the most widespread one is Control Objectives for Information and related Technology (CobiT), developed by the ITGI (ITGI 2007). CobiT introduces a framework for IT Governance which is built upon a set of 34 high level processes grouped into four domains; detailing the control objectives, metrics, maturity models, and other management guidelines for each of these processes.

The 34 high level processes are grouped into the following domains:

- Plan and Organize
- Acquire and Implement
- Deliver and Support
- Monitor and Evaluate

These domains can be followed in an iterative cycle through which the defined processes are successively executed to achieve adequate governance.

CobiT has become a "de facto" standard for IT auditing, offering a structured guideline of relevant processes and control objectives that need to be analyzed within the IT auditory. But going a step further from an auditing tool to an IT Governance tool, CobiT can be used by any company to achieve a higher degree of IT Governance. An organization may choose which of the 34 processes decides to implement and follow its control objectives to guarantee its success. Also, once the processes are deployed, CobiT's maturity models offer a benchmarking of the fulfilment degree of each matter inside the enterprise, which can result in a performance indicator of IT Governance.

CobiT framework identifies five focus areas on IT Governance:

- Strategic alignment
- Value delivery
- Resource management
- Risk management
- Performance measurement

These five areas are clearly aligned with the five elements of IT Governance highlighted when the definition was presented.

OVERVIEW OF INFORMATION security GOVERNANCE

Information Security Governance (ISG) is focused in the appropriate governance and management of any company's information assets. As indicated in the previous section, ISG is broadly considered a component of IT Governance because many Information Security aspects are related with IT (electronic data bases, information systems, etc.). But ISG is also considered a direct component of Corporate Governance, when dealing with aspects not related with IT; for example with legal issues, human resources or physical security. This double dependence appears because of the multidimensional nature of Information Security, which in many ways relies on IT procedures, but also includes some separate aspects.

Introduction to Information Security

Information has become a critical asset of any organization. The fast adoption of IT by all the business activities of every enterprise has arisen the necessity to manage carefully the company's information. Nowadays, information is an asset as important as capital or work. This reality is even more pressing on new generation companies in which information is part of their core business.

Enterprise security is a classical term that reflects the efforts performed to avoid business risks, letting the company to surpass any threat that may jeopardize its survival. The traditional security concept needs to be expanded in order to include the mentioned information assets, whose combination is known as Information Security.

Security and information are therefore two closely linked terms, which is shown in the fact that any company's information is as good as the security mechanisms it has implemented over it. Unreliable information due to wrong security policies generates uncertainty and mistrust, impacting negatively on every business area. Otherwise, secure information is a sign of certainty which contributes to generate value inside and outside the company.

Information Security is a business function whose mission is to establish security policies and their associated procedures and control elements over their information assets, with the goal of guaranteeing their authenticity, confidentiality, availability and integrity. Ensuring these four characteristics is the core function of Information Security:

- Authenticity allows trustful operations by guaranteeing that the handler of information is whoever it claims to be
- Confidentiality is understood in the sense that only authorized users access the information, avoiding its spreading among users without the proper rights
- Availability refers to being able of accessing information whenever is necessary, guaranteeing that offered services can be used when needed
- Integrity is the quality which shows that the information has not been modified by third parties, and assures its correctness and completeness

As stated previously, Information Security has a multidimensional nature because it involves many different subjects that must be implemented coordinately in order to secure the information assets. In (Solms and Solms 2009) authors identify a list of dimensions, some of which are:

- Governance Dimension
- Management Dimension
- Ethical Dimension
- Legal Dimension
- Insurance Dimension
- Personnel/Human Dimension
- Technical Dimension
- Audit Dimension
- IT Forensics Dimension

The elements of this list may be clearly differentiated between those related with IT and those more connected to other enterprise areas. This is the reason why Information Security, although very linked with IT, goes beyond its boundaries into other crucial aspects. This point of view of Information Security is developed in the following section to introduce a definition of ISG.

What is Information Security Governance?

After introducing Corporate Governance and IT Governance we are now in conditions of understanding Information Security Governance (ISG) as part of the governance activities that every enterprise should develop. Through the previous steps of this introduction, we have positioned ISG under the concepts of both Corporate Governance and IT Governance. So having set the scope of ISG, it is time to continue with its definition.

A first approach to ISG is given by the ITGI: *Information security governance consists of the leadership, organisational structures and processes that safeguard information. Information security governance is a subset of enterprise governance that provides strategic direction, ensures that objectives are achieved, manage risks appropriately, uses organisational resources responsibly, and monitors the success or failure of the enterprise security programme* (ITGI 2006). This definition stresses the dependency of ISG with respect to Corporate Governance, and includes the global objectives proposed in IT Governance, which are inherited (strategic alignment, risk management, resource management, performance measurement, and value delivery).

Following the governance argumentation, ISG can be defined as *an overarching category directly affecting the entire policy management process; doing so also stresses that governance is not merely an internal organizational process but can consist of external attributes such as the involvement of a board of directors* (Knapp, Morris et al. 2009). In this case, authors highlight that the governance aspect is not just some internal matter of the company, but it must be projected to its exterior.

A clear introduction of the stakeholders' roles can be found in (Rastogi and Solms 2006): *ISG consists of the frameworks for decision-making and performance measurement that Board of Directors and Executive Management implement to fulfil their responsibility of providing oversight, as part of their overall responsibility for protecting stakeholder value, for effective implementation of Information Security in their Organization*. Therefore, the responsibility of the board of directors and high executives within ISG is unquestionable, as with other governance areas.

The National Institute of Standards and Technology (NIST) proposes: *ISG can be defined as the process of establishing and maintaining a framework and supporting management structure and processes to provide assurance that information security strategies are aligned with and support business objectives, are consistent with applicable laws and regulations through adherence to policies and internal controls, and provide assignment of responsibility, all in an effort to manage risk* (Bowen, Hash, et al., 2006). This approach focuses on the compliance on current legislation, due to the public nature of the NIST, and also introduces the concept of risk management specifically applied to Information Security.

Finally, deepening in its relationship with Information Security, ISG is defined as *the establishment and maintenance of the control environment to manage the risks relating to the confidentiality, integrity and availability of information and its supporting processes and systems* (Moulton and Coles 2003), where the main objectives of Information Security are recalled (confidentiality, integrity, and availability).

Why is Information Security Governance Important?

A direct consequence of the multidimensional nature of Information Security, it can no longer be considered just as a technical issue that can be assessed through hardware implementations, but as a process that involves the whole company (Pasquinucci 2007). Responsibility for security management has traditionally been limited to operational and technical managers, but it is essential to extend it to the governance levels. A greater involvement of boards of directors, executive management and business process owners is required, so that senior directors understand the risks and opportunities, and assure that these are being properly and continuously managed (Williams 2001).

A first motivation to introduce Information Security into the governance level is explained by the legal responsibility for security breaches. Both companies and individuals are everyday more aware of the necessity of increasing security in everyday activities. This increasing concern has not only forced companies to tackle this security issues, but has also reached legislators to take action. Actually, governments have already established a significant legislative and regulatory regime around Information Security (BSA 2003), most of which focus the security responsibilities around the governance bodies. The main drawback, especially for non-local organizations, is that no uniform regulatory framework exists in every country, so that the ISG area must consider specific implications of each applicable region.

Besides legal constrictions, information assets are too valuable for any enterprise to allow unnecessary risks that can threaten its own survival. On the one hand, security breaches can damage seriously the image of the firm, which is not easily recovered, or can result in substantial penalties. On the other hand, an adequate management of Information Security and its related assets may be perceived positively by clients and result in a competitive advantage to the organization.

When Information Security is addressed at the corporate level as part of the enterprise planning process, it is afforded greater ownership by employees of the firm. Greater ownership means that employees are more responsible and accountable for the security of their assets, and view security not as a barrier to success, but as an enabler. Improved ownership also contributes to an organizational culture of secure computing (Johnston and Hale 2009).

Therefore, developing an ISG programme is not just a matter of legal compliance, but an investment on the company's self-interest. However, when organizations delegate Information Security on lower management and technical levels, they can not expect to receive enough attention in proportion to the magnitude of the handled risks. These intermediate levels usually do not have at their disposal the budgets to tackle these security threats, and lack of the decision level to manage these responsibilities.

Additionally, to help organizations in implementing ISG there have been developed numerous guidelines. Each approach focuses on different specific aspects of ISG, but it does not exist a recognized standard that may aid companies defining what activities should be accomplished and how to perform them.

AIMS OF THIS BOOK

This book aims to provide a theoretical and academic description of IT Security Governance issues, and practical and innovative guidelines, models and techniques for implementing IT security governance practices in organizations.

The book covers the following topics:

- An in-depth review of the major IT security governance frameworks, IT security governance legal issues, and IT security governance overview in e-banking.
- Approaches based on main IT security governance standards, guidelines, and models, both theoretical and practical perspectives, will be presented.
- Practical and innovative guidelines, models, and techniques for implementing IT security governance practices in organizations will be described.

ORGANIZATION OF THIS BOOK

This book is divided into three sections and eleven chapters, each section addressing a state-of-the-art topic in IT Security Governance. They are as follows: IT Security Governance Landscape, Security Standards and Guidelines in the IT Security Governance, and IT Security Governance Innovations.

Section 1: IT Security Governance Landscape

1. Overview of Key Information Security Governance Frameworks

This chapter tries to provide an overview of state of the art of the most current relevant security governance frameworks by means of a comparison through a set of comparative criteria that have been defined and applied to every proposal, so that strengths and weaknesses of each one can be pointed out. Most of the selected frameworks can be used as a starting point towards integrating security inside their processes, but this paper helps managers to be aware of its limitations and the gaps which need to be covered in order to achieve a complete integration.

2. IT Security Governance in E-Banking

In this chapter the authors are focused on an analysis of reputed best standards, guidelines on governance, Risk Management methods, and internal controls currently used for e-banking (one of the most important sectors in IT security governance) as means to research which satisfies best Information Security Governance (ISG) objectives. They propose an ITSG framework for e-banking as a continuous process for assuring ISG objectives. They also highlight the importance of consistent measurement of metrics of ITSG performance with the aid of Security Content Automation Protocol.

3. IT Security Governance Legal Issues

IT must fulfill the privacy protection regulations currently in force and the companies using it must carry out the international auditing standards. But intellectual property rights cannot protect simple data and information, apart from the substantial investment made in either obtaining, verification or presentation of data, by sui generis right over databases (or database right). This chapter examines and compares the current legislations of developed countries in order to find the characteristics -and the criticism- in common.

Section 2: Security Standards and Guidelines in the IT Security Governance

4. Information Technology Service Management

ITIL® (Information Technology Infrastructure Library) is the most used and extended model related to IT service management. The purpose of this chapter is to describe briefly the main phases and processes related to the ITIL® service lifecycle, detailed information related to the information security management process, and the qualifying system for IT Service Management with ITIL®, with regard to IT Security Governance.

5. Assessing the Maturity of Control Objectives for Information and Related Technology (COBIT) Framework in the Egyptian Banking Sector

Banking sector is one of the most important sectors in IT security governance and in Egypt is one of the largest business sectors in terms of contributing to country economic growth and in terms of investing in IT. Thus, implementing a good IT security governance framework inside Egyptian banks is a rather critical issue. The purpose of this chapter is to assess the importance and the implementation of Control Objectives for Information and Related Technology (COBIT) high level processes in the Egyptian banking sector under a practical perspective.

6. Adoption of ISO 27001 in Cyprus Enterprises: Current State and Challenges

This chapter presents the findings of an investigation on current IT security governance practices in Cypriot organizations, including enterprises and public sector divisions. In order to gain knowledge on the deployed security technologies by organizations, a survey was conducted and concluded in late 2010. The survey primarily examined compliance of enterprise current security policies and procedures with ISO/IEC 27001 security guidelines. A research analysis has been performed, which identified that security mechanisms and the management of IT resources may be improved on a number of aspects. Based on the research findings, an assessment of the viability of ISO/IEC 27001 in Cyprus is given as well as recommendations on the further deployment of ISO/IEC 27001.

7. An Information Governance Model for Information Security Management

The purpose of this chapter is to propose an IS security governance model to enhance the security of information systems in an organisation by viewing security from a holistic perspective of encompassing information security, information assurance, audit, governance and compliance. This is achieved through the strategic integration of appropriate frameworks, models, and concepts in information governance, IS service management, and information security. The frameworks identified are Control Objectives for Information and related Technology (COBIT), Information Technology Infrastructure Library (ITIL), ISO 27002, Risk IT and Payment Card Industry Data Security Standard (PCI DSS).

Section 3: IT Security Governance Innovations

8. Information Security Governance Using Biometrics

To establish the identity of an individual is very critical with the advancement of technology in networked society. Thus there is need for reliable user authentication technique to solve the growing demand for high level of Information Security Governance (ISG) depending on the requirement. Biometrics can be explained as the method to recognize an individual based on physical (face, fingerprint, ear, iris, etc.) or behavioral (voice, signature, gait, etc.) to identify an individual person. Nowadays, biometric systems are being used for different purposes for information security like commercial, defense, government, and forensic applications as a means of establishing identity and to mitigate the risk which is one of the important objectives of Information Security Governance. In this book chapter, an attempt has been made to explain the use and proper selection of biometric trait to help in Information Security Governance.

9. Ontology Based Multi Agent Modelling for Information Security Measurement

In this chapter the authors discuss a framework for building a multi agent information model that captures the notion of compliance semantics and present it using event ontology. The authors also present a methodology for computing the compliance measure of organizational practice with regulatory/standards requirements capturing the relevance of the ontological concepts using fuzzy weights towards estimating the compliance. Without any loss of generality the authors show their technique applied in some particular cases of Information Technology - Security Techniques (AS/NZS ISO/IEC 17799:2006 & CobiT4.1) where the authors present an ontology, construct semantic model, and derive compliance rules from the information security controls. Finally the authors compare the two standards and discuss how the model can be used as a decision support system tool at the hands of auditors in the chosen domain in order to improve the auditory of the security governance of Information Systems.

10. Using Indicators to Monitor Security Risk in Systems of Systems: How to Capture and Measure the Impact of Service Dependencies on the Security of Provided Services

In this chapter, the authors put forward a method for the capture and monitoring of impact of service dependencies on the security of provided services. The method is divided into four main steps focusing on documenting the system of systems and it service dependencies, establishing the impact of service dependencies on risk to security of provided services, identifying measureable indicators for dynamic monitoring, and specifying their design and deployment, respectively. The authors illustrate the method in an example-driven fashion based on a case within power supply.

11. Information Security Governance: The Art of Detecting Hidden Malware.

The goal of this chapter is, firstly to unearth the recent obfuscation strategies employed to hide malware. Secondly, this chapter proposes innovative techniques that are implemented as a fully-automated tool, and experimentally tested to exhaustively detect hidden malware that leverage on system vulnerabilities. Based on these research investigations, the chapter also arrives at an information security governance plan that would aid in addressing the current and future cyber-crime situations.

Daniel Mellado
Rey Juan Carlos University, Spain

Luis Enrique Sánchez
University of Castilla – La Mancha, Spain

Eduardo Fernández-Medina
University of Castilla – La Mancha, Spain

Mario Piattini
University of Castilla – La Mancha, Spain

REFERENCES

Bowen, P., & Hash, J. (2006). Information security governance . In *Information security handbook: A guide for managers* (pp. 2–19). National Institute of Standards and Technology.

BSA. (2003). *Information security governance: Toward a framework for action.*

ITGI. (2003). *Board briefing on IT governance* (2nd ed.).

ITGI. (2006). *Information security governance: Guidance for boards of directors and executive management* (2nd ed.).

ITGI. (2007). *Control objectives for information and related technology* (COBIT 4.1).

Johnston, A. C., & Hale, R. (2009). Improved security through information security governance. *Communications of the ACM, 52,* 126–129.

Knapp, K. J., & Morris, M. F. (2009). Information security policy: An organizational-level process model. *Computers & Security, 28,* 493–508.

Moulton, R., & Coles, R. S. (2003). Applying information security governance. *Computers & Security, 22*(7).

OECD. (2004). *OECD principles of corporate governance.*

Pasquinucci, A. (2007). Security, risk analysis and governance: A practical approach. *Computer Fraud & Security, 7,* 12–14.

Rastogi, R., & van Solms, R. (2006). Information security governance - A re-definition. *International Federation for Information Processing, 193,* 223–236.

van Solms, S. H., & van Solms, R. (2009). *Information security governance.* Springer.

Webb, P., Pollard, C., et al. (2006). Attempting to define IT governance: Wisdom or folly? *Proceedings of the 39th Hawaii International Conference on System Sciences.*

Weill, P., & Ross, J. W. (2004). *IT governance on one page.*

Wikipedia. (2011). *Corporate governance.* Retrieved from http://en.wikipedia.org/wiki/Corporate_governance

Williams, P. (2001). Information security governance. *Information Security Technical Report, 6*(3), 60–70.

Acknowledgment

This book is part of the following projects: MEDUSAS (IDI-20090557) and ORIGIN (IDI-2010043(1-5), financed by the Centre for Industrial Technological Development (CDTI) and the FEDER, MAGO-PEGASO (TIN2009-13718-C02-01) awarded by the Spanish Ministry for Science and Technology and SERENIDAD (PEII11-0327-7035) and SISTEMA (PII2I09-0150-3135) financed by the Council of Education and Science of the Castilla-La Mancha Regional Government.

The editors would like to thank all the people that collaborated in making this book a reality. First, we would like to thank the team of IGI Global. In particular, we would like to thank Myla Harty for guiding throughout the editing process; and the members of the Editorial Advisory Board, Julia H. Allen, Haris Mouratidis, Jan Jürjens, Sushil Jajodia, Antoni Bosch, and Javier Garzás for their constant support and advice.

We would like also to express our gratitude to the authors of the chapters for their insights and contributions to this book. Most of them also served as reviewers for chapters written by other authors. We wish to thank all of them their productive and complete reviews. We would like also to thank Prof. Ernesto Damiani for accepting to write the Foreword of this book.

Section 1
IT Security Governance Landscape

Chapter 1
Overview of Key Information Security Governance Frameworks

Oscar Rebollo
Ministry of Labour and Immigration, Spain

ABSTRACT

Security awareness has spread inside many organizations leading them to tackle information security not just as a technical matter, but from a corporate point of view. Information Security Governance (ISG) provides enterprises with means of dealing with the security of their information assets in a comprehensive manner, involving every stakeholder through the whole governance and management processes. Boards of Public and Private Entities cannot remain unaware of this development and should make efforts to include ISG into their business processes. Realizing of this relevant role, scientific literature contains a variety of proposals which define different frameworks to foster ISG inside any corporation. In order to facilitate the adoption of any of them by the public sector, this chapter compiles existing approaches, highlighting the main contributions and characteristics of each one. Senior executives and security managers may need support on their decisions about adopting one of these frameworks, so a comparative analysis is performed. This chapter tries to provide an overview of state of the art of the most current relevant security governance frameworks by means of a comparison through a set of comparative criteria that have been defined and applied to every proposal, so that strengths and weaknesses of each one can be pointed out. These criteria have been selected from a deep analysis of existing ISG papers, including both governance and management aspects.

DOI: 10.4018/978-1-4666-2083-4.ch001

INTRODUCTION

As results show, each proposal mentioned in the abstract focuses on different aspects of ISG giving priority to some of the defined criteria, and none of them covers the entire required spectrum. Most of the selected frameworks can be used by any public or private organization as a starting point towards integrating security inside their processes, but this paper helps managers to be aware of its limitations and the gaps which need to be covered in order to achieve a complete integration. Special attention has been given to public sector due to the importance of security on this sector.

Consequently, more investigation is needed to fulfill detected gaps and define an ISG framework that organizations can rely on, and which offers security guarantees of covering every information asset of the company.

Information Technology (IT) security can no longer be considered as a technical issue that can be assessed through hardware implementations, but it is a process that involves the whole company (Pasquinucci, 2007). It is widely accepted that security needs to reach the governance level so that senior directors understand the risks and the opportunities, and have assurance that these are being properly and continuously managed (Williams, 2001). The motivations to introduce IT in the corporate executive agenda is twofold: many countries have developed legislation to hold responsibilities for security breaches (BSA, 2003, Hardy, 2006), and achieving a higher security degree may become a competitive advantage to the organization (Humphreys, 2008, Johnston and Hale, 2009).

Public entities are also involved with these considerations, as higher IT security usually strengthens the trust relationship between Administrations and their citizens. A recent European Union research shows existing gaps related with security and privacy concerns that need to be fulfilled in the field of electronic governance and policy modeling (Crossroad, 2010).

All these objectives may be achieved through Information Security Governance (ISG) which is an overarching category directly affecting the entire policy management process (Knapp et al., 2009). There is not a unique definition of ISG, but among the most widespread conceptions it is generally accepted that ISG consists of the leadership, organizational structures and processes that safeguard information (ITGI, 2006b). ISG can also be defined more specifically as the process of establishing and maintaining a framework and supporting management structure and processes to provide assurance that information security strategies are aligned with and support business objectives, are consistent with applicable laws and regulations through adherence to policies and internal controls, and provide assignment of responsibility, all in an effort to manage risk (Bowen et al., 2006). Finally, focusing on the stakeholders' roles, ISG consists of the frameworks for decision-making and performance measurement that Board of Directors and Executive Management implement to fulfill their responsibility of providing oversight, as part of their overall responsibility for protecting stakeholder value, for effective implementation of Information Security in their Organization (Rastogi and Solms, 2006).

In order to secure their information assets, companies need to adopt an ISG framework that assures effective implementation and makes process operational (Corporate Governance Task Force, 2004). Although there exist a variety of proposed frameworks, organizations neither know which one to adopt nor which one tailors to their own necessities. To help managers in their decisions, the following three comparative reviews have been found: (Rastogi and Solms, 2006) provide existing guidance on ISG and use four frameworks to propose a new definition of ISG; (Park et al., 2006) develop a literature review to look for ISG definitions and use this research to find which security management approaches cover governance success factors, and to know their limitations; (Mahncke et al., 2009) offer a literature review of approaches to measure ISG, and evaluate their suitability to general medical practice.

The analysis presented in this chapter will show the most relevant ISG frameworks, their characteristics, and the gaps that need to be filled in future research. Achieved results may help security professionals identifying the proposal that best suits their organizations; and lay the foundations of new researches focused on the thorough development of these frameworks.

The research has lead to a set of criteria that allow performing an objective comparison and the repeatability of the results. These criteria have been selected from existing ISG definitions through the extraction of compulsory and desirable features that every framework should accomplish.

During the process, specific and differentiating characteristics of the public sector were taken into account. While E-government is subject to the same threats as e-business, E-government operates within different constraints(Stibbe, 2005). Government entities exist for the purpose of serving society, while commercial firms exist for the benefit of their shareholders (Conklin and White, 2006); therefore the resulting security implementation must have specific considerations. Public organisms may be bound to security considerations according to applicable legislation, but an ISG framework can complement them or even be a substitute in case of lack of regulation (Ozkan and Karabacak, 2010).

This paper is structured as follows: next section offers a brief description of the nine frameworks that have been studied; section 3 presents the comparative criteria that have been defined and the analysis performed; finally, our conclusions and future works are set out on section 4.

INFORMATION SECURITY GOVERNANCE APPROACHES

A literature review has been performed in depth to locate existing ISG frameworks. The nine most relevant ones are summarized in this section.

A Practical Guide to Implement and Control Information Security Governance

In (de Oliveira Alves et al., 2006), authors propose a framework for implementing ISG. It focuses on selecting metrics and indicators to track information security evolution, and also on measuring the maturity level of information security inside the organization.

The approach considers the integration of corporate governance indicators, such as Balance Scorecard, with IT and security governance best practices, such as those included in COBIT and ISO/IEC 17799. The practical guide to implement ISG is composed of five stages, which are divided in activities, detailing the actions to be taken and who is responsible of performing each one.

Business Software Alliance

The Business Software Alliance (BSA) formed the Information Security Governance Task Force whose goal is to frame a response in terms that organizations can understand and implement. This Task Force has resumed in two white papers many ideas and concepts contained in other reports, legislation and guidelines.

Firstly, in (BSA, 2003), the authors state that there is already a legislative and regulatory regime around IT security and it must be enough so that companies stop treating security as a technology issue and start dealing with it as a corporate governance issue. They recommend adopting best practices and standard procedures such as ISO/IEC 17799 (later included in ISO/IEC 27000 family) and recognize the lack of an ISG framework that organizations can adopt. The Task Force proposes a framework where each management role knows what his functions are, how to accomplish his objectives and how to measure and audit the activities performed.

Secondly, proposal (Corporate Governance Task Force, 2004) expands the framework introduced formerly detailing the functions and responsibilities of every stakeholder involved in security. To implement this framework, the authors propose the IDEAL model which is based in five steps: Initiating, Diagnosing, Establishing, Acting and Learning. Finally, tools are provided for the assessment, verification and compliance of the corresponding implementation.

Information Security Policy: An Organizational-Level Process Model

The proposal (Knapp et al., 2009) focuses on the policy side of ISG. Following a different approach from other studies, author´s methodology includes data collection from security experts and some interviews and questionnaires with security professionals. The result is an information security policy model based on a set of interrelated processes that can be implemented in a repeatable cycle.

Similar to other governance proposals, the model considers the impact of external and internal influences, as well as the role of corporate governance. Also, there is a great emphasis on training and awareness of developed policies through out the whole cycle.

Information Security Governance (Von Solms)

Authors have been researching the field of ISG, and as a result they have published a wide variety of papers and a compendium book.

In (Posthumus and Solms, 2004), authors introduce the motivation why information security should be considered as a corporate governance issue. They propose an information security framework clearly distinguishing between the governance and management sides.

The approach (Posthumus and Solms, 2006) gives more detail on ISG and Information Security Management, as a part of the corporate governance; and describes the tasks, roles and responsibilities of any key individual in an organization.

As stated in (Solms and Solms, 2006), considering that Corporate Governance can be modeled using the Direct-Control Cycle, the same model is applied to Information Security Governance. Each of the steps of this cycle is analyzed through the three management levels: strategic, tactical and operational.

All these results are compiled in the book (Solms and Solms, 2009), where authors describe ISG as part of Corporate Governance and also sharing some aspects of IT Governance. The Direct-Control Cycle anticipated in the previous paper is applied to a group of dimensions of information security and is combined with COBIT and ISO/IEC 27000 as best practices. Also, a methodology of 14 steps is developed to establish an ISG environment.

Information Systems Audit and Control Association (ISACA)

The Information Systems Audit and Control Association (ISACA) has proposed (ISACA, 2009), where they define a generic model to tackle Information Security within a corporation. The model is based on systems theory and, therefore, consists of processes with inputs and outputs viewed holistically as a complete function unit.

The model has the structure of a tetrahedron (four sided pyramid) with four elements situated on its vertexes and six dynamic interconnections between them that link the elements together. The four elements are:

- Organization Design and Strategy.
- People.
- Process.
- Technology.

The six dynamic interconnections are:

- Governing.
- Culture.
- Enabling and support.
- Emergence.
- Human factors.
- Architecture.

ISO/IEC Standards

The International Organization for Standardization (ISO) has a wide portfolio of standards. Among these, the ISO/IEC 27000 family is dedicated to Information Security Management Systems, which can be used by organizations to develop and implement a framework for managing the security of their information assets and prepare for an independent assessment applied to the protection of their information. These standards provide guidelines to protect information assets through defining, achieving, maintaining, and improving information security; what is achieved implementing suitable controls and treating unacceptable information security risks.

Although at first instance, it may seem that this publication only deals with management issues, there are some proposals to integrate them with information security governance. The paper (Solms, 2005) recognizes the broader scope of COBIT, as it covers the whole field of IT Governance, but states that COBIT focuses on what to do but without giving details on how to do it. Here is where the ISO/IEC 27000 family has a chance, as it focuses on Information Security and gives more detail on how to do things. Both frameworks complement each other as shown in (ITGI, 2006a).

Standard ISO/IEC 27014, currently under development, pretends to be a proposal on an ISG framework. Its scope includes defining ISG clarifying its relationship with corporate and IT governance; and developing a framework establishing its objectives, principles, and processes.

The ISO/IEC 38500 family (ISO/IEC, 2008), which is related to Corporate Governance of information technology, can also be taken into consideration when dealing with ISG. The governance framework proposed in this standard, can be exported to information security implementations.

ITGI

The IT Governance Institute (ITGI), established in 1998 by the ISACA to focus on original research on IT governance and related topics, has developed COBIT (ITGI, 2007), which is a framework for IT Governance. COBIT 4.1 introduces a set of 34 processes grouped in four domains; detailing the control objectives, metrics, maturity models and other management guidelines for each of these processes.

Although COBIT is mainly focused on IT Governance, four of its processes are more related to ISG, namely:

- **PO6:** Communicate management aims and directions.
- **PO9:** Assess and manage IT risks.
- **DS4:** Ensure continuous service.
- **DS5:** Ensure systems security.

Surrounding COBIT, there are a group of products which complement it beyond the main framework (i.e. implementation guide, assurance guide, value of IT investments, etc). The most relevant ones in relation with ISG are the following guides:

- In (ITGI, 2006b) ITGI describes what is ISG and why is it important; details what should the Board of Directors and Senior

Executives do, how can it be implemented and what, as consequence, can be achieved.

- The proposal (ITGI, 2008b) is based on the foundations presented in the previous one. It provides more detail in the definition of Information Security Objectives, and the strategies and action plans that can be used to reach them. Furthermore, critical success factors and metrics are introduced to monitor and measure Information Security, showing that this guide is directed to a lower management level than the aforementioned one.

NIST

The National Institute of Standards and Technology (NIST), an agency of the U.S. Department of Commerce, has published many guidelines related with Information Security. The guide (Bowen et al., 2006) has its second chapter dedicated to ISG.

According to this book, there are five components of ISG:

- Strategic Planning.
- Organizational Structure.
- Roles and Responsibilities.
- Enterprise Architecture.
- Policies and Guidance.

All of these components of the governance must be linked to the current implementation of security through on-going monitoring. In order to achieve this result, a description of activities and supporting processes to perform this monitoring is offered.

In another NIST publication (Bowen et al., 2007), the focus is pointed towards developing an Information Security Program, so the key activities of this task are detailed. Among these activities, ISG is highlighted. Also, applicable laws and regulations to security programs, from the U.S. point of view, are resumed.

Software Engineering Institute

The Software Engineering Institute, from the Carnegie Mellon University, has published the guide (Allen and Westby, 2007), as part of the Computer Emergency Response Team (CERT) program. This guide defines the governance for enterprise security and what are the characteristics of effective ISG so that readers can distinguish between effective and ineffective security governance.

To succeed on ISG, the guide proposes defining an Enterprise Security Program within the corporation. This program involves personnel at all levels throughout the organization, so different roles are identified pinpointing their functions and responsibilities. Each role has associated a set of activities with their correspondent outputs and supporting documents, which are described in a sequential way.

COMPARATIVE ANALYSIS

This section contains a comparative analysis of the most relevant approaches to Information Security Governance described previously. There is not any standardized framework to compare this kind of proposals so a set of criteria from different research fields will be utilized. These criteria have been selected taking into account the wide variety of existing literature definitions related to ISG. Most of these definitions place this subject as closely linked with IT Governance, Corporate Governance and Information Security, among other areas. Considering these three points of view, a comprehensive group of criteria has been defined, which covers both governance and management aspects.

Selected criteria facilitate performing an objective analysis of the nine identified frameworks. With the proposed comparison topics, the whole spectrum of desirable characteristics related to

ISG that can be found in literature is taken into account. To achieve unbiased results, some of the criteria are subdivided in different sub-criteria as a second aggregation level, so that each proposal may be easily classified.

Furthermore, besides these three comparison groups, which are shared by every organization, public sector distinct characteristics have been considered. This constitutes a fourth criterion, which reflects the fact that governance processes have their own peculiarities within institutional units.

Therefore, the comparative analysis will be based on the criteria detailed in the following subsections.

IT Governance Criteria

Literature review shows that there are many definitions of IT Governance. Papers such as (Webb et al., 2006) and (Dahlberg and Kivijärvi, 2006) analyze more than a dozen definitions and highlight five elements, which provide the foundations of IT Governance. These elements are:

- Strategic Alignment: information security must be aligned with business strategy towards the goals of the organization.
- Delivery of business value through IT: optimization of security investments delivering the promised benefits.
- Performance Management: monitoring security strategies to ensure reaching the organization´s goals in time.
- Risk Management: security risk awareness, indentifying threats, vulnerabilities and impacts to control and reduce risks over the whole enterprise.
- Control and Accountability: every person of the organization needs to be involved in the security controls and has to know the responsibilities he owns inside the defined framework.

Corporate Governance Criteria

As a part of Corporate Governance, the following domains will be considered, taken from (Simonsson and Johnson, 2006):

- **Goals:** Strategy decisions, development of information security policies and guidelines, and controls to monitor whether the goals are achieved.
- **Processes:** Implementation and management of information security processes, with their related activities and procedures.
- **People:** The structure within the organization, and defining roles and responsibilities of the different stakeholders.
- **Technology:** Linking between Information Security Governance and the physical IT assets that the organization manages (inside and outside).

Security Criteria

Information Security Governance is obviously related to Information Security field, so a set of security criteria have been selected:

- Standards integration: some proposals refer to controls and best practices included in security standards (i.e. ISO/IEC 27000).
- Information Security Management: policies and procedures defined in the governance side can be linked to the management and operative side of information security.
- Tools and techniques: usually frameworks utilize tools to facilitate their implementation, such as metrics to measure de degree of compliance or maturity models to enable benchmarking between organizations.
- Practical implementation guidelines: theoretical approaches may be distinguished from practical ones; the latter involve de-

tailing implementation activities, include case studies and even practical examples.

Public Sector Suitability

Although every identified ISG framework may be adapted to a public organism, some of them include differentiating characteristics that makes them more suitable for the public sector. These particularities range from the compliance with specific laws, policies and regulations to requirements originated from multiple governing bodies; going through funding limitations in budgets and investments.

Public institutions need to consider security beyond technical aspects in four domains: social, political, cultural and legal (Wimmer and Bredow, 2002). This fourth criterion evaluates these domains so that it may help boards in their decisions, avoiding unnecessary efforts in tailoring an ISG framework to a public entity.

Analysis Results

The former defined criteria have been applied to the nine frameworks presented in section 2. The result is summarized in Table 1, which has been elaborated assigning three levels of conformance (high, medium and low) to each of the criteria.

Table results can be analyzed from two different perspectives. On one hand, horizontally, some of the proposed criteria are more widespread over the ISG frameworks than others. Among the governance criteria, nearly all of the proposals deal with strategic alignment, risk management, goals and processes; however, delivery of business value through IT is only deeply developed by the IT Governance Institute on the Val IT Framework (ITGI, 2008a), and technology relations with physical IT implemented assets are seldom considered. Generally speaking, security criteria seem to be less relevant than the previous ones, as authors tend to offer high level solutions, distant from implementation details.

On the other hand, vertically, three of the frameworks seem to be more aligned with the groups of criteria and could be considered as reference starting points. Namely: IT Governance Institute focuses on IT Governance, ISACA is mainly related to Corporate Governance, and ISO Standards deal principally with Security criteria. The rest of the approaches are situated in intermediate positions, leveraging the importance each one gives to every comparative aspect.

With respect to public sector suitability, most of the frameworks do not detail the specific implications of implementing ISG into a public entity. The guidelines proposed by the NIST are the main exceptions which take into account these considerations, but they are much localized as a consequence of having their foundations based on United States regulation and laws. Therefore, additional efforts are needed when adapting this framework to other country´s organisms. Also, some guidance is included in BSA´s proposal, which offers some key notes when adopting information security by education and non-profit institutions.

Public organizations are usually bound to a specific regulatory framework which results in different governance processes. This is the consequence of the application of the corresponding legislation which emanates from various level authorities (national, regional, etc). In most cases, selected ISG proposal needs to be localized to the regulations where the organism resides.

CONCLUSION AND FUTURE WORKS

The security of any organization´s asset must involve every stakeholder from senior executives to operational personnel. Information Security Governance helps to this task providing a framework which can be adopted by enterprises. The board of governance of any company that relies on this methodology can be confident of compliance with a wide set of security measures

Table 1. Comparison of ISG frameworks

Criteria	A practical guide to implement and control Information Security Governance	Business Software Alliance	Information security policy: An organizational-level process model	Information Security Governance (Von Solms)	ISACA	ISO Standards	IT Governance Institute	NIST	Software Engineering Institute
IT Governance									
Strategic Alignment	medium	medium	high	medium	high	medium	high	high	high
Delivery of business value through IT	medium	low	low	low	medium	low	high	low	medium
Performance Management	low	medium	medium	medium	medium	high	high	medium	low
Risk Management	high	high	high	high	low	high	high	high	high
Control and Accountability	medium	low	medium	high	low	medium	high	low	high
Corporate Governance									
Goals	medium	medium	high	medium	high	medium	high	high	high
Processes	high	high	high	high	high	high	high	high	high
People	high	high	low	high	high	medium	medium	high	medium
Technology	high	low	medium	medium	high	medium	low	low	medium
Security									
Standards integration	high	medium	low	high	low	high	low	high	medium
Information Security Management	medium	low	medium	high	low	high	medium	medium	medium
Tools and techniques	high	high	medium	low	low	high	medium	low	low
Practical implementation guidelines	medium	high	low	medium	medium	high	low	medium	medium
Public Sector Suitability	low	medium	low	low	low	low	low	high	low

(Table header spanning group: ISG Frameworks)

and even regulation requirements; furthermore, information security becomes a process inside the organization covering all of the information assets and provides alignment with business strategy.

The nine most relevant ISG frameworks existing in literature have been reviewed in this paper, performing a comparative analysis between them using a comprehensive set of conformance criteria. The performed revision has shown that none of the approaches, even the most recent ones, fulfill every necessity field that organizations need to tackle. Although these proposals include desirable features, their main lacks have been highlighted.

Special attention has been given to public sector suitability, but most ISG proposals are more focused on private corporations than public organizations. This issue may be considered by the directors of any public institution when adopting one of these methodologies.

Additional investigation work is needed to develop a general ISG framework which fills the detected gaps. Either taking any of the approaches included in the comparative as a starting point, or building it from scratch, it is imperative that such a task is undertaken. Future work will follow this line, complementing existing proposals to reduce their weaknesses and achieve a comprehensive framework that can be systematically extended to any organization.

ACKNOWLEDGMENT

This research is part of the following projects: MEDUSAS (IDI-20090557), financed by the Centre for Industrial Technological Development (CDTI), ORIGIN (IDI-2010043(1-5)) financed by the CDTI and the FEDER, BUSINESS (PET2008-0136) awarded by the Spanish Ministry for Science and Technology and SEGMENT (HITO-09-138) and SISTEMAS (PII2I09-0150-3135) financed by the Council of Education and Science of the Castilla-La Mancha Regional Government.

REFERENCES

Allen, J. H., & Westby, J. R. (2007). *Governing for enterprise security implementation guide*. Software Engineering Institute - CERT.

Bowen, P., Chew, E., & Hash, J. (2007). *Information security guide for government executives*. National Institute of Standards and Technology.

Bowen, P., Hash, J., & Wilson, M. (2006). Information security governance. In *Information security handbook: A guide for managers*. National Institute of Standards and Technology.

BSA. (2003). *Information security governance: Toward a framework for action*.

Conklin, A., & White, G. B. (2006). E-government and cyber security: The role of cyber security exercises. *Proceedings of the 39th Annual Hawaii International Conference on System Sciences*.

Corporate Governance Task Force. (2004). *Information security governance: A call to action*.

Crossroad. (2010). *Updated gap analysis report: A participative roadmap for ICT research in electronic governance and policy modelling*.

Dahlberg, T., & Kivijärvi, H. (2006). An integrated framework for IT governance and the development and validation of an assessment instrument. *Proceedings of the 39th Hawaii International Conference on System Sciences*.

de Oliveira Alves, G. A., Rust da Costa Carmo, L. F., & Ribeiro Dutra de Almeida, A. C. (2006). *Enterprise security governance: A practical guide to implement and control information security governance*. Business-Driven IT Management.

Hardy, G. (2006). Using IT governance and CO-BIT to deliver value with IT and respond to legal, regulatory and compliance challenges. *Information Security Technical Report, 11*, 55–61.

Humphreys, E. (2008). Information security management standards: Compliance, governance and risk management. *Information Security Technical Report*, 13.

ISACA. (2009). *An introduction to the business model for information security.*

ISO/IEC. (2008). *ISO/IEC 38500:2008 Corporate governance of information technology.*

ITGI. (2006a). *COBIT mapping to ISO/IEC 17799:2000 with COBIT.*

ITGI. (2006b). *Information security governance: Guidance for boards of directors and executive management* (2nd ed.).

ITGI. (2007). *Control objectives for information and related technology (COBIT 4.1).*

ITGI. (2008a). *Governance of investments, the val IT framework 2.0.*

ITGI. (2008b). *Information security governance: Guidance for information security managers.*

Johnston, A. C., & Hale, R. (2009). Improved security through information security governance. *Communications of the ACM, 52*, 126–129.

Knapp, K. J., Morris, R. F., Marshall, T. E., & Byrd, T. A. (2009). Information security policy: An organizational-level process model. *Computers & Security, 28*, 493–508.

Mahncke, R. J., McDermid, D. C., & Williams, P. A. H. (2009). Measuring information security governance within general medical practice. *Proceedings of the 7th Australian Information Security Management Conference.*

Ozkan, S., & Karabacak, B. (2010). Collaborative risk method for information security management practices: A case context within Turkey. *International Journal of Information Management, 30*, 567–572.

Park, H., Kim, S., & Lee, H. J. (2006). General drawing of the integrated framework for security governance. *Lecture Notes in Computer Science, 4251*, 1234–1241.

Pasquinucci, A. (2007). Security, risk analysis and governance: A practical approach. *Computer Fraud & Security, 7*, 12–14.

Posthumus, S., & Solms, R. v. (2004). A framework for the governance of information security. *Computers & Security, 23*, 638–646.

Posthumus, S., & Solms, R. v. (2006). *A responsibility framework for information security.* International Federation for Information Processing.

Rastogi, R., & Solms, R. v. (2006). Information security governance - A re-definition. *International Federation for Information Processing, 193*, 223–236.

Simonsson, M., & Johnson, P. (2006). Assessment of IT governance - A prioritization of COBIT. *Proceedings of the Conference on Systems Engineering Research.*

Solms, B. v. (2005). Information security governance: COBIT or ISO 17799 or both? *Computers & Security, 24*, 99–104.

Solms, R. v., & Solms, S. H. B. v. (2006). Information security governance: A model based on the direct–control cycle. *Computers & Security, 25*, 408–412.

Solms, S. H. v., & Solms, R. v. (2009). *Information security governance.* Springer.

Stibbe, M. (2005). E-government security. *Infosecurity Today, 2*, 8–10.

Webb, P., Pollard, C., & Ridley, G. (2006). Attempting to define IT governance: Wisdom or folly? *Proceedings of the 39th Hawaii International Conference on System Sciences.*

Williams, P. (2001). Information security governance. *Information Security Technical Report*, *6*(3), 60–70.

Wimmer, M., & Bredow, B. v. (2002). A holistic approach for providing security solutions in e-government. *Proceedings of the 35th Hawaii International Conference on System Sciences*.

Chapter 2
IT Security Governance in E-Banking

Theodosios Tsiakis
Alexandrian Technological Educational Institute of Thessaloniki, Greece

Theodoros Kargidis
Alexandrian Technological Educational Institute of Thessaloniki, Greece

Aristeidis Chatzipoulidis
University of Macedonia, Greece

ABSTRACT

Most industries have been influenced in different ways by e-commerce, and the banking industry is no exception. Particularly, banks are embracing electronic banking (e-banking) as a service to reach a wider market share, increase customer satisfaction and lower operational costs. This increased supply and demand in e-banking services has caused not only opportunities but also risks. The need to manage and regulate those risks calls for a sound Information Technology Security Governance (ITSG) program as means to deliver value business and mitigate Information Technology (IT) risks. In this regard, the chapter's objectives are to explore, evaluate, and compare the current status and characteristics of Information Security Governance (ISG) approaches for e-banking. Therefore, the authors focus on an analysis of reputed best standards, guidelines on governance, risk management methods, and internal controls currently used for e-banking as means to research which satisfies best ISG objectives. Results show that banks should not be restricted to currently used approaches to ISG for e-banking but should take into consideration benefits and shortcomings other approaches possess. In this regard, the authors propose an ITSG framework for e-banking as a continuous process for assuring ISG objectives. They also highlight the importance of consistent measurement of metrics of ITSG performance with the aid of security content automation protocol.

DOI: 10.4018/978-1-4666-2083-4.ch002

INTRODUCTION

Since the beginning of modern network technology, especially the Internet, financial institutions have renovated their communication and business infrastructure in order to take benefit of advances in technology. It is evident that electronic banking (e-banking) has contributed substantially to the success and profitability of many banks (Kondabagil, 2007). Nevertheless, the parallel expansion of digital attacks has made stakeholders lose confidence on e-banking operations (Gikandi and Bloor, 2010).

The evolution of e-banking has moved banking services from back-end applications to customer-centric network ends. Particularly, the open networked environment provides instant global access to information products and services so now the consumer can access the bank to conduct financial services instantly. Common e-banking services include but are not limited to financial information news, ATM (Automated Teller Machine) locators, insurance, credit cards, cash management, funds transfer, investment services and others (Baten and Kamil, 2010).

With society's dependence on technology the risks as well as the failures to assure information has increased in a high rate. Particularly, the total amount of security breach and computer viruses cost globally $1.6 trillion a year and 39,363 human years of productivity for financial institutions (Symantec, 2010). Another incident in 2007 accused three cyber thieves for stealing $450.000 from the City National Bank in North Carolina (Vijayan, 2010) when recently in New Jersey, an attempt to steal information from more than 500.000 bank accounts got a bank employee arrested (MSNBC, 2010).

Banks ability to take advantage of the proliferation of technology often depends on open, accessible, available, and secure network services. Financial institutions depend on human notions such as customer trust, confidence, and satisfaction

that appear to be the key indicators correlated to the growth of a business. As a result, retaining a good reputation for safeguarding information will increase market share and profit. In this respect, there is typically nothing that causes customer dissatisfaction more that compromised accounts or stolen identities, all purviews of security (Tan et al., 2010). For this reason and because banks should mitigate the information technology (IT) risks to an acceptable level, the concept of Information Technology Security Governance (ITSG) concept is tested as the main objective of this chapter under the prism of e-banking.

Particularly, we stress the importance for a financial institution to have a much more sophisticated and structured approach to ITSG as part of a wider Risk Management approach. In this regard, we focus on strengthening the relationship between Risk Management methods and ISG frameworks to approach the objectives of Security Governance in e-banking. Therefore, our main research objectives are to:

1. Empirically examine congruent terminology, role and implementation of ITSG in e-banking.
2. Research on e-banking risks with emphasis on outsourcing risk because it causes and affects other e-banking risks.
3. Focus on an overview of reputed approaches to ISG to meet the specific needs of e-banking systems.
4. Propose an ITSG framework for e-banking helping small banks achieve higher business value.

Just as new trends in information security (IS) require consistent measurement of metrics, we also consider how ITSG performance in e-banking can be measured. We summarize the chapter by supporting the argument that "*Security is a management problem, not a technical problem*" (Brotby, 2009, pp.15) especially in e-banking due to the interaction nature. This chapter is organized into ten sections. This section introduces the reader with the evolution of e-banking and main research concerns. Section two portrays the literature review of ITSG and e-banking in general and emphasizes on congruent terminology. Section three discusses the objectives of Information Security Governance (ISG) and most reputed approaches. Section four describes the role of ITSG in e-banking and proposes an ITSG framework as a basis for banks wishing to govern information security in the e-banking domain. Section five describes and summarizes most common e-banking risks and section six describes why outsourcing risk is considered the most critical e-banking risk among others. Section seven describes the main concepts around Risk Management in e-banking and section eight compares the most reputed ISG frameworks in the banking industry. In section nine we describe emerging trends in measuring ITSG performance such as the Security Content Automation Protocol (SCAP). In section ten we summarize the findings of the chapter and propose future research.

Research Contribution: We focus on the rising demand of electronic banking to highlight how a sound Information Technology Security Governance program can actually add business value and mitigate IT-related risks. In this respect, we a) analyze and compare approaches not only to standard ISG objectives but also to other related IS criteria as means to discover which one best fits the e-banking environment and b) propose an ITSG framework as a continuous process for assuring ISG objectives. Results show that each approach/method has its own benefits and shortcomings. Moreover, following recent trends in measuring security we exemplify how to measure ITSG performance in e-banking in a consistent and automated manner with the aid of Security Content Automation Protocol.

BACKGROUND

We emphasize from the very beginning that it is important to use the terminology accurately because our words define our understanding. Therefore, before describing in detail the role of ITSG in e-banking, we need at least a literature review over e-banking and ITSG as separate contexts.

Fundamentally, banking services has evolved in a service of "anytime/anywhere/anyhow" (Chen, 2009) and the term e-banking is used to describe banking applications, including products and services, with the use of technology. Specifically, the proliferation of Internet technology has led the development of new products such as aggregation of services, bill presentment and personalized financial services. Today the competition in the banking sector is determined by the success of a bank to adopt and deliver innovative products and services that meet the changing needs of a customer (Daniel, 1999). In this respect most banks has some type of Web presence however this is restricted primarily for marketing purposes (Ho Bruce and Wu, 2009). However, e-banking can offer much more than a static banking presence online. Specifically, e-banking has the potential to:

- Eliminate physical or geographical boundaries, enabling a wider market share.
- Use a variety of devices (e.g. phone, personal computer) for instant admission to banking services without the expenses of facilities or labor.
- Satisfy consumer demands via mass-customization and self-service.
- Lower operational, transaction and production costs via the use of technology.
- Showcase community activities and attractions offering multilingual sites.
- Build public relations and reputation by supporting social welfare and local needs.
- Provide effortless (all time) accessibility for disabled people.

Figure 1. Retail banking services and distribution channels; Source: Adopted from Akinci et al., 2004

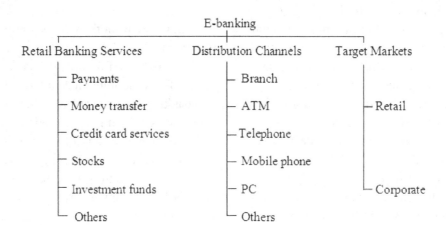

While there are various definitions in the literature about e-banking (Insley et al., 2003; Kolondisky et al., 2004; Shah and Clarke, 2009; Angelakopoulos and Mihiotis, 2011) we conclude that e-banking is an umbrella term including all possible transactions of a bank which are performed with the use of electronic means, mainly through the Internet but also via VPNs (Virtual Private Networks), Intranet, Extranet, phone and mobile phone and other devices such as ATMs, and these transactions do not require the customer to visit a bank branch. According to (Akinci et al., 2004; Aggelis, 2005) there are a number of retail banking services, distribution channels and target markets included in an e-banking environment (see Figure 1) but three major types of e-banking distinguish depending on the channel by which the transactions are performed: 1. Internet banking, 2. Phone banking, 3. Mobile banking.

1. Internet banking (or web banking), as its name implies, is operated mainly through the Internet. The customer of the bank must have access to a personal computer and to the network of the bank. Usually, due to the increased security requirements regarding e-transactions, banks must ensure that e-banking customers' records remain safe under all conditions. In this regard, banks use security tools such as tokens, specialized software, digital signatures and other security defenses to protect the security requirements (confidentiality, integrity, availability) of the assets supporting e-banking.

2. Phone banking services are processed via a phone device that is not mobile. This service is divided (Aggelis, 2005) into two categories a) manually via real-person contact and b) automatically through IVR (Interactive Voice Response) systems where the customer responds to voice messages.

3. Mobile banking (m-banking) is a relative new channel which has not reached as much a penetration rate in usage as it should have. The main reasons are lack in security and marketing strategy. M-banking is performed thought the installation of specialized software program in the user's mobile device and precautions for safeguarding security such as the usual change of the password are essential.

According to (Nsouli and Schaechter, 2002), e-banking is considered an electronic financial service that belongs to the wider e-commerce area. E-commerce is conceived as a broad term that

Figure 2. Position of e-banking in relation to e-commerce; Source: Adopted from Nsouli and Schaechter, 2002

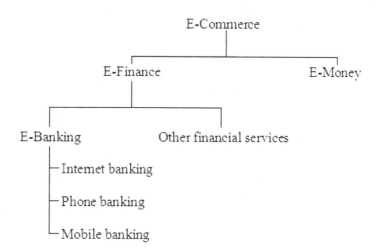

includes all business through the use of electronic networks. E-commerce is divided in two broad categories namely a) e-finance, a term which includes financial services via e-channels and b) e-money, a term that includes all the mechanisms for stored value or pre-paid payment. The main difference between e-money and e-banking is that the former balances are not kept in financial accounts within banks but are rather seen as digital money or cash. Direct deposit and electronic funds transfer (EFT) are usual examples of e-money. E-finance includes e-banking and other financial services and products such as insurance and online brokering. Figure 2 summarizes this notion.

E-banking cannot operate without the aid of technology and specifically the Internet. Therefore, the role of technology in supporting the e-banking function has become increasingly complex. In this respect, IT operations have become highly dynamic and usually include distributed environments, integrated applications, telecommunication options, Internet connectivity, different computer operating platforms as well as increased reliance on third parties (e.g. vendors, partners) for delivering e-banking solutions (Rao

et al, 2007). For this reason, IT security can no longer be regarded as a purely technical issue since it involves different stakeholders with different security behavior (e.g. investors, employees, society) and unfortunately, security is rarely at the forefront of stakeholders concerns, with the exception to comply with standards and /or legal requirements (Mellado et al., 2010). Particularly, IT security is a subset of information security (IS), a concept which has become an integral part of daily life and banks need to ensure that their information as well as the delivery of services are adequately secured (Saint-Gemain, 2005). For this reason, the purpose is to set the "desired state" of security to achieve the Information Security Governance (ISG) objectives for e-banking (Kondabagil, 2007; Solms and von Solms, 2009) namely:

1. Strategic alignment.
2. Risk Management.
3. Business process assurance/convergence.
4. Value delivery.
5. Resource management.
6. Performance measurement.

It is time to describe the ITSG concept, a term which derives from the ITG (Information Technology Governance) term with an emphasis on the technological factor. In trace of its roots, Rastogi and Von Solms (2006) use a number of references such as Weill and Woodham (2002, p. 4) to define IT Governance as: *'specifying the decision rights and accountability framework to encourage desirable behavior in the use of IT,"* moreover, Van Grembergen (2002, p. 1) defines IT Governance as: *"the organizational capacity exercised by the Board, executive management and IT management to control the formulation and implementation of IT strategy and in this way ensuring the fusion of business and IT."*

There is a variety of definitions in the literature about the role of ITSG in general, however, most academicians and practitioners have lack of consensus in the definition and adherence of this term and some others use the term ISG to describe both the technological aspect in an institution (Monks and Minow, 2004; Kritzinger and von Solms, 2006; Rao et al., 2007). Moulton and Cole (2003) defined ITSG as the establishment and maintenance of the control environment to manage the risks relating to the confidentiality, integrity and availability of information and its supporting processes and systems. The IT Governance Institute (2006) supports that ITSG is compliment to ISG and is the set of responsibilities various stakeholders possess with the goal of providing strategic direction, ensuring that risks and resources are managed efficiently. In addition, Rastogi and Von Solms (2006) describe ITSG as a decision-making process including protection of stakeholder value and the most valuable assets of a financial institution. This definition matches well with this chapter's work since the objective is to examine how an ITSG program can benefit an e-banking system. To make this definition more accurate in the context of e-banking, we extend the aforementioned description and clarify the role of ITSG in e-banking as a *"cognitive process that adds value to the business and IT infrastruc-* *ture resulting in a set of actions among several stakeholders towards managing e-banking risks."*

It is argued that the assurance of protecting information in financial services should not become an "one-man responsibility" but should be treated as a government issue (Abu Masa, 2010). For this reason, the term "Corporate Governance" (CG) is used to specify the relationships between, and the distribution of rights, information and responsibilities among, the four main groups of participants in a corporate body naming 1. Board of directors, 2. Managers, 3. Employees, and 4. Various stakeholders. CG can also be defined as the system by which business operations are directed and controlled (Biri and Tentra, 2004). According to the same author, examples of international best practices for CG are: The King 2 Report and The Organization for Economic Co-operation and Development (OECD) Principles of CG. A highly related term that compliments and consists an integral part of ITSG, and thereby ISG, is the enterprise governance (EG) concept. According to IFAC (2004) EG is a more generic term, closely related to corporate governance (CG), referring to the organizational structures and processes that aim to ensure the organization's business objectives and IT sustains and delivers business value to the financial institution and stakeholders.

Moreover, relevant aspects of ISG include accountability to stakeholders, compliance with legal requirements, setting clear security policies, spreading security awareness and education, defining roles and responsibilities, contingency planning and instituting best practice standards (Monks and Minow, 2004). In other words, the scope of ISG is to describe the rules and procedures for making decisions regarding corporate affairs and the structure through which the corporate objectives are set. Moreover, it aims to fulfill the security objectives (confidentiality, availability and integrity), monitor corporate performance against those objectives and communicate it to the stakeholders (Long et al., 2008). However, there are sound examples that ISG has failed to live up to expectations due to high visibility failures such as Enron, Tyco, WorldCom, and Arthur Andersen (Ralph Spencer Pool, 2005). For this reason, the need for ITSG has become apparent in an attempt to support ISG achieve its role. At its core, ITSG is concerned with two things namely delivery of value to the business and mitigation of IT risks (Moreira et al., 2008). A comprehensive definition of ITSG (Solms and von Solms, 2009) is as an integral part of enterprise (corporate) governance consisting of the leadership and organizational structures that ensure the organization's IT infrastructure sustains and extends the organization's strategies and objectives.

From a theoretical perspective ITSG is compliment to ISG, which is a subset of CG, but these two terms are not congruent. Particularly, ITSG focuses on the application of technology to business and how and to what degree this application provides value to the business. In practice, this concept reflects more the arguments of the technology itself (e.g. computer failures, technology obsolescence) rather than of the information itself. But because the primary purpose of any governance program within a financial institution is to hold management accountable for the assurance of information therefore, it must also assure the protection and ethical use of the information assets (Poore, 2005).

In literature there are attempts to build holistic ISG frameworks in order to simplify the variety of components and bring together the existing

Figure 3. Information security governance framework; Source: Adopted from Da Veiga and Eloff, 2007

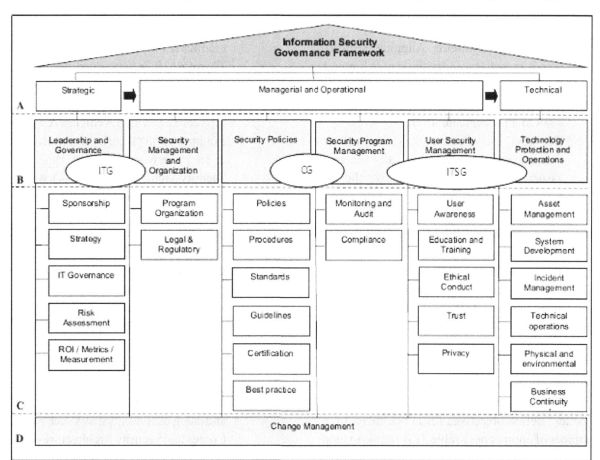

approaches such as (Tan et al., 2010, Trompeter and Eloff, 2001; Tudor, 2000). In this regard, wishing to further clarify the meaning of congruent terms such as CG, ITSG, ITG and ISG we use the framework as depicted in Da Veiga and Eloff (2007) (Figure 3) because it represents ISG based on four approaches namely, a) ISO 17799 (2005), b) PROTECT, c) the Capability Maturity Model, and the d) Information Security Architecture (ISA). The authors see ISG as a triangle pyramid (see Figure 3) shape consisting of three layers with distinct components.

INFORMATION SECURITY GOVERNANCE OBJECTIVES

According to literature (Moreira et al., 2008; Solms and von Solms, 2009) an effective ISG program, has six objectives summarized in the next bullets:

- **Strategic Alignment:** Aligning security activities with business strategy to support organizational objectives.
- **Risk Management:** Actions to manage risks to an acceptable level.
- **Business Process Assurance/ Convergence:** Integrating all relevant assurance processes to maximize the effectiveness and efficiency of security activities.
- **Value Delivery:** Optimizing investments in support of business objectives.
- **Resource Management:** Using organizational resources efficiently and effectively.
- **Performance Measurement:** Monitoring and reporting on security processes.

In this section, we will consider the most reputed methods used to describe the ISG objectives. Therefore, in our quest for which approach can "better" define objectives for ITSG, there are a number of approaches (Table 3) available to help

define a desired state of ISG. Here "better" means "in a more holistic way." Reputed approaches to ISG objectives described in (Da Veiga and Eloff, 2007; Brotby, 2009; Koons and Minoli, 2010) are summarized below.

1. **Sherwood Applied Business Security Architecture (SABSA):**

   Given the increasing complexity that surrounds the e-banking environment, the variety of cyber risks, the increasing regulatory pressures, and the ever more problematic security administration, one solution calls for the function of a "security architecture" as a tool of modern business capable to provide a framework within which complexity can be managed successfully. Particularly, it can offer simplicity and clarity through layering and modularization of business functions. Therefore, it is concerned with what the institution wants to achieve along with the environmental factors that will influence those achievements. A sound example of a "security architecture" is the Sherwood Applied Business Security Architecture (SABSA), which has been developed to address issues such as the design, management, implementation, and monitoring of business activities against security incidents. The approach is a framework that is compatible with and can utilize other IT Governance frameworks such as CobiT as well as ITIL and ISO/IEC 27001. The SABSA Model comprises of six layers each layer representing the view of a different player in the process of specifying, designing, constructing, and using business systems such as the Contextual Security Architecture - The

Business View and the Conceptual Security Architecture - The Architect's View. The "security architecture" concept is closely related to the "enterprise architecture" concept that typically provides a layered organized view of the IT assets. Such models include the Zachman Framework for Enterprise Architectures, The Open Group Architecture Framework (TOGAF) and the Federal Enterprise Architecture (FEA).

2. **CobiT:**

CobiT (Control Objectives for Information and Related Technology) is an IT governance framework that allows managers to bridge the gap between control requirements, technical issues, and business risks as defined by the IT Governance Institute (ITGI, 2007). CobiT is developed by the Information Systems Audit and Control Association (ISACA) and enables policy development and good practice for IT control (Heschl, 2004). CobiT 4.0 was released in November 2005, CobiT 4.1 in 2007 and CobiT 5 is the latest strategic improvement towards enterprise governance of IT and address governance and management of information and related technology to achieve the business objectives of stakeholders. CobiT defines 34 high level control objectives under four domains namely 1) plan and organize 2) acquire and implement 3) deliver and support 4) monitor and evaluate. CobiT also aims to fulfill the COSO requirements for the IT control environment. CobiT also supports Risk Management principles from ISO 27002, specifi-

cally, in the "PO 9 Control Objective" CobiT focuses on the assessment of risk for the scope to reduce them to an acceptable level. This framework can be used in ensuring proper control and governance over information and the systems that create, store, manipulate, and retrieve it. CobiT 4.1 is organized with 34 IT processes, giving a complete picture of how to control, manage, and measure each process. CobiT is, therefore, clear on the aspect of monitoring and ensuring compliance as part of ISG. CobiT appeals to different users namely from Executive management (to obtain value from IT investments and balance risk and control investment), to auditors (to validate their opinions and provide advice to management on internal controls). In particular, high level processes such as ME 1 and ME 4 and DS 5 are referring to Monitoring, Surveillance and Evaluating respectively.

3. **The Capability Maturity Model (CMM):**

This model is used to measure two things: The maturity of processes (specific functions) that produce products (e.g., identified vulnerabilities, countermeasures, and threats) and the level of compliance as a process with respect to the IATRP (InfoSec Assurance Training and Rating Program) methodology. In other words, a CMM is a measurement of the level of assurance that an organization can perform a process consistently. In this respect, a CMM identifies nine process areas related to performing information security assurance services. For each of the nine process areas, the CMM defines six levels of process maturity from Level 0 to Level 5. The higher the maturity levels, the more likely the process will be performed consistently.

4. ISO/IEC 27001:2005 and ISO/IEC 27002:2005:

These are ISO standards suited to develop a management approach. Both using the ISMS processes and control objectives in ISO 27001; and the code of practice and controls in ISO 27002, these standards can support useful governance guidance and can be effectively used to establish the current state of security for an organization. Specifically, the ISO 27001 was published in October 2005 and as a standard defines the requirements for ISMS. An ISMS is a management system for dealing with IS risk exposures namely, a framework of policies, procedures, physical, legal, and technical security controls forming part of the organization's overall Risk Management processes. ISO 27001 incorporates Deming's Plan-Do-Check-Act (PDCA) cycle have to be continually reviewed and adjusted to incorporate changes in the security threats, vulnerabilities and impacts of information security failures. The organization who adapts ISO 27001 can receive certification by an accredited certification body. ISO 27002 (aka ISO 17799) is used to describe two distinct documents: ISO 27002, which is a set of security controls (a code of practice), and ISO 27001 (formerly BS7799-2), which is a standard "specification" for an Information Security Management System (ISMS). This standard and code of practice can serve to provide an approach to ISG, although, to some

extent by inference. That is, ISO 27001 is a management system with a focus on control objectives, not a strategic governance approach. The linkage between control objectives and strategic business objectives is not explicitly addressed. CobiT shares similarities with ISO 27001 and ISO 27002 regarding the depth of functional territory, although organized differently. In this respect, CobiT covers IT governance extensively. ISO 27002 is concerned with the security of information assets as a group and in its view this is well beyond just the IT systems. Therefore the standard implicitly view that the IT domain has the majority proportion of the organization's information assets and is charged with securing them. However, there is also a vast quantity of information that resides outside IT such as financial information. ISO 27002 identifies 133 security controls to satisfy 39 security objectives in order to address IS risk exposures in the area of confidentiality, integrity, and availability. ISO 27002 is an advisory document, not a formal specification. In particular, Clause 15 of ISO 27002 is totally dedicated to compliance and ISG objectives specifying controls related with legal requirements (control 15.1), security policies (control 15.2) and information systems audit compliance (control 15.3). ISO 27002 sees Risk Management as an essential part of Best Practices in IT and as a process to ensure Information Security Governance (Pretorius and Solms, 2004).

5.   **The National Cyber Security Summit Task Force Corporate Governance Framework (CGTF):**

This is an ISG framework, formed in 2003, to promote global, regional and local corporate governance (CG) reform initiatives, improve institutional framework for good CG and facilitate improved CG practices in developing countries towards organizational compliance. In particular, item 3 in the framework refers to the security responsibilities for the Board, senior management and workforce towards compliance and governance objectives. The details described in the framework can be used to identify whether the security conditions exist, to what extend and how can the organization reach a higher level of compliance. CGTF supports that information security is not only a technical issue but also a governance challenge that involves Risk Management, reporting and accountability. As such, it requires the active engagement of executive management. (CGTF, 2004). CGTF has developed CG codes of best practice as generic recommendations with the aim to improve and guide the governance practices of corporations within a country's specific legal environment and business context.

THE ROLE OF ITSG IN E-BANKING

Prophetically, Dewan and Seidmann (2001) predicted the e-banking will consist of two classes namely very large banks and small niche banks. This distinction was clarified in a study from Southard and Siau (2004) in which depicted that smaller banks can actually compete with larger

national banks at the same level through the use of technology. This capability to obtain a market share regardless of size shows how the banking industry is polarizing with very large banks and small niche banks at either end of the spectrum. As Figure 4 illustrates, banks will need to focus their Internet technology strategy along this continuum. Movement along the continuum is only toward the upper left. This restricted movement foretells the future of e-banking. Banks will either maintain their positions or will be forced, through acquisition or merger, towards the upper-left segment of the continuum.

Information security (IS), which may include protection of consumers' personal data and safe transactions to prevent misuse, is paramount for the growth of any sort of online trade, including e-banking. This factor has been cited as the most critical success factor for e-banking among others (Shah and Siddiqui, 2006). The same author outlines the importance of upgrading the technological infrastructure of e-banking, not only with advanced legacy systems but also with policies and user management practices that will enable a safer e-banking environment. Along with IS the strategic nature of e-banking has been identified as a success factor for the adoption and usage of e-banking however, little empirical evidence exists in the literature (Gikandi and Bloor, 2010).

In a real-world context banks refuse to publish security incidents to the general public for fear of losing customers and reputation. In this respect, they frequently lack in a sound ITSG program capable to assure that e-banking will satisfy business and security requirements. An ITSG program can actually increase IT performance and Risk Management in e-banking through management or leadership processes where visibility to the effectiveness of the security program will be the key to verify results and promote a security culture. In other words, organizational accountability for security is the pathway to future security and business investments in the e-banking domain (ITSG, 2007). In Figure 5 we represent the role

Figure 4. E-banking continuum; Source: Adopted from Southard and Siau (2004)

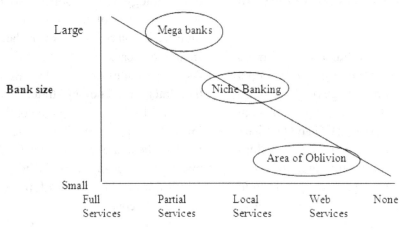

Web site usage/features

of ITSG in e-banking taking into consideration the e-banking continuum described in Figure 4.

This figure indicates that smaller banks that usually lack in resources contrary to larger banks, can build an ITSG framework which will differentiate them from competition and gain the *relative* advantage in the e-banking services. Relative advantage is the degree to which consumers perceive a new product or service as different as and better than its substitutes in which the theory "diffusion of innovation" stands (Rogers, 1962).

In this respect the security culture requires active participation and a shared understanding among stakeholders in order to coordinate activities and adapt to changing circumstances including social, technological and business environment. Training and security awareness programs are of paramount importance from the Board of Directors to future customers but this may not be sufficient enough if banks do not publicize their improvements through the media and press in order to increase consumer confidence in e-banking (Gikandi and Bloor, 2010). The security culture highly depends on the security strategy the bank employs for e-banking. Small, niche banks focused more on external portals can create a dynamic and constantly evolving security strategy which will enable them to compete with larger banks. Most critical factors included in a security strategy usually are a) Business integration, b) Building e-trust c) Obtain support from upper management and d) Promote and protect

Figure 5. ITSG framework for e-banking

the functional areas of e-banking (Shah and Siddiqui, 2006). Within the security strategy, clear policies should be formed in compliance with industry-related standards based on the unique environment of the service provider.

Security is useless if it cannot be communicated in clear and unambiguous terms. This is highly important in e-banking since the complexity of technological advances usually distracts users and inhibits adoption of e-banking. For this reason, monitoring and communication can increase performance, user satisfaction and minimize security incidents. New trends in monitoring complex systems such as e-banking include automated methods with consistent metrics such as the Security Content Automated Protocol (SCAP) from the National Institute of Standards and Technology (NIST) which is described later.

Smaller banks that concentrate on local accessibility as their niche advantage rather than full e-banking services can enhance their e-banking status by focusing on the service quality. Contrary to larger banks which focus on mass-customization, small banks through their own unique security strategy can compete on a local level with a greater service quality. Key components that are considered important in the quality of service in e-banking, with an emphasis on Internet banking, include speed of service (e.g. download e-banking content), enhanced navigation and interactivity (Vachirapornpuk and Broderick, 2002).

Therefore, the main purpose of ITSG in e-banking is to offer a shield against the diversity of risks that can impact the security objectives of e-banking, however, the security objectives for e-banking do not include the usual triad namely the confidentiality, integrity, availability but extend to non repudiation and authentication of information (Basel Committee, 2003). Moreover, the role of ITSG in e-banking is to combat risks and result in tangible benefits such as improved internal processes and controls, potential lower audit and insurance costs, market and customer differentiation and as tool for competitive advan-

tage (Reserve Bank of India, 2011). An ITSG program for e-banking should rely on a well-defined organization structure to eliminate gaps between business and IT and also to minimize overlaps in technology management (Kondabagil, 2007).

E-BANKING RISKS

The vast majority of best known Risk Management methods, frameworks and best practices in e-banking suggest security policies, procedures, standards, and guidelines as the key components in order to provide management, support compliance and direct employees with what is expected as security behavior (Kouns and Minoli, 2010). Up to this point, there is no distinct Risk Management approach for this domain but only generic models modified to suit the e-banking environment (Tanampasidis, 2008). However, the e-banking environment is characterized as highly dynamic and involves perceptible changes such as product and service innovation, the unprecedented speed of technological change, the increasing dependence of banks on third-party service providers and the ubiquitous nature of open electronic networks. For these reasons the Basel Committee has acknowledged e-banking risks under two main categories with four subcategories each namely traditional risks or financial risks under credit, market, interest rate, and liquidity risk, and as inherently new risks or non financial risks namely operational, reputation, legal and strategic (Kondabagil, 2007). Figure 6 and following paragraphs provide an overview of the e-banking risks.

Strategic risks can derive when management does not efficiently plan, manage and monitor the performance of the e-banking services and products. In this regard, the need for an effective ITSG process will enable value delivery, performance measurement and management of IT-related risks. This will in turn create competitive advantage, increase customer satisfaction, and improve cost efficiency and innovation (Kondabagil, 2007).

Figure 6. E-banking risks

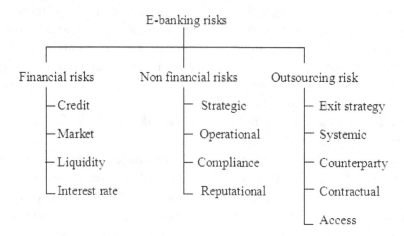

Factors influencing strategic risk include, but not restricted, to the adequacy of information systems, the increased dependence on outsourcing and third parties and the adequacy of technical, operational, compliance and marketing support. Particularly, outsourcing risk and third parties dependencies have become integral part of e-banking therefore, will be analyzed separately.

Operational risk can be defined under the Basel Committee principles as the risk of loss resulting from inadequate processes, people and systems or from external events. This broad definition is also found on literature as transaction risk, security risk or IT risk (Kouns and Minoli, 2010). Examples of operational risk involve but not limited to internal and external fraud, human factors, and erroneous transaction processing and product and service liability. Operational risk affects the financial institution in the ability to deliver e-banking services and has a direct impact on customer service and satisfaction. Major factors affecting the nature of operational risk are the structure and complexity of the bank's processing environment, complexity of supportive technology and failed outsourced processes. In this regard, a sound ITSG process can mitigate operational risks by acting as an internal control process thereby increasing business value.

Legal risk arises mainly from violations or non-conformance with laws, rules, regulations and ethical standards. Legal risk is also found in the literature as compliance risk (Shah and Clarke, 2009) where non compliance may indicate serious consequences including rating downgrades, monetary fines, enforced penalties, reputational damage and in extreme cases withdrawal of authorization to operate. E-banking is a highly dynamic channel that necessitates a strong governance program where the laws, rules, policies and procedures are clear and implemented in a daily basis. However, since e-banking is still evolving the risk associated with legal issues is considered highly complex because the changing technological environment and the cross-border transactions are deliberate causes for concern.

Reputational risk is described as the risk of significant negative public opinion where the image and the reputation of the bank are badly damaged. Factors affecting the reputation of e-banking system are, but not limited, the loss of trust due to an unauthorized activity on customer accounts, failure to deliver marketing objectives, confusion between services, lack on online communication and the modification of the bank's website (Kondabagil, 2007). For this reason, an ITSG program can help improve reputational risk

Table 1. E-banking risks categorization

Strategic Risk: Associated risk with Board and management decision-making.	Non finan-cial risks
Operational Risk: Associated risk with implementation of e-banking functions.	
Legal Risk: Associated risk with non adherence to law enforcement.	
Reputational Risk: Associated risk with damage to e-trust and image of e-banking services.	
Credit Risk: Associated risk with the bank's inability to meet its obligations in accordance with agreed terms.	Financial risks
Market Risk: Associated risk resulting from changes in market prices, interest rates, foreign exchange rates, equity and commodity prices.	
Interest Rate Risk: Associated risk resulting from falling bond prices due to variability of interest rates.	
Liquidity Risk: Associated risk with a bank's inability of funding.	
Outsourcing Risk: Associated risk resulting from third parties dependence.	

by establishing monitoring procedures capable not only to prevent failures but educate the customer along with formal incident responses.

Financial risks such as credit, market, liquidity and interest rate risks are considered as traditional e-banking risks. However, their practical implications may be of a different magnitude for banks than non financial risks (Rao et al., 2007). This is true in the case where banks cover a variety of banking activities as compared to banks or solely Internet banks that focus exclusively on e-banking services. For example a liquidity risk may emerge if a bank lacks in resources and has inability to meet its obligations whereas credit risk emerges from a bank's inability to make payments as promised. It should be pointed out here that specific problems may occur at different risk categories. For example an internal fraud can be classified as operational risk but such an event also exposes a bank to reputational and legal risk. Table 1 summarizes the categorization of e-banking risks with the addition of outsourcing risk that will be explained in detail in the next section since it has the ability to affect traditional risks and also cause other risks in the e-banking environment.

OUTSOURCING RISK IN E-BANKING

Public confidence in e-banking is a cornerstone in the stability and reputation of a financial institution. Systems reliability and assurance of security requirements (availability, confidentiality and integrity) is therefore the responsibility of the bank even though the e-banking system is operated elsewhere, either domestically or abroad. The main drivers to outsource for banks have been the potential for cost savings and the need to focus on core competencies. Other benefits involve lower personnel costs, instant access to talent and the need not to do extensive training (Angelakopoulos and Mihiotis, 2011). For these reasons, e-banking systems are based not solely on operational efficiencies but also on third party service providers. Therefore, as the range and relative complexity of such outsourced activities increase, so are the risks.

Outsourcing can be defined as any activity that is not performed by the bank itself, but it is supported by a contracted third party (Rao et al., 2007). The most common way for a bank to mitigate outsourcing risks is via an ITSG process in due diligence. This means that a bank needs to ensure that the supported vendors are trusted third parties and through an ITSG process to assess the quality and reputation of their products and services. Particularly, the Federal Financial

Institutions Examination Council (FFIEC, 2004) specifies recommendations about selecting a third party service provider when performing due diligence. The most important include a) qualifications and background of the vendor, b) financial status and reputation, c) adherence to legal and regulatory compliance and d) insurance coverage. According to (Arshad et al., 2007) Information Computer Technology (ICT) outsourcing is an act of delegating or transferring a proportion of IT-related decision making rights, business process and material to external providers, who will be responsible to develop, manage and administer these activities in accordance with agreed upon deliverables as explicitly set in contractual agreement. Usually, most commonly outsourced are ISP services, web hosting, ICT application maintenance and support, ICT infrastructure, programming, e-business solutions, application analysis, application support end user, staff/user training, ICT security audit and security policy or standards development.

Outsourcing requires a contract or a solid deal with the third party to ensure smooth cooperation. Particularly the contract arrangements should indicate the type and the range of the arrangement between the bank and the third party namely the terms and conditions of the agreement, ownership of information, limitations, dispute resolution, cost of transition and periodic reviews of the agreement. Normally outsourcing arrangements are classified into either IT outsourcing or business process outsourcing (BPO). More usually occurs the first arrangement since banks prefer to transfer the technological equipment outdoors (material outsourcing) and keep the business processes performed and managed internally (indoors). Another subset of outsourcing include the "offshore outsourcing" where the arrangement with the third service provider is based outside the bank's territory, mostly because to take advantage of the labor costs. Another type of outsourcing contract is a service level agreement (SLA). This type of contract emphasizes the requirements a bank anticipates from the vendor as far as bandwidth, response time and business expectations are concerned (Shah and Siddiqui, 2006). Outsourcing and the perceived risks affect significantly financial and non financial risks as described in the previous section. For example strategic risks may emerge from the inadequacy of a financial institution to control the activities of the service provider. Moreover, reputation risk may arise when the service provider fail to deliver the promised results and the quality of the service is poor. This has a direct impact on the e-banking system operability and of course on the reputation of the bank. In addition, legal risk (compliance risk) may also manifest if the service provider fail to abide and conform to legal and regulatory provisions. In this respect, operational risk also arises because bank's internal processes are downgraded due to the lack of support from the third party service provider.

Furthermore, outsourcing risk may give rise to *other* risks such as the "Exit strategy risk" which occurs when a bank has high reliance on a vendor and lack in exit strategies. In addition, *other* risks include the "Country risk" which may occur due to offshore outsourcing because economic, political, social and legal climate of the host country, where the service provider is located, prevent to fulfill the contract agreement. Outsourcing risk may also cause "Concentration and Systemic risk" which refers to the risk incidents that happen within the overall banking industry or sector. For example, if e-banking functional areas are dependent upon a certain number of external service providers this cause a number of banks to be indirectly dependent on the same service provider. Other types of risks include "Counterparty risk" which arises due to bad quality of services, "Contractual risk" when the agreement between the parties is not fulfilled as it should be and "Access risk" when the outsourcing arrangement hampers the ability of regulated entity to provide timely data

Figure 7. Outsourcing risk relationships

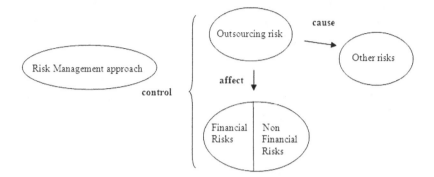

and other information to regulators (Basel Committee on Banking Supervision, 2005). Managing outsourced services in e-banking imply the need for a sound Risk Management approach which will entail a comprehensive ITSG process for managing the whole range of e-banking risks including outsourcing and other third party dependencies.

The role of ITSG will be a) to enforce compliance functions, b) combat anti-money laundering, c) improve the reputation between the trusted parties and d) ensure the privacy of customer information. Figure 7 shows that outsourcing risk affect traditional (financial) and nontraditional (nonfinancial) risks such as strategic risks but can also cause other risks such as "country risk" or "counterparty risk." Therefore, evaluation of outsourcing decisions should begin with a proper Risk Assessment namely a) identification of the role of outsourcing in the overall business strategy and objectives of the financial institution, b) analysis due diligence on the complexity and nature of the vendor, c) analysis of risk-return benefits of outsourcing against the vulnerabilities and threats that may emerge upon the possibility of a security incident (Arshad et al., 2007).

Financial institutions relying on e-banking systems should mitigate the overall risk by developing appropriate contingency plans thereby plan for processing alternatives. The contingency planning for outsourced activities could be part

of a Business Continuity Planning (BCP). BCP needs to ensure the sustainability of the e-banking system itself and of the activities outsourced. The BCP is a comprehensive written plan of action provides with specific requirements for the staff and infrastructure and establishes the procedures necessary to deal with a disruption and recovery of business functions within the estimated timeframes. At the same time, a Business Continuity Management (BCM) is a trade-off process between costs and benefits and can be included in a wider Risk Management approach (Kondabagil, 2007).

RISK MANAGEMENT IN E-BANKING

The Risk Management is considered by some resources (SANS Institute, 2003; BSI Standard 100-1, 2006) a discipline and part of information security management. This point of view is also shared by ENISA (2006), naming that Risk Management and Risk Assessment are major components of Information Security Management. Moreover, according to Peltier (2004), Risk Management is the process that allows balancing operational and economic costs of protective measures and achieving gains in mission capability by protecting business process that supports the business objective or mission of the enterprise. In a similar way, (Tsoumas and Tryfonas, 2004) defines Risk Management process as a framework for determining and implementing acceptable security controls. To take things from the beginning and rationalize the purpose of conducting a Risk Management approach in e-banking we must understand the elements and relationships of risk in e-banking. Therefore we explicitly refer to the definitions of risk elements in e-banking such as risk […] the possibility of any deliberate or undesirable action that could cause and result in a negative impact in the e-banking system or the combination of the probability of an event and its consequence (Kondabagil, 2007, ISO 27005). Threat as […] any situation or event that has potential to harm the e-banking system. Threats materialize when they exploit vulnerabilities (Kondabagil, 2007; ISO 27001). Vulnerability as […] a weakness, which is susceptible to be used by a threat to gain unauthorized access to information or disrupt processing. Vulnerabilities can be human errors, weakness in software from the information system, system security practices and procedures, internal controls etc. (Kouns and Minoli, 2010). The threat – vulnerability

pairs leads to an unwanted risk, which is subject of likelihood to be estimated or measured. This likelihood is the probability that a vulnerability will be exploited by a threat which leads to a harm or damage.

Figure 8 shows a semantic net of key concepts related to the management of e-banking risks. The relationship between the likelihood of a threat materializing vulnerability determines the intensity of the risk. An asset is anything that has value to the bank and is part of the e-banking system, therefore, requires protection. Assets can be categorized as *tangible* such as software, hardware and *intangible* such as reputation, user confidence. Normally, assets with higher value will suffer greater risk and will require more protection. The existence of risk requires the satisfaction of security requirements or objectives within the e-banking system namely the availability, confidentiality, integrity, authentication, and non-repudiation (Basel Committee on Banking Supervision, 2003). As most risks cannot be controlled or mitigated fully, some *residual* risk is normally left. Usually the residual risk is accepted

Figure 8. Relationship of key elements of risk in e-banking

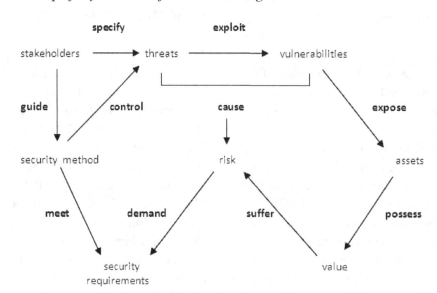

by the bank, transferred or insured. The security method is a Risk Management process able to meet the security requirements and decrease the risk to an acceptable level. Stakeholders guide the security method in terms of analysis and results and also identify possible threats to e-banking. This notion is supported by (Solms and von Solms, 2009) who support that Risk Management should involve various stakeholders (from the Chairman of the Board to the youngest worker) to consider the different security behavior towards the system.

ISO 13335-1 defines Risk Management as the total process that entail identifying, controlling, and eliminating or minimizing uncertain events that may affect IT systems. CobiT and ISO 27001 support the utilization of Risk Assessments, as part of Risk Management, to determine what risks need to be mitigated and to what extent. Also CobiT and ISO 27002 sees Risk Management as a core element of an ITSG process. Risk Assessment in e-banking is [...] the systematic process of identifying the nature and causes of risks to which e-banking activities could be exposed and assessing the likely impact and probability of these risks occurring (Aggelis, 2005). Moreover, according to Soliman (2006) Risk Assessment is an *"objective analysis of the current security controls that protect an organization's assets and a determination of the probability of losses to those assets."*

ISO 27001 and ISO 27005 regard Risk Assessment as part of Risk Management with risk identification, risk analysis and risk evaluation described as Risk Assessment phases. Risk treatment is more part of a wider Risk Management approach since it follows the assessment of risks in order to manage and control the residual risks (Brotby, 2009). The risk analysis is conducted to show that a due diligence is performed. Risk analysis also requires a deep knowledge of the financial institution and its surroundings as well as a deep understanding of strategic and operational objectives (Tanampasidis, 2008). For this reason, identification of information assets is required.

The risk identification consists of the identification of critical assets to be risk-managed, threats, and vulnerabilities in order to control the consequences of risk event realization. To sum up, Risk Assessment in e-banking is a distributed process that involves steps including (Shah and Siddiqu 2006, Rao et al., 2007; ISO 27005):

- Identification of risk elements in the e-banking processing environment.
- Analysis and magnitude of the risk elements in the e-banking processing environment.
- Outsourcing dependencies and country risks in offshoring.
- Business impact analysis for the BCP in the e-banking processing environment.
- Compliance requirements for the e-banking processing environment.

Thereby, it within the responsibility of the Board and Executive Management to implement a comprehensive Risk Management approach. All risks that could possibly have a negative effect on the well-being of the e-banking system (if and once they materialize) are definitely the responsibility of management. Therefore, all levels of organizational management should be involved in the process of Risk Management (Tan et al., 2010). This notion is also supported by (Brotby, 2009) who suggest separate frameworks for each major category of risk in e-banking such as outsourcing risk, legal risk, operational risk etc. Therefore, an effective Risk Management framework should be built on a formal governance process, rely on individual responsibility and collective oversight, use a combination of advances analysis and be backed by comprehensive reporting and monitoring.

ITSG APPROACHES FOR E-BANKING

We expand important studies (Da Veiga and Eloff, 2007; Rao et al., 2007; Holmquist, 2008) to pres-

Table 2. ITSG approach/method comparison

ITSG Approach / ISG Objectives	Basel Committee	Joint Forum	ISO 27002	COBIT	CORAS	OCTAVE	COSO	PCI	FATF	CGC	FFIEC	CGTF	OECD	ISSA	CISWG	ISO 27005	ISO 38500	ISO 15489	NIST 800-39	SABSA	CMM
Strategic alignment	✓	✓	✓	✓	✓	✓	✓	x	✓	✓	x	✓	✓	/	/	✓	✓	✓	✓	✓	✓
Risk Management	✓	✓	✓	✓	✓	✓	✓	✓	x	✓	✓	✓	/	✓	✓	✓	/	✓	✓	✓	✓
Business process assurance	✓	x	✓	✓	✓	✓	✓	x	/	✓	x	✓	✓	✓	✓	✓	✓	✓	✓	✓	✓
Value delivery	✓	x	✓	✓	✓	✓	✓	x	x	✓	✓	✓	✓	✓	✓	✓	✓	✓	✓	✓	✓
Resource management	✓	x	✓	✓	✓	✓	✓	x	✓	✓	✓	✓	✓	✓	✓	✓	✓	✓	✓	✓	✓
Performance measurement	/	x	✓	✓	✓	✓	✓	x	✓	✓	✓	✓	✓	/	✓	✓	✓	✓	✓	✓	✓
User awareness & training	✓	x	/	✓	x	✓	/	✓	/	✓	x	✓	✓	✓	x	x	✓	✓	✓	✓	✓
Certification	x	x	✓	✓	x	x	x	✓	x	x	x	x	x	✓	x	x	✓	✓	✓	✓	x
Internal audit	✓	x	✓	x	✓	✓	✓	x	✓	✓	✓	✓	✓	x	✓	x	✓	✓	✓	✓	✓
Best practice	✓	x	✓	✓	x	x	x	/	✓	✓	✓	✓	✓	✓	✓	✓	✓	✓	✓	✓	✓
Corporate governance	✓	✓	✓	✓	/	✓	✓	✓	✓	✓	✓	✓	✓	✓	✓	x	✓	✓	✓	✓	✓
Incident management	✓	/	✓	x	✓	✓	✓	x	✓	✓	x	✓	✓	x	x	✓	✓	✓	✓	✓	✓
Business continuity planning	✓	✓	✓	✓	✓	✓	✓	x	/	✓	✓	x	✓	✓	x	✓	✓	✓	✓	✓	✓
Ethical codes	✓	x	/	x	x	x	x	x	✓	✓	x	x	✓	✓	x	x	✓	x	/	/	x
Compliance	✓	x	✓	✓	✓	✓	✓	✓	✓	✓	✓	✓	✓	✓	✓	✓	✓	✓	✓	✓	✓
	✓		✓	✓	✓	✓	✓	✓	✓	✓	✓	✓	✓	✓	✓	✓	✓	✓	✓	✓	✓

✓ = yes / = partial x = no

ent the reader with the most commonly used ISG frameworks. The first eight in the row along with CobiT and ISO 27002 have evidence as direct fits in an e-banking environment (Kondabagil, 2007) however we expand into other well known approaches so as to evaluate (Table 2) which one can satisfy ISG objectives more holistically. We consider for comparison not only common ISG objectives/criteria such as strategic alignment and value delivery but also related IS criteria such as IS awareness programs and compliance as means to enhance the applicability of an approach to the specific needs of e-banking.

Basel Committee on Banking Supervision

The Basel Committee objective is to formulate broad supervisory standards and guidelines about the banking industry in the areas of system supervision and regulation. The Committee does not possess any formal supranational supervisory authority and does not enforce any kind of compliance however it offers comprehensive coverage of Risk Management and ISG issues relating to e-banking such as operational Risk Management, outsourcing, business continuity management, anti-money laundering, privacy of customer information and audit procedures. Specifically in a 2003 report (Basel Committee, 2003), the Committee describes Risk Management challenges, requirements and principles in the area of e-banking. Risk Management principles for e-banking include a) Board and Management oversight, b) identification and evaluation of security controls c) legal and reputational Risk Management principles. Among the challenges the Committee considers to e-banking activities are the complex characteristics of the Internet delivery channel, the speed of change relating to customer innovation and the e-banking trends such as outsourcing diversify the applicability of these principles. Moreover, the Committee in a series of documents expects that such principles must be tailored to fit the exact needs of a bank.

The Joint Forum

The Joint Forum is considered as an advisory group formed under the guidance of the Bank for International Settlements, Basel, Switzerland and consists of three members namely the Basel Committee on Banking Supervision, the International Organization of Securities Commissions (IOSCO) and the International Association of Insurance Supervisors (IAIS). The Joint Forum mainly provides recommendations for the insurance, securities, and banking industries worldwide setting high level principles including Risk Assessment guidelines. Relevant principles about e-banking also refer to outsourcing of e-banking activities and to the importance of a Business Continuity Planning (BCP).

Operationally Critical Threat, Asset, and Vulnerability Assessment (OCTAVE)

OCTAVE stands for the "Operationally Critical Threat, Asset and Vulnerability Assessment," a risk-based strategic assessment and planning technique for IS developed by the Software Engineering Institute of the Carnegie Mellon University Computer Emergency Response Team. This framework is team-driven from business department and IT that cooperate to address the security needs of an organization. OCTAVE is also an asset-driven method and represents visually the range of threats during the evaluation in tree structures. Currently, there exist three variations of the OCTAVE method namely the original OCTAVE method as a comprehensive suite of tools, the OCTAVE-S for smaller organizations and the OCTAVE-Allegro as a streamline approach for IS and assurance. OCTAVE is based on interactive workshops to accumulate the different knowledge perspectives of the employees, the Board and Executives and other stakeholders for the purpose to measure current organization security practices and develop security improvement strategies and risk mitigation planning (OCTAVE, 2003). The OCTAVE approach is driven by two of the aspects: operational risk and security practices. Technology is examined only in relation to security practices. The OCTAVE also characterizes certain criteria as set of principles, attributes, and outputs. Important principles, among others, are the fundamental concepts driving the nature of the evaluation, for example, self direction, integrated management and open communication. OCTAVE also consists of three phases namely *Phase 1*: Build Asset-Based Threat Profiles (organizational evaluation),

Phase 2: Identify Infrastructure Vulnerabilities (information infrastructure evaluation and *Phase 3:* Develop Security Strategy and Plan (evaluation of mitigation plans). The OCTAVE methods acquire certain benefits namely it is *self-directed* since the method is guided by stakeholders, *flexible* since it can be tailored to suit a unique risk environment and, *evolving* since it moves the operational risk-based view of security into a business context supporting the organization's mission and priorities.

Committee of Sponsoring Organization of the Treadway Commission (COSO)

COSO stands for the "Committee of Sponsoring Organization of the Treadway Commission," formed in 1985 to sponsor the National Commission on Fraudulent Financial Reporting (the Treadway Commission) and in 1992 issued the Internal Control – Integrated Framework to help businesses assess and improve their security posture via internal control systems. COSO emphasize on the concept of Enterprise Risk Management (ERM) as a "*process effected by an entity's board of directors, management and other personnel, applied in strategy setting and across the enterprise, designed to identify potential events that may affect the entity, and manage risk to be within its risk appetite, to provide reasonable assurance regarding the achievement of entity objectives*" (Committee of Sponsoring Organizations of the Treadway Commission, 2004). In this regard, COSO is an enterprise Risk Management framework with four distinct categories namely 1) Strategic (high levels business goals aligned with its mission), 2) Operations (effective use of resources), 3) Reporting (in support to documentation) and 4) Compliance (with applicable laws and regulations). In addition, the ERM framework is built on eight interrelated components namely 1) internal environment, 2) objective setting, 3) event identification, 4) Risk Assessment, 5) risk response, 6) control activities, 7) information and communication and 8) monitoring. COSO and similar compliant frameworks (such as CobiT) are generally accepted as internal control framework for enterprises. CobiT is more accepted as an internal control framework for IT. One concern about COSO is the overwhelming nature which can appear for some organizations or systems, such as e-banking, as a heavy task especially if they lack a Risk Management culture (Kondabagil, 2007).

Payment Card Industry Data Security Standard (PCI DSS)

The PCI DSS is an acronym for the "Payment Card Industry Data Security Standard," released in 2004 as a joint effort between all major credit card associations to enhance payment account data security by driving education and awareness about cardholder data security. It includes guidelines for user authentication, firewalls, encryption, anti-virus measures, policy issues and others (Koons and Minoli, 2010). In other words, PCI DSS is a widely accepted set of policies and procedures intended to optimize the security of creditcard holders. The latest version of the standard is PCI DSS 2.0 and institutions compliant with this standard show to customers that sensitive credit card information being processed is protected against fraud or financial terrorism. The standard contains twelve major requirements supported by 175 sub-requirements that apply to system components, which are defined as "any element attached to cardholder data environment" (PCI, 2010). The new version supports a prolonged lifecycle of three years (compared to two years in the previous versions) to ensure multiple opportunities for stakeholder input and feedback in order to remain ahead of the threat landscape.

Financial Action Task Force (FATF)

FATF is an acronym for the "Financial Action Task Force," based in Paris, an inter-governmental body with the purpose to develop and promote policies to combat money laundering and terrorist financing. Forty Recommendations were developed in 1996 by FATF as a policy document issued to provide a set of security controls against money laundering covering from criminal justice to law enforcement (FATF, 1996). In 2001, the FATF expanded its mandate to deal with the issue of financing of the terrorism by creating the Eight Special Recommendations on Terrorism Financing. These recommendations are supportive set of countermeasures to the Forty Recommendations. The security objective of FATF is to set standards against "dirty" money from corruption, terrorism or tax evasion (Task Force on Financial Integrity and Economic Development, 2011). The purpose is to expand and strengthen the bank's ability to handle money from high level political officials, prevent the creation of anonymous companies that cannot be traced to a real person and stop tax evasion as a trigger crime for money laundering.

Corporate Governance Codes (CGC)

CGC is an acronym for "Corporate Governance Codes" issued from the European Corporate Governance Institute. Among the most important governance codes is the "Dey Report," developed in 1994, recommended 14 best practice guidelines for financial institutions. The guidelines provide directions for the Board of Directors about stewardship, strategic planning, Risk Management and internal audits. Another well recognized CGC was the Sarbanes-Oxley Act of 2002 in the United States. This was a legal framework for CG and internal controls. Other CGCs principles about CG are available as full texts from the website of the European Governance Institute. (www.ecgi.org).

Federal Financial Institutions Examination Council (FFIEC)

FFIEC is an acronym for the "Federal Financial Institutions Examination Council," established in

1979 authority with the purpose to set principles, standards, and report forms for the federal examination of financial institutions. FFIEC guidelines have replaced previously issued Banking Circulars BC-177 and BC-226 (Brotby, 2009). The FFIEC publication "Authentication in an Internet Banking Environment" is used by federal financial institutions for compliance with their obligations regarding e-banking systems operability (FFIEC, 2005). The objectives of the publication are to ensure proper identification and assessment of risks associated with Internet-based services as well risk mitigation actions to strengthen authentication controls for e-banking systems. This publication is consistent with the FFIEC "Information Technology Examination Handbook" which presents generic guidance for assessing information technology (IT) risks including corporate governance, internal audit controls and others.

A Platform for Risk Analysis of Security Critical Systems (CORAS)

CORAS is an acronym for "A Platform for Risk Analysis of Security Critical Systems" and is a model-driven risk analysis method developed by the European Union (EU) for the purpose to improve security during the systems design process (Lund et al., 2010). CORAS uses the Unified Modeling Language (UML) to model and target the analysis results in terms of reporting and documenting. CORAS provides a standard for the safety requirements of high security information systems, such as e-banking, supporting Risk Assessments process. The CORAS framework is based on the Australian/New Zealand Standard for Risk Management AN/NZS4360:2004 and is inspired by the asset-driven strategy of CRAMM. CORAS has eights steps in the risk analysis namely 1) Preparation for the analysis, 2) Customer presentation of the target, 3) Refining the target description using asset diagrams, 4) Approval of the target description, 5) Risk identification using threat diagrams, 6) Risk estimation using threat diagrams, 7) Risk evaluation using risk diagrams and 8) Risk treatment using treatment diagrams. CORAS covers an extensive range of security objectives from business context goals to IS compliance and legal requirements. The main concern about CORAS and other Risk Assessments, such as OCTAVE and CRAMM, is that the focus is not on trade-offs and calculated risks meaning that there has been no prior activity on determining what are acceptable risks based on budget, time and resource constraints (Houmba et al., 2010)

Organization for Economic Co-Operation and Development (OECD)

OECD is an acronym for "Organization for Economic Co-operation and Development" established in 1947 and its publication of "OECD Principles of Corporate Governance" recommends policies and actions against financial terrorism, tax evasion, money laundering and other actions that can harm the well-being of the society. The principles are a living instrument offering non-binding standards and best practices towards implementation of good CG. Examples of such principles are 1) Ensuring the basis for an effective corporate governance framework, 2) The rights of shareholders and key ownership functions, 3) The equitable treatment of stakeholders, 4) The role of stakeholders, 5) Disclosure and transparency, and 6) The responsibilities of the Board. The OECD also provides a forum in which governments policy makers, investors, corporations and other stakeholders worldwide can work together to share experiences and seek solutions to common problems (OECD, 2004).

Information Systems Security Association (ISSA)

ISSA is an acronym for the "Information Systems Security Association," a not-for-profit international organization of IS professionals and practitioners. The primary goal of the ISSA is to promote management practices that will ensure the confidentiality, integrity and availability of information resources. ISSA has published GAISP V3.0 in 2003 – the Generally Accepted Information Security Principles project - in an attempt to address the challenges that IS faces in front of new changes in regulatory compliance and upcoming risks. Among the benefits and goals of the GAISP are the comprehensive guidance on good CG practice throughout industry, commerce, and government globally; increase the effectiveness and efficiency of business, promote trade and commerce, and improve productivity through good IS practice; enable certification and self-policing of practitioners against a Common Body of Knowledge (CBK); help preserve public trust in the ability to leverage modern information technology while avoiding unintended consequences; ensure global harmonization of culturally diverse IS principles to minimize artificial barriers to the free flow of information that can result from conflicting standards and controls; promote increased customer confidence, trust, and acceptance of vendor products conforming to GAISP (GAISP, 2003).

Corporate Information Security Working Group (CISWG)

CISWG is an acronym for the "Corporate Information Security Working Group" established by Adam H. Putnam in 2003 as an actionable program on the development of information security and compliance metrics to monitor whether or not information security is being effectively managed (CISWF, 2004). The responsibility resides with the Board of Directors/Trustees in its role to adhere to a governance framework. Organizations follow the CISWG guidelines should conduct a Risk Assessment with emphasis placed on key corporate assets and functions. While total risk elimination is impossible, risk mitigation strategies should indicate the amount of residual risk as the level of risk tolerance to executive management in a meaningful way.

ISO/IEC 27005:2008

ISO 27005 is a key IS Risk Management standard that supports the concepts specified in ISO 27001 and is designed to assist the implementation of IS based on a Risk Management approach. ISO 27005 offers general advice for IS Risk Management in an organization supporting the requirements of an ISMS in conjunction with ISO 27001 and ISO 27002. ISO 27005 is applicable to all types of organizations and systems with an intention to manage IT risks that could compromise the organizations information security. ISO 27005 indicate how a Risk Assessment should be conducted without however indicating a certain type of method (ISO/IEC 27005:2008).

ISO/IEC 38500:2008

ISO 38500 is a "Corporate Governance of Information Technology" standard with the objective to provide a framework which comprises of definitions, principles and a model for the Board of Directors to use when evaluating, directing and monitoring the use of IT in their organizations. ISO 38500 is a high level advisory standard applicable to the governance of management processes (and decisions) relating to the information and communication services used. The purpose of this standard is a) to assure stakeholders for a sound CG program if the standard's framework is attained, b) guide directors in governing the use of IT and c) provide a basis of objective evaluation of the CG of IT. Among the principles supported by this standard include the responsibility of stakeholders, a Risk Management strategy for CG of IT and guidelines on human behavior (ISO/IEC 38500:2008).

AS ISO 15489:2002

ISO 15489 is a standard designed to meet records management requirements in businesses and governments. The standard is an Australian codi-fication of the International Standard on Records Management and consists of two parts namely part 1 which describes generally the standard itself and part 2 which describes guidelines for the implementation of the standard. Specifically, part 1 describes a framework for record management with legal and audit considerations (ISO 15489-1:2001). Part 2 is a technical report supports part 1 by providing additional guidance on records management policies and the responsibilities to be defined and assigned to stakeholders (ISO 15489-2:2001). Additionally, the alignment of ISO 27001 to ISO 15489 strengthens the delivery of existing records management systems and its drivers. This is critical to build strong information governance projects, which enable risks to be assessed in an ever-changing information management world (Lomas, 2010).

NIST SP 800-39

NIST 800-39 Special Publication is a standard that describes a Risk Management framework (RMF) as a structured process for managing risks related to the operation and use of information systems. NIST 800-39 has a similar approach with ISO/IEC 27001:2005 in Risk Management with focus on selecting and documenting security controls for information systems. Additionally, the RMF process describes risk-based protection strategies support the overall goals and objectives of organizations, can be tightly coupled to enterprise architectures, and can operate effectively within system development life cycles. The RFM framework is based on a combination of other NIST Special Publications (e.g. NIST SP 800-53, NIST SP 800-70 and NIST SP 800-37) to support assessment authorization and monitoring of information systems (NIST SP 800-39, 2011).

In Table 2 we compare each approach against a number of ISG objectives under a scale: "yes," "partial" and "no" - levels of fulfillment. For example, the Basel Committee of Banking Supervision for e-banking provides guidelines for monitoring and reporting, however, it does not provide performance measurement in the sense of exact metrics. Most of the aforementioned frameworks, best standards and Risk Management methods suggest security policies, procedures, and guidelines as key components in order to provide management, support compliance and direct employees with what is expected as behavior. Every single approach has its own strengths and weaknesses but none covers all ITSG components. Thereby, according to literature (Rao et al., 2007; Brotby, 2009) customization seems to be a solution when we deal with complex IT environments such as the e-banking environment. This table is intended to outline not only the baseline ISG objectives (namely the first six in the row) but also other objectives related to the concept of ITSG in order to enforce the applicability of a method in the e-banking domain. Thereby, the ISG Objectives and requirements depicted in this table define the internal configuration and management issues for each approach, to a level that is granular enough to be implemented.

EMERGING TRENDS IN MEASURING ITSG PERFORMANCE

In this section we provide insights about the emerging trends in measuring ITSG performance from the perspective of e-banking. Therefore, the significance of an ITSG program relies on constant monitoring, reporting and on the ability to articulate the results in clear and consistent metrics. However, the lack of performance-measuring systems for ITSG makes more prone the risk of incidents such as deficiencies in information systems, human errors and technical breakdowns. The key elements of a sound ITSG program in the e-banking context include a comprehensive Risk Management function capable to deliver the necessary checks and balances for the supporting infrastructure. In this regard, new trends in

Table 3. Security content application protocol components

SCAP Components
Vulnerabilities (CVE)
Configurations (CCE)
Platforms (CPE)
Vulnerability Scoring System (CVSS)
Checklist Language (XCCDF)
Assessment Language (OVAL)

measuring ITSG include automated IT security methods, such as the Security Content Automation Protocol (SCAP) from NIST, to measure policy compliance evaluation (e.g. FISMA compliance).

SCAP consists of six inter-related components (Table 3) that shape the security requirements of the method namely a) automated vulnerability management, b) standardized reporting and c) conformity with the NIST Validation program. SCAP components integrate information into an automated flow making security more measurable and comply with NIST federal security requirements (NIST, 2011). SCAP is usually being used to enable enterprise reporting within the U.S. Federal Government but for the purpose of this chapter we briefly describe the role of SCAP as an ITSG tool for generating stronger data control within an e-banking environment.

CVE (Common Vulnerabilities and Exposures)

CVE is a dictionary list of information security vulnerabilities and exposures. This standard defines "vulnerability" as a condition in a system that allows an attacker to a) execute commands as another user b) access restricted data c) pose as a different entity d) conduct a denial-of-service. Every publicly known information security vulnerability or exposure has a unique identification code which includes the following characteristics:

- CVE Identifier numerical figure (e.g., "CVE-1333-1234").
- Status description (e.g. default password).
- Short analysis (e.g. remote command execution).
- Relevant references (e.g. OVAL-ID).

CCE (Common Configuration Enumeration)

Similar to the CVE purpose, CCE (2011) is a complementary standard with an aim to automate the management of vulnerabilities and also provide conformity with policies such as federal information technology security requirements (e.g. NIST). CCE can correlate configuration data across multiple information sources. Each entry contains the following five attributes:

- CCE Identifier numerical figure (e.g."CCE-5678-122").
- Short status description of the configuration issue (e.g. operating system)
- Theoretical Parameters of the tested system (e.g. time, space, specification and settings).
- Viable technical solutions to a given configuration issue (e.g. download a security update).
- Relevant references (e.g. OVAL-ID).

CPE (Common Platform Enumeration)

A method of naming software (e.g. vendor, title, version). Purpose is to foster automation towards identification of the IT platforms to which a vulnerability or element of guidance applies. CPE uniform naming specification encourages community members generate names for new IT platforms in a consistent and formal manner. A CPE Name is a unique collection of components (URI scheme name) given to a specific platform type that is made up of hardware, applications, an operating system, and other possible parts e.g. cpe://microsoft:windows:2000

CVSS (Common Vulnerability Scoring System)

CVSS is a universal open and standardized method for vulnerability scoring. CVSS uses multiple fields for evaluating the overall risk of an individual vulnerability. Two common uses of CVSS are: a) prioritization of vulnerability remediation activities and b) calculation the severity of vulnerabilities discovered on a system. Metrics used to score and prioritize a vulnerability are a) Base Score Metrics (inherent characteristics of the vulnerability) b) Exploitability Metrics (related exploit range, attack complexity, and level of authentication needed) c) Impact Metrics (confidentiality, integrity, availability and impact value weighting) d) Environmental Metrics (effect of a vulnerability on the system environment) e) Temporal Metrics (elements about the vulnerability that change over time e.g. availability of exploit, type of fix available and level of vulnerability verification).

XCCDF (eXtensible Configuration Checklist Description Format)

XCCDF is a selection of documents or checklists for automated policy compliance. XCCDF uses an XML specification language to provide compliance with recommendations for minimum security controls under NIST guidelines. This method describes a process for measuring system configuration to a specified document or checklist. Audience of the XCCDF specification is primary *government* and secondary industry security analysts and product developers. Specifically, XCCDF goals are to a) generate documentation b) express policy-aware configuration rules c) support complex systems that may require complex rules d) support compliance scoring e) support customization.

OVAL (Open Vulnerability and Assessment Language)

A method for performing structured tests for reporting purposes. The purpose of OVAL is to create and update a database of system characteristics against OVAL definitions so as to evaluate a system for a specified machine state. OVAL supports, homogenizes and transfers the communication of security content across the whole system. OVAL actual use is similar to a common Risk Assessment process namely: identify and collect configuration data (OVAL System Characteristics); analyze a "specified machine state" such as a vulnerability (OVAL Definition schema) and document and report the final results about the state of a system (OVAL Results schema). OVAL uses a language (in XML format) for storing system configuration information in local systems.

In summary, the purpose of SCAP in measuring ITSG performance in e-banking is to

1. Identify the context of e-banking, existing and new risk elements (vulnerabilities and exposures) in automated fashion and constantly update the candidate list.
2. Analyze and configure the data from the IT platforms used based on existing controls (policies and settings) and user-system interaction.
3. Score and prioritize ITSG performance.
4. Facilitate community involvement via an enhanced role as a cognitive resource and
5. Insure compliance with NIST 800-53 controls. This integration of efforts can help standardize a highly complex environment and provide real-time risk management.

Other metrics, such as the number of persons trained in security awareness, reduction in fraud losses, in audit findings, or in security incidents (e.g., computer viruses, reported unauthorized data), may also portray the effectiveness of an ITSG program (Solms and von Solms, 2009).

Important factor is the experience and security behavior of different stakeholders and the use of the method to acquire the results (qualitative, semi, quantitative, combination).

In addition, attempts to measure ITSG performance using statistics tools, such as the Standard deviation, are not new however there are arguments against their effectiveness (Frankland, 2008). In addition, experts opinion may well be a more sufficient indicator of the effectiveness of an ITSG program however, opinion may be tampered with corrupted practitioners who rely on the FUD (Fear, Uncertainly and Doubt) principle. In this respect, best practices and international standards have already progressed in clearly defining a series of core metrics that characterize an ITSG program. For example ISO 27004 (ISO/IEC 27004:2009), part of ISO/IEC 27000 series, provides guidance on the development and use of measures and measurement for the assessment of an implemented information security management system, in alignment with ISO 27001 and ISO 27002. Furthermore, NIST SP 800-55 makes reference to security metrics for IT systems and NIST SP 800-80 is a relevant guide for developing performance metrics for IS (US Department of Commerce, 2006).

At this moment, there is no formal approach used across financial institutions about the effectiveness of an ITSG program in e-banking. Any reasonable approach should be satisfactory as long as the methods used are consistent (Brotby, 2009). To be successful, the widespread e-banking sector would have to agree on the metrics to be used and the collection of statistics. In this respect, the effectiveness of an ITSG program should be measured by whether or not defined objectives are achieved. As with any other process, increased productivity and compliance, greater resource utilization, customer satisfaction and successful risk mitigation can be indicators of an effective ITSG program. Another indicator might be trends in strategic, proactive security activities as opposed to purely tactical, reactive ones. For this reason effective policies and procedures must be the foundation for reliable security metrics and measurements.

CONCLUSION

The way Bill Gates in 2008 announced that "banking is essential, banks are not" shows the traditional bank branch is going to phase out and gradually be replaced by e-banking services which will continue to attract new users in favor of lower costs, instant accessibility and reliable customer service. However, as the financial sector and society embraces these new opportunities they have to contend with issues and face challenges that arise in the context of e-banking risks. Therefore, the main question of this chapter is whether an ITSG program can mitigate e-banking risks, increase business value and achieve compliance with industry-related best practices without severe organizational problems. So far, no study has been carried out to establish the ISG objectives influencing the adoption and effectiveness of e-banking or to evaluate relevant ITSG approach features. Therefore, this study was designed to evaluate reputed approaches such as ISG frameworks, best practices and principles, international standards, internal controls and Risk Management methods against standard ISG objectives and additional criteria in order to indicate which approach/method suits best in e-banking. The results of the study indicate benefits and shortcomings each ITSG approach possesses. Customization may be the preferable solution according to each e-banking system security strategy.

Although the majority of financial institutions recognize the importance of an ITSG program as an indispensable factor for the success of IT and corporate governance, they usually equate effective governance with meeting the demands of regulators without recognizing that sound ITSG can actually boost business. In this regard, they avoid using consistent metrics to measure the ef-

fectiveness of an ITSG program. New trends in measuring ITSG effectiveness include collection of metrics in a standard and automated fashion using security methods such as SCAP. Particularly, each financial institution is different in risk appetite, scope, complexity and resources therefore analysis of existing frameworks and best standards may indicate further areas for improvement and future research in order to combat the diversity of risks and the different view of stakeholders. For example, it is interesting to see in a future research whether user awareness, education and training programs are in accord with ethical codes proposed from current ITSG approaches.

In this respect, since there is no officially accepted ITSG framework for the e-banking domain, this chapter focused on establishing a strong relationship between Risk Management in e-banking and ISG in order to govern the information security in e-banking. To achieve this, we highlighted on the concept of Risk Management in e-banking and ISG. We further examined and compared elements from the most commonly used ISG frameworks, standards and best practices to a number of objectives/criteria that satisfy a sound ITSG program. This comparison leads us to safely propose that no single approach is a "best fit" for e-banking because the state of e-banking varies depending on a number of core capabilities such as country, culture and bank's reputation. Thereby, the main proposals for governing the information security in e-banking is to

- Develop an ITSG framework based on guidance from Figure 5 which can help banks govern information security in e-banking.
- Embrace a security strategy based on the results from Table 2 in order to fit each unique e-banking environment.
- Focus on outsourcing risk since this type of risk possesses more threat and impact for e-banking.

We summarize the chapter by supporting the argument set in the introduction that "*Security is a management problem, not a technical problem*" and in simple economic terms, it is cheaper and more effective to find and eliminate security problems when the system is developed rather than after have been employed (Villaroel et al, 2005). On the contrary, IS is an issue with multiple key dimensions (e.g. business, economic, culture, legal, politics, standards, technology) that need to be taken into account. Undoubtedly, the existence of many viewpoints ensures a holistic approach towards effectiveness of an ITSG program in e-banking but the final responsibility lies on the hands of the Board Management and stakeholders. In the foreseeable future there will continue to be a need for brick-and-mortar facilities because the current generation of customers still require the personal contact and also because there are still some functions such as cash withdrawals that require a physical facility and personnel. However, the future of e-banking is more than promising and depends heavily on the development of technology. Future research on the state of relationships (e.g. dependencies) among the multiple key dimensions (business, culture etc.) that affect an ITSG program, will offer useful insights about which dimension is more critical than other.

REFERENCES

Abu-Musa, A. (2010). Information security governance in Saudi organizations: An empirical study. *Information Management & Computer Security*, *18*(4), 226–276.

Aggelis, V. G. (2005). *The bible of e-banking*. Athens, Greece: New Technologies Publications. (in Greek)

Akinci, S., Aksoy, S., & Atilgan, E. (2004). Adoption of Internet banking among sophisticated consumer segments in an advanced developing country. *International Journal of Bank Marketing*, *22*(3), 212–232.

Angelakopoulos, G., & Mihiotis, A. (2011). E-banking: Challenges and opportunities in the Greek banking sector. *Electronic Commerce Research*, *11*, 1–23.

Arshad, N. H., May-Lin, Y., Mohamed, A., & Affandi, S. (2007). Inherent risks in ICT outsourcing project. *Proceeding of the 8th WSEAS Conference, 8*(4), 141 – 146. Retrieved July 20, 2011, from http://www.wseas.us/elibrary/transactions/economics/2007/24-107.pdf

Basel Committee on Banking Supervision. (2003). *Risk management principles for electronic banking*. Retrieved July 20, 2011, from http://www.bis.org/publ/bcbs98.pdf

Basel Committee on Banking Supervision. (2005). *Outsourcing in financial services*. Retrieved July 20, 2011, from http://www.bis.org/publ/joint12.pdf

Baten, M. A., & Kamil, A. A. (2010). E-banking of economical prospects in Bangladesh. *Journal of Internet Banking and Commerce*, *15*(2).

Biri, K., & Tentra, G. M. (2004). *Corporate information security governance in Swiss private banking*. Master's Thesis University of Zurich, Retrieved July 20, 2011, from http://www.isaca.ch/files/DO7_Diplomarbeiten/Diplom_CorporateInfSecGovernance_E.pdf

Brotby, K. (2009). *Information security governance: A practical development and implementation approach*. Wiley.

BSI-Std. BSI Standard 100-1. (2006). *Information security management systems*. Bonn, Germany: Bundesamt für Sicherheit in der Informationstechnik.

Chen, X. (2009). The challenges and strategies of commercial bank in developing e-banking business. In *Proceedings of the International Conference ICHCC 2009-ICTMF 2009*, Sanya, Hainan Island, China, December 13-14, 2009, (pp. 68-74).

Committee of Sponsoring Organizations of the Treadway Commission. (2004). *Enterprise risk management — Integrated framework*. Executive Summary, September. Retrieved July 20, 2011, from http://www.coso.org/documents/COSO_ERM_ExecutiveSummary.pdf

Corporate Governance Task Force (CGTF). (2004). Corporate governance task force report: Information security governance - A call to action. Retrieved July 20, 2011, from http://www.cyber.st.dhs.gov/docs/Information%20Security%20Governance-%20A%20Call%20to%20Action%20%282004%29.pdf

Corporate Information Security Working Group (CISWG). (2004). *Report of the best practices and metrics team*. Retrieved July 20, 2011, from http://net.educause.edu/ir/library/pdf/CSD3661.pdf

Da Veiga, A., & Eloff, J. H. P. (2007). An information security governance framework. *Information Systems Management, 24*(4), 361–372.

Daniel, E. (1999). Provision of electronic banking in the UK and Republic of Ireland. *International Journal of Bank Marketing, 17*(2), 72–83.

Dewan, R., & Seidmann, A. (2001). Current issues in e-banking. *Communications of the ACM, 44*(6), 31–329.

ENISA. (2006). *Risk management: Implementation principles and inventories for risk management/risk assessment method and tools*. European Network and information Security Agency - Technical Department Heraklion, Greece. Retrieved July 20, 2011, from http://www.enisa.europa.eu/rmra/files/D1_Inventory_of_Methods_Risk_Management_Final.pdf

Federal Financial Institutions Examination Council (FFIEC). (2004). *Outsourcing technology services*. Retrieved July 20, 2011, from http://www.enpointe.com/assets/pdf/Outsourcing_Booklet.pdf

Federal Financial Institutions Examination Council (FFIEC). (2005). *Authentication in an Internet banking environment*. Retrieved July 20, 2011, from http://www.ffiec.gov/pdf/authentication_guidance.pdf

Financial Action Task Force (FATF). (1996). *The forty recommendations of the financial action task force on money laundering*. Retrieved July 20, 2011, from http://www.fincen.gov/news_room/rp/files/fatf_40_recommendations.pdf

Frankland, J. (2008). IT security metrics: Implementation and standards compliance. *Network Security, 6*, 6–9.

Generally Accepted Information Security Principles, Version 3.0 (GAISP). (2003). Retrieved July 20, 2011, from http://all.net/books/standards/GAISP-v30.pdf

Gikandi, J. W., & Bloor, C. (2010). Adoption and effectiveness of electronic banking in Kenya. *Electronic Commerce Research and Applications, 9*, 277–282.

Heschl, J. (2004). COBIT in relation to other international standards. *Journal of Information Systems Control, 4*.

Holmquist, E. (2008). *Which security governance framework is the best fit?* TechTarget ANZ Australia. Retrieved July 20, 2011, from http://searchcio.techtarget.com.au/articles/24787-Whichsecurity-governanceframework-is the-best-fit-.htm

Houmba, S. H., Franqueira, V. N. L., & Engum, E. A. (2010). Quantifying security risk level from CVSS estimates of frequency and impact. *Journal of Systems and Software, 83*, 1622–1634.

IFAC. (2004). *Enterprise governance: Getting the balance right.* International Federation of Accountants, Professional Accountants in Business Committee. Retrieved July 20, 2011, from www.ifac.org/Members/DownLoads/Enterprise-Governance.pdf

Insley, R., Al-Abed, H., & Fleming, T. (2003). *What is the definition of e-banking?* Retrieved July 20, 2011, from http://www.bankersonline.com/technology/gurus_tech081803d.html

ISO 15489-1:2001. (2001). *International standard, information and documentation – Records management, part 1: General.* Retrieved July 20, 2011, from http://www.javeriana.edu.co/archivo/07_eventos/preservaciondigital/memorias/index_archivos/norma/iso_15489-1.pdf

ISO 15489-2:2001. (2001). *Technical report, information and documentation – Records management, part 2: Guidelines.* Retrieved July 20, 2011, from http://www.javeriana.edu.co/archivo/07_eventos/preservaciondigital/memorias/index_archivos/norma/iso_15489-2.pdf

ISO-Std. ISO/IEC TR 13335-1. (1996). *Information technology - Guidelines for the management of IT security - Concepts and models for IT security.* International Organization for Standardization (ISO), Switzerland, 1996.

ISO-Std. ISO/IEC 27001:2005(E). (2005). *Information technology - Security techniques - Information security management systems - Requirements.* International Organization for Standardization (ISO), Switzerland, 2005.

ISO-Std. ISO/IEC 27005:2008. (2008). *Information technology – Security techniques - Information security risk management.* International Organization for Standardization (ISO), Switzerland, 2008.

ISO/IEC 27004:2009. (2009). *Introduction to ISO 27004.* The ISO 27000 Directory. Retrieved July 20, 2011, from http://www.27000.org/iso-27004.htm

ISO/IEC 38500:2008. (2008). International standard, corporate governance of information technology. Retrieved July 20, 2011, from http://webstore.iec.ch/preview/info_isoiec38500%7Bed1.0%7Den.pdf

ISO/TC-Std. 31000:2008. (2008). *Risk management- Principles and guidelines on implementation* (draft). International Organization for Standardization (ISO), Switzerland, 2008.

ITGI. (2006). *Information security governance: Guidance for boards of directors and executive management* (2nd ed.). Rolling Meadows, IL: IT Governance Institute.

ITGI. (2007). *COBIT 4.1 excerpt: Executive summary – Framework.* Retrieved July 20, 2011, from http://www.isaca.org/KnowledgeCenter/cobit/Documents/COBIT4.pdf

Kolondisky, J. M., Vermont, B., Hogarth, M. J., & Hilgert, M. A. (2004). The adoption of electronic banking technologies by US consumers. *International Journal of Bank Marketing, 22*(4), 238–259.

Kondabagil, J. (2007). *Risk management in electronic banking: Concepts and best practices.* Wiley Finance.

Kouns, J., & Minoli, D. (2010). *Information technology risk management in enterprise environments: A review of industry practices and a practical guide to risk management teams.* Wiley.

Kritzinger, E., & von Solms, S. H. (2006). E-learning: Incorporating information security governance. *Issues in Informing Science and Information Technology, 3,* 319–325.

Lomas, E. (2010). Information governance: Information security and access within a UK context. *Records Management Journal, 20*(2), 182–198.

Long, X., Qi, Y., & Qianmu, L. (2008). Information security risk assessment based on analytic hierarchy process and fuzzy comprehensive. In *Proceedings of the International Conference on Risk Management& Engineering Management*, (pp. 404-409).

Lund, M. S., Solhaug, B., & Stølen, K. (2010). *Model-driven risk analysis: The CORAS approach*. Springer.

Mellado, D., Blanco, C., Sanchez, L. E., & Fernandez-Medina, E. (2010). A systematic review of security requirements engineering. *Computer Standards & Interfaces*, *32*, 153–165.

Monks, R. A. G., & Minow, N. (2004). *Corporate governance* (3rd ed.). Malden, MA: Blackwell.

Moreira, E., Martimiano, L. A. F., Brandao, A. J., & Bernardes, M. C. (2008). Ontologies for information security management and governance. *Information Management & Computer Security*, *16*(2), 150–165.

Moulton, R., & Coles, R. S. (2003). Applying information security governance. *Computers & Security*, *22*(7), 580–584.

MSNBC. (2010). Massive bank security breach uncovered in New Jersey. Retrieved July 20, 2011, from http://www.msnbc.msn.com/id/3303539

National Institute of Standards and Technology (NIST). (2011). *Special publication 800-126 Rev. 1: The technical specification for the security content automation protocol (SCAP): SCAP Version 1.1*. February. Retrieved July 20, 2011, from http://csrc.nist.gov/publications/nistpubs/800-126-rev1/SP800-126r1.pdf/

NIST Special Publication 800-39. (2011). *Managing information security risk organization, mission, and information system view*. Retrieved July 20, 2011, from http://csrc.nist.gov/publications/nistpubs/800-39/SP800-39-final.pdf

Nsouli, S. M., & Schaechter, A. (2002). Challenges of the E-banking revolution. *International Monetary Fund: Finance & Development*, *39*(3). Retrieved July 20, 2011, from http://www.imf.org/external/pubs/ft/fandd/2002/09/nsouli.htm

OCTAVE. (2003). *Operationally critical threat, asset, and vulnerability evaluation*. Retrieved July 20, 2011, from http://www.cert.org/octave/approach_intro.pdf, Organization for Economic Co-operation (OECD). (2004). *Principles of corporate governance*. Retrieved July 20, 2011, from http://www.oecd.org/dataoecd/32/18/31557724.pdf

PCI. (2010). *About the PCI data security standard (PCI DSS)*. Retrieved July 20, 2011, from https://www.pcisecuritystandards.org/security_standards/pci_dss.shtml

Peltier, T. (2004). Risk analysis and risk management. *Information Systems Security*, *13*(4), 44–56.

Poore, R. S. (2005). Information security governance. *EDPACS*, *33*(5), 1–8.

Pretorius, E., & Solms, B. (2004). Information security governance using ISO 17799 and COBIT. *Integrity and Internal Control in Information Systems*, *6*(140), 107–113.

Rao, H. R., Gupta, M., & Upadhyaya, S. J. (2007). *Managing information assurance in financial services*. Hershey, PA: IGI Publishing.

Rastogi, R., & Von Solms, R. (2006). *Information security governance a re-definition. International Federation for Information Processing, 193*. Boston, MA: Springer.

Reserve Bank of India. (2011). *Working group on information security, electronic banking, technology risk management and cyber frauds*. Retrieved June 20, 2011, from http://www.rbi.org.in/scripts/PublicationReportDetails.aspx?UrlPage=&ID=609

Rogers, E. M. (1962). *Diffusion of innovations*. New York, NY: The Free Press.

Saint-Gemain, R. (2005). Information security management best practice based on ISO/IEC 17799. *Information Management Journal, 39*(4), 60–65.

SANS Institute. (2003). *Using a capability maturity model to derive security requirements.* Retrieved July 20, 2011, from http://www.sans.org/reading_room/whitepapers/bestprac/capability-maturity-model-derive-security-requirements_1005

Shah, M., & Clarke, S. (2009). *E-banking management: Issues, solutions, and strategies.* Hershey, PA: IGI Publishing.

Shah, M. H., & Siddiqui, F. A. (2006). Organisational critical success factors in adoption of e-banking at the Woolwich bank. *International Journal of Information Management, 26*, 442–456.

Soliman, K. (2006). Managing information in the digital economy: Issues & solutions. In *Proceedings of the 6th International Business Information Management Association (IBIMA) Conference 19-21 June 2006, Bonn, Germany,* (pp. 227- 232).

Solms, S. H., & von Solms, R. (2009). *Information security governance.* Springer.

Southard, P. B., & Siau, K. (2004). A survey of online e-banking retail initiatives. *Communications of the ACM, 47*(10).

Tan, T. C. C., Ruighaver, A. B., & Ahmad, A. (2010). Information security governance: When compliance becomes more important than security. In *Proceedings of the 25th IFIP TC 11 International Information Security Conference,* (pp. 55–67).

Tanampasidis, G. (2008). A comprehensive method for assessment of operational risk in e-banking. *Information Systems Control Journal, 4.*

Task Force on Financial Integrity and Economic Development. (2011). *Response to FATF consultation paper: Review of the standards.* Preparation for the 4th Round of Mutual Evaluations. Retrieved July 20, 2011, from http://www.financialtaskforce.org/wpcontent/uploads/2011/02/Task_Force_on_Financial_Integrity_and_Economic_Development_Response_to_FATF_Consultation_Paper.pdf.pdf

Trompeter, C. M., & Eloff, J. H. P. (2001). A framework for the implementation of socio-ethical controls in information security. *Computers & Security, 20*(5), 384–391.

Tsoumas, V., & Tryfonas, T. (2004). From risk analysis to effective security management: Towards an automated approach. *Information Management & Computer Security, 12*(1), 91–101.

Tudor, J. K. (2000). *Information security architecture—An integrated approach to security in an organization.* Boca Raton, FL: Auerbach.

US Department of Commerce. (2006). *NIST (Draft) SP 800-80: Guide for developing performance metrics for information security.*

Vachirapornpuk, S., & Broderick, A. J. (2002). Service quality in internet banking: The importance of customer role. *Marketing Intelligence & Planning, 20*(6), 327–335.

Vijayan, J. (2010). *Five indicted in cybertheft of city's bank account.* Retrieved July 20, 2011, from http://www.computerworld.com/s/article/9177409/Five_indicted_in_cybertheft_of_city_s_bank_accounts

Villarroel, R., Fernandez-Medina, E., & Mellado, D. (2005). Secure information systems development – A survey and comparison. *Computers & Security, 24*, 308–321.

Chapter 3
IT Security Governance Legal Issues

Gemma María Minero Alejandre
University Autónoma of Madrid, Spain

ABSTRACT

The protection of the investment and creativity made in producing computer programs and databases by intellectual property rights is still not harmonised internationally. Taking into account that IT is used not only to produce these goods, but also to infringe their intellectual property rights, national laws nowadays also protect the so-called technological protection measures, such as passwords, encryption or copy-protection software, created to protect the intellectual property rights. Besides, IT must fulfill the privacy protection regulations currently in force and the companies using it must carry out the international auditing standards. But intellectual property rights cannot protect simple data and information, apart from the substantial investment made in either obtaining, verification, or presentation of data, by sui generis right over databases (or database right). This chapter examines and compares the current legislations of developed countries in order to find the characteristics -and the criticism- in common.

INTRODUCTION: IT SECURITY GOVERNANCE LEGAL ISSUES

With the development of new information and communication technologies new challenges but also new problems lie ahead. This chapter addresses the most relevant areas of intellectual property law in relation to IT and describes other legal issues regarding information security and data protection.

Nowadays, as a rule, intellectual property rights and information are the greatest corporate assets. Intellectual property rights cannot protect simple data and information, apart from the substantial

DOI: 10.4018/978-1-4666-2083-4.ch003

investment made in either obtaining, verification or presentation of data, by sui generis right over databases (or database right). However, other specific laws and statutory agreements deal with protection of corporate information.

The term "information security" means protecting information and information systems -particularly, computer programs and databases- from unauthorized access, use or modification, in order to provide integrity, confidentiality and availability for its lawful users.

Why do we need a supra-national protection or, at least, some common worldwide standards in these fields? The answer, nowadays, is self-evident: in the current global marketable place, national borders do not exit any more in a practical way, so maintaining them in a formal, theoretical or legal perspective does not make any sense.

This chapter analyses whether this aim has been fulfilled or not and compares the currents methods available for the protection in order to find an adequate type and level of protection. Society's challenge is to find that adequate protection. The implications of under-protection or over-protection are both ill-fated. Left with insufficient protection, producers do nor invest for fear of free-riding. But too much protection can lead to monopolies abuses. Both scenarios are detrimental to society.

As we have seen in previous chapters, companies today face a global revolution in governance that directly affects their information and intellectual property rights management practices. Organisations are more and more dependent on their information systems and on their intellectual property capital. Regulators and the public are increasingly concerned about proper use of information, particularly personal data, and intellectual property rights. The threats to them from criminals are increasing. A single laptop lost or stolen from a firm compromised identifying information of hundreds or thousands of customers and employees. Given this situation, many companies are identifying information as an area of

their operation that needs to be protected through corporate governance plans as part of their system of internal control.

History has demonstrated that improvements in governance and compliance typically come as a result of scandals. Following the high-profile organizational failures of the past decade, legislatures, statutory authorities, private international organizations and regulators have created a complex array of the new laws and binding agreements designed to force improvement in organizational governance, security and transparency. Coupled with previous regulations and pacts in these areas and intellectual property protection and information retention and privacy, these new laws and agreements, together with significant threats of information system disruptions from hackers and virus perpetrators create and unprecedented need for a governance approach to information management.

Nevertheless, most developing nations, where the majority of IT outsourcing occurs, have no national governance or policies related to IT security or privacy.

Finally, we have to take into account that many regulations follow the principle of territoriality -all of them, except the international treaties-, which means that those rules do not have extra-territorial effect abroad the country of its legislature. A similar principle is applied to private agreements -e.g. some of the agreements on the management and supervision of operational risk of the financial sector-, so only signatories or companies which want to profit from them are bound by these pacts (Goldstein, 2001; Gaster, 2006).

While there are global actions such as the Basel banking accords -issued by the Basel Committee On Banking Supervision- and the International Financial Reporting Standards -adopted by the International Accounting Standards Board-, emerging as global generally accepted accounting principles, the vast majority of actions will occur at a local level. However, the cumulative effect of these local actions, even though they seem insignificant, will be to improve GRC on a global level. In short, there is no such thing as an isolated event in improving GRC.

Unfortunately, also local constraints on information rights do not occur on isolation, but the contrary. They have worldwide repercussions, at least indirectly. Therefore, process of improved GRC is and will continue to be unstoppable. The goal of this chapter is to provide a summary that touches the current state in the GRC process. It summarizes the global legal framework for information security. It is written from a perspective of a company that needs to comply with many laws in many jurisdictions, and needs to understand the general framework of legal security requirements, so it can evaluate how local law fits in and what it might do to become generally compliant under many laws.

METHOD

To achieve this aim, the author of this chapter makes an analysis from two relevant perspectives. On the one hand, the interests of companies which are the right-holders of computer programs databases and other information systems. Secondly, the public or the individuals, right-holders of privacy rights. The first group looks for investment promotion and protection against free riding. They use information created by them, but also information provided by individuals. Therefore, the first group of interests try to avoid other companies from accessing, collecting and processing substantial amounts of information. Acts which are remarkably simple and inexpensive on the Internet. To this effect, the author uses criteria based on a combination of the human rights to intellectual property and to information access and the public interests.

Apart from that, in order to elaborate a global model or some international parameters, a comparison of the manner in which the Laws of several countries protect both intellectual property

rights, informational privacy and, in general, information security issues is in order. Besides, the abundant literature facing the same problems in the United States, in the European Union and in many others countries all around the world cannot be ignored. Most of the study is a theoretical analysis of the statutory Law in force and judicial cases pronounced.

Protecting Information and Information Systems by IPR?

Protecting the security of corporate information and computer systems was once just a technical issue to be addressed by a company's IT department. Nevertheless, today, what we call information security has become a legal obligation, and responsibility for compliance has been put directly on the shoulders of senior management. Regulations governing information security typically focus on the protection of both information systems -networks, databases, software- and the data that those systems process, communicate, receive or share (Figure 1). Therefore, firstly, we will study the means of protecting corporate information and computer systems: the Intellectual Property Rights (IPR). Despite the general principle that IPR do not protect mere data, we will see that actually, in relation to databases, at least in the European context, this principle is not entirely in force. Afterwards, we will study the private data protection and the general objectives of laws and regulations governing information security.

Some Preliminary Notes

Taking into account the above-mentioned principle of territoriality, this chapter will focus on national laws and regulations of developed countries, particularly U.S., E.U., Canada and Japan.

In the international level, we must mentions the two leading organizations which have produced the main texts on this field during the twenty century. Firstly, the World Trade Organization (WTO)

Figure 1. Intangible corporate assets

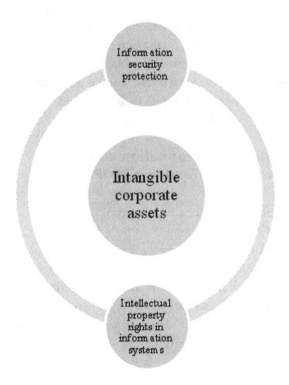

adopted the so-called TRIPS Agreement (Trade-Related Aspects of Intellectual Property Rights), given the support of the U.S. and the E.U., both grown highly concerned with increasing piracy of software (Louwers & Chow, 2009). The TRIPS Agreement covers all principal areas of IPR, particularly databases and computer programs. It requires the contracting parties to establish, at least, the levels of protection required under the Agreement. Therefore, as we will see in the next sections of this chapter, the different national laws do not differ in their main issues (Louwers & Chow, 2009). Afterwards, the World Intellectual Property Organization (WIPO) adopted the WIPO Copyright Treaty (WCT), similar to the TRIPS Agreement, mentioned above.

The former EU has undertaken a number of initiatives in the field of international copyright. The US has also upheld a pro-active position in this field up to now. Nowadays, both of them are members of, and participate in, the WTO and,

accordingly, in the TRIPs' Council, and have ratified the WIPO Treaties.

Protection of Computer Programs

Introduction: International, US - EU Background

Debates regarding the eligibility of computer programs for copyright protection carried out for a long time both in national and international level as to whether computer programs qualified as works (and, if so, as what kind of work), or whether they should be protected by a sui generis right or were outside copyright law (Von Lewinski, 2008). The US opted for the strongest possible protection, that is, under the copyright law. Taking into account the fact that the computer program's source code was written, the US considered that software should be protected as a literary work within the meaning of the Berne Convention (an old international treaty on copyright ratified by the vast majority of developed countries). During the TRIPS' negotiations, the US pleaded for internationalizing this protection all around the world (Reinbothe, 1992). Therefore, the rest of the industrialized countries -and, particularly, their technology industries- strongly advocated for this option too (Gervais, 2008), particularly the EU, adopting the Computer Program Directive on 1991, although some of its Member States had followed the protection provided by the US on an earlier date. In France, Germany and the UK, since 1985 (Aplin & Davis, 2009). In contrast to developing countries, which wanted to restrict protection as far as possible, because they were aware of their technologically limited capacities, and, therefore, of the fact that stronger protection of computer programs would only benefit developed countries. Despite this opinion, the EU Directive on the Legal Protection of Computer Programs, the US Copyright Act, the WIPO Copyright Treaty and the above-mentioned TRIPS do all provide nowadays that computer programs are to be protected by copyright, without excluding other means of protection related to patent law and other legal instruments of protection.

What is a Computer Program in Legal Terms?

The lack of legal definition of the concept of computer program, literature holds that copyright covers the computer program in all its extent, whether in source or object code, and regardless the mode, form or method by which it is expressed. In practical terms, it means that the legal concept, and, therefore, the legal protection, cover not only software, but also hardware, that is, anything that can be stored electronically and any device or display device were the computer program can be stored might be protected by IPR. It includes also its preparatory design material. This wide interpretation has been underline by national judges in the string of cases analyzed up to now (US judgments *Williams Electronics, Inc. v. Arctic International, Inc.,* 685 F.2d 870 (3d Cir.); and *Apple Computer, Inc. v. Franklin Computer Corp.,* 714 F.2d 1240 (3d Cir.)). As a jurisprudential doctrine, the specific code or language is immaterial. Source code, object code, binary notation, hexadecimal notation, machine language, high level languages, low-level languages, will all be protected (Halpern, 2010).

However, as a general rule, what will never be covered under this copyright protection are the ideas or principles which underline any element of the computer program, including its interfaces. (Walter & Von Lewinski, 2010). The problem in determining copyrightability lies in specifying where in the array of activities, unprotected ideas end and protected expression begins. This, which is often a difficult task on the IPR general context, is made all the more difficult when evaluating a computer program and its essentially utilitarian nature (US cases *Whelan Associates, Inc. v. Jaslow Dental Laboratory, Inc.,* 797 F.2d 1222 (3d Cir.); and *Computer Associates, Inc. v. Altai, Inc.* 982

F 2d 693 (2d Cir.). EU cases of the EU Court of First Instance of 17 September 2007, case T-201/04 *Microsoft v. Commission*; and the judgment of the EU Court of Justice of 22 December 2010, case *Bezpecnostní softwarová asociace v. Ministerstvo Kultury.* Andermann, 2008; Minero, 2011).

How is a Computer Program Protected by Copyright?

Both the U.S. and the European systems and, following them, the majority of countries, require to meet the condition: Computer programs, as the rest of the works, shall only be protected in the case that they were original. The standard for originality is low, it does not suffice to have made an economic effort, but it is enough to demonstrate that the computer program has been independently created by the author and posses a modicum of creativity (US judgment *Feist Publications Inc v. Rural Telephone Service Company Inc.,* 111 s. Ct, 1282). Thus, originality does not signify novelty: a computer program may be original even though it closely resembles other computer programs so long as similarity is not the result of copying. Therefore, in practical terms, originality means absence of copying. Consequently, many of the current corporate information systems are protected by copyright, despite organizations do not know it. Provided the originality, every use of the computer program needs the previous authorization of the relevant copyright holder, either explicit or implicit. The simple access and start of the computer program is an infringement of its copyright, in case it was not previously authorized by the right-holder.

Given this regulation, the question is the following: why is copyright protection important in relation to information security issue? As we will see in next sections, information security involves protecting corporate information systems, so the mere access, when the user was not previously authorized, is *per se* considered an infringement.

But when that specific information system is also protected by copyright, the infringement is double.

When it comes to computer programs created by employees in the execution of their duties or following the instructions given by their employer, it is the employer who will have the exclusive economic rights. This default rule may, however, be altered by contract, though it is not very usual.

At first, most national regulations provided a term of protection of fifty years after the creation of the corporate computer program. Despite many authors had stated that this period of protection was far too long, it was extended up to seventy years by the Directive of 1993 harmonizing the Term Protection, which is the term applied to every copyright protected work. This option was also followed by the US and by many other countries all around the world, except Japan, which nowadays maintains the rule of fifty years (Lloyd, 2004).

Other Forms of Protection

Patents and Computer Programs

Notwithstanding the present prohibition expressly contained in the European Patent Convention, there is no doubt that software-related inventions can be patented. Patents have a significant role to play in the field of IT. Indeed, since the middle of the eighties, national patents offices, as well as European Patent Office and, above all, the US Supreme Court (judgments *Diamond v. Diehr*, 450 US 175, 101 S. Ct. 1048; and *Diamond v. Bradley*, 450 US 381) and the US Patent and Trademark Office (Mathematical Algorithms or Computer Programs, Manual of Patent Examining Procedures, Sec.2110(1981)), have been granted patents for software-related inventions. Besides, a new term has been created in order to afford this issue: the computer-implemented inventions, which are usually defined as an invention that works by using a computer or a computer network and that have one or more features which are realized wholly or partly by means of that computer program. The

trend throughout the world is, therefore, clearly to accept that software should be brought within the ambit of the patent system. In some senses, there is almost an element of competition between States as to who can provide the strongest protection (US judgment *Lotus v. Paperback,* 740 F Supp 37).

The protection term of patents lasts only twenty years. However, it seems to be sufficient to protect corporate information systems, due to its changeable nature.

The main difference between the approach of the EU system and the situations in the U.S. and Japan lies in the requirement of a technical contribution. In Japan, the invention needs to be a highly advanced creation of technical ideas by which a law of nature is utilized. In the U.S., the requirement differs: a patentable invention must fall within the technological arts but no specific technological contribution is needed. Both in Japan and the U.S., claiming patents of software that implements patentable inventions is permitted (Louwers & Chow, 2009). The patenting process for the computer-implemented inventions at the European Patent Office is much more restrictive, as it puts emphasis on new technical solutions. The most striking consequence of this definition is that computer programs or computer-implemented business methods that make no technical contribution to the level of existing technology, as the ones that provide a business process or solve business problems rather than technical problems, are not patentable in Europe. The current systems allow the same computer program to be cumulatively protected both by patents and by copyright. Therefore, in some cases, corporate information systems could be protected in the U.S. and Japan, but not in the E.U.

Trade Secrets

The trade secrets protection of computer software is available in some form or another in many countries. Trade secrets laws protect against unauthorized use of a corporate secret by those whom it has been confided under the terms of an agreement or by those who gained it by improper means, such as an employee's breach of trust or industrial espionage. The duration of trade secret protection is unlimited until the secret is disclosed.

In most countries, the labor relationship imposes a duty on the employee not to use or disclose the employer's confidential information to the detriment of the employer. In the late 1970s a number of cases of this nature were raised in courts in the United Kingdom and the U.S. Commonly, the facts can be explained simply, as follows. A person would have been employed to work on the development of a particular computer program or information system. The employment would come to an end and the individual, either in his own or as an employee of another company, would be involved in the development of a similar software or information system. Besides, in this case the act also constituted a contractual infringement (Lloyd, 2004). Therefore, the best way to protect the corporate information systems is a written employee contract that expressly binds the employee to non-disclosure of secret or confidential information obtained in the course of the employee's work or an agreement not to compete in an specific period of time, geographical area and type of precluded activity. Besides, some countries such as the U.S. have criminal laws dealing with certain issues of trade secrets protection (Louwers & Chow, 2009).

Protection of Databases

Introduction: International, US - EU Background

Nowadays, the leading role of information in society and trade creates the necessity of some form of protection against unauthorized accessing and copying of compilations of data. Information is not protected by copyright, but databases are certainly covered both by copyright and sui generis right.

However, until 1996, Member States of the E.U. regulated databases protection in a national level. On that date, the volume of disparities among their Laws were such -e.g. some of them do not protect databases whose contents were mere data, in contrast to the U.S.- that the European legislator decided to make them uniform. With this purpose, it adopted the E.U. Directive on the Legal Protection of Databases, of 1996. By this norm, the E.U. created the so-called sui generis right, which protects the contents of the database as a whole, and is, therefore, complementary or additional to the copyright, which protects only the structure of the database, provided it is original. The actual purpose of the E.U. was obvious: it had been observed that Europe strongly lagged behind the production of databases, compared with the U.S.

The U.S., on the contrary, maintain the exclusively copyright protection of database's structure, but not of its contents as a whole. Following the criticisms of large parts of US research and scientific circles against the European sui generis protection, the legislative projects on the regulation of an equivalent protection in the U.S. were abandoned (Gotzen, 2007). However, economic studies carried out in the course of these years have shown the clear maintenance of a U.S. supremacy in this field (European Commission, 2005).

The sui generis right only exits in the EU, not in the international level. Indeed, what the above-mentioned international treaties and many other national laws mean to protect is much more closer to the referred U.S. protection.

What is a Database in Legal Terms?

Both the E.U. Database Directive and the U.S. Copyright Act -and the vast majority of countries all around the world- define the term databases in a very similar and expansive way, including in this concept products that cannot be qualified as such databases in a technical or computing language. Being a database, from a legal point of view, a collection or assembling of data or other materials, any corporate compilation of information could be included in this concept, regardless of its format, electronic or not (Minero, 2011).

The protection foreseen in the Databases Directive -both copyright and *sui generis* right- does not cover computer programs used in the making or operation of databases. It follows that the protection under the Directive does not extent to software which provides access to and enables searching in corporate electronic databases. Therefore, it is exclusively protected under the Computer Program Directive, as was seen above (Beunen, 2007; Reichman & Samuelson, 1997; Minero, 2012).

How is a Database Protected?

As explained above, there are two forms of protection of databases by IPR in the European context. The first one, is the copyright. The second, the *sui generis* right. Whereas the copyright covers the original database's structure, meaning its selection and/or arrangements of its contents -but not those contents themselves-, the *sui generis* right, on the contrary, protects the investment in processing the database's contents as a whole. However, in the U.S. context there is only one protection: the copyright, with the same requirement of originality above-mentioned. Mexico and South Korea have also regulated a right similar to sui generis right.

Copyright

The criterion for considering original a database's structure is that its selection and/or arrangement is the author's own intellectual creation, as in computer programs. Databases, to be considered works, must be original in the sense that they must be independently created by the author and not copied from other works, and must be works of at least minimal authorship. It means that copyright will not protect such product in which the creative component is lacking or so trivial as to be virtually non-existent, such as the alphabetical or chronological order in databases' arrangement.

Although these kinds of arrangement criteria are the more common among today's databases, web databases and other kind of current digital corporate databases usually do not suffer from the lack of copyright protection, as the web format, unlike the physical one -which has been explored over and over again-, provides their authors -that is, the web developers or programmers-, with much more -almost infinitive- new creation opportunities. In practical terms, all this means that common physical corporate telephone directories do not grant of copyright, but its digital format do can fulfill the originality requirement by introducing in the database's structure of the firm's website some changes. E.g. a searching engine that makes users' searches and combinations possible -so that users may be able to look for a telephone number or identity by introducing a combination of terms, previously chosen by the users-. The resulting database's structure may be, therefore, protected as such database by copyright, without prejudicing the possible copyright protection that may cover the mentioned search engine as a computer program. The organization gets, therefore, a double protection on its information system.

The author, that is, the person who has created or designed the original database's structure enjoys a list of exclusive economic rights, which are, in short, the right of reproduction, adaptation, distribution and communication to the public from the creation until 70 years after the death of the author or the last living author or, in case it was created by the firm itself, 70 years after the creation of the database. In other words, it means that anyone who pretends to use that structure must be licensed or authorized by its author.

Even so, a corporate database's structure can be used without its author's consent in two cases: for the illustration for non commercial reaching or scientific research and for public security or administrative or judicial procedures. The first is not very common in practice, but the second usually takes place in almost every creditors' meeting.

Sui Generis Right

Since 1996, in the European context a new *sui generis* right is given to database maker provided its production -the obtaining, verification and/or presentation of the database's contents- required a substantial investment. Thus, the object of protection is the database itself -the sum of its contents as a whole-, while the reason for protection -and its condition at the same time- is the substantial nature of the investment made. As opposed to copyright, no originality is needed. A mere investment suffices. The investment can be substantial either in a quantitative or a qualitative way, what means that not only the amounts paid in order to obtain a software license, but also aspects such as the effort and time spent by the technicians, their salaries or their qualification, as appropriate (Hugenholtz, 2005).

The sui generis protection is the right to prevent the unauthorized extraction and or re-utilization of all or a substantial part of the databases' content, which means any kind of use, either public or private, of a substantial part -or the whole- of the database's content. Thus, it does not cover the use of individual material or data contained in the database, but only the exploitation of a substantial part of the whole database's content. Therefore, sui generis right includes the mere act of on-screen display of the contents of a database when it necessitates the transfer of all or a substantial part of the contents of the database. The substantial character of the part used depends directly on the volume of this part or on the investment made by the maker on that concrete part. Its holder, which is called maker of the database, is the person who takes the initiative and the risk of investing.

This *sui generis* right lasts for 15 years from the date of the database's completion, but this term of protection may start anew after the database has been substantially changed -resulting from successive additions, deletions or alterations- through a substantial investment. In order to get this benefit, for databases which are constantly being updated,

it may be recommendable that makers adequately document, date -or- register successive versions, because it may otherwise be difficult to prove the (substantial) difference between an older database version and a new one (Beunen, 2007). However, determining it on a daily changeable database is almost impossible.

About its beneficiaries, this is a right only given to makers who are EU nationals or residents, although it may be extended to nationals of third countries who give equivalent protection to the databases of EU origin, which currently would probably exclude the US, after the US Congress's defeat of the similar proposed legislation.

Technological Measures of Protection and Rights Management Information

As was said before, information security means protecting information and information systems in order to provide confidentiality. Confidentiality is the property that data and information is not available or disclosed to unauthorized persons or processes. It involves controlling access to information. The so-called "technological protection measures" (TPM) carry out this function. Thus, a loss of confidentiality is the unauthorized disclosure of information. But it can also be an infringement of the intellectual property rights that protect TPM.

The legal protection of these kind of measures was established within the copyright system, in order to protect the use of copyrighted work on the Internet. Establishing that copyright holders have the right to make their works available via the Internet or other digital networks is one thing, but enforcing this right is another when the infringing activity reaches the current scale, with the widespread use of peer-to-peer technology. Given this situation, copyright owners began to look at other non-legal tools for trying to protect their works against unauthorized digital access and exploitation of them. One of these means were the technological protection measures, which protect IPR by either encrypting the works so that they can only be accessed by authorized users, or by marking the works with a digital watermark or similar method so they cannot be freely exploited. Legislatures reinforced these measures through anti-circumvention protection.

The aforementioned WIPO Treaties were the first international instruments establishing the prohibition of TPMs circumvention and circumvention means. As most important advocate of anti-circumvention rules, the U.S. introduced the Digital Millennium Copyright Act in 1998 and the EU -its 27 Member States and the European Economic Area- enacted the Information Society Directive three years later, in 2001. Many others developed countries have also adopted anti-circumvention rules, which are very similar to their counterparts in the US and EU Laws. Obviously the decision of whether to employ such technological protection measures and, if so, which one to use in which situations, is entirely left to the right-holders.

In relation to IT, ensuring confidentiality requires implementing policies and controls to protect information against unauthorized access or use. It involves protecting information so that unauthorized persons cannot have access to it and, in some cases, protecting information so that even if unauthorized access is obtained, the information is unreadable (e.g. encrypted). Therefore, two key requirements for ensuring the confidentiality of information are access control and authentication. On the one hand, access control involves determining who can access an information system and what they can do once they are granted access. It requires implementation of controls, such as user ID and password procedures. On the other hand, authentication is the process of determining whether someone or something is, in fact, who or what it is declared to be (Smedinghoff, 2008).

In legal terms, TPMs are generously define as any technology, device or component that, in the normal course of its operation, is designed to prevent or restrict acts, in respect to works or other subject-matter, which are not authorized by the right-holder of any copyright. Thus, this general definition is technology-neutral to the extent that it does not specify the type of mechanism that will be protected.

The Laws ban the manufacture and provision of tools, including software and even information that could help another to bypass TPMs. E.g., in relation to IPR, posting on one's website a copy of a computer program usable for circumvention information security measures or linking to other websites where these programs could be easily found (US judgments *Universal City Studios, Inc. v. Reimerdes*, 111 F.Supp.2d 294 (S.D.N.Y.), known as *Universal I*; and *Universal City Studios, Inc. v. Corley*, 273 F.3d 429 (2d Cir.), known as *Universal II*), or, in relation to IT, copying user ID and passwords by unlawful users.

It should be noticed that the mere act of TPMs circumvention attracts liability, regardless of whether or not it leads afterwards to a violation of trade secrets, information or data privacy, copyright on databases or sui generis right, corporate know-how or unfair competition, among others. Therefore, by mean of technological mechanisms and the above-mentioned proscriptions, companies can control the mere access to their information and/or their information systems, even when they are not protected by IPR.

This peculiarity is captured in the U.K. case *Kabushiki Kaisha Sony Computer Entertainment Inc. and Others v. Ball and Others* [2004] EWHC 1738. Sony's consoles were designed to only work with authorized games, which means that a game can only be used in the specific geographical region where it was purchased, but not in others. The defendant was involved in the design, manufacture, sale and installation of an electronic chip, which, attached to the consoles, allows games to be played regardless their purchase place. The English court held that this kind of chip infringed the TPM inserted both in the consoles and the games (Duran, Krieger, Maistry, Manasterski, & Whetton, 2008).

For some commentators, it is reprehensible that TPMs can be applied to any digital content such as personal data and mere information. According to these authors, it should only be applied regarding work protected by IPR (Dussolier, 2005; Luo, 2005; Samuelson, 2003).

However, many disadvantages of DRMs have been identified during this time in three main fields. Firstly, in the practice, the circumvention acts are carried out generally by means of computer programs or computer applications, capable of being used also for legitimate activities. Thus, in this particular case, judges would declare that concrete computer program or application illegal as a whole. A well-known example is the American case Adobe *Software v. Elcomsoft & Dmitry Sklyarov eBook Reader. Elcomsoft* (Duran, Krieger, Maistry, Manasterski, & Whetton, 2008).

Secondly, TPMs are used to control acts or block access to mere data, limiting, therefore, the right of access to information (Koelman & Helberger, 1998).

Finally, the implementation of TPMs has profound implications for privacy and for consumers' rights. The current practices appear very threatening even to users who had not the intention of circumventing them. Particularly, the information stored by DRMs can be used for user profiling about the consumption patterns of its products or services to facilitate, in particular, advertising, including spam e-mails. While consumers could benefit in receiving a customized service, they are exposed to the risk of losing privacy and the expression of non-conformist opinions and preferences is inhibited. Indeed, there is no dude that the potential to collect and process personal information of consumers through technology can constitute privacy invasion (COHEN, 2003). Even so, in the European context, the Information-Society Directive expressly requires that all these technical means should incorporate safeguards in accordance with the Data Protection Directive,

so data can be collected and processed only after having explained to consumers such purpose, and having acquired their consent. Next section describes the current legal framework for data protection.

INFORMATIONAL PRIVACY OR DATA PROTECTION

This section will discuss the various privacy elements that make up the international privacy framework and help corporations better understand their compliance requirements and privacy considerations.

Data protection -also known as informational privacy- is a type of privacy protection and, therefore, a fundamental human right. However, unlike general privacy right, which was internationally recognized as a human right by a large number of international human rights instruments protecting civil and political rights in the period immediately following the Second World War -such as the 1948 Universal Declaration of Human Rights-, data protection laws did not emerge until the 1970s, in response to some public fears about the potentially privacy-invasive consequences of computer technologies.

As the Privacy Working Group stated in 1995, also nowadays, data protection is "a scarce commodity in cyberspace", given the fact that accessing, collecting and processing substantial amounts of information are remarkably simple and inexpensive acts. Besides, the means of collecting personal information has become increasingly sophisticated and less easily detectable. E.g. spyware installed in PCs by web-sites to which they have been connected which collects information about user's habits (Samuelson, 2000). Our societies are even more dependent on the continuous and widespread use of information and telecommunications technologies. However, an important part of those data undoubtedly is constituted of personal data. They are kept in various records for the benefit of both the private (e.g. direct marketing) and the public (e.g. national administration, tax services, social security) sectors. Apart from that, there is question of money. With the growing importance of personalization services, it is clear that the ownership rights in personal data -creating people's profiles- has become a valuable asset and a key commercial access for businesses (Louwers & Chow, 2009). Given this context, individuals must be given a property right that would enable them to control the use of their personal data. Concern at privacy implications of information technology has been constantly expressed either by political and scholarly circles. (United Kingdom Information Commissioner Office, 2006; Lloyd, 2004; Cavoukian & Tapscott, 1997; Balz and Hance, 1996; Kirby, 1999. Kirby, chairman of the two expert groups which prepared the OECD principles on this subject, warmed of this circumstance more than a decade ago).

More than just policy, privacy is a growing risk center for every organization that collects, manages or maintains information (Figure 2). With complex and ever-increasing regulations, the impact of a breach can damage customer relations and corporate credibility. This issue is further complicated by international operations or outsourcing relationships in developing countries where security and privacy policies are often non-existent.

As the European Data Protection Supervisor, Hustinx alerts, while IT is a source of economic growth, it also raises the need for more effective informational privacy protection (Hustinx, 2011. B).

The regulation has to balance two often opposing, interests. On the one hand, protecting informational privacy. But, on the other hand, promoting the flow of information for corporate or socially useful purposes, so that duties imposed by law on unlawful personal data processing do not constrain the IT industry. In practice, it means prohibiting, as a general rule, the recourse to protection of privacy by argumentations to block international data flows.

Obviously, given the supra-national nature of these information flows, the national efforts alone cannot deal with the problems arising out of data processing, so that coordinated steps need to be taken not on a national, but on an international

Figure 2. Intellectual property rights infringement regarding corporate information and information systems

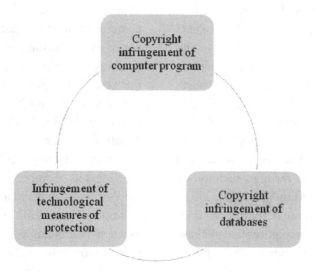

level. Although this global consensus on data protection standards is developing in practice, it is far from perfect.

But what is informational privacy? How is it effectively protected in relation to IT? It has to be said that the notion of informational privacy -as the general notion of privacy- cannot be absolutely fixed to a certain temporal fact. Indeed, the content of this term lends itself to different extent, according to the concrete situation or sector in which the act in question is placed (European Commission, 2003; Louwers and Chow, 2009). However, it can be stated that the essential component of informational privacy may be stated in terms that an individual has the right to control the extent to which personal information is disseminated to other people.

Well over twenty countries have now enacted data protection laws, most of them European, but also important countries outside Europe, such as the US, Japan, Canada, Australia and New Zealand. In addition to national data protection laws, a range of data protection instruments have been adopted at an international level. The most influential has been the Organization for Economic Cooperation and Development (OECD), an international organization which has among its members the majority of developed countries -Australia, Austria, Belgium, Canada, Chile, Czech Republic, Denmark, Estonia, Finland, France, Germany, Greece, Hungary, Iceland, Ireland, Israel, Italy, Luxembourg, the Netherlands, New Zealand, Poland, Slovakia, Slovenia, Sweden, Switzerland, Turkey, the United Kingdom and the United States of America-. It established in 1980 and in 1992 the so-called *Guidelines Governing the Protection of Privacy and Transborder Flows of Personal Dada* and the *Guidelines on Security of Information Systems,* currently in force (Holvast, MADSEN and Roth, 2001).

These very same principles also underline the regulation regime adopted by the E.U., by means of the its 1995 Data Protection Directive (Directive 95/46/EC of the European Parliament and of the Council of 24 October 1995), Canada, with the Personal Information Protection and Electronic Documents Act, and the U.S., by means of its Privacy Act of 1974 -mainly amended by the Electronic Communications Privacy Act- and the narrowly-focused Federal and State laws as well as self-regulatory rules existing in the U.S. (such as the Fair Credit Reporting Act and the Financial Services Modernization Act, also known as Gramm-Leach-Bliley Act). These regulations were designated to ensure that everyone has an appropriate degree of control over the collection and use of his or her personal data. The above mentioned European Directive has been updated by other two e-privacy Directives, to reflect developments in the trade practices in general and in IT, in particular, as to provide an equal level of protection of personal data, regardless the technologies used. Many other developed countries have taken similar measures. They are, among others, the following:

1. **Openness Principle:** The data subject must be informed about the existence of automatic processed personal data files and the identity of the data controller.

2. **Minimization Principle:** The amount of data gathered should be limited to what is necessary to achieve the purpose of gathering the data.

3. **Individual Access Principle:** The data subject should be informed of, and given access to, data on him or her kept by the data controller, within a reasonable time and in a reasonable manner.

4. **Collection Limitation Principle:** The gathering of personal dada has to be fair and legal. Particularly, the collection of certain sensitive data (such as racial origin, political opinions, health, sexual life, etc.) must be prohibit. Derogation is tolerated under very specific circumstances, but national law should provide solid safeguards.

5. **Purpose Specification Principle:** Personal data can only be collected and processed if it is necessary for a specific lawful purpose and based on legitimated grounds. The data keeper has the duty to inform the data subject about his or her concrete aim and also the duty to acquire his or her consent.

6. **Use Limitation Principle:** The data should be used in correspondence with that aim. Use of these data for purposes other than those specified should occur only with the consent the data subject or if such a provision exits within the law.

7. **Individual Participation Principle:** Any subject has the right to check data relating to him or her, to correct them and to have them removed from the file if necessary.

8. **Information Management Principle:** Data have to be adequate, correct, complete and up-to-date and have to be secured against destruction, disclosure, intrusion and alteration by unauthorized people.

9. **Accountability Principle:** The data keeper is accountable for ensuring the living up to these principles.

However, for the reasons that will be explained bellow, there is no solid basis in the U.S. law for the purpose limitation and data minimization principles. Administrative interpretation of the U.S. Privacy Act allows disclosure of data for routine use, that is, for a purpose which is compatible with the aim for which it was collected (Electronic Privacy Information Center - EPIC, 2006). Therefore, the main problem when it comes to international transfer of personal data, is that -according to European officials- none of the numerous private sector efforts as well as US privacy laws match the general protection level set in Europe, with exception of the credit and banking sectors, as we will see bellow. Therefore, the U.S. and the E.U. adopted the so-called International Safe Harbor Privacy Principles, resulting that those companies that adhere to them are considered to provide the

requisite level of protection and allowed to receive personal data from EU companies. In applying the principles by means of a self-certifying system, companies have a presumption of adequacy. This system came into effect in 2000, but it has not received so much support from the U.S. IT industry (Louwers & Chow, 2009). Even so, the general solution developed for providing the European level of data protection is by closing agreements between senders and receivers of those personal data.

However, despite the aforementioned common ground, national data protection regulations differ on their application. E.g. most of the main national privacy laws only apply to private bodies, excluding any case to processing operations concerning public security, defence, etc. Besides, there are some *ad hoc* data protection rules and transatlantic agreements on data protection and public agencies. On the contrary, the U.S. Privacy Act is limited to data collecting and processing by public sector bodies, so the U.S. has no comprehensive legal framework covering the private sector. Therefore, although the U.S. government is subject to omnibus privacy requirements for personal information through the Privacy Act of 1974, the private sector is not subject to any overarching privacy law similar to the E.U.'s Directive and the Canada's Personal Information Protection Act. It only applies to U.S. government agencies and government contractors operating on behalf of government (Westby, 2004.A). However, the U.S. Congress has passed several laws covering different economic sector or regulating surveillance activities, such as credit and banking reporting, health insurance portability and accountability or foreign intelligence surveillance. This fact has pushed several commentators to claim that the main focus and concern of the U.S. privacy legislation is the control of government data management.

Besides, the US Privacy Act does not protect individuals that are neither US citizens nor permanent residents. Such a lack of protection has represented a major obstacle in transatlantic negotiations U.S.-E.U. for privacy protection agreements. Apart from that, the US provisions on civil remedies for privacy invasions are framed in a way that strongly limits the possibility to legal redress. It disregards the basic European idea that data protection concern is not only about blocking and prosecuting illegitimate use of data, but also to channel legitimate use of data and to create redress for problems arising with it (De Hert & Gutwirth, 2006). Indeed, in order to start a civil action against the U.S. public agency, the behavior of the agency must have had an adverse effect on the individual, but it is very difficult to proof, particularly when invisible technologies of control were used (Bignami, 2007. B.). Moreover, the court should determine that the agency acted in a manner which was intentional (De Hert & Bellanova, 2008).

Finally, differences also exit with respect to the supervisory regime established pursuant to each law. Most national laws provide the establishment of a special independent data protection authority to monitor their laws' application. E.g. in the E.U. context, there are one or more data protection authorities in each Member State and, above all of them, the European Data Protection Supervisor. However, this is not the case with respect of the US, where there is neither a global nor an independent authority, but various agencies at a federal and state level, political appointed and responsible for enforcing privacy issues only under the regulations that are within their jurisdiction, which lack powers to investigate and sanction privacy violations in general (Bignami, 2007. A.).

As a conclusion, we must state that there is actually a need for a reasonable and flexible interpretation of certain concepts and provision foreseen in informational privacy regulations. Firstly, the concept of personal data, which is an essential element determining the scope of the legal principles for data protection. It is generally defined as any information relating to an identified or identifiable natural person. It ensures, there-fore, a wide scope of application, but it is subject to two main conditions: the information should relate to an individual and that individual should at least be identifiable. However, the first of these conditions is not always properly understood. It applies when information is about someone, but also when information has an impact on someone, either intended or resulting, such as data about a device which is used to draw conclusions about its users. This is highly relevant for many emerging technologies that will thus involve the applica-tion of legal safeguards, such as many custom-ized financial services or other banking products which involve automated decisions using personal data processes by automatic means. E.g. when an individual applies for a loan on-line, the bank website uses algorithms and auto-credit searching to provide an immediate yes/no decision on the application (Hustinx, 2011. A).

Secondly, another aspect that has prompted calls for a flexible interpretation in relation to the exercise is the right of subject data to access to information held about them. Sometimes, the access request concerns data processed in com-plex networks, extremely difficult and expensive to retrieve and clearly excluded from the normal operation of the controller, so maybe the solution would require the assistance of the data subject (European Commission, 2003).

Another area of special attention is how to activate responsible controllers, so that they are able to demonstrate that they have taken the ap-propriate technical and organizational means to build compliance with data protection principles into all phases of development of their relevant systems and projects. An additional problem that has emerged is the difficulty of recognizing which products are genuinely privacy-enhancing tech-nologies -PETs- and how can they be recognized as such by users, taking into account that some current systems presenting themselves as PETs are not even privacy-compliant, in a scale of privacy-compliant, privacy-friendly and privacy-enhancing technologies.

In addition to -or further specification of- these elements, it is interesting to require impact assessments or regular audits for cases with specific risks, such as those involving banking and financial actors, as we will see in next sections. Other ideas would include the use of certifications for privacy relevant goods or services to ensure effective fulfillment of the abovementioned data controllers' obligations, based on real independent verification. This one is an important factor that contribute to the awareness about privacy issues by consumers in the U.S. This also explains why more U.S. websites than websites of European companies work with privacy seals and privacy statements, such as TRUSTe and BBOnline or some other programs which require companies that place the seal on their website to adhere to certain fair personal data practices (Louwers & Chow, 2009).

A particular problem is the increasing use of various methods of risk assessment, including the development of indicators or profiles suggesting that someone may qualify for further investigation of other kind of special treatment, by means of biometrics and data mining programs, particularly those ones either developed or used by Governments for national security purposes. Some interesting examples deal with banking data and travel data, such as the so-called Passenger Name Records (PNR), which contains data requested by an airline company when buying a ticket and which has been processing for security process by the U.S. for more than a decade -and in relation to which both the U.S. and the E.U. have concluded two agreements up to now-, or the former *United States Visitor and Immigrant Status Indicator Technology* program (De Hert & Bellanova, 2008).

The E.U. is currently planning not to reinvent, but to review the current legal framework for data protection in order to give much attention to making data protection more effective in practice, in view of the challenges posed by IT in the last 15 years. In the spring of 2009, the European Com-

mission launched a public consultation on the need to review of current E.U. regulation. The outlines of the Commission proposal were presented in a Communication -*A comprehensive approach on personal data protection in the UE*- in November 2010. On the basis of the input received from various stakeholders, the European Commission is now likely to present a proposal -or a package of proposals- later this year, so the discussion in the European Parliament and Council may well happen in 2013. It is in parallel with the announcement of the U.S. Administration to work towards a future Bill of Rights for Privacy and Data Protection. This purpose has been foreseen also at international level, in the last G-8 meeting in May 2011 (Hustinx, 2011. C). The coincidence of these major reviews is an opportunity for undertaking in synergy. Besides, some relevant private initiatives and agreements are being developed all around the world, including those adopting some kinds of binding corporate rules and mutual recognition rules, such as the *Law of the Future Project* and the *ETICA (Ethical Issues of Emerging ICT Applications) Project.*

OTHER IT SECURITY GOVERNANCE LEGAL ISSUES

Commonly Accepted Principles of Corporate Governance

Regardless of the national jurisdiction and local conditions, there are some principles of corporate governance that have been widely embraced over the years.

1. **Fair Treatment of Shareholders:** Companies need to respect shareholders rights. This includes open communication and shareholders' involvement in general board meetings. Being information a right of every shareholder, so its infringement would be adequate grounds for lawsuits.

2. **Responsibilities of the Board of Directors:** Robust corporate boards need a mix of independent members with ample credentials and internal skilled members with company expertise.

3. **Financial Transparency and Disclosure:** Companies need well-documented controls to consistently provide full transparency in financial reporting. Results must be audited by internal and external experts. They must be qualified enough to provide frank assessments without the fear of any kind of retaliation.

4. **Internal Controls:** Internal controls are a key component to improve corporate governance in general, to reduce risks and to provide consistent financial transparency.

All of these principles are included in the recently enacted security regulations. A list of the main laws and regulations addressing corporate obligations to implement information security requirements is set out in the Appendix at the end of this chapter. Besides, recent U.S. case law also recognizes that there may be a Common-law duty to provide information security, the breach of which constitutes a tort (e.g. *Wolfe v. MBNA America Bank,* 485 F. Supp. 2d 874).

In fact, evolving U.S. case law suggests that, by virtue of their fiduciary obligations to the company, corporate directors will find that their duty of care includes responsibility for the security of the company's information systems. E.g. *In re Caremark International Inc. Derivative Litigation,* 698 A. 2d. 959. In this case, the shareholders of Caremark International Inc. brought a derivative action, alleging that directors breached their duty of care by failing to put in place adequate internal control systems. This in turn was said to enable the company's employees to commit criminal offences, resulting in substantial fines and civil penalties. Chancellor William T. Allen, of the Delaware Court of Chancery, stated that, since *Smith v. Van Gorkom*, 488 A. 2d 858, it was clear

that "relevant and timely information is an essential predicate for satisfaction of the board's supervisory and monitoring rule under the Law". Allen considers that "directors must be assuring themselves that information and reporting systems exist in the organization, that are reasonably designed to provide senior management and to the board itself timely and accurate information sufficient to allow management and the board, each within its scope, to reach informed judgments concerning both the corporation's compliance with law and its business performance". "Failure to do so under some circumstances may render a director liable for losses" (paragraphs 969-971). Taking recent U.S. case law into account, companies are beginning to recognize that the responsibility for information security lies with upper management and the board of directors.

Legal Obligation to Provide Information Security

The legal issues surrounding information security are rooted in the fact that electronic communications have become the preferred way of doing business and networked computer technology has become the primary mean for storing information. But the resulting dependence on a networked computer infrastructure also creates significant vulnerabilities regarding ensuring individual privacy, protecting sensitive business data, accountability for financial information and the authenticity of transaction data are driving the enacted of Laws (Smedinghoff, 2008. B).

The companies obligation to provide information security is expansive in scope. It means that all types of corporate information need to be protected, including personal information, employee information, financial information, tax-related records and all kinds of confidential information. Besides, corporate obligation to provide information security extends not only to the data in a company's possession but also to a company's data in the possession of a third-party service provider. Thus, third-parties should also be subject to the same measures of the first company (Westby, 2004. B).

What is at risk and what concrete security measures must the company implement vary greatly from case to case. In fact, laws and regulations rarely specify the security measures a company should implement to satisfy its legal obligations. Most simply obligate firms to maintain and/or establish "appropriate" and/or "reasonable" security controls, but give no further guidance. Therefore, companies must engage in an ongoing process that assesses risk and implements security measure and must constantly evolve in light of changes in threats and information security technology (Smedinghoff, 2008. B; Westby, 2004. B). Despite law does not require companies to implement specific security measures or use a particular technology, some procedures are widely used in practice, such as procedures to ensure employee honesty and to prevent them from compromising security systems and procedures to protect infor-

mation from unauthorized access, alteration or disclosure of data during storage or transmission.

The first step is to define what information communications and processes are to be protected and what are the potential risk to the organization's information systems and data.

Many of the legal requirements are data-specific (Figure 3). Those considerations include the following: i) Legislation designed to protect public companies and their shareholders and business partners; ii) Legislation and regulation designed to protect personal interests of individual employees and customers; and iii) Sector-specific regulations. In the U.S., the Sarbanes-Oxley Act requires public companies to ensure controls with respect to their financial information and regarding personal data. In the private sector, several U.S. laws require companies to implement information security measures to protect certain personal data they maintain about individuals. This package of measures includes the Fair Credit Reporting Act and the Financial Services Modernization Act, in the financial sector, and the Health Insurance

Figure 3. Legal framework for information security

Portability and Accountability Act, regarding the healthcare industry. (Smedinghoff, 2008. B; Westby, 2004. B).

Using IT for Identifying, Assessing, and Ranking Risk: Industry-Specific Requirements Regarding Corporate Information Security Obligations

The process oriented legal standard for corporate information security was first set forth in a series of financial industry security regulations, which were required by public and media after some national and international financial scandals. Indeed, the currently rising interest in IT governance is partly due to compliance initiatives, for instance, the so-called Sarbanes-Oxley Act in the US and the Basel Accords in the international level, and the awareness of the need for greater accountability for decision-making around the use of IT in the best interest of all stakeholders, due to the major corporate and accounting scandals of *Enron, WorldCom* and *Tyco International*, among others, in the early 2000s. In the European context, we can stress *Parmalat* and *Ahold* scandals. After these widely reported scandals, the duties and responsibilities of auditors and managers for public and private corporations were questioned. To attempt to prevent similar situations from happening again, these regulations were written to stress the importance of business control and auditing.

The U.S. National Institute of Standards and Technology, which has statutory responsibilities to provide IT guidelines for U.S. federal agencies, published the *Risk Management Guide for Information Technology Systems* (July 2002). It provides IT risk management recommendations that are a good foundation for any IT organization to follow.

The Sarbanes-Oxley Act, also known as Public Company Accounting Reform and Investor protection Act or Corporate and Auditing Accountability and Responsibility Act, is a U.S. Federal law enacted on July 2002. It is commonly called

Sarbanes-Oxley Act, as its sponsors were the U.S. Senator P. Sarbanes and the US Representative M. G. Oxley. Prior to Sarbanes-Oxley Act, auditing firms were self-regulated. This act defines the codes of conduct for securities analyst and requires disclosure of knowable conflicts of interest and requires management and the external auditor to report on the adequacy of the company's internal control over financing reporting. It sets new standards for all U.S. public companies boards, management and public accounting firms-it does not apply to privately held companies-. It requires all organizations, large or small, registered with the Securities and Exchange Commission (SEC) to report on the effectiveness of their internal controls over financial reporting (US Security and Exchange Commission, 2007). It establishes standards for external auditor independence, to limit conflict of interest. One of the measures is the restriction of auditing companies from providing others non-audit services -such as consulting-from the same clients they audited. In the past, most of these consulting agreements were far more lucrative than the auditing engagement, thus arising evident conflict of interest. This law also creates the Public Company Accounting Oversight Board (PCAOB), a new quasi-public organization charged with regulating, guiding and inspecting accounting firms in their roles as auditors of public companies over financial reporting. Finally, it mandates that senior executives take individual responsibility for the accuracy and completeness of corporate financial reports and describes specific criminal penalties for manipulation or destruction of financial records or investigations.

Following corporate collapses in Australia around the same time, working groups adopted during the five-year period 2003-2008, the *Australian Standards for Corporate Governance of Information and Communication Technology*, with contractual rather than legal nature.

This contractual nature is also found in the aforementioned Basel Accords, which are recommendations on banking laws and regulations issued by the Basel Committee on Banking Supervision (BCBS), which was established by the so-called Group of ten countries-Belgium, Canada, France, Germany, Italy, Japan, the Netherlands, Sweden, the United Kingdom and the U.S.- in 1975 and formulates broad supervisory standards of best practice in banking supervision in the expectation that its members and other third countries will implement them trough their own national systems. Nowadays, its member are much more than ten: Argentina, Australia, Belgium, Brazil, Canada, China, France, Germany, Hong Kong, India, Indonesia, Italy, Japan, Korea, Luxembourg, Mexico, the Netherlands, Russia, Saudi Arabia, Singapore, South Africa, Spain, Sweden, Switzerland, Turkey, the United Kingdom and the U.S. Basel II is the second of these accords. Its aim is to generate an international standard that banking regulators can use when adopting regulations about how much capital banks need to put aside to guard against the financial and operational risks while maintaining sufficient consistency so that this does not become a source of competitive inequality among internationally active banks. For this, Basel II sets up risk and capital management

requirements designed to ensure that a bank holds capital reserves adequate to the concrete risk bank exposes itself to through its investment practices.

In response to a questionnaire released by the Financial Stability Institute, almost 100 national regulators indicated that they were to implement this accord, whether in statutory form or otherwise, by 2015. The EU has already implemented it by means of the so-called EU Capital Requirements Directives and many European banks have already applied them, reporting their capital adequacy ratios according to the new system. The US is also to implement it, with the difficulty there are various regulators, and that they have had to reach a final approach applicable for the largest banks and another standardized approach applicable for the smaller ones. Australia has already implemented it too. See Figure 4 fo rissues regarding intangible corporate assets.

CONCLUSION

Nowadays, information security has become a legal obligation, and responsibility for compliance

Figure 4. Issues regarding intangible corporate assets

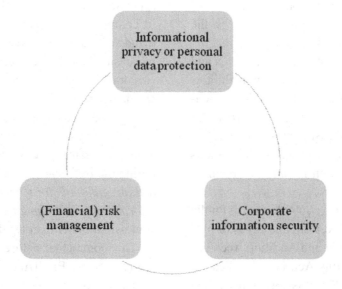

has been put directly on the shoulders of senior management. Despite the territoriality principle and the differences among the developed countries legislatures, all the major regulations of the past few years directed towards corporate obligations to implement information security measures show an amazing consistency in approach. Following the above-mentioned case-law, companies are beginning to recognize that the responsibility for information security lies with upper management and the board of directors. Nevertheless, according to *Guin v. Brazos Higher Education Service Corp. Inc.,* No. Civ. 05-668, when a proper risk assessment has been done and responsive security measures implemented, the inability to foresee and stop a specific security breach does not constitute a failure to satisfy the duty to provide reasonable security.

But, apart from laws regarding information security, there are other means of protecting corporate information and computer systems: the IPR. Particularly, in the European context, the so-called sui generis right protects the mere investment in either obtaining, verification or presentation of data contained in databases.

REFERENCES

Andermann, H. (2008). Microsoft v. Commission and the interoperability issue. *European Intellectual Property Review*, 395.

Aplin, T., & Davis, J. (2009). *Intellectual property law. Text, cases and materials*. Oxford, UK: Oxford University Press.

Balz, S. D., & Hance, O. (1996). Privacy and the Internet: Intrusion, surveillance and personal data. *International Review of Law Computers & Technology*, *10*(2), 219–230.

Beunen, A. (2007). *Protection for databases: The European database directive and its effects in the Netherlands, France and the United Kingdom*. Nijmegen, The Netherlands: Wolf Legal Publishers.

Bignami, F. (2007A). *The US privacy act in corporative perspective,* (p. 7). Paper presented at the European Parliament Public seminar PNR/SWIFT/Safa Habour, Are Transatlantic Data Protected? Retrieved August 25, 2011, from http://europarl.europa.eu/hearings/20070326/libe/bignami_en.pdf

Bignami, F. (2007B). European versus American liberty: A comparative privacy analysis of antiterrorism data mining. *Boston College Law Review. Boston College. Law School, 48,* 609–698.

Bornkamm, J. (2000). *Time for a European copyright code*. Retrieved August 25, 2011, from www.europa.eu.int/comm/internal_market/copyright/docs/conference/2000-07-strasbourg-proceedings_en.pdf

Business Software Alliance. (2003). *Eight annual BSA global software piracy study: Trends in software piracy 1994-2002*. Retrieved August 25, 2011, from http://www.bsa.org/country/Research%20and%20Statistics/~/media/Files/Research%20Papers/GlobalStudy/2003/IPR_GlobalStudy2003.ashx

Bygrave, L., & Koelman, K. (1998). *Privacy, data protection and copyright: Their interaction in the context of electronic copyright management systems*. IViR Publications. Retrieved August 25, 2011, from http://www.ivir.nl/publicaties/koelman/privreportdef.pdf

Cavoukian, A., & Tapscott, D. (1997). *Who knows: Safeguarding your privacy in a networked world*. New York, NY: McGraw-Hill.

Chander, A., Gelman, L., & Radin, M. J. (2008). *Securing privacy in the Internet age*. Stanford, CA: Stanford University Press.

Cohen, J. E. (1996). A right to read anonymously: A closer look at copyright management in cyberspace. *Connecticut Law Review, 28*, 981–991.

Cohen, J. E. (2003). DRM and privacy. *Berkeley Technology Law Journal, 18*, 575–617. Retrieved August 25, 2011 from http://www.law.georgetown.edu/faculty/jec/drmandprivacy.pdf

De Hert, P., & Bellanova, R. (2008). *Data protection from a transatlantic perspective: The EU and US towards an international data protection agreement?* Study requested by European Parliament, (PE 408.320). Retrieved August 25, 2011, from http://www.europarl.europa.eu/studies

De Hert, P., & Gutwirth, S. (2006). Privacy data protection and law enforcement. Opacity of the individual and transparency of power. In Claes, E., Duff, A., & Gutwirth, S. (Eds.), *Privacy and the criminal law* (pp. 61–104). Antwerp, Belgium: Intersentia.

Derclaye, E. (2008). *The legal protection of databases: A comparative analysis*. Cheltenham, UK: Edward Elgar Publishing.

Dreier, T., & Hugenholtz, P. B. (2006). *Concise European copyright law. Alphen aan den Rijn*. The Netherlands: Kluwer Law International.

Duran, L., Krieger, M. J., Maistry, U., Manasterski, A., Whetton, L., et al. (2008). *Technological measures to prevent the illegal uses of intellectual property rights*. MAS-IP Diploma Papers & Research Reports. Retrieved August 25, 2011, from http://e-collection.library.ethz.ch/eserv/eth:2193/eth-2193-01.pdf

Dusollier, S. (2005). Technological as an imperative for regulating copyright: From the public exploitation to the private use of the work. *European Intellectual Property Review, 27*(6), 201–205.

Electronic Privacy Information Center – EPIC. (2007). *Privacy and human rights. An international survey of privacy laws and developments*. Washington, DC: Author. Retrieved August 25, 2011, from https://www.privacyinternational.org/article/phr2006-foreward

European Commission. (2003, May 15). *First report from the European Commission on the implementation of the Data Protection Directive*, (p. 15). Brussels, Belgium: Author. Retrieved August 25, 2011, from http://europa.eu/legislation_summaries/information_society/data_protection/l14012_en.htm

European Commission. DG Internal Market and Services. (2005). *First evaluation of directive 96/9/EC on the legal protection of databases*. Brussels, Belgium: Author. Retrieved August 25, 2011, from http://ec.europa.eu/internal_market/copyright/docs/databases/evaluation_report_en.pdf

European Patent Office. (2008). *Patents for software?* Retrieved August 25, 2011, from http://www.epo.org/news-issues/issues/computers/software.html

Ganley, P. (2002). Access to the individual: Digital rights management systems and the intersection of informational and decisional privacy interest. *Journal of Law and Information Technology, 10*(3), 241–293.

Gaster, J. L. (1999). *Der Rechtsschutz von Datenbanken: Kommentar zur Richtlinie 96/9/ EG: mit Erläuterungen zur Umsetzung in das deutsche und österreichische Recht*. Köln, Germany: Heymans Verlag.

Gaster, J. L. (2006). Das urheberrechtliche Territorialitätsprinzip aus Sicht des Europäischen Gemeinschaftsrechts. *Zietschrift für Urheber- und Medienrecht (ZUM), 1*, 8-14.

Geiger, C. (2009). Intellectual property shall be protected!? Art. 17(2) of the charter of fundamental rights of the European Union: A mysterious provision with an unclear scope. *European Intellectual Property Preview*, *31*, 113–117.

Gervais, D. (2008). *The TRIPS agreement: Drafting history and analysis*. London, UK: Sweet & Maxwell.

Ghidini, G., & Arezzo, E. (2005). Patent and copyright paradigms vis-à-vis derivative innovation: The case of computer programs. *International Review of Intellectual Property and Competition Law*, *36*, 159–170.

Ginsburg, J. (1999). Copyright legislation for the digital millennium. *VLA Journal of Law & the Arts*, *23*, 137–143.

Goldstein, P. (2001). *International copyright*. Oxford, UK: Oxford University Press.

Gotzen, F. (2007). *The industrial property right protection of the producer of a database. Some reflections in the future of European and Japanese protection schemes*. Tokyo, Japan: Institute for Intellectual Property.

Gotzen, F., & Minero, G. (2011). Comentario a la estrategia de la Comisión Europea para 2011-2014 en materia de propiedad intelectual, "Un mercado común para los derechos de propiedad intelectual. *Revista de Propiedad Intelectual*, *38*, 115–126.

Halpern, S. W. (2009). *Copyright law. Protection of original expression*. Durham, NC: Carolina Academic Press.

Holvast, J., Madsen, W., & Roth, P. (2001). *The global encyclopedia of data protection regulation*. The Hague, The Netherlands: Kluwer Law International.

Hugenholtz, P. B. (2005). *The database right file*. IViR Publications. Retrieved August 25, 2011, from http://www.ivir.nl/files/database/index.html

Hustinx, P. (2011A). *A citizen's agenda for fundamental rights*. Paper presented at the ETICA Conference on Ethics and Governance of Future and Emerging ICTs, European Parliament. Retrieved August 25, 2011, from http://www.edps.europa.eu/EDPSWEB/edps/cache/off/EDPS/Publications/SpeechArticle/SA2011.

Hustinx, P. (2011B). *Data protection and privacy*. Paper presented at the International Data Protection Conference. Retrieved August 25, 2011, from http://www.edps.europa.eu/EDPSWEB/edps/cache/off/EDPS/Publications/SpeechArticle/SA2011.

Hustinx, P. (2011C). Data protection -A critical success factor for other important policy facts. *Engineering & Technology Magazine*, 35-38.

Kirby, M. (1999). *International dimensions of cyberspace law*. Paris, France: United Nations Educational, Scientific and Cultural Organization (UNESCO).

Koelman, K., & Helberger, N. (1998). *Protection of technological measures*, (pp. 8-12, 30). IViR Publications. Retrieved August 25, 2011, from http://www.ivir.nl/publicaties/koelman/technical-pdf

Koelman, K. J. (2001). *The protection of technological measures vs. the copyright limitations*. Paper presented at the ALAI Congress Adjuncts and Alternatives for Copyright, New York, NY. Retrieved August 25, 2011, from http://www.ivir.nl/publicaties/alaiNY.html

Lloyd, I. J. (2004). *Information technology law*. Oxford, UK: Oxford University Press.

Louwers, E. J., & Chow, S. T. (2009). *International computer law. A practical guide to international information technology law*. New York, NY: Bender.

Luo, L. (2005). *Legal protection of technological measures. A comparative study of US, European and Chinese anti-circumvention rules.* Hauser Global Law School Program, working paper 08/05. Retrieved August 25, 2011, from http://www.nyulawglobal.org

Minero, G. (2011). Protección jurídica de las bases de datos: Estudio de la aplicación de la Directiva 96/9/CE tres lustros después de su aprobación y comentario a la primera evaluación realizada por la Comisión Europea en 2005. *Revista de Propiedad Intelectual, 37,* 13–101.

Minero, G. (2012). Reflexiones acerca de la protección jurídica de las páginas web y la posible aplicación de la tutela de las bases de datos. *Revista de Propiedad Intelectual, 39.*

Privacy Working Group. (1995). *Information infrastructure task force, privacy and the national information infrastructure: Principles for providing and using personal information.* Retrieved August 25, 2011, from http://www.ntia.doc.gov/legacy/ntiahome/privwhitepaper.html

Reichman, J. H., & Samuelson, P. (1997). Intellectual property rights in data? *Vanderbilt Law Review, 50,* 132–134.

Reinbothe, J. (1992). Der Schutz des Urheberrechts und der Leistungsschutzrechte im Abkommensentwurf GATT/TRIPS. *GRUR International, 1992,* 709.

Samuelson, P. (2000). Privacy as intellectual property? *Stanford Law Review, 52,* 1125–1173.

Samuelson, P. (2003). Mapping the digital public domain: Treats and opportunities. *Law & Contemporary Problems, 66,* 147-172. Retrieved August 25, 2011, from http://www.law.berkeley.edu/phpprograms/faculty/facultyPubsPDF.php?facID=346&pubID=131

Shaw, T. J. (2011). *Information security and privacy: A practical guide for global executives, lawyers and technologists.* USA: American Bar Association, Section of Science & Technology.

Smedinghoff, T. J. (2008A). *Information security law: The emerging standard for corporate compliance.* Ely, UK: IT Governance Publishing.

Smedinghoff, T. J. (2008B). Defining the legal standard for information security. In Chander, A., Gelman, L., & Radin, M. J. (Eds.), *Securing privacy in the internet age* (pp. 15–40). Stanford, CA: Stanford University Press.

United Kingdom Information Commissioner Office. (2006). *A surveillance society report.* Retrieved August 25, 2011, from http://news.bbc.co.uk/1/hi/uk_politics/6260153.stm

US Security and Exchange Commission. (2007). *Spotlight on Sarbanes-Oxley rulemaking and reports.* Retrieved August 25, 2011, from http://www.sec.gov/spotlight/sarbanes-oxley.htm

Van Compel, S., Guibault, L., Helberger, N., & Hugenholtz, P. B. (2009). *Harmonizing European copyright law. The challenges of better lawmaking. Alphen aan den Rijn.* The Netherlands: Kluwer Law International.

Von Lewinski, S. (2008). *International copyright law and policy.* Oxford, UK: Oxford University Press.

Walter, M. M., & Von Lewinski, S. (Eds.). (2010). *European copyright law. A commentary.* Oxford, UK: Oxford University Press.

Westby, J. R. (Ed.). (2004A). *International Guide to Privacy.* American Bar Association, Section of Science & Technology.

Westby, J. R. (Ed.). (2004B). *International guide to cyber security.* American Bar Association, Section of Science & Technology.

Westby, J. R. (Ed.). (2005). *Roadmap to an enterprise security program.* American Bar Association, Section of Science & Technology.

KEY TERMS AND DEFINITIONS

BCBS: Basel Committee on Banking Supervision.

DRM: Digital rights management.

ETICA: Ethical Issues of Emerging ICT Applications.

GRC: Governance, risk management and compliance.

IASB: International Accounting Standards Board.

IFRS: International Financial Reporting Standards.

ICT: Information and Communication Technologies.

IPR: Intellectual Property Rights.

IT: Information Technology.

OECD: Organization for Economic Cooperation and Development.

PCAOB: U.S. Public Company Accounting Oversight Board.

PET: Privacy-enhancing technology.

SEC: U.S. Securities and Exchange Commission.

SOX Act: Sarbanes-Oxley Act.

TPM: Technological protection measures.

TRIPS Agreement: Trade-Related Aspects of Intellectual Property Rights Agreement.

WCT: WIPO Copyright Treaty.

WIPO: World Intellectual Property Organization.

WTO: World Trade Organization.

APPENDIX

National Laws and Regulations and International Agreements Regarding Information Security and Data Protection

1. US
    a. Privacy Act of 1974, Public Law 93-579, 5 U.S.C, amended. Available at: http://www.justice.gov/opcl/privstat.htm.
    b. Electronic Communications Privacy Act Amendments Act of 2011. S 1011. Available at: http://www.gpo.gov/fdsys/pkg/BILLS-112s1011is/pdf/BILLS-112s1011is.pdf
    c. Fair Credit Reporting Act, Public Law 91-508, 15 U.S.C. Available at: http://www.ftc.gov/os/statutes/031224fcra.pdf.
    d. Financial Services Modernization Act, also known as Gramm-Leach-Bliley Act, Public Law 106-102. Available at: http://www.gpo.gov/fdsys/pkg/PLAW-106publ102/pdf/PLAW-106publ102.pdf
    e. Health Insurance Portability and Accountability Act, Public Law 104-191, 42 U.S.C. Available at: http://www.gpo.gov/fdsys/pkg/PLAW-104publ191/pdf/PLAW-104publ191.pdf.
    f. Sarbanes-Oxley Act, Public Law 107-204, 15 U.S.C. Available at: http://www.gpo.gov/fdsys/pkg/PLAW-107publ204/pdf/PLAW-107publ204.pdf.
2. European Union (The following Directives, Decisions and Regulations have also been regulated into the national level by the legislatures of the twenty-seven Member States. National naming of each one is not cited in this Appendix)
    a. Directive 2006/48/EC of the European Parliament and the Council of 14 June 2006, relating to the taking up and pursuit of the business of credit institutions. Consolidated version, Official Journal 30.03.2010. Available at: http://eur-lex.europa.eu/LexUriServ/LexUriServ.do?uri=CONSLEG:2006L0048:20100330:EN:PDF.
    b. Directive 2006/49/EC of the European Parliament and the Council of 14 June 2006, on the capital adequacy of investment firms and credit institutions. Consolidated version, Official Journal 07.12.2009. Available at: http://eur-lex.europa.eu/LexUriServ/LexUriServ.do?uri=CONSLEG:2006L0049:20091207:EN:PDF.
    c. European Parliament and Council Directive 95/46/EC of 24 October 1995 on the protection of individuals with regard to the processing of personal data and the free movement of such dada (Official Journal L 281 of 23.11.1995). Available at: http://eur-lex.europa.eu/LexUriServ/LexUriServ.do?uri=OJ:L:1995:281:0031:0050:EN:PDF.
    d. Regulation EC No. 1882/2003 of the European Parliament and of the Council of 29 September 2003. Available at: http://eur-lex.europa.eu/LexUriServ/LexUriServ.do?uri=CONSLEG:1995L0046:20031120:EN:PDF.
    e. Directive 2002/58/EC of the European Parliament and of the Council of 12 July 2002 concerning the processing of personal data and the protection of privacy in the electronic communications sector (Known as Directive on privacy and electronic communications). Official Journal L 201 of 31.07.2002. Available at: http://eur-lex.europa.eu/LexUriServ/LexUriServ.do?uri=OJ:L:2002:201:0037:0047:EN:PDF.
    f. European Commission Decision 2004/915/EC of 27 December 2004 amending Decision 2001/497/EC as regards the introduction of an alternative set of standard contractual clauses

for the transfer of personal data to third countries (Official Journal L 385 of 29.12.2004). Available at: http://eur-lex.europa.eu/LexUriServ/LexUriServ.do?uri=OJ:L:2004:385:0074:0085:EN:PDF.

g. European Commission Decision 2001/497/EC of 15 June 2001 on standard contractual clauses for the transfer of personal data to third countries under Directive 95/46/EC (Official Journal L 181 of 04.07.2001). Available at: http:// http://eur-lex.europa.eu/LexUriServ/LexUriServ.do?uri=OJ:L:2001:181:0019:0031:EN:PDF.

h. Regulation EC No. 45/2001 of the European Parliament and of the Council of 18 December 2000 on the protection of individuals with regard to the processing of personal data by the Community institutions and bodies and on the free movement of such data (Official Journal L 8 of 12.01.2001). Available at: http:// http://eur-lex.europa.eu/LexUriServ/LexUriServ.do?uri=OJ:L:2001:008:0001:0022:EN:PDF.

3. Canada

a. Personal Information Protection and Electronic Documents Act (S.C. 2000, c. 5). Available at: http://laws-lois.justice.gc.ca/eng/acts/P-8.6/.

4. International Agreements

a. Basel I, Basel II and Basel III, issued by the Basel Committee on Banking Supervision (BCBS).

b. U.S.-E.U. International Safe Harbor Privacy Principles.

c. Australian Standards for Corporate Governance of Information and Communication Technology.

d. ETICA (Ethical Issues of Emerging ICT Applications) Project.

5. Case Law

a. US:
   i. *Apple Computer, Inc. v. Franklin Computer Corp.*, 714 F.2d 1240 (3d Cir. 1983).
   ii. *Computer Associates, Inc. v. Altai, Inc.* 982 F 2d 693 (2d Cir.).
   iii. *Diamond v. Bradley*, 450 US 381.
   iv. *Diamond v. Diehr*, 450 US 175, 101 S. Ct. 1048.
   v. *Feist Publications Inc v. Rural Telephone Service Company Inc.*, 111 s. Ct, 1282.
   vi. *Guin v. Brazos Higher Education Service Corp. Inc.*, No. Civ. 05-668.
   vii. *In re Caremark International Inc. Derivative Litigation*, 698 A. 2d. 959.
   viii. *Lotus v. Paperback*, 740 F Supp 37.
   ix. *Smith v. Van Gorkom*, 488 A. 2d 858.
   x. *Whelan Associates, Inc. v. Jaslow Dental Laboratory, Inc.*, 797 F.2d 1222 (3d Cir.).
   xi. *Williams Electronics, Inc. v. Arctic International, Inc.*, 685 F.2d 870 (3d Cir.).
   xii. *Wolfe v. MBNA America Bank*, 485 F. Supp. 2d 874.

b. EU:
   i. EU Court of First Instance of 17 September 2007, case T-201/04, *Microsoft v. Commission*.
   ii. EU Court of Justice of 22 December 2010, case C-393/09, *Bezpecnostní softwarová asociace v. Ministerstvo Kultury*.

c. UK:
   i. *Kabushiki Kaisha Sony Computer Entertainment Inc. and Others v. Ball and Others* [2004] EWHC 1738.

Section 2
Security Standards and Guidelines in the IT Security Governance

Chapter 4
Information Technology Service Management

Magdalena Arcilla
*Universidad Nacional de Educación a Distancia,
Spain*

Mercedes de la Cámara
Universidad Politécnica de Madrid, Spain

Jose A. Calvo-Manzano
Universidad Politécnica de Madrid, Spain

Javier Sáenz
Universidad Politécnica de Madrid, Spain

Luis Sánchez
Universidad Politécnica de Madrid, Spain

ABSTRACT

Nowadays, there is an increasing dependence on information and on the systems that provide such information. So, for many organizations, the information and technology that supports them represent the most valuable assets of the company. Research on Information Technology (IT) management practices in many organizations around the world has revealed that most of them are not optimizing their investment on IT. The differentiating factor between those who succeed and those who failed is the participation of management in key IT decisions that must be aligned with the strategic and operational business plans and a proper corporate governance of IT. Corporate governance evaluates and directs the use of IT to support the organization, monitoring its use to achieve plans, and provides guidance to advising, informing or assisting directors, and assuring the compliance with laws and regulations. Some frameworks and models have been developed related to the governance and service management of IT. ITIL® (Information Technology Infrastructure Library) is the most used and extended model related to IT service management. The purpose of this chapter is to describe briefly the main phases and processes related to the ITIL® service lifecycle, detailed information related to the information security management process, and the qualifying system for IT Service Management with ITIL®.

DOI: 10.4018/978-1-4666-2083-4.ch004

INTRODUCTION

ICT (Information and Communications Technologies) are present in any organization. There's no need to be in contact with technological environments to see how in these days we all use technology. If we go to a hospital we can see many electronic devices, or systems that improve our lives or that help us in our work. And the same occurs for public administrations or private organizations.

This means that there are organizations that, without a technological base, have a lot of technology available and, in many cases, they are not able to take full advantage of it, or they simply need people or more powerful tools to help them in their day to day with the technologies they use regularly.

In the past, it was a common practice to consider the role of IT (Information Technology) in an organization as a mere supporting one. Currently, most investment in infrastructure and new IT applications are related to business lines and functions of the organization. Therefore, the CEOs (Chief Executive Officer) and CIOs (Chief Information Officer) are increasingly feeling the need to enhance the relationship between IT and business. But how can be addressed this strategic challenge? The key issues are:

- Is there a framework to help business and technology leaders in their effort to change the role of IT and reduce the gap between IT and the business that it must sustain and support?
- What are the responsibilities at the managerial and management levels?

A key element for the success and survival of any organization is the effective management of its information and related IT. In this global society (where information travels through the "cyberspace" without the constraints of time, distance and speed) this criticality arises from:

- The increasing dependence on information and on the systems that provide such information.
- The increasing vulnerability due to a wide spectrum of threats, such as the "cyber" and information warfare.
- The cost of current and future investments on information and IT.
- The potential of technologies to dramatically change organizations and business practices, creating new opportunities and reducing costs.

For many organizations, the information and technology that supports them represent the most valuable assets of the company. Moreover, in our current competitive and rapidly changing environment, the government has increased its expectations regarding the delivery of IT services. Therefore, the government requires services which help to increase the quality, functionality and ease of use of services, as well as a continuous improvement and a reduction in delivery time, while demanding that this be done at a lower cost.

It is necessary a change in the role of IT to obtain the most efficiency from an IT investment and to use technology as a competitive weapon. Thus, IT attitude related to business changes from being merely reactive to proactive, anticipating the needs of the organization.

Research on IT management practices in hundreds of companies around the world has revealed that most organizations are not optimizing their investment on IT. The differentiating factor between those who succeed and those who failed is the participation of management in key IT decisions. Proper management participation in these decisions provides real value to IT investments while serving to prevent IT-related disasters. It must be distinguished between strategic and operational decisions and these decisions must be aligned with the strategic and operational plans of the business.

If IT is to be managed like a business within the business, the concept of government (a process that helps management to achieve their goals) also applies to IT management. In many organizations, IT is critical to maintain and make grow the business. As a result, management needs to understand the strategic importance of IT and should have in their agenda the IT governance. The main objective of IT governance is to understand the issues and the strategic importance of IT to enable the organization to maintain its operations and implement the necessary strategies to manage its projects and future activities in an appropriate way.

Corporate governance of IT involves evaluating and directing the use of IT to support the organization and monitoring this use to achieve plans (ISO/IEC 38500:2008, 2011). It includes the strategy and policies for using IT within an organization. Governance is distinct from management. IT governance must provide guidance for advising, informing, or assisting directors (including senior managers; members of groups monitoring the resources within the organization; external specialists, such as legal or accounting; professional bodies; vendors of hardware, software, communications and other IT products; internal and external service providers; or IT auditors) (Van Grembergen, 2009). And IT Services Management (ITSM) establishes a processes set for supporting and providing IT services into the organization.

In the same way, corporate governance of IT may assist directors in assuring conformance with obligations such as: regulatory legislation or contractual law concerning the acceptable use of IT (Yip, 2006). For example, directors could be held accountable for breaches of: security standards; privacy legislation; spam legislation; trade practices legislation; intellectual property rights, including software licensing agreements; record keeping requirements; environmental legislation and regulations; health and safety legislation; accessibility legislation; social responsibility standards. Finally, a proper corporate governance of IT assists directors to ensure that IT use contributes positively to the performance of the organization, through:

- Appropriate implementation and operation of IT assets.
- Clear responsibility and accountability for both the use and provision.
- Of IT in achieving the goals of the organization.
- Business continuity and sustainability.
- Alignment of IT with business needs.
- Efficient allocation of resources.
- Innovation in services, markets, and business.
- Good practice in relationship with stakeholders.
- Reduction in the costs for an organization.
- Actual realization of the approved benefits from each IT investment.

IT governance provides the structures that support the IT processes, IT resources and information according to the strategies and objectives of the company. Furthermore, IT governance integrates and institutionalizes good (or best) practices for planning and organization, acquisition and implementation, service delivery and support, and monitors IT performance to ensure that company information and related technologies support its business objectives. IT governance helps the company to take full advantage of its information, maximizing its profits, capitalizing on its opportunities and improving the competitive advantage. IT governance must also encourage the definition and implementation of a frame for security aligned with the objectives of the organization. IT governance constitutes a subgroup of action inside the corporative governance that facilitates the strategic axis, assures the fulfillment of the objectives, manages the risk appropriately, uses the resources of the organization, defines responsibilities and monitors the success or fail of the corporative program for information security. The actions and processes aimed at security governance of Information Technology should be integrated into the governance of IT (Gregory, 2009).

The core of IT has two main responsibilities: delivering value to the business and mitigating risks associated with IT. The management of the organization needs to expand their governance responsibilities to IT, and provide structures and processes to ensure that Information Technologies are capable of supporting the strategies of the organization and help to achieve its goals.

Business and IT governance cannot be considered separately nor different disciplines in order to succeed in this information economy. The effective governance of the company focuses on the knowledge and experience of individuals and groups, the way to be more productive, how to monitor and measure the performance, as well as provide the assurance for critical areas. IT, for long time considered isolated in the achievement of the objectives of the company, must now be considered as an integral part of the strategy.

Management must lead and manage IT activities to achieve an effective balance between risk and benefits in order to ensure that business goals are reached. To accomplish this, management needs to identify the most important activities to be developed, measuring progress toward meeting the goals and determining how well they are developing IT processes. Furthermore, management needs the ability to assess the maturity level of the organization related to industry best practices and international standards.

To solve the problems related to the governance, different frameworks have been provided, being COBIT (Control Objectives for Information Technology and related) one of them (ITGI, IT Governance Institute, 2007).

As it was indicated above, technological progress has meant that companies now heavily rely on IT. This growing dependency, necessary to improve the efficiency of their business and strategy processes, leads to the upcoming need to build quality services that will meet both the business requirements and the arising necessities of the users.

It is essential that IT departments are aware of how the alignment with the infrastructure directly affects the quality, quantity and availability that the company is able to provide to users.

IT Service Management has a major impact on business processes and represents one of the most valuable assets. Organizations have less hierarchical and more flexible structures, supported by a reference framework or model to identify and relate the various activities that make up the operational processes of IT Service Management. ITIL® (Information Technology Infrastructure Library) is one of these models.

ITIL® provides a set of best practices for covering the objectives of good service management through a variety of roles, tasks, procedures and responsibilities that can be adapted to any organization. ITIL® is a set of concepts and best practices for service management of information technology, development of information technology and operations related to IT in general. ITIL® provides detailed descriptions of an extensive set of management procedures designed to help organizations in achieving quality and efficiency of IT operations. These procedures are supplier independent and have been developed to serve as a guide covering all infrastructure, development and operations of IT.

ITIL® embodies best practices for IT Service Integral Management. It is applied by numerous organizations around the world and provides a supporting professional qualification scheme that allows that each professional profile acquires the more adequate knowledge. ITIL® describes, through the life cycle of the service, every process implied in obtaining the organization goals and objectives.

The objectives of this chapter are to describe the processes associated to each of the phases of the service lifecycle. For each process, its objectives, benefits obtained by an adequate implementation of the process, difficulties when implementing the process and the main activities are enumerated. Also, a more detailed view of the information security management process will be given, as well as the qualifying system for IT Service Management.

BACKGROUND OF ITIL® V3

Although ITIL® was developed during the 80's, it was not widely adopted until the mid-90's, as other best practices frameworks, such as Information Services Procurement Library (ISPL, Information Services Procurement Library, 2011), the Application Services Library (Van Der, 2009), Dynamic Systems Development Method (Stapleton, 1999), the Capability Maturity Model (Integration) (SEI, 2009) (SEI, 2010), and often it is related to the governance of information technology through COBIT (ITGI, IT Governance Institute, 2007).

ITIL® is built around a process-control model and operations management. The ITIL® recommendations were developed in the 80's by the Central Computer and Telecommunications Agency (CCTA) of the British Government in response to the growing dependence on information technologies and the recognition that, without standard practices, contracts of government agencies and private sector, had independently created their own IT management practices, duplicating efforts in their IT projects and resulting in common mistakes and increased costs.

One of the main benefits of ITIL® within the IT community is that it provides a common vocabulary consisting of a glossary of terms precisely defined and widely accepted.

What is now called ITIL® version 1, developed under the auspices of the CCTA, was titled Method Government Information Technology

Infrastructure and described in thirty-one books. These publications were renamed mainly due to the desire of being saw as a guide and not as a formal method, and as a result of the increasing interest of different organizations, not only of those related to the British Government.

In order to make ITIL® more accessible (and cheaper) to those wishing to explore it, one of the objectives of the ITIL® version 2 update project was to group the books according to some logical features for dealing with the management processes covered by everyone. Thus, various aspects of ICT systems, applications and service are presented in thematic sets.

Although Service Management (Service Support and Service Delivery) (OGC, Service Soport: Best practice, 2006), (OGC, Service Delivery: Best Practice, 2006) is the most widespread and implemented part of ITIL®, a full set of practices, that includes processes, operational and technical requirements, strategic management, operations and financial management for any modern organization.

The eight books of ITIL® v2 and their topics are:

- IT Service Management.
  - Service Delivery best practices.
  - Service Support best practices.
- Other Operating Guidelines.
  - IT Infrastructure Management.
  - Security Management.
  - Business perspective.
  - Application Management.
  - Software Asset Management.

To assist in the implementation of ITIL® practices, an additional book was published with implementation guides (mainly of Service Management):

- Planning to implement Service Management.

In addition to the eight original books, more recently a guide was added with recommendations for smaller ICT departments:

- Implementing ITIL® at a small scale.

The Service Support book is concerned with ensuring that the user has access to appropriate services that support business functions. Topics covered in the book are:

- User Service Centre.
- Incident Management.
- Problem Management.
- Configuration Management.
- Change Management.
- Delivery Management.

In the Service Delivery book it is analyzed what service requires the provider business in order to provide adequate support to users and/or business customers. The book covers the following topics:

- Service Level Management.
- Financial Management for IT Services.
- Capacity Management.
- Continuity Management for IT Services.
- Availability Management.

ITIL® V3

In ITIL® v3, the model is restructured towards a "service lifecycle," separating and expanding some subprocesses until they become specialized processes.

In recent years, the pragmatic approach to ITIL® has allowed IT organizations to get good results. ITIL® V3 has a complete view of the supply chain of IT services.

ITIL® v3 has five books based on the service life cycle (see Figure 1):

- Service Strategy (OGC, "Service Strategy", 2007)
- Service Design (OGC, "Service Design", 2007)
- Service Transition (OGC, "Service Transition", 2007)
- Service Operation (OGC, "Service Operation", 2007)
- Continual Service Improvement (OGC, "Continual Service Improvement", 2007)

Next, an overview of each of the books as well as its associated processes is presented.

Service Strategy

It is focused on market research and new opportunities by seeking innovative services that meet the customer necessities, considering the feasibility of its real implementation. It also discusses potential improvements to existing services. Contracts based on the new offerings from former suppliers and potential new suppliers are verified, including the renewal or revocation of existing contracts.

It is essential to first determine what services should be provided and why they should be provided from a customer and market perspective.

Services are defined in ITIL® as a way of adding value to the customer without assuming the specific risks and costs of its delivering.

But the value does not depend exclusively on the economic aspect associated with the specific outcome of each service. This includes some other intangibles like the customer's perception.

Provider must take into account that the value for the customer is the result of the service delivered and the impact it has on its business and not the service itself.

Utility and warranty of a service are often interdependent and, when designing a new IT service, an organization must try to reach a balance between them and, at the same time, minimize those issues that potential customers may perceive negatively.

Utility requires that the service:

Figure 1. ITIL® service lifecycle

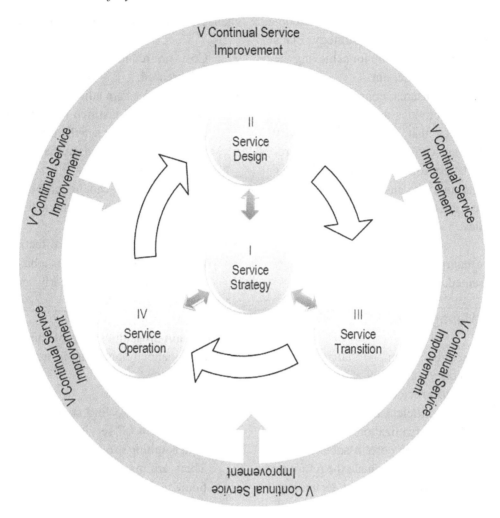

- Meets customer requirements.
- Increases performance.

And it should result in a benefit for the customer by lowering costs directly or by helping to increase revenues.

The warranty implies that the service:

- Will be available when needed.
- Is correctly sized to meet its objectives.
- Is safe.
- Will have backup mechanism to allow its continuity.

An appropriate service strategy requires:

- A perspective that clearly determines the objectives and decisions to be taken to achieve them. The general rules of the game, both within the IT organization and for the relationships with its customers must be established. Communication is an essential part since all stakeholders must understand easily what the selected perspective is.
- The position must define what services will be provided, how and to whom, differentiating them from those of the competence.

- Planning is essential in a constantly evolving environment that will force us to constantly evolve our service strategy. Plans must establish a road map for achieving the general objectives set out.
- The pattern ensures consistency in the undertaken activities and establishes procedural rules that ensure the necessary activities are carried out as and when required. Patterns outline the profile of the IT organization to the customer and facilitate resource allocation and prioritization of activities.

Next, the main processes of the service strategy will be presented.

Financial Management

The main objective of Financial Management is to assess and control the costs associated with IT services and to provide a quality service to customers with an efficient use of required IT resources. If the IT organization and/or its clients are not aware of the costs associated with services, they may neither evaluate the return on investment nor provide consistent technology spending plans. Generally, the higher the quality of services, greater cost, so it is necessary to carefully assess the needs of the client in order to reach an optimal balance.

To achieve this objective, Financial Management must:

- Evaluate the actual costs associated with the provision of services.
- Provide the IT organization all financial information required for decision-making and pricing.
- Advise the client on the added value provided by IT services.
- Assess, in collaboration with the Service Portfolio Management, a financial analysis of return on investment (ROI).

The main benefits of an adequate financial management of IT services are summarized as:

- Costs are reduced and service profitability is increased.
- Service prices are adjusted, controlled, appropriated and justified (if applicable), increasing customer satisfaction.
- Clients contract services that offer a good cost/profitability ratio.
- IT organization can better plan their investments by knowing the actual costs of IT services.
- IT services are used more effectively.
- IT organization operates as a business unit and it is possible to clearly assess their overall performance.

The main difficulties in implementing the IT Services Financial Management are summarized as follows:

- It is difficult to find staff that is familiar with both the IT services and financial and/or accounting aspects.
- There are many hidden costs that are difficult to assess because of poor financial organization.
- There is no clear strategy to develop budgets adjusted to it.
- An increase in costs.
- There is no organization-wide commitment to the process.

The main activities of Financial Management of IT services are summarized as follows:

- **Budgets:** Analyzing the financial situation, establishing financial policies, and budgeting.
- **Accountability:** Identifying costs, defining cost elements, and monitoring costs.

- **Fixing Prices:** Developing a pricing policy, and establishment of rates for services or products offered.

Portfolio Management

The main objective of Service Portfolio Management is to define a service strategy that will generate maximum value by controlling risks and costs. It is also in charge of evaluating the quality requirements and the related costs.

To achieve this objective, Service Portfolio Management must:

- Know and analyze the market in which the service will develop its activities, identifying opportunities, competence, etc.
- Raise strong strategic lines that guide all business activities towards a set of clear objectives.
- Define, in detail, the services to be offered to customers. It is also a task of the Service Portfolio Management to choose, among all possible services the IT organization can offer, those which best meet the stated objectives, provide better business prospects, and provide more value to customers.

The main benefits of a good Service Portfolio Management are summarized as:

- The organization is able to optimize their ability to offer added value, obtaining optimal levels of ROI at a low cost when knowing in depth the resources available and the risks facing.
- The danger of excessive business diversification of disparate services is avoided when having clear the objectives that must govern the organization's strategic lines, a situation which is often interpreted by customers as a sign of inconsistency.

The main difficulty faced by the Service Portfolio Management is that the management of the IT organization is reluctant to define the services in advance for considering this procedure limits the business.

The main activities of Service Portfolio Management are summarized as follows:

- **Defining the Business:** What services are offered by competitors, what opportunities the market offers, which are the "strengths" of the organization, and so on.
- **Analyzing Services:** Objectives, services needed to achieve them, capabilities and associated resources, etc.
- **Approving Decisions for the Future on Services:** Retention, substitution, rationalization, refactoring, renewal and disposal.
- **Updating Service Portfolio and Planning:** Definition of services, priorities, risks, schedules, intended costs and so on.

Demand Management

Demand management is responsible for predicting and regulating the cycles of use of services, adapting production to higher demand peaks to ensure that the service is being provided according to the times and quality levels agreed with the client. Usually, the better the service works the more increases the demand. The demand, in turn, causes the necessity of a higher capacity that must be compensated by increasing the service assets. A cycle is generated in which use is a positive stimulus for production and vice versa.

A proper Demand Management provides a number of improvements and substantial benefits to both the service and the business itself:

- Management Capacity can optimize planning to fit the patterns of use based on the reports of Demand Management.

- Service Portfolio Management may approve investment in extra capacity, new services or changes in services based on use.
- The Service Catalogue can also trace patterns of demand for certain services.
- Operation of the Service may adjust the allocation of resources and make better plans just finding common patterns of demand.
- Financial Management may approve incentives to influence demand.

The main activities of Demand Management are summarized as follows:

- Analysis of business activity to determine demand patterns and customer segments.
- Developing the offer with options for each market segment according to their needs, packaging essential and support services separately.

Service Design

Once a service is identified, the next step is to analyze its feasibility. This is done by analyzing factors such as available infrastructure, staff training and planning issues (e.g., security and disaster prevention). To start, it is necessary to take into account the reallocation of employee positions (hiring, firing, promotions, retirements, etc.), the infrastructure and the software to implement.

The primary mission of the Service Design phase is to design new services or modify the existing ones for their incorporation into the service catalogue and then deploying them into the production environment.

Service Design should follow the guidelines set out in the Strategy phase, and must in turn work with it in order to designed services:

- Fit into market needs.
- Be cost efficient and profitable.
- Meet the adopted quality standards.

- Add value to customers and users.

Next, the main processes of the service design are presented.

Service Catalogue Management

Service Portfolio provides a key strategic and technical reference within the IT organization, showing a detailed description of all services provided and resources allocated for them. Service Catalogue does exactly the same function, but externally.

The main objective of the Service Catalogue is to summarize all the information concerning the services that customers need to know to ensure a good understanding between them and the IT organization.

To achieve this objective, the Service Catalogue Management must:

- Describe the services provided in a comprehensible way for non-specialized people, being careful to avoid technical language.
- Be used as guidance to guide and direct customers.
- Include the Service Level Agreements (SLAs) and current prices. It should also reflect other policies and conditions for provision of services as well as responsibilities associated with each of them.
- Record existing customers of each service.
- Be available to the Service Centre and personnel in contact with customers.

The main benefit of creating, maintaining and using a Service Catalogue is that the relationship between the organization and the customer is more fluid and solid.

The main activities of Service Catalogue Management are:

- Define the main groups of services to be provided, and record the active services and the documentation associated with them.
- Maintain and update the Service Catalogue.

Service Level Management

Service Level Management should ensure IT service quality by aligning technology and business processes at reasonable costs.

To achieve its objectives, Service Level Management must:

- Know the needs of its customers.
- Define correctly the services offered.
- Monitor service quality related to the objectives established in Service Level Agreements.

The main benefits of a proper Service Level Management are:

- IT services are designed to meet their true objectives, that is, to meet customer needs.
- Communication with customers is facilitated and misunderstandings about the nature and quality of the services offered are prevented.
- Clear and measurable objectives are established.
- Responsibilities of both customers and service providers are clearly defined.
- Customers know and accept the quality levels offered and establish clear protocols for action in case of service deterioration.
- Monitoring constantly the services provided to detect the "weakest links in the chain" for improving them.
- IT management knows and understands the services offered, which facilitates arrangements with suppliers and subcontractors.
- The Service Centre staff has the necessary documentation (Service Level Agreement

-SLA, Operation Level Agreement - OLA, etc.) for an ongoing relationship with customers and suppliers.
- SLAs help IT Management to estimate the cost and to justify its price to customers.

The main difficulties when implementing the Service Level Management are summarized as:

- There is no good communication with customers and users, so that the agreed SLAs do not reflect their real needs.
- Service level agreements are based more on customer needs and expectations than in services that IT infrastructure can provide with a sufficient level of quality.
- IT services are not properly aligned to the client's business processes.
- SLAs are too wordy and technical, not fulfilling its primary objectives.
- There are not enough resources dedicated, as management considers them as an added expense and not as an integral part of the service offered.
- Communication problems: not all users know the characteristics of service and the agreed levels of quality.
- SLAs compliance is not monitored properly and consistently, making difficult to improve service quality.
- There is no real commitment with IT service quality offered in the organization.

The main activities in Service Level Management are summarized as:

- Planning.
- Implementing Service Level Agreements (SLAs), Operation Level Agreements (OLAs) and Underpinning Contracts (UC).
- Monitoring and reviewing Service Level Agreements.

Availability Management

Availability Management is responsible for optimizing and monitoring IT services in order they work continuously and reliably, meeting SLAs and at a reasonable cost. Customer satisfaction and profitability of IT services depend largely on its success. The main objective of Availability Management is to ensure that IT services are available and work properly as long as customers and users want to use them as is described in the SLAs in place.

To achieve the objective, Availability Management must:

- Determine availability requirements in close collaboration with customers.
- Ensure the availability level established for IT services.
- Monitor the availability of IT systems.
- Suggest improvements in infrastructure and IT services with the aim of increasing the availability levels.
- Monitor the fulfillment of the agreed OLAs and UCs with the internal and external suppliers.

The main benefits of an appropriate Availability Management are:

- Fulfillment of the agreed availability levels.
- Costs associated with a high level of availability are reduced.
- The customer receives a higher quality of service.
- Availability levels are steadily increasing.
- The number of incidents is reduced.

The main difficulties when implementing Availability Management are summarized as:

- Actual availability of the service is not monitored properly.

- There is no commitment to the process within the IT organization.
- There are no software tools and suitable personnel.
- Availability objectives are not aligned with customer needs.
- Lack of coordination with other processes.
- Internal and external providers do not recognize the authority of the Availability Manager due to lack of management support.

The main activities of Availability Management are summarized as:

- Determining the actual availability requirements of the business.
- Developing an availability plan where future short and medium term availability needs are estimated.
- Keeping the service operating and recovering in case of failure.
- Performing periodic diagnostics on the availability of systems and services.
- Assessing the capacity of service for internal and external suppliers.
- Advising Change Management on the possible impact of a change in availability.

Capacity Management

It is responsible for all IT services are backed by a sufficient and correctly sized process and storage capacity. Without an adequate capacity management, resources are not used properly and unnecessary investments that entail additional costs of maintenance and management are made. Or worse, the resources are insufficient and therefore the quality of service degrades.

The main objective of Capacity Management is to make available the IT resources needed by customers, users and IT department itself to efficiently perform their tasks, and all without incurring in disproportionate costs.

To achieve this objective, Capacity Management must:

- Know the current state of technology and expected future developments.
- Know the business plans and service level agreements to provide the necessary capacity.
- Analyze the performance of the infrastructure to monitor the use of the existing capacity.
- Perform capacity models and simulations for predictable different future scenarios.
- Size applications and services properly, aligning them to business processes and real customer needs.
- Manage demand for IT services rationalizing their use.

The main benefits of a proper capacity management are:

- The performance of computing resources is optimized.
- The capacity required at the appropriate time is available preventing the quality of service may be affected.
- Unnecessary expenses resulting from purchases of "last minute" are avoided.
- The growth of the appropriate infrastructure for the real needs of business is planned.
- The maintenance and management costs associated with hardware and software that are obsolete or unnecessary are reduced.
- Possible incompatibilities and IT infrastructure failures are reduced.

The main difficulties in implementing the Capacity Management are summarized as follows:

- Insufficient information for realistic capacity planning.

- Unjustified expectations about cost savings and performance improvements.
- Insufficient resources for proper monitoring of performance.
- Distributed computing infrastructures and excessively complex that make difficult to access the data properly.
- There is not enough commitment from management to implement rigorously the associated processes.
- The rapid evolution of technologies may force a continuous review of plans and considered scenarios.

The main activities in Capacity Management are summarized as:

- Developing the capacity plan and modeling different capacity scenarios.
- Monitoring the IT infrastructure resources.
- Overseeing the capacity and management of the capacity database.

Service Continuity Management

It is concerned of preventing that an unexpected and severe disruption of IT services due to natural disasters or other force majeure has catastrophic consequences for the business.

The main objectives of Continuity Management are to ensure the earliest recovery of critical IT services after a disaster, and to establish policies and procedures to prevent, as far as possible, the harmful consequences of a disaster or force majeure.

The main benefits of a proper Continuity Management are summarized as follows:

- Risks are adequately managed.
- The period of service interruption due to force majeure is reduced.
- The confidence in the quality of service of customers and users is improved.

The main difficulties when implementing the Continuity Management are:

- There may be resistance to investments whose profitability is not immediate.
- The associated costs are not properly budgeted.
- Not enough resources are allocated.
- There is not enough commitment to the process within the organization and the involved tasks and activities are perpetually delayed just for addressing only "urgent activities".
- A proper risk analysis is not performed, and actual threats and vulnerabilities are obviated.
- Staff is not familiar with the actions and procedures taken in case of serious disruption of services.

The main activities of Continuity Management are summarized as:

- Establishing policies and scope of the IT Service Continuity Management.
- Assessing the business impact of an interruption of IT services.
- Analyzing and predicting the risks the IT infrastructure is exposed to.
- Establishing the strategies of IT service continuity.
- Taking proactive measures to prevent risks.
- Developing contingency plans.
- Testing contingency plans.
- Training staff on procedures for prompt service recovery.
- Periodically reviewing the plans to adapt them to the real needs of the business.

Suppliers Management

Suppliers Management is responsible for managing the relationship with suppliers of services on which the IT organization depends. Its main objective is to achieve the highest quality at an appropriate price.

The main objectives of Suppliers Management are:

- To provide maximum value at the lowest cost for those services provided by suppliers.
- To ensure that contracts and agreements with suppliers are aligned with the strategy and business needs of the organization.
- To manage the relationships with suppliers.
- To manage supplier performance.
- To negotiate contracts with suppliers and manage them throughout their life cycle.
- To maintain a policy of suppliers and a database of suppliers and contracts.

The main benefit of an adequate Supplier Management is that the IT organization obtains more benefits when hiring those suppliers that provide the best service at the lowest cost.

The main difficulties when implementing Suppliers Management are:

- When Demand Management does not provide basic guidelines to streamline spending, Supplier Management is forced to improvise the levels of capacity to contract to the suppliers.
- The current contracts are too vague and do not provide easily quantifiable goals such as working hours, number of deliverables, etc.
- Suppliers Management does not have performance indicators relate to service performance or receive them too late. If there are delays or reductions in quality of supply, it is impossible to act effectively to correct it.

Suppliers Management is in charge of defining and managing:

- Procurement requirements that are going to be required to suppliers.
- The processes to evaluate and select suppliers.
- The classification and documentation of the relationship with suppliers into a database of suppliers and contracts.
- The performance management of suppliers.
- The renewal or termination of the contracts.

Information Security Management

Security Management must ensure that the information is correct and complete, is always available to the business and will be used only by authorized users.

The main objectives of Security Management are summarized as:

- Designing a security policy in collaboration with customers and suppliers, and properly aligned with business needs.
- Ensuring compliance with security standards agreed in the SLAs.
- Minimizing security risks threatening the continuity of service.

The main benefits of an adequate Security Management are:

- Service interruptions caused by viruses, hackers, etc. are avoided.
- The number of incidents is minimized.
- Access to information is obtained when needed and the integrity of data is preserved.
- Data protection regulations are met.
- Perception and confidence of customers and users as regards the quality of service is improved.

The main difficulties when implementing Security Management are summarized as follows:

- There is no sufficient commitment of all IT organization members with the process.
- Security policies excessively restrictive are established and adversely affect the business.
- There are not available tools necessary to monitor and ensure the security of service (firewalls, antivirus, etc.).
- Staff does not receive adequate training for the implementation of security protocols.
- Lack of coordination between different processes, which prevents a proper assessment of risks.

The main activities of Security Management are summarized as follows:

- Establish a clearly defined security policy that guides all other processes.
- Develop a Security Plan that includes appropriate levels of security both in the services provided to clients as well as in the service agreements signed with internal and external suppliers.
- Implement the Security Plan.
- Monitor and evaluate the compliance with the plan.
- Oversee proactively levels of security to analyze trends, new risks and vulnerabilities.
- Perform regular security audits.

Service Transition

Before starting the service, testing should be performed. To this end, the available information about the actual level of user training, state of infrastructure, IT available resources, among others, are analyzed. Then, a scenario for testing is prepared; databases are replicated, rollback plans are prepared; and tests are performed. The results of testing are analyzed because the service implementation will depend on them, and compared with the expected results.

The mission of the Service Transition phase is to integrate products and services defined in the Service Design phase into the production environment and to make them accessible to authorized customers and users.

Next, the main processes of the service transition are presented.

Transition Planning and Support

Planning and Support is responsible for coordinating the resources of the IT organization to launch the service on time, with the quality and cost previously defined. This includes the definition of the deliverables (content, timing, quality levels) as well as workflows and actors involved in service delivery, protocols of quality control, testing, mechanisms for monitoring, reporting and so on.

The main benefits of applying an appropriate Transition Planning and Support are:

- It increases the organization's ability to handle simultaneously a large volume of changes and versions.
- The service provided is better aligned with customer and suppliers requirements, and even with the internal strategy of the organization.
- Downtime is minimized and therefore the delays because all processes have knowledge of a general schedule.

The main difficulties when implementing Transition Planning and Support are:

- The relationship between the available resources to provide the service and the required quality in the requirements is unbalanced, resulting in missed deadlines or agreements with the client.
- Information about the configuration items related to the change is not updated.

- The assessment of the RFC (Request For Change) in their impact and resources it needs is incomplete or inaccurate.
- Service Acceptance Criteria are not aligned with the design requirements.
- Configuration items involved in the change are not prepared at the right time, causing delays in planning.
- Each step of the transition is monitored, but unless the client demands it, it is not needed a final reflection on the performance, suitability to the initial requirements, etc.

The main activities of Transition Planning and Support are:

- Defining the transition strategy.
- Preparing for the transition.
- Planning the transition.

Change Management

The main objective of Change Management is the evaluation and planning of the change process to ensure that, if it takes place, it is made in the most efficient manner, following established procedures at all times and ensuring the quality and continuity of IT service.

The main benefits by applying an appropriate change management are:

- The number of incidents and problems potentially associated with any change is reduced.
- It is possible to return to a stable configuration quickly and easily if the change has a negative impact on the IT structure.
- The real costs of change are evaluated, and therefore it is easier to assess the real return on investment.
- The Configuration Management Database is properly updated, which is essential for the adequate management of other IT processes.

- Standard change procedures that enable rapid updating of non-critical systems are developed.

The main activities of Change Management are summarized as follows:

- Record, assess and accept or reject RFCs received.
- Plan and implement the change.
- Arrange meetings of the Change Advisor Board, except for minor changes, for the approval of the RFCs and the development of the Forward Schedule of Change.
- Evaluate the results of the change and close it in case of success.

Configuration Management and IT Asset

It is essential to know in detail the IT infrastructure of the organization to get the most benefit from it. The main task of Configuration Management and IT Asset is to keep an updated record of all configuration items of the IT infrastructure, along with their interrelationships.

The main objectives of Configuration Management and IT Assets are to:

- Provide accurate and reliable information to the rest of the organization related to all the elements that make up the IT infrastructure.
- Update the database related to Configuration Management and IT Assets.
- Record all configuration items and their relationships (including the services they provide).
- Support the other processes, specifically Incident Management, Problem Management and Change Management.

The benefits of an appropriate Configuration Management and IT Assets are:

- Faster resolution of problems, resulting in a higher quality of service. A common source of problems is the incompatibility between different Configuration Items (CIs), outdated drivers, etc. The detection of these errors without an updated Configuration Management Database considerably extends the life cycle of a problem.
- A change management more efficient just for knowing the previous structure of CIs to design a change that does not generate new inconsistencies and/or problems.
- Reduction in costs (for example, knowing all CIs can eliminate unnecessary duplicates).
- Control of licenses. Illegal copies of software can be identified avoiding dangers to both the IT infrastructure in the form of viruses, etc., as well as non-compliance of legal requirements.
- Higher levels of security. For example, an updated Configuration Management Database allows detect vulnerabilities in the infrastructure.
- Faster recovery of services. If all configuration items and their interrelationships are known, it will be much easier to recover the operation configuration in the shortest possible time.

The main difficulties when implementing Configuration Management and IT Assets are:

- Incorrect planning: it is essential to plan correctly the necessary activities to avoid duplication or inaccuracies.
- Inadequate Configuration Management Database structure: keep updated an overly detailed and comprehensive configuration management and IT assets database can be cumbersome and consume too many resources.
- Inadequate tools: it is necessary to get the right software to streamline the record-

ing processes and get the most out of the Configuration Management Database.

- Lack of Coordination with Change Management and Release and Deployment, which prevents the proper maintenance of the Configuration Management Database.
- Lack of infrastructure: it is important to have a proper allocation of resources and responsibilities. It is preferable that the Configuration Management and IT Assets is carried out by independent and specialized staff.
- Lack of commitment: the benefits of Configuration Management and IT assets are not immediate and are often indirect, which may cause the lack of management of the company and, consequently, of the agents involved.

The main activities of Configuration Management and IT Assets are:

- Plan the objectives and strategies of Configuration Management and IT Assets.
- Record CIs.
- Monitor and control the Configuration Management Database to ensure that all authorized components are appropriately recorded and its current state is known.
- Perform regular audits.
- Prepare reports to assess the performance of the Configuration Management and IT Assets.

Release and Deployment Management

It is responsible for the implementation and quality control of all software and hardware installed on the operation environment. Release and Deployment Management must collaborate closely with Change Management and Configuration Management and IT Assets.

The main objectives of the Release and Deployment Management are:

- Establish a policy for implementing new versions of hardware and software.
- Implement new software and hardware versions in the operation environment after Validation and Test have verified them in a realistic environment.
- Ensure that the change process meets the specifications of the related RFC.
- In collaboration with Change Management and Configuration Management and IT Assets, ensure that all changes are properly reflected in the Configuration Management Database.
- Archive identical copies of the software in production, as well as all related documentation, in the Definitive Media Library.
- Maintain the Definitive Spare updated.

The benefits of an appropriate Release and Deployment Management are:

- The change process is performed without deterioration of the service quality.
- New versions meet the objectives.
- Proper Definitive Media Library maintenance prevents loss of copies of the source files.
- Reduction in the number of illegal software copies.
- Centralized control of software and hardware deployed.
- Protection against viruses and problems associated with uncontrolled software versions.

The main difficulties when implementing Release and Deployment Management are:

- There is no clear allocation of responsibilities and/or the IT organization does not accept the dominant figure of the Release and Deployment Management throughout the process of change implementation.

- There is no adequate test environment where new versions of software and hardware can be realistically tested.
- There is resistance in the different departments to centralize the process of change. It is usual that there is no commitment to adopt standardized systems across the organization, especially when it has not been the traditional policy.
- Changes are made without regard to the Release and Deployment Management arguing that these changes are only responsible for a particular workgroup or that its "urgency" required it.
- There is resistance to accept any "back out" plan. Certain operation environments can choose to "ignore" the problems that a new version may provoke on other areas and do not return to the last stable version.

The main activities of Release and Deployment Management are:

- Establish a planning policy for the implementation of new versions.
- Develop or acquire the new versions from third parties.
- Implement the new versions in the operation environment.
- Carry out the back-out plans or withdrawal of this new version if necessary.
- Update the Definitive Media Library, Definitive Spare and Configuration Management Database.
- Communicate and train customers and users about the functionalities of the new version.

Validation and Testing

It consists in ensuring that new versions meet the minimum quality requirements agreed with the client and, of course, they will not cause any unexpected error when operational. Service Vali-

dation and Testing is in charge of testing each new version into an environment identical to the real one prior to deployment. The ultimate objective of the process is to detect and prevent those errors caused by unforeseen incompatibilities, and verify compliance with the established levels of utility and warranty.

To achieve this objective, Service Validation and Test must:

- Design and maintain a test environment, i.e. an exact replica of the scenario in which the service will operate.
- Understand the service functionalities and maintain updated lists of all use cases in order to make full checks.
- Understand service quality requirements agreed with the customer to ensure that new versions satisfy them.
- Plan and carry out a test schedule that covers all the functionalities registered for the service.

The benefits of an appropriate Service Validation and Testing are summarized as follows:

- The number of incidents due to incompatibilities with other software or hardware is reduced.
- With fewer incidents, the volume of incoming calls to the Service Centre is also significantly reduced.
- The problems and known errors can be detected, isolated and diagnosed in the test environment much better than in the real environment.
- Costs are saved, because it is much less "expensive" fix bugs in a test environment than in a real one.
- The associated testing process not only ensures the quality of software and hardware to install, but also reveals the user feedback on functionality and usability of new versions.

The main difficulties for implementing Service Validation and Testing are:

- The Technical Service Catalogue omits some functionalities of the service, either because they are not updated enough or because lack of detail, so the service validation and testing does not include them in the test plan.
- Release and Deployment Management does not update often enough the development environment, resulting in the need for several tests prior to refine the version from a technical point of view before considering its utility and security.
- Release and Deployment Management does not know in depth the requirements defined in the SLAs and SLRs (Service Level Requirement), making preliminary assessments necessary to achieve the minimum performance level.
- The methodology to be used during testing is not defined clearly enough, or it deviates too far from the SLRs agreed with the client, so the tests are ineffective.

The main activities of Service Validation and Testing are:

- Validation of service packages, offers and contracts. Definition of the test model, planning and testing protocols.
- Construction of test scenarios and access to the items to be tested.
- Testing of new versions in an identical environment to the real environment related to the development of the new or improved service.
- Acceptance of data and reporting the results to record errors, if occurred.
- Cleaning the test environment and close the process.

Evaluation

Evaluation is responsible for collecting and analyzing all available information about the change in a service or a new service and developing the reports needed to make these decisions. The evaluation should not be conceived as a specific activity, but as an iterative process. Preliminary reports of service performance are helpful when planning the transition, but they must be contrasted with later reports once they have been implemented.

The main objective of the evaluation is to provide enough information to determine with certainty whether an aspect of the service is useful for business or not, either because it increases their quality or because it provides an improvement in productivity.

The main difficulties when implementing the activities of Evaluation are:

- Evaluations are not handled quickly enough and bottlenecks that delay the implementation of change are generated.
- The results of the Service Validation and Testing are incomplete or not detailed, which can result in a biased assessment.
- The performance model does not reflect the service in all its complexity, resulting in a constant mismatch between the initial estimates of expected and actual service performance once changes are implemented.

The main activities of Evaluation are summarized as follows:

- Plan the evaluation to analyze the effects, both intended and unintended, of the implementation of a change or new service.
- The expected performance evaluation is done prior to implement the change and it consists on predicting the effects of the change once it is operational.
- The actual performance evaluation is done once the change has already been imple-

mented and it consists on analyzing the effects that its implementation has caused.

Knowledge Management

Knowledge Management is responsible for establishing criteria to record and undertake regular work classification, evaluation and improvement of the available data. Knowledge Management is responsible for collecting, analyzing, storing and sharing knowledge and information of the organization.

The main objective is to improve process efficiency, reducing the need to rediscover knowledge. Knowledge management helps to improve the quality of decisions made in an organization in order to ensure that those who take them have accurate and reliable information.

The main benefits of an appropriate Knowledge Management are:

- Work is not duplicated unnecessarily. If there is a problem that occurred in the past, it can be easily recovered the details of the solution applied previously, saving time and effort.
- Better use of existing resources.
- Prevention of any misinformation in the case of missing the "owners" of access data to an application, the contact with a client, and so on.

The main difficulties when implementing the Knowledge Management are:

- Staff members are overworked and have no time to document the data or give priority to other more urgent tasks.
- Staff members do not trust the records, so they turn to other options when looking for information.
- Data are poorly structured, incomplete or not suited to the audience they are intended, so in practice they are useless.

- Data are recorded but not checked, so that the available information is outdated or incomplete.

The main activities of Knowledge Management are summarized as follows:

- Define a strategy for knowledge management and disseminate it to the entire IT organization.
- Assist in the transference of knowledge among individuals, teams and departments.
- Manage information and data to ensure its quality and utility.
- Use the Service Knowledge Management System.

Service Operation

In this phase, the operation of the service is monitored actively and passively, and events, incidents, problems, service requests and service access are recorded.

The main objectives of the Operation phase are:

- Coordinate and implement all the necessary processes, activities and functions to provide the agreed services with the quality levels approved.
- Support all service users.
- Manage the technology infrastructure for service delivery.

Next, the main processes and functions of Service Operation are presented.

Event Management

Event is a detectable occurrence that has significance for the IT organizational structure, for the provision of a service or for its evaluation. Typical examples of events are notifications created by services, configuration items or tools for monitoring and control.

The main objective of Event Management is to detect and escalate exception conditions thus contributing to a normal service operation:

- Providing entry points for various processes of the operation phase (e.g. Incident Management).
- Enabling the comparison between the actual performance of the service and the design standards and SLAs.
- Contributing to the Continual Service Improvement with reports of improvement.

The benefits of an appropriate Event Management are:

- It helps the early detection of incidents, even to prevent their appearance to users.
- In addition, direct coordination with other processes enables them to react more quickly, resulting in greater efficiency throughout the IT organization.
- It allows an automated monitoring of certain activities. It is cheaper than real-time monitoring and significantly reduces the period of inactivity of the service between the appearance of the incident and its final resolution.
- It provides the basis for automated operations, which increases the efficiency and offloads human resources that can be used in other tasks such as designing new functionalities.

The activities of the Event Management are:

- Appearance of events.
- Event notification.
- Detection and filtering of events.
- Event classification.
- Correlation.
- Triggers.
- Response options.
- Action review and closure.

Incident Management

Incident Management aims to resolve, as quickly and efficiently as possible, any incident that causes an interruption in service. Incident Management is not concerned about finding and analyzing the underlying causes of a particular incident but only to restore the service as soon as possible.

Incident Management is also different from Request Management, which is concerned about the different request from users to improve the service, not when the service fails.

The main objectives of Incident Management are to:

- Detect any alteration in IT services.
- Record and classify these alterations.
- Assign personnel to restore the service as defined in the related SLA.

An incident is any event that is not part of the standard operation of a service and which causes or may cause an interruption or a reduction in the quality.

Any change that requires a modification of the infrastructure is not considered a standard service and it requires the initiation of a RFC to be treated according to the principles of Change Management.

The main benefits of an appropriate Incident Management are:

- Improvement of the user productivity.
- Compliance with service levels agreed in the SLA.
- More control of processes and monitoring of services.
- Optimization of available resources.
- An accurate *Configuration Management Database*, as incidents are recorded in relation to the configuration items.
- Improvement of customers and users satisfaction.

The difficulties when implementing Incident Management are:

- Reduction of service levels.
- Valuable resources are wasted: too many people or people of an inadequate level working concurrently in the resolution of the incident.
- Loss of valuable information on the causes and effects of incidents for future restructurings and developments.
- Unsatisfied customer and users because of a poor o slow management of their incidents.

Request Management

It is responsible for attending requests from users by providing information and quick access to standard services of the IT organization.

A service request is:

- A request for information or advice.
- A request for standard changes (for example when the user forgets their password and requests for a new one).
- A request for access to IT services.

The benefits of an appropriate Request Management are:

- Commercial department can quickly and effectively access to standard services. This improves productivity, quality of business services and the products themselves.
- Bureaucracy associated with the process of request for access to new and existing services and costs are reduced.
- The level of control over services is increased by centralizing a granted access to them.
- Costs are reduced by centralizing negotiations with suppliers regarding access to

services, and also by reducing the cost of support.

The main objectives of Request Management are to:

- Provide a communication channel through which users can request and receive standard services previously approved.
- Provide information to users and customers about the availability of services and the way to use them.
- Locate and distribute the components of the standard service requested.
- Assist in resolving complaints or comments providing general information.

The activities of Request Management are:

- Request selection.
- Financial approval of the request.
- Processing.
- Closure.

Problem Management

The main objectives of Problem Management are to:

- Investigate the underlying causes of any alteration, real or potential, of the IT service.
- Identify possible solutions.
- Propose the necessary RFC to restore the quality of service.
- Conduct post-implementation review to ensure that changes have had the desired effect without creating problems of secondary importance.

It is necessary to distinguish between:

- **Problem:** Underlying cause, not yet identified, of a series of incidents or an isolated incident of significant importance.

- **Known Error:** A problem becomes a known error when its causes have been determined.

To achieve the objectives, Problem Management must:

- Identify, record, and classify problems.
- Support Incident Management, providing information and workarounds or patches.
- Analyze and determine the causes of problems and propose solutions.
- Raise RFCs to Change Management to carry out the necessary changes in the IT infrastructure.
- Track post-implementation of all changes to ensure they are working properly.
- Make reports documenting not only the origins and solutions of a problem but also to support the IT structure as a whole.
- Analyze trends to prevent potential incidents.

The main benefits of an appropriate Problem Management are:

- An increase in the overall quality of IT services.
- Minimization of the number of incidents.
- Incidents are resolved more quickly and, generally, in the first line of IT support, saving resources and unnecessary escalations.
- Documentation obtained is useful for Capacity Management, Availability and Service Levels.

The main activities of Problem Management are:

- Problem Control.
- Error Control.

The main objective of Problem Control is to ensure that they become known errors in order to Error Control can propose appropriate solutions.

Access Management

Access Management for IT Services is the process by which a user will be provided with the necessary permissions to make use of the services documented in the Service Catalogue of the IT organization. Sometimes it is called Rights Management or Identity Management.

The main objective of the Access Management for IT Services is granting permits for access to those authorized users and preventing unauthorized users.

The benefits of an appropriate Access Management are:

- More assurance of information confidentiality, through controlled access to services.
- Increased employee effectiveness by minimizing conflicts and problems resulting from the assignment of permits.
- Less likelihood of errors in critical services related to the activity of non-skilled users.
- Ability to monitor the use of services and to identify cases of misuse.
- Increased speed and efficiency to revoke permits if necessary, something that can be critical to security in certain circumstances.
- Access Management can also be a prerequisite for the compliance to certain standards of quality and even to the law.

The main activities of Access Management can be summarized as follows:

- Request for access, which can be reached by different routes such as the Human Resources department, a change request, an authorized instruction, and so on.
- Verification of the identity of the user requesting access, as well as those that allow it.
- Monitoring of identity.
- Recording and monitoring the access.
- Removing and restricting rights.

Service Operation Functions

A function is a specialized unit for performing a certain activity and is responsible for its outcome. Functions incorporate all the resources and capabilities necessary for the proper developing of this activity.

The functions involved in the operation phase of the service are responsible for ensuring that services meet the objectives requested by clients and manage all the technology needed for the provision of such services:

- Service Centre: it is responsible for all the processes that interact with users of IT services.
- IT Operation Management: responsible for the daily operation of the service.
- Technical Management: a functional unit that includes all teams, groups and departments involved in managing and supporting IT infrastructure.
- Application Management: this functional unit is responsible for managing the life cycle of IT applications.

Service Centre

The main objective of the Service Centre is to serve as an interface between users and IT Service Management.

The point of contact with the client can take different forms depending on the breadth and depth of the services offered: call centre, help desk and service desk.

The main benefits of implementing a Service Centre are:

- Lower costs through efficient resource allocation.
- Better customer service, which drives to a greater degree of satisfaction and loyalty of the customer.
- New business opportunities.

- Centralization of processes that improve information management and communication.
- Proactive service support.

When selecting the structure of a Service Centre, it is necessary to take into account the needs of the service: local, global, 24/7.

Operation Management

Operation Management is the unit responsible for maintenance and ongoing management of IT infrastructure of the organization, and mainly focuses on ensuring that services meet agreed levels.

The main objectives of the IT Operation Management are:

- Maintaining the status quo of the processes and activities of the organization to achieve stability day by day.
- Regular scrutiny and improvements to deliver better services at a reduced costs while maintaining stability.
- Early implementation of operational skills to diagnose and resolve any faults during operation.

The two functions of the Operation Management tend to form organizational structures: operation control (in charge of assuring that routine tasks are carried out) and facilities management (in charge of supervising the maintenance of all physical equipment).

Technical Management

Technical Management provides technical skills and resources needed to support the service operation phase.

The main objective of the Technical Management is to assist in planning, implementing and maintaining a stable technical infrastructure to support business processes of the organization.

The main activities of the Technical Management are to:

- Identify the knowledge and experience necessary to deliver services and manage the IT infrastructure.
- Design and develop training programs related to technical resources.

Application Management

Application Management is responsible for supporting and maintaining the applications that take part in the service operation.

The main objective is to identify the functional requirements of software applications, to support the design and development of such applications and to assist in the support and improvement after their deployment.

While most teams/departments of Application Management are dedicated to specific applications or sets of them, there are certain common activities:

- Assist the Technical Management in the task of identifying the knowledge and experience needed to manage applications in delivering IT services.
- Design and develop (but not provide) training programs for end users.

Continual Service Improvement

Measurement tools and feedback are used to document information regarding the operation of the service, the results obtained, problems, implemented solutions, and so on. This requires verifying the level of awareness of users about the new service, encouraging registration and investigation related to the service and making available the information to other users.

The main objectives of the Continual Service Improvement can be summarized as follows:

- Recommend improvements to all processes and activities involved in the management and delivery of IT services.

- Monitoring and analysis of the parameters of Service Level and contrasting them with SLAs in place.
- Propose improvements to increase ROI and Value On Investment associated with IT services.
- Support the strategy and design phases for the definition of new services and processes/activities associated with them.

PDCA Cycle: Plan, Do, Check and Act, also known as the Deming cycle, is the backbone of all continuous improvement processes.

The process of continuous improvement requires a series of goals and objectives to determine the forward direction and serve as pillars for the rest of the activities involved in it. But the determination of those goals and objectives depends on a process of constant review as part of a cycle described by the CSI model.

Next, the processes associated with the Continual Service Improvement are presented.

Continual Improvement

The objective of the Continual Service Improvement Process (CSI) is to implement the Deming cycle to improve IT services. The CSI enables the IT organization to:

- Know in depth the quality and performance of IT services offered.
- Identify opportunities for improvement.
- Propose corrective actions.
- Monitor its implementation.

The improvement process of CSI consists of seven steps for elaborating, from the obtained data, the Service Improvement Plans in order to modify activities or process that can be optimized.

- **Step 1:** What we must measure.
- **Step 2:** What we can measure.
- **Step 3:** Collect the needed data.

- **Step 4:** Process data (information).
- **Step 5:** Analyze data (knowledge).
- **Step 6:** Propose corrective actions (wisdom).
- **Step 7:** Implement corrective actions.

Report Management

The main objective of the Report Management process is to provide to all those involved in IT service management an objective view, based on data and metrics, related to the quality and performance of the services provided.

The benefits of an appropriate management of this process are summarized as:

- Provide the entire IT organization a periodic snapshot of the status of IT services provided.
- Facilitate strategic decision-making based on objective information.
- Communicate the perception of customers and users about the quality of services offered.

The main activities of the IT Service Report Management are summarized as follows:

- Selecting and collecting data needed for reporting.
- Processing and analyzing data for later use.
- Preparing contents for different target audiences.
- Publication of the default reports.

INFORMATION SECURITY MANAGEMENT

The objective of the Information Security Management (ISM) is to align IT to ensure business processes, information security and IT processes.

Corporate governance is a set of responsibilities and practices for the executive management to pro-vide a strategy to ensure reaching the objectives, determining risks to be managed and ensuring that the company uses the resources effectively. Also, it ensures the security of information, a proper risk management and a responsible use of information resources. The objective of the ISM is to establish a central point for the security and management of all IT security activities.

The term "information" is used as a general one that includes data warehouses, databases and metadata. ISM protects the interests of those who trust the information and communication systems from damages resulting from the lack of availability, confidentiality and integrity.

Security must deal with all business processes and meet the technical and physical issues, deciding what should be protected and the level of protection of the company.

ISM must establish and maintain a policy of information security covering the use and abuse of all IT systems and services, including:

- Production, maintenance, distribution and execution of an information security policy and its support.
- An understanding of current and future agreements in the security requirements of enterprises, regulations and security policies for the existing businesses.
- Implementation of security controls to support the information security policy and management of risk associated with the access to services, information and systems.
- Documentation of all security controls, its implementation and maintenance, and risk assessment of suppliers management and contracts related to access to systems and services.
- Management of all security violations and incidents related to all systems and services.
- Improvement of security and risk controls.
- Integration of security issues in all other IT processes.

To achieve an adequate information security, it must be established and maintained an Information Security Management System (ISMS) to guide the development and management of a comprehensive program related to information security that meets the objectives of the company.

From the governance point of view, all processes within an IT organization must include security considerations. The most important and basic concepts are:

- Security Framework: it includes policies for information security, security strategy, ISM and everything related to storage and security management.
- Information Security Policy: it covers all areas of security and meets business needs. These policies should be available to all customers and users, and its compliance should be referred in the SLR, SLA, UCs and agreements. All must be reviewed and approved by the executive management.
- Information Security Management System (ISMS): it provides the basis for developing cost efficient information security program that supports business objectives. It involves the 4Ps (People, Processes, Products and Technologies, Sponsors or Providers – "Partners") to ensure a high level of security. The ISO 27001 family provides the standard formal framework with which organizations must compare their ISMS so as its management.

The ISM framework is based on a model with five subprocesses:

- Control: it is related to the organization and management of security. It defines a security policy and determines the organization of information security. At the same time, it sets out what plans will be created and how often updated.

- Planning: it defines and designs appropriate security measures based on business needs. The requirements are drawn from various sources: business, service risk, plans and strategies, SLAs, OLAs and moral and ethical responsibilities of information security. And all of this well documented and updated by the Information Security.
- Implementation: it implements the security measures defined in the previous phase. ITIL® provides a list of measures:
  ○ Classification and management of IT resources.
  ○ People security.
  ○ Security management.
  ○ Access control.
- Maintenance: applying the PDCA cycle, as suggested by ISO 27000 (ISO/IEC 27001:2005, 2005), (ISO/IEC 27002:2005, 2005) to establish the ISMS in order to improve:
  ○ Security agreements as are specified in SLAs, OLAs, UCs, etc.
  ○ Implementation of controls and security measures.
- Evaluation: it assesses the performance and measurement of the security management, monitoring and checking compliance with security policies and requirements set out in the various contracts (SLAs, etc.). It provides information to external auditors if necessary. Based on assessments, new measures can be agreed (with the client or internally) that could be implemented following the Change Management.

The main activities for an effective and efficient ISM are:

- Develop, review and provide a new vision of a global information security policy as well as a set of specific support policies.

- Communicate, implement and enforce security policies.
- Evaluate and classify all information assets and documentation.
- Review, improve and offer a new vision of security controls and risk assessment.
- Monitor and manage all security violations and major security incidents.
- Analyze, report and reduce the impact of violations and security incidents.
- Extract conclusions from security reviews, audits and tests.

Information Security Management processes, along with methods, tools and techniques, constitute the security strategies. The security manager is responsible for the security architecture, authentication, authorization, administration and recovery.

The results of the security measures can be used in a specific phase for the prevention and management of security incidents. Security incidents are not the only ones caused by technical threats. Statistics show that the vast majority result from human error (intentional or not) or procedural errors, and often have implications in other organizational, legal or health scopes.

In general, the process usually goes through several states. At the beginning there is a risk that a threat can be materialized. A threat can be anything that disrupts the business or impact negatively on it. When a threat materializes, we talk about a security incident. This security incident can result in a damage that must be repaired or corrected. The choice of the measure type will depend on the importance and information status. According to OGC (OGC, "ITIL The Official Introduction to the ITIL Service Lifecycle", 2007), some types of measures are:

- Preventive: they are used to prevent the occurrence of a security incident. The best known example of preventive measures is to assign access rights to a limited group of

authorized persons. A requirement associated to this measure is controlling access rights (granting, maintenance and removal of rights), authorization (to identify who is allowed access to information using tools), identification and authentication, and access control (ensuring that only authorized personnel can access).

- Reductive: to minimize any damage that may occur. An example of reduction measures is to make regular backups, and the development, testing and maintenance of contingency plans.
- Detective: if a security incident occurs, it is important to discover it as soon as possible. An example is monitoring with alerts or virus checking software.
- Repressive: establishing the policies and protocols for access to information. It is used to counteract any security incident that is recidivist. For example, an account is temporarily blocked after numerous failed attempts to log on.
- Corrective: the damage is repaired, if possible, using corrective measures. For example, corrective actions include restoring the backup or return to a previous stable situation. These measures are essential for IT Service Continuity Management.

Reporting of security incidents is needed to assess the effectiveness and efficiency of existing security measures. It is very useful the information obtained from the maintenance log files, audit files and, of course, the event log of the Services Desk. Statistical analysis on security issues should lead to actions that improve outcomes and reduce the volume of security breaches and incidents.

Some events that can trigger the processes of ISM are:

- Modification/New business security policy in the corporate governance guidelines, the processes of enterprise risk management, business needs or services, SLAs, SLRs, OLAs or UCs.

- Reviews of strategies, IT and business plans and designs and strategies.
- Security violations, events, alerts, events associated with thresholds, exception reporting about components or services.
- Notification of changes in risk assessment or impact in a critical business process.
- Security requirements of other management processes.

The effective and efficient implementation of an information security policy in an organization depends largely on a good security management in all management processes:

- Incident and Problem Management: it assists, solves, justifies and corrects incidents security problems.
- IT Service Continuity Management: it assesses the impact and business risk, and provides security mechanisms. An IT Service Continuity Management work plan is a mandatory requirement for ISO 27001.
- Service Level Management: it determines the security requirements and responsibilities under SLAs and SLRs, enclosing reports of research and resolution of security breaches on components and services.
- Change Management: it evaluates the impact of each change on security and controls to be performed. It also provides information on changes authorized on components and services.
- Configuration Management: it provides accurate information about security assets helping to classify them. Similarly, an updated Configuration Management System provides to the ISM very useful information about CIs.
- Availability Management: it makes risk analysis.

- Capacity Management: it considers security implications in the selection and introduction of new technology or software.
- Financial Management: it provides enough funding for security requirements.
- Supplier Management: it ensures that supplier's access to services and systems are made in the terms and conditions included, along with responsibilities, in supplier contracts.

Conversely, ISM needs to obtain information from various areas:

- Business information: strategy, implementation plans, current and future requirements.
- Corporate governance: corporate security policies, security plans, risk analysis.
- IT Information: strategy, plans and current budgets.
- Service Information provided by Service Level Management, Service Portfolio and Catalogue, SLA, SLR.
- Availability Management and Continuity: risk analysis and reports.
- Details of all events and security breaches reported in all areas of IT, especially Incident and Problem Management.
- Change: information of changes in processes, plans and controls, impact of changes in security policies.
- System Configuration Management: relationships between business processes, IT services, and technology.
- Availability and Suppliers Management: details of levels and client and suppliers access permits.

ISM products needed for other management processes are:

- Global and specific Information Security Management policies.

- A Security Management Information System (SMIS) with all the information related to the ISM.
- A set of security controls, including details of operation, maintenance and associated risks.
- Report and security audits.
- Calendars and security test plans and reports.
- Reviews and reports of security violations and serious incidents.
- Policies and procedures for managing access to services and information for partners and suppliers.

ISM quality, in terms of effectiveness and efficiency, is set by the Key Performance Indicators-based metrics of security. Measurements are made on services, clients and business prospects. The most prominent are:

- Protection against breaches in the company:
  ◦ Reduction (%) of reported security breaches in Service Desk
  ◦ Reduction (%) of incidents related to security failures.
- Reduction (%) in the number of non-conformities of the ISM process with security policies and business processes.
- Security procedures justified and supported by the management:
  ◦ Increase (%) of the acceptance and compliance of security procedures.
- Mechanism for improvement:
  ◦ Increase (%) of the proposed improvements for security procedures and control.
  ◦ Decrease (%) of non-conformities found during security audits and testing.
- ITSM integration with all services:
  ◦ Increase (%) of services and processes because of security procedures and controls.

- Knowledge of the requirements and procedures and technology to support the security:
  ◦ Increase (%) of organizational awareness of security policy and its contents.
  ◦ Increase (%) of security technical services.
  ◦ Increased of IT components registered that support security.
  ◦ Increase (%) of services supported by Service Desk.

One of the biggest challenges of the ISM is to ensure support from management and staff. Conversely, it is useless to have good policies, procedures and security controls if they are not assumed as corporate culture.

Just as information systems can generate benefits, both direct and indirect, they are subject to risks, direct and indirect, which open a gap between the need to be protected and the degree of protection given to them. The difference is caused by factors such as widespread use of technology, increased business dependency on IT, the increasing complexity and interconnection of systems, the disappearance of clear limits of the traditional organizations and regulatory requirements. This means there are new areas of risk that could have a significant impact on critical business operations, such as:

- Increased of availability and robustness needs.
- Potential increase of misuse and abuse of information systems affecting privacy and ethical values.
- External hazards of hackers that can cause denial of service, virus attacks, extortion, industrial espionage and the loss of information or private data of the organization.

Other major risks associated with the ISM are:

- Lack of business support to the procedures of ISM.
- Lack of information on future security strategies and plans.
- Lack of resources and/or budget for the ISM process.
- ISM process focuses too much on technology issues and not enough on the business needs and priorities.
- Risk assessment and management are performed in isolation, not related to availability management and IT Service Continuity Management.
- ISM policies, plans, risks and information lose their alignment with business processes.

As we have seen previously, the adoption of the family of standards ISO/IEC 27000 provides a framework for information security management applicable to any organization, public or private, large or small.

- ISO/IEC 27001:2005 (ISO/IEC 27001:2005, 2005) is a certifiable standard specification for the ISM process. It establishes a definition of terms, general requirements for an ISMS, activities related to the ISM implementation and operation, monitoring and review, and maintenance and improvement; documentation requirements, recording of control data, responsibilities management and commitments, provision and management resources, training and competence, internal audits, management reviews, and continual improvement.
- ISO/IEC 27002:2005 (ISO/IEC 27002:2005, 2005) provides a code of good practices for ISMS management. It describes what you need to do to meet the specifications of ISO 27001. It provides recommendations for reducing risk

and incident management with a clearer structure. The standard establishes a set of controls in each ISM area offering implementation guidance for controlling objectives. The intention is that these controls are applied against the risks identified through risk assessment. The areas covered are: security policy, security organization, asset management, human resources security, physical and environmental security, security of communications and operations management, access control, information retrieval systems, development and maintenance security, incident management, continuity management and compliance.

- ISO/IEC 27006:2011 (ISO/IEC 27006:2011, 2011) specifies requirements and provides guidance for bodies providing audit and certification of an information security management system (ISMS). It is a complement to the requirements contained within ISO/IEC 17021 and ISO/IEC 27001, in order to support the accreditation of certification bodies providing ISMS certification.

ISO/IEC 27006:2011 contains the requirements to demonstrate the competence and reliability of any body providing ISMS certification, and represents a guidance for the interpretation of requirements in ISO/IEC 27001 for any body providing ISMS certification.

- ISO/IEC 27005:2011 (ISO/IEC 27005:2011, 2011) provides a guide for information security risk management. It is based in ISO/IEC 27001 and is designed as helpful to the satisfactory implementation of information security based on a risk management approach. Knowing of the concepts, models, processes and terminologies described in ISO/IEC 27001 and ISO/IEC 27002 is important for a complete understanding of ISO/IEC 27005:2011. It is applicable to all types of organizations that intend to manage risks that could compromise the organization's information security certification.

QUALIFYING SYSTEM FOR IT SERVICE MANAGEMENT IN ITIL ®

When designing a governance framework, some organizational key factor such as people and culture, communications, training, roles and responsibilities, can improve the likelihood of implementing a successful ITSM.

Organizations must have the right people in required areas with defined responsibilities for: Senior Management; Users throughout the organization; suppliers; Customers; Owners of information; Information Technology, providing adequate training to all stakeholders, and communicating information security within their organizational culture. The training and qualification are so good for the candidates as for their organizations.

Nowadays every organization needs the enthusiasm and commitment of their staff more than ever. The ITIL® Qualification Scheme is a personal development map for IT Service Management professionals.

Each exam has credits to be awarded. Once candidates have a sufficient number of credits they will be an ITIL® Expert in IT Service Management.

ITIL® provides a training system for IT service management, based on credits in order to obtain different levels of qualification (OGC, English-ITIL V3 Qualification Scheme Brochure, 2009). The system is divided into 4 levels of theoretical and practical knowledge (see Figure 2).

- **ITIL® Foundation:** Suited for those who need basic understanding of the framework and vocabulary knowledge of ITIL ®.

- **ITIL® Intermediate:** This level can be achieved by two different and complementary ways.

The first alternative consists of 5 modules (3 credits per module) where each of the 5 phases of the lifecycle (strategy, design, transition, operation and continual service improvement) is studied in detail.

The second alternative is to acquire specific skills for intermediate through 4 modules (4 credits per module) focused on daily execution of ITIL® best practices in various areas of service management. It contains the following modules:

- Service Offerings and Agreements.
- Release, Control and Validation.
- Operational Support and Analysis.
- Planning, Protection and Optimization.

The qualification module "ITIL® Managing Across the Lifecycle" (5 credits) complete the intermediate level. This module is compulsory and common for any of the training routes chosen to achieve the highest level of service management expert in the ITIL® Expert Level. Thus, ITIL® Expert level requires at least 22 credits obtained in the foundation and intermediate levels of the qualification system.

- **ITIL® Master:** The highest level. It is obtained with the ITIL® Expert certificate and demonstrating practical application experience through a peer assessment system.

Master Certification in ITIL® Service Management enables an expert manager of IT services to demonstrate his knowledge of ITIL® and apply them in the real world. A deep understanding of the concepts and their application in real situations on different areas of service management is showed. It targets three types of candidates:

Figure 2. ITIL® qualifying system

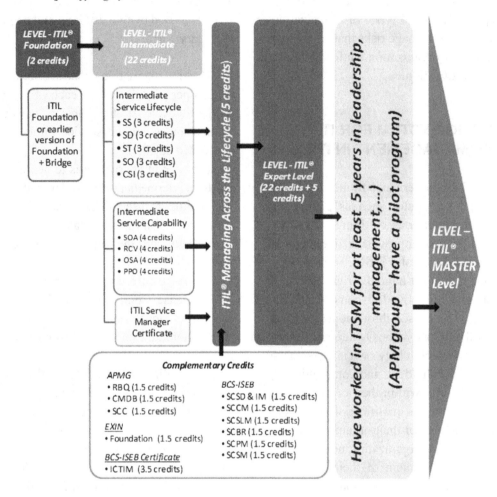

- Project managers that have implemented service management.
- High level professionals who are specialized in specific areas of IT.
- High level managers and CIOs.
    ○ **ITIL® Complements:** Recently the OGC has approved a set of specific training complements related to different subjects of ITIL®. Each course represents additional and cumulative credits for the ITIL® Expert Level, and is taught by different certifying organizations recognized by the OGC. Some of this organizations are:

APMG-International:

- Role Based Qualifications: Change Analyst Certification (1.5 credits for ITIL® V3). The objective of this module is to acquire the knowledge and confidence to assess, authorize and manage changes.
- CMDB (Configuration Management Database) Certification (1.5 credits for ITIL® V3). The objective of this module is to obtain a specific understanding of the terminology, concepts and best practices associated with ITIL® CMDB. It provides a complete overview of the concepts behind Service Asset and the process of configuration management in relation to other processes in the service lifecycle.

- Service Catalogue Certification. It is a complementary course with 1.5 credits for ITIL® V3. The International Qualifications and Certification Executive Sub Committee (IQC) recommends it. The objective of this module is enable candidates to:
  - ○ Analyze and adopt new ways of controlling the demand.
  - ○ Publish and keep track of prices and cost of services.
  - ○ Automate application management and service compliance.

BCS-ISEB: It offers 6 modules of 1.5 credits each, with the objective of deepening the basic processes of ITIL® life cycle and referred to in ISO 20000.

- Specialist Certificate in Service Desk and Incident Management.
- Specialist Certificate in Change Management.
- Specialist Certificate in Service Level Management.
- Specialist Certificate in Business Relationship Management.
- Specialist Certificate in Problem Management.
- Specialist Certificate in Supplier Management.

EXIN:

- Foundation Certificate in ITSM according to ISO/IEC 20000 (1.5 credits). The objective is to know the basic principles, processes and practices related to IT service management, from the point of view of quality and the standard ISO 20000 (ISO/IEC 20000-1:2005, 2005) (ISO/IEC 20000-2:2005, 2005) (OGC, Best Management Practice: ITIL V3 and ISO/IEC 20000, 2008).

BCS-ISEB Certificate:

- ICT Infrastructure Management (ICTIM) (3.5 credits). The objective of this module is to know and apply the involved process in ICT infrastructure management, focusing on the definition and management of the interface between processes.

CONCLUSION

Good management of IT services vertebrates and articulates the most important areas of an organization through its business units. We have seen how ITIL® provides a framework of good practices enabling organizations to integrate the IT processes focusing them to the business, its customers and users. Organizations are subject to continuous changes of various kinds in the changing global environment that surrounds them, and ITIL® makes easier its implementation. ITIL® helps to conceive, design, make operative, and improve a service according to the strategy, returning added value, a rapid response to potential disruptions, ensuring the security of their processes and reducing the risk to guarantee business-continuity.

ITIL® is conceived in an integrated business environment with other management and security standards, such as ISO 20000 and ISO 27000, and governance frameworks, such as ISO 38500 and COBIT. Therefore, it is focused on ensuring the quality of IT services governance and management processes integrated in the continuous improvement of organizations and its business processes.

REFERENCES

Gregory, H. J. (2009). *Comparison of corporate governance guidelines and codes of best practice.* New York, NY: Weil, Gotshal & Manges.

ISO/IEC 20000-1:2005. (2005). *ISO/IEC*. Retrieved from www.iso.org

ISO/IEC 20000-2:2005. (2005). *ISO/IEC*. Retrieved from www.iso.org

ISO/IEC 27000 doc_iso27000_all.pdf. (2011). *ISO International Organization for Standardization*. Retrieved from http://www.iso27000.es/download/doc_iso27000_all.pdf

ISO/IEC 27001:2005. (2005). *ISO International Organization for Standardization.*

ISO/IEC 27002:2005. (2005). *ISO International Organization for Standardization.*

ISO/IEC 27005:2011. (2011). *ISO International Organization for Standardization.* Retrieved from http://www.iso.org/iso/iso_catalogue/catalogue_tc/catalogue_detail.htm?csnumber=56742 ISO/IEC 27006:2011. (2011). *ISO/IEC 27006:2011. Information technology. Security techniques. Requirements for bodies providing audit and certification of information security management systems Edition: 2. JTC 1/SC 27 ICS: 35.040.*

ISO/IEC 38500:2008. (2011). *Corporate governance of information technology.* Retrieved from www.iso.org: www.iso.org

ISPL, Information Services Procurement Library. (2011). Retrieved from http://projekte.fast.de/ISPL/

ITGI. IT Governance Institute. (2007). *COBIT 4.1 en Español.* Retrieved from http://www.isaca.org/

OGC. (2006). *Service delivery: Best practice.* itSMF.

OGC. (2006). *Service Soport: Best practice.* itSMF.

OGC. (2007). *Service Operation. Office of Government Commerce.* TSO.

OGC. (2007). *Continual service improvement. Office of Government Commerce.* TSO.

OGC. (2007). *ITIL: The official introduction to the ITIL service lifecycle.* London, UK: Office of Government Commerce, TSO.

OGC. (2007). *Service design. Office of Government Commerce.* TSO.

OGC. (2007). *Service strategy. Office of Government Commerce.* TSO.

OGC. (2007). *Service transition. Office of Government Commerce.* TSO.

OGC. (2008). *Best management practice: ITIL V3 and ISO/IEC 20000. Office of Government Commerce.* TSO.

OGC. (2009). *English-ITIL V3 qualification scheme brochure.* Retrieved from http://www.itil-officialsite.com/nmsruntime/saveasdialog.aspx

SEI. (2009). *CMMI for services process area quick reference from CMMI-SVC, v1.2.* (SEI, Ed.) Retrieved from www.sei.cmu.edu/

SEI. (2010). *CMMI for services,* vol. 1.3. Retrieved from http://www.sei.cmu.edu/library/abstracts/reports/10tr034.cfm

Stapleton, J. (1999). DSDM: Dynamic systems development method. *TOOLS '99 Proceedings of the Technology of Object-Oriented Languages and Systems.* Washington, DC: IEEE Computer Society.

Van Der, P. (2009). *ASL 2: A framework for application management.* Zaltbommel, The Netherlands: Van Haren Publishing.

Van Grembergen, W. a. (2009). *Enterprise governance of IT: Achieving strategic alignment and value.* Springer.

Yip, F. (2006). *Corporate security compliance in a heterogeneous environment.*

Chapter 5
Assessing the Maturity of Control Objectives for Information and Related Technology (COBIT) Framework in the Egyptian Banking Sector

Hisham M. Abdelsalam
Cairo University, Egypt

Ahmed M Marzouk
IBM Egypt, Egypt

Haitham S. Hamza
Cairo University, Egypt

ABSTRACT

Banking sector in Egypt is one of the largest business sectors in terms of contributing to country economic growth and in terms of investing in information technology (IT). Thus, implementing a good Information Technology (IT) governance framework inside Egyptian banks is a rather critical issue. The purpose of this chapter is to assess the importance and the implementation of Control Objectives for Information and Related Technology (COBIT) high level processes in the Egyptian banking sector. A total of 25 working banks in Egypt which are registered in the Central Bank of Egypt (CBE) from (public sector, private and joint venture and foreign) banks were interviewed in a series of one-to-one interviews. The results of this study showed that although the majority of interviewed Chief Information Officer (CIO), IT Managers, IT Auditors and others perceived the importance of COBIT high level processes in their organizations, the majority of the Egyptian banks have a below average maturity level for most of the COBIT processes.

DOI: 10.4018/978-1-4666-2083-4.ch005

INTRODUCTION

Information systems do not exist in isolation. Clearly, they are developed and operate within an environmental – most commonly business - context that has a significant effect on them. This environment is increasingly complex and dynamic. But, few organizations have realized the full potential of their information assets, although most consider their information to be essential to the operation. So, as Information Technology (IT), in general, contributes a larger and more noticeable role in driving business success, senior executives are under mounting pressure to clearly demonstrate the business value of IT, and to prove that IT investments can generate a positive return while supporting business objectives (Sarvanan and Kohli, 2000). Despite of a lot of talk about business alignment of ICT, a permanent link between the mandates of business and IT management remains yet to be established, even in organizations well aware of their information management and the business alignment issue (Pulkkinen and Hirvonen, 2005).

The past few years witnessed an increased attention to many standards and worldwide accepted frameworks that support the assessment and the implementation of IT governance in various organizations. These include: (1) Control Objectives for Information and Related Technology (COBIT) with a focus on the IT processes in organizations; (2) Information Technology Infrastructure Library (ITIL) with a focus on IT service management; and (3) ISO/IEC 17799:2000 which is an information security standard. The objectives, the scope, and the structure of each framework vary considerably. But, these all aim toward – or can be used for – improving IT governance in organizations.

Corporate governance is "a general term that is defined as "the system by which companies are directed and controlled" (Cadbury Report, 1992). Among the various aspects of corporate governance, IT governance is the one responsible for guaranteeing the effective alignment between

use of (and investments in) IT and organization's business objectives. IT governance is, thus, a subset regulation of Corporate Governance (Dellit, 2002; Hamaker, 2003), which is focused on IT systems and their performance and risk management and it has developed into a discipline of its own. IT governance provides "specifying the decision rights and accountability framework to encourage desirable behavior in the use of IT," (Weill and Ross, 2004) and is "an integral part of enterprise governance and consists of the leadership and organizational structures and processes to ensure that the organization sustains and extends its strategy and objectives." (ITGI, 2000)

The value of IT governance to corporate governance has raised based on the understanding that the most important IT issues in the near future are not technology-related, but governance-related (Guldentops 2002), IT governance is the capability of organization's senior management to direct, measure and evaluate the use of IT resources to support the achievement of the organization's strategic goals (Gray, 2004).

The primary goal for IT governance is to (1) ensure that the money invested in IT would be able to produce the expected business value, and (2) ensure the risks associated with IT are well mitigated (Williams, 2006). Good IT governance system can help organizations manage their IT internal and external costs by running efficient IT processes, aligning these processes with business objectives, introducing needed control and monitoring these processes to provide better visibility and feedback over IT (Gray, 2004).

Among various IT governance frameworks and standards, COBIT has shown as a strong and powerful framework and has been used increasingly by many organizations in public and private sectors throughout the world. COBIT was developed by the Information Systems Audit and Control Association (ISACA) and the IT Governance Institute (ITGI) in 1992. The first edition of COBIT was published in 1996, COBIT was intended to serve as an IT process and control framework linking

IT to business requirements, the 2nd edition was published in 1998. Since then, COBIT is being used as a framework for IT governance, providing management tools such as metrics and maturity models to complement the control framework.

The third version was released in 2000. In this edition, COBIT has been focused on IT governance because management guidelines were added to it. Since its original release, COBIT was enhanced with emerging international technical, professional, regulatory and industry-specific standards. In 2005, the 4th version of COBIT has released. And in May 2007, the IT Governance Institute (ITGI) has released an incremental update 4.1 of the COBIT, which has transitioned from an IT tool to an IT governance framework. The main changes introduced with COBIT 4.1 included streamlined control objectives, streamlined application controls, improved process controls, and an enhanced explanation of performance measurement.

COBIT is a comprehensive framework of 34 control objectives (high-level processes) divided into four categories which are: Plan and Organize (PO), Acquire and Implement (AI), Deliver and Support (DS) and Monitor and Evaluate (ME). The 34 high-level processes are linked to 318 tasks and activities to define an internal control framework that is powerful for communicating effectiveness and value to the business.

The COBIT framework was created with the main characteristics of being business-focused, process-oriented, controls-based and measurement-driven. To satisfy business objectives, information needs to conform to some control criteria, which COBIT refers to as business requirements for information, control criteria. These are: effectiveness, efficiency, confidentiality, integrity, availability, compliance and reliability. While these criteria provide generic business requirements, COBIT defines a set of generic business and IT goals to offer a business-related and more refined basis for establishing business requirements and developing the metrics that identifies the performance of the seven information criteria;

as well as which of the IT resources (people, applications, technology, facilities and data).

For the management and control over IT processes in the organization, COBIT defines six maturity levels of these processes:

0. **Non-Existent:** Management processes are not applied at all
1. **Initial:** Processes are ad hoc and disorganized.
2. **Repeatable:** Processes follow a regular pattern.
3. **Defined:** Processes are documented and communicated.
4. **Managed:** Processes are monitored and measured.
5. **Optimized:** Good practices are followed and automated.

Maturity levels are not designed for use as a threshold model, where one cannot move to the next higher level without having fulfilled all conditions of the lower level, but rather as a means to identify where issues are and how to set priorities for enhancements.

Banking sector is one of the major contributors to Egypt economic growth, and it is one of the largest sectors in investing in information technology. Investing in IT should add value to business and this is where IT governance importance came into view. COBIT is one of the important and famous IT governance frameworks today. The current research aims to assess the implementation of the Control Objectives for Information and Related Technology (COBIT) high-level processes in Egyptian banking sector and therefore to better understand the IT governance performance and importance in this sector.

Following the introduction section, the rest of this book chapter is organized as follows. Section 2 provide a review on related research work on IT governance and COBIT in particular, followed by a brief introduction to the context (Egyptian banking sector) in Section 3. Objectives, data collection, and analyses methods are provided in

Section 3, while detailed results and discussions are presented in Section 4. Finally, conclusions are given in Section 5.

LITERATURE REVIEW

Although IT governance in general and COBIT in particular is a hot topic at the present time because of the continuous raise of the governance awareness and importance, there are no many published studies and researches about it (Ridley et al., 2004; Williams, 2006).

Sohal and Fitzpatrick (2002) investigated the IT governance and management of information in Australian organizations using a questionnaire survey that was mailed to the most senior IT officer within the organization. The respondents were categorized into three groups based on the intensity with which the company uses information, namely high tier, medium tier and low tier industries. The findings showed some interesting differences among the three groups regarding the measurement and accountability of IT delivery. The majority of senior IT executives surveyed believed it was imperative that their organizations addressed aligning their IT with their business strategy in the near future. Hadden (2002) studied the role of audit committees in monitoring IT risks. Their instrument was developed from the 34 high-level control objectives identified in the COBIT model and the results of the study showed that audit committee oversight assessments were partially affected by prior COBIT experience.

The IT Governance Institute (ITGI) had a study that covered 335 Chief Executive Officers (CEOs) and Chief Information Officers (CIOs) in 21 countries. It was reported that while more than (91%) of executives recognise that IT is vital to their business success, more than two-thirds of CEOs were not comfortable answering questions about governance and control over their IT processes. The paper validates that the major problem continues to be "the inadequate view of how well IT is performing" (Son et al., 2005). Another study by ITGI for the entities currently using COBIT revealed that 75% of these researched entities found COBIT somewhat useful or very useful, and 15% were unsure and fewer than 10% showed a negative response. The main negative problem identified by the respondents was the perceived complexity of the framework (Williams, 2006).

The role of information technology (IT) governance in corporate strategy was discussed in Brown (2006). The study examined the four elements of IT governance, including value delivery, managing risk, maintaining accountability, and measurement of on-going programs and activities. This research showed that management' commitment and involvement with IT development at the senior management level, the IT management level, and the project management level significantly enhances the probability of success.

Luthy and Forcht (2006) compared COBIT and COSO in their study for the purpose of compliance with rules and regulations. The results of the comparison showed that both COSO and COBIT take an organization-wide view. However, COBIT only considers an organization-wide view to the extent of ensuring that IT governance is aligned with overall business objectives and organization governance. COBIT also provides very detailed IT control suggestions within its presentation of detailed control objectives. The study also concluded that COSO on its own might not provide sufficient guidance for organizations and auditors as they consider compliance with laws and regulations. The study also suggested that it might be useful, if not needed, to use more than one framework for assessing compliance with rules and regulations.

The factors influencing the IT governance effectiveness in an organization has been studied by Bowen et al. (2007). This study addresses the gap that exists between theoretical frameworks, prior empirical research, and contemporary practices on effective IT governance. Tuttle and Vandervelde (2007) studied internal consistency of the conceptual model that lies beneath the CO-

BIT internal control framework as it applies to an audit setting (including operational, compliance, and financial audit settings). The study studied the auditor perceptions of audit risks. From a practical standpoint, the results of this study suggested that it is very important and potentially very useful for the audit profession to seek academic examination of its practices. The findings suggest that the COBIT framework is significantly related to overall risk assessments of the COBIT processes for which they are associated. The results should give auditors and policy-makers assurance that COBIT is an appropriate supplement to COSO in an IT setting.

Abu-Musa (2008) researched the importance and implementation of the COBIT processes in Saudi organizations. The study showed that the majority of respondents perceive the importance of the COBIT processes and domains, but a lower percentage believe that such processes are adequately implemented in their organizations. It is observed that banks, financial institutions, and service organizations show more concern and application of COBIT processes compared with other organizations. The results also showed that IT specialists, internal auditors, and executive managers perceive and appreciate the importance of COBIT processes more than the others.

In Egypt, El-Morshedy (2008) developed a framework that enables effective and efficient application of the COBIT within audit and assessment activities. The proposed framework integrates four methodologies which they are: (1) Soft Systems Methodology (SSM), (2) Viable System Model (VSM), (3) Balanced Scorecard (BSC), and (4) Quality Function Deployment (QFD).

CONTEXT: EGYPTIAN BANKING SECTOR

The banking sector in Egypt is among the oldest and largest in the region. It has gone through many stages since the establishment of the first bank in 1856, followed by the emerging private sector and joint venture banks during the period of the Open Door policy in the 1970s (Egypt State Information Service, 2009). In June 1998, major amendments to the Banking Law, which permitted private ownership in public banks were approved by the Parliament.

Later in the nineties, as part of Egypt's economic and financial reform program, the banking sector has been undergoing reforms, privatization, mergers and acquisitions and was completely liberalized. The goal of this banking reform was creating an efficient banking sector which offers better quality services. The reform program was mainly based on promoting transparency and use of adequate accounting and supervision standards. According to the law, banks are required to publish their financial statements on quarterly basis in compliance with the International Accounting Standards (IAS). Also, the Law requires all banks to be audited by two different independent auditors, with auditors changing every two years.

Banks are supervised by the Banking Control Department of the Central Bank of Egypt (CBE), which has made considerable progress in developing its supervisory framework and staff using materials, procedures, and techniques obtained from other countries' supervisory systems. According to the Financial Sector Assessment Program (FSAP) report of 2003, CBE complied with most of the Basel Core Principles for Effective Banking Supervision.

Based on central bank of Egypt reports, Egyptian banking sector currently consists of thirty nine banks composed from (5) five public sector banks, (27) twenty seven private and joint venture banks and (7) seven branches of foreign banks.

Many Egyptian banks are making huge investments in technology to maintain and upgrade their infrastructure, not only to provide new electronic information-based services, but also to manage their risk positions and pricing. At the same time, new off-the-shelf electronic services, such as on-line retail banking, are making it possible for very small institutions to take advantage of new technologies at quite reasonable costs. These developments might in the end change the competitive landscape in financial services in ways that we cannot predict today.

More than other industries, financial institutions rely on gathering, processing, analyzing, and providing information to meet their customers' needs. Given the importance of information in banking, it is not surprising that Egyptian banks were among the earliest adopters of automated information processing technology. Leveraging information technology assets can help institutions manage risks more efficiently, as outlined by Basel II. The financial sector will, therefore, rely significantly on IT service providers to provide a more coherent architecture for process automation, integration, and cost reduction mechanisms.

The IT Governance Institute, US (Pathak, 2005), outlines 11 potential business drivers for COBIT adaptation. Among these, four drivers would be the reason behind potential interest of the Egyptian banking sector in COBIT. These are; (1) there is a need for IT governance; (2) mergers and acquisitions are taking place; (3) a considerable part of the IT function is outsourced; and (4) compliance with external requirements is of concern - CBE has directed banks to start building their own internal rating systems in preparation for Basel II (Egyptian Banking Sector Reform Policy: Areas of Future Actions, 2003).

RESEARCH METHODOLOGY

Objectives

This paper intends to explore the current status of COBIT practice in the Egyptian banking sector. More specifically, the paper attempts to: (1) assess how the importance of COBIT high-level processes are perceived; (2) measure the extent to which these processes are performed; (3) ex-

amine whether any significant differences among respondent groups regarding their perception of the importance of COBIT high-level processes; and (4) examine whether any significant differences among respondent groups regarding the implementation of these processes.

Three variables will be considered as moderating ones, these are: bank type, familiarity of IT governance inside the bank, and the number of IT employees. In Egypt, there exists three types of banks; public sector, private and joint venture, and branch of foreign banks.

Data Collection and Analysis

In this research, a questionnaire was developed to assess and evaluate the importance and implementation of Control Objectives for Information and Related Technology (COBIT) high-level processes in the Egyptian banking sector. The questionnaire was developed based on the COBIT standard domains and 34 high-level processes which were introduced in COBIT 4.1 edition. The questionnaire was pre-tested on selected sample of Egyptian banks (2 public sector banks and 3 private and joint venture banks). Comments and suggestions were considered in the development and revision of the final questionnaire version.

A series of sixty one-to-one interviews with managerial levels in the IT departments of the Egyptian banks have been conducted in order to collect questionnaire data and to correctly assess the implementation of the COBIT high-level processes inside the Egyptian banks. The managerial levels involved in these one-to-one meeting included IT CIOs, IT Directors, IT Managers, IT Project Managers, IT Quality Assurance Managers, IT Governance Managers and IT Auditors.

The questionnaire consisted of three main sections: demographic data, questions regarding the importance of COBIT high level processes, and questions regarding the maturity if these processes. While the importance of different processes represents how such importance is perceived in different

Table 1. Research sample

Type of Bank	Population	Respondents	Respondents % to Total Sample	Respondents % to Total Population
Public Sector Banks	5	3	12 %	7.7 %
Private and Joint Venture Banks	27	18	72 %	46 %
Branches of Foreign Banks	7	4	16 %	10.3 %
Total	25	39	100%	64 %

banks, maturity assessment was conducted by the researchers and included examination of related evidences of IT governance practice.

In this research, the sample unit is a 'bank.' A total of 25 banks from the 39 registered banks in Central Bank of Egypt (public sector, joint venture and foreign) have been interviewed and included in the research sample representing 64% of banks.

The collected data were processed using the Statistical Package for Social Sciences (SPSS) version 16. Descriptive statistics of the collected data were analyzed for the purpose of understanding the main characteristics of the research variables. To investigate the significant differences among independent groups of respondents related to the investigated COBIT's processes, two non-parametric tests (Kruskal-Wallis and Mann–Whitney–Wilcoxon) were used.

RESULTS AND DISCUSSION

Sample Characteristics

The research sample, as Table 1 depicts, was stratified as following: (1) three public sector banks out of 5 working public sector banks (60%) registered in Central Bank of Egypt (CBE); (2) four foreign banks out of 7 working foreign banks (57%) registered in CBE, and (3) eighteen private banks out of 27 working private banks (66.7%) registered in CBE.

Importance of COBIT High-Level Processes

Overall

Table 2 provides summary statistics of how the respondents perceived the importance of various COBIT high level processes. Generally, as the Table shows, the majority of these processes (33 out of 34) were seen as above 'medium' importance with a tendency towards 'important' and 'critical'; 12 process were seen as 'important' and 'critical.' This can be further illustrated with Figure 1 that provides the average importance of these processes. As shown, all of them are above 2.5 (on a 5 point scale). On the domains' level, the four of them; Plan and Organize, Acquire and Implement, Deliver and Support, and Monitor and Evaluate have shown to have the same importance with averages of 3.28, 3.29, 3.21, and 3.2, respectively.

On the processes level, however, Figure 2 depicts that the first three highest processes belong to the Deliver and Support domain while the highest ranked Plan and Organize process (PO1) came the 7th followed by PO2. On the other hand, the lowest three processes from the important perspective were also from the Deliver and Support domain. In fact, 5 out of the lowest 10 processes belong to the Deliver and Support domain.

Effect of Moderating Variables

Table 3 illustrates summary statistics of respondents group difference regarding their perception

Table 2. Importance of COBIT high-level processes in Egyptian banks – Summary statistics

COBIT High Level Processes	Importance									
	Not Important		Low Important		Medium		Important		Critical	
Plan and Organize	No.	%	No.	%	No.	%	No.	%	No.	%
PO1 Define a Strategic IT Plan	0	0	0	0	0	0	13	52	12	48
PO2 Define the Information Architecture	0	0	0	0	0	0	23	92	2	8
PO3 Determine Technological Direction	0	0	0	0	1	4	15	60	9	36
PO4 Define the IT Processes, Organisation and Relationships	0	0	0	0	1	4	23	92	1	4
PO5 Manage the IT Investment	0	0	0	0	2	8	12	48	11	44
PO6 Communicate Management Aims and Direction	0	0	0	0	3	12	20	80	2	8
PO7 Manage IT Human Resources	0	0	0	0	0	0	17	68	8	32
PO8 Manage Quality	0	0	0	0	0	0	16	64	9	36
PO9 Assess and Manage IT Risks	0	0	0	0	1	4	11	44	13	52
PO10 Manage Projects	0	0	0	0	2	8	11	44	12	48
Acquire and Implement										
AI1 Identify Automated Solutions	0	0	0	0	1	4	19	76	5	20
AI2 Acquire and Maintain Application Software	0	0	0	0	0	0	21	84	4	16
AI3 Acquire and Maintain Technology Infrastructure	0	0	0	0	0	0	21	84	4	16
AI4 Enable Operation and Use	0	0	0	0	1	4	11	44	13	52
AI5 Procure IT Resources	0	0	0	0	1	4	17	68	7	28
AI6 Manage Changes	0	0	0	0	1	4	16	64	8	32
AI7 Install and Accredit Solutions and Changes	0	0	0	0	1	4	10	40	14	56
Deliver and Support										
DS1 Define and Manage Service Levels	0	0	0	0	9	36	16	64	0	0
DS2 Manage Third-party Services	0	0	0	0	0	0	12	48	13	52
DS3 Manage Performance and Capacity	0	0	0	0	0	0	22	88	3	12
DS4 Ensure Continuous Service	0	0	0	0	0	0	8	32	17	68
DS5 Ensure Systems Security	0	0	0	0	0	0	0	0	25	100
DS6 Identify and Allocate Costs	0	0	1	4	13	52	10	40	1	4
DS7 Educate and Train Users	0	0	1	4	3	12	18	72	3	12
DS8 Manage Service Desk and Incidents	0	0	0	0	1	4	22	88	2	8
DS9 Manage the Configuration	0	0	0	0	3	12	18	72	4	16
DS10 Manage Problems	0	0	0	0	1	4	20	80	4	16
DS11 Manage Data	0	0	0	0	0	0	3	12	22	88
DS12 Manage the Physical Environment	0	0	0	0	3	12	9	36	13	52
DS13 Manage Operations	0	0	0	0	3	12	20	80	2	8
Monitor and Evaluate										
ME1 Monitor and Evaluate IT Performance	0	0	0	0	4	16	14	56	7	28
ME2 Monitor and Evaluate Internal Control	0	0	0	0	0	0	17	68	8	32
ME3 Ensure Compliance With External Requirements	0	0	0	0	0	0	11	44	14	56
ME4 Provide IT Governance	0	0	0	0	2	8	22	88	1	4

Figure 1. Importance of COBIT high-level processes in Egyptian banks - Means

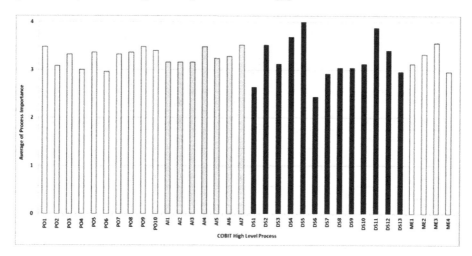

of the importance of the COBIT high-level processes based on three moderating variables; bank type, familiarity of IT governance inside the bank, and the number of IT employees in the bank.

The effect of bank type was tested using Kruskal-Wallis test. The results of the test showed that there are no significant differences among respondent groups regarding their perception of the importance of the COBIT 34 high-level processes based on bank type.

Mann-Whitney test was used to test the effect of the second variable – familiarity of IT governance

inside the bank – and as shown in the table, there was a significance difference in five processes (PO10, AI4, AI5, AI7, and DS1) only.

Finally, the effect of the number of IT employees was tested using Kruskal-Wallis test and the results showed no significant differences among respondent groups regarding their perception of the importance of the COBIT high-level processes based on that variable.

Figure 2. Importance of COBIT high-level processes in Egyptian banks – Ranked means

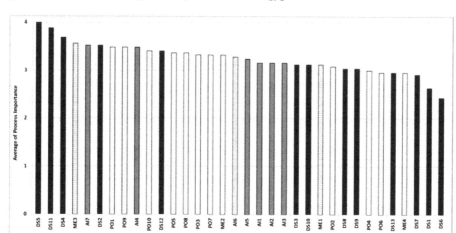

Table 3. Importance of COBIT high-level processes – Testing the moderating variables

COBIT High-Level Processes	Bank Type (Kruskal Wallis Test)		Familiarity of IT Governance inside the bank (Mann-Whitney)		Number of IT Employees (Kruskal Wallis Test)	
Plan and organize	x^2	p	W	P	x^2	P
PO1 Define a Strategic IT Plan	4.98	0.083	141.0	0.079	5.35	0.254
PO2 Define the Information Architecture	5.52	0.063	144.0	0.165	6.61	0.158
PO3 Determine Technological Direction	2.16	0.340	157.0	0.448	3.66	0.454
PO4 Define the IT Processes, Organisation and Relationships	3.67	0.160	169.0	1.000	3.20	0.525
PO5 Manage the IT Investment	0.19	0.911	142.5	0.108	3.45	0.485
PO6 Communicate Management Aims and Direction	2.07	0.354	152.0	0.185	2.33	0.675
PO7 Manage IT Human Resources	0.72	0.699	142.0	0.069	0.40	0.983
PO8 Manage Quality	0.27	0.872	148.0	0.170	5.88	0.209
PO9 Assess and Manage IT Risks	1.57	0.456	150.0	0.711	3.51	0.476
PO10 Manage Projects	1.45	0.484	114.0	0.001	0.92	0.922
Acquire and Implement						
AI1 Identify Automated Solutions	2.72	0.257	157.0	0.380	2.12	0.714
AI2 Acquire and Maintain Application Software	1.38	0.501	144.5	0.325	3.64	0.456
AI3 Acquire and Maintain Technology Infrastructure	1.38	0.501	144.5	0.325	4.24	0.375
AI4 Enable Operation and Use	4.14	0.126	133.0	0.026	2.66	0.617
AI5 Procure IT Resources	0.88	0.646	133.0	0.016	2.38	0.667
AI6 Manage Changes	1.81	0.405	163.0	0.698	9.66	0.047
AI7 Install and Accredit Solutions and Changes	1.05	0.591	139.0	0.061	1.99	0.738
Deliver and Support						
DS1 Define and Manage Service Levels	2.70	0.259	127.5	0.007	3.17	0.530
DS2 Manage Third-party Services	0.50	0.780	140.5	0.330	1.63	0.804
DS3 Manage Performance and Capacity	2.54	0.281	150.5	0.595	3.70	0.449
DS4 Ensure Continuous Service	2.19	0.335	146.0	0.122	2.60	0.626
DS5 Ensure Systems Security	0.00	1.000	169.0	1.000	0.00	1.000
DS6 Identify and Allocate Costs	3.82	0.148	144.0	0.128	5.57	0.234
DS7 Educate and Train Users	0.91	0.635	142.0	0.063	0.64	0.958
DS8 Manage Service Desk and Incidents	0.14	0.932	150.0	0.563	4.89	0.298
DS9 Manage the Configuration	2.06	0.357	153.0	0.270	2.51	0.643
DS10 Manage Problems	0.60	0.739	150.0	0.639	4.76	0.313
DS11 Manage Data	1.27	0.529	163.5	0.595	3.55	0.471
DS12 Manage the Physical Environment	3.90	0.142	163.0	0.717	6.70	0.152
DS13 Manage Operations	7.60	0.022	163.5	0.668	4.29	0.368
Monitor and Evaluate						
ME1 Monitor and Evaluate IT Performance	0.19	0.910	152.5	0.316	4.96	0.291
ME2 Monitor and Evaluate Internal Control	0.10	0.950	154.5	0.329	2.60	0.626
ME3 Ensure Compliance With External Requirements	0.84	0.657	153.0	0.312	6.53	0.163
ME4 Provide IT Governance	0.14	0.932	151.5	0.092	0.54	0.969

Table 4. Maturity of COBIT high-level processes in Egyptian banks – Summary statistics

COBIT High Level Process Name	Maturity											
	Non-existent		Initial/ Ad Hoc		Repeat-able		Defined		Managed		Optimized	
Plan and Organize	No.	%	No.	%	No.	%	No.	%	No.	%	No.	%
PO1 Define a Strategic IT Plan	0	0	0	0	2	8	3	12	20	80	0	0
PO2 Define the Information Architecture	0	0	2	8	2	8	18	72	3	12	0	0
PO3 Determine Technological Direction	0	0	0	0	4	16	12	48	9	36	0	0
PO4 Define the IT Processes, Organisation and Relation-ships	0	0	0	0	4	16	19	76	2	8	0	0
PO5 Manage the IT Investment	0	0	3	12	11	44	5	20	6	24	0	0
PO6 Communicate Management Aims and Direction	0	0	2	8	16	64	7	28	0	0	0	0
PO7 Manage IT Human Resources	0	0	5	20	8	32	10	40	0	0	2	8
PO8 Manage Quality	0	0	9	36	2	8	8	32	5	20	1	4
PO9 Assess and Manage IT Risks	0	0	0	0	11	44	6	24	8	32	0	0
PO10 Manage Projects	0	0	2	8	2	8	11	44	8	32	2	8
Acquire and Implement												
AI1 Identify Automated Solutions	0	0	5	20	11	44	7	28	2	8	0	0
AI2 Acquire and Maintain Application Software	0	0	1	4	5	20	14	56	5	20	0	0
AI3 Acquire and Maintain Technology Infrastructure	0	0	0	0	5	20	5	20	15	60	0	0
AI4 Enable Operation and Use	0	0	0	0	2	8	9	36	12	48	2	8
AI5 Procure IT Resources	0	0	0	0	2	8	13	52	8	32	2	8
AI6 Manage Changes	0	0	3	12	8	32	10	40	3	12	1	4
AI7 Install and Accredit Solutions and Changes	0	0	0	0	0	0	5	20	20	80	0	0
Deliver and Support												
DS1 Define and Manage Service Levels	0	0	11	44	9	36	5	20	0	0	0	0
DS2 Manage Third-party Services	0	0	0	0	0	0	4	16	13	52	8	32
DS3 Manage Performance and Capacity	0	0	1	4	9	36	5	20	10	40	0	0
DS4 Ensure Continuous Service	0	0	1	4	0	0	12	48	11	44	1	4
DS5 Ensure Systems Security	0	0	0	0	0	0	5	20	18	72	2	8
DS6 Identify and Allocate Costs	5	20	14	56	1	4	5	20	0	0	0	0
DS7 Educate and Train Users	0	0	3	12	7	28	12	48	3	12	0	0
DS8 Manage Service Desk and Incidents	1	4	2	8	5	20	6	24	11	44	0	0
DS9 Manage the Configuration	0	0	2	8	6	24	9	36	8	32	0	0
DS10 Manage Problems	0	0	6	24	9	36	8	32	2	8	0	0
DS11 Manage Data	0	0	0	0	0	0	2	8	21	84	2	8
DS12 Manage the Physical Environment	0	0	0	0	4	16	5	20	16	64	0	0
DS13 Manage Operations	0	0	0	0	4	16	14	56	7	28	0	0
Monitor and Evaluate												
ME1 Monitor and Evaluate IT Performance	0	0	4	16	9	36	9	36	1	4	2	8
ME2 Monitor and Evaluate Internal Control	0	0	0	0	2	8	8	32	15	60	0	0
ME3 Ensure Compliance With External Requirements	0	0	0	0	1	4	7	28	17	68	0	0
ME4 Provide IT Governance	2	8	12	48	4	16	5	20	2	8	0	0

Figure 3. Maturity of COBIT high-level processes in Egyptian banks – Means

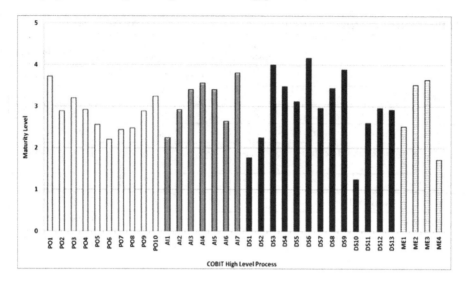

Maturity of COBIT High-Level Processes

Overall

Table 4 provides summary statistics of the how mature is the implementation of COBIT 34 high level processes. Overall, as the Table shows, there is a noticeable range of variability in the maturity of these processes; from 'non-existent' to 'optimized.' This variability is further illustrated in Figure 3 that the average maturity of these processes. As shown, average score of process maturity ranges from 1.24 (DS10) to 4.16 (DS6).

On the average, the Acquire and Implement domain showed the highest maturity with 3.14, followed by the Deliver and Support domain with 2.98 and then by the Plan and Organize and Monitor and Evaluate domains with 2.85 for both of them.

Figure 4. Maturity of COBIT high-level processes in Egyptian banks – Ranked means

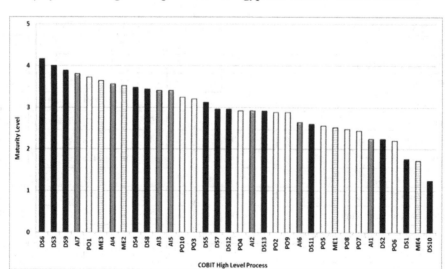

Table 5. Maturity of COBIT high-level processes – Testing the moderating variables

COBIT High Level Process Name	Bank Type (Kruskal Wallis Test)		Familiarity of IT Governance inside the bank (Mann-Whitney)		Number of IT Employees (Kruskal Wallis Test)	
Plan and organize	X^2	p	W	p	X^2	p
PO1 Define a Strategic IT Plan	5.182	0.075	150.5	0.149	4.239	0.375
PO2 Define the Information Architecture	1.891	0.388	153.5	0.286	2.340	0.673
PO3 Determine Technological Direction	2.450	0.294	123	0.006	2.190	0.701
PO4 Define the IT Processes, Organisation and Relationships	2.605	0.272	136	0.016	3.879	0.423
PO5 Manage the IT Investment	1.198	0.549	125.5	0.012	1.809	0.771
PO6 Communicate Management Aims and Direction	6.296	0.043	139	0.054	1.306	0.860
PO7 Manage IT Human Resources	1.252	0.535	118	0.003	1.063	0.900
PO8 Manage Quality	4.070	0.131	129.5	0.025	3.599	0.463
PO9 Assess and Manage IT Risks	7.307	0.026	119	0.004	2.480	0.648
PO10 Manage Projects	6.185	0.045	125.5	0.012	1.639	0.802
Acquire and Implement						
AI1 Identify Automated Solutions	5.788	0.055	124.5	0.010	3.744	0.442
AI2 Acquire and Maintain Application Software	2.315	0.314	115.5	0.001	1.757	0.780
AI3 Acquire and Maintain Technology Infrastructure	3.433	0.180	124	0.005	4.000	0.406
AI4 Enable Operation and Use	3.531	0.171	132.5	0.031	1.046	0.903
AI5 Procure IT Resources	1.162	0.559	112.5	0.001	2.635	0.621
AI6 Manage Changes	4.089	0.129	129	0.022	3.070	0.546
AI7 Install and Accredit Solutions and Changes	2.333	0.311	139	0.019	4.600	0.331
Deliver and Support						
DS1 Define and Manage Service Levels	10.389	0.006	135	0.046	6.426	0.169
DS2 Manage Third-party Services	5.868	0.053	119.5	0.003	3.239	0.519
DS3 Manage Performance and Capacity	3.263	0.196	109	0.001	6.475	0.166
DS4 Ensure Continuous Service	7.470	0.024	132	0.025	2.351	0.671
DS5 Ensure Systems Security	2.805	0.246	131	0.009	3.669	0.453
DS6 Identify and Allocate Costs	9.580	0.008	125.5	0.009	4.717	0.318
DS7 Educate and Train Users	3.072	0.215	121.5	0.005	3.892	0.421
DS8 Manage Service Desk and Incidents	3.702	0.157	124.5	0.010	5.822	0.213
DS9 Manage the Configuration	5.102	0.078	137	0.068	2.337	0.674
DS10 Manage Problems	6.468	0.039	127.5	0.018	5.944	0.203
DS11 Manage Data	1.833	0.400	157.5	0.327	3.000	0.558
DS12 Manage the Physical Environment	1.756	0.416	140.5	0.069	4.391	0.356
DS13 Manage Operations	2.778	0.249	133	0.029	5.940	0.204
Monitor and Evaluate						
ME1 Monitor and Evaluate IT Performance	5.032	0.081	122	0.007	4.480	0.345
ME2 Monitor and Evaluate Internal Control	5.968	0.051	120.5	0.002	4.037	0.401
ME3 Ensure Compliance With External Requirements	1.802	0.406	133	0.016	3.400	0.493
ME4 Provide IT Governance	4.420	0.110	104.5	0.000	1.061	0.900

On the processes level, Figure 4 depicts that the first three highest processes belong to the Deliver and Support domain and the lowest process is D10. Out of the lowest 10 processes, 5 belong to the Plan and Organize domain.

Effect of Moderating Variable

Table 5 illustrates summary statistics of group difference regarding the maturity of COBIT high-level processes based on the three moderating variables; bank type, familiarity of IT governance inside the bank, and the number of IT employees in the bank. While Kruskal-Wallis test showed no significant differences based on the number of IT employees, significant difference were shown in 7 processes based on bank type (using Kruskal-Wallis test), and significant difference were shown in 28 processes based on bank type (using Mann-Whitney test).

COBIT Domains' Maturity: Comparison of Different Bank Types

Plan and Organize

This domain covers strategy and tactics as proper organisation and technological infrastructure should be put in place. This domain tackles management areas related to the alignment of IT and business strategy, quality, projects, risk assessment, and human resources.

In this study, Plan and Organize (PO) processes shown to be considerably high matured as for of them were repeatable and higher. Two processes (PO7 and PO 10) showed optimized maturity in two banks. On the average, as shown in Figure 5, all PO processes showed almost the same maturity levels in different bank types with exception to PO8, PO9, and PO10 that showed increase maturity in foreign banks compared to public and private banks.

Defining a strategic IT plan (PO1) was a process that showed high maturity as 80% of banks were in the "Managed" level. This can be reasoned to that fact that this process is highly monitored by the bank board of directors and also by the managerial business levels in the bank, it is the most important link between IT and business from CIO and IT managers perspective, its importance also came from the fact that it the initial stone in planning for future business needs.

PO3 process is more matured in foreign banks compared to private and public mainly because of the existence of IT architecture board, who is responsible for providing architecture guidelines and technology directions for the bank, and the existence of technology infrastructure plan that

Figure 5. COBIT domains – Plan and organize processes

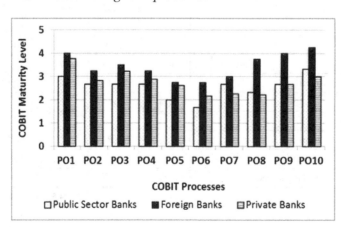

includes directions for acquisition of technology infrastructure and responsiveness for changes in the competitive environment, in the studied public sector banks, this process was more of the time (66.67%) in the "Defined" level, because of the absence of technology direction in the public sector bank, also the IT department responds very slowly to competitive changes in the environment after taking many procedures and precautions to minimize the investments and the risks, another thing is that there is no preferred technology direction for the public sector bank in general, most of the time these banks are adapting the same successful technology direction in private and foreign banks.

Foreign banks showed more maturity for PO4 compared to private and public sector banks because of the existence of the IT process framework that ensures transparency and control as well as involvement of senior executives and business management, also foreign banks showed that processes, procedures and administrative policies are in place for all functions and especially for control, quality assurance, risk management functions. In addition to this all job descriptions for IT staff are clearly defined and stated, as well as supervision and segregation of duties. Private and public sector banks do have the same process but in less maturity level due the absence of most of the controls for that process.

Managing quality (PO10) process is highly matured in foreign banks compared with public sector and private banks because of the existence of Quality Management System (QMS) and quality assurance department in foreign banks responsible for ensuring IT is delivering the expected value to business stakeholders without any deviations. In public sector bank, the QMS is still under development and construction

The case was the same for managing project (PO10) that is highly matured in foreign banks compared with public sector and private banks because of the existence of a project management framework that ensures the correct prioritisation

and coordination of all projects. All sampled foreign banks have now a project management unit for all IT projects or at least project management function.

Finally, the critical process of assessing and managing IT risks (PO9) is also highly matured in foreign banks compared with public sector and private banks because of the existence of a risk management framework, which is responsible about identifying and mitigating IT risks, many foreign banks have risk management function which is responsible about ensuring the proper working of this process.

Acquire and Implement

Realizing the IT strategy requires potential IT solutions to be identified, developed or acquired, as well as implemented and integrated into the business process. In addition to these processes, this domain covers areas related to the maintenance of existing systems, management of systems' changes, procurement, operation and use of new and current systems, and verification of installed solutions.

Comparing the maturity of this domain process in the three bank types in Egypt, Figure 6 indicates an even maturity in the range of (4) of almost all process. Unlike the PO domain, public banks outperformed foreign ones in two processes AI 1 and AI2. Foreign banks, however, showed better performance on the following four processes.

Acquire and maintain technology and infra-structure (AI3) is highly matured in foreign banks compared to public sector and private banks because of the existence of processes for acquisition, implementation and upgrade of technology infra-structure. The same

Enable operations and use (AI4) is also highly matured in foreign banks compared to public sector and private banks because of the existence of processes that produces documentation and manuals for users and IT, and provides training for IT and end users.

Figure 6. COBIT domains – Acquire and implement processes

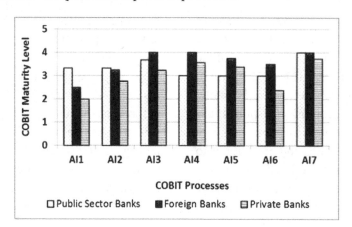

Deliver and Support

This domain is concerned with the delivery of required services, which includes service delivery, management of security and continuity, service support for users, and management of data and operational facilities. It management issues related to alignment of delivered It services with business priorities, cost optimization, users' capacity, and security.

Results of this study showed that public banks had higher maturity than foreign banks in four processes (DS2, DS8, DS12, DS 13) while their maturity in the rest of processes was lower than those of the foreign banks.

Despite the fact that define and manage service level (DS1) is an important process from the IT governance perspective as it links business with IT, this study showed very low maturity level for the examined banks sample, the result was even worse in public and private banks, till now there is no formalized process in these banks which is responsible about measuring service level agreements between business and IT.

With respect to another critical process (DS5), all examined bank in this research showed very high attention to this process importance, all respondent banks reported that they consider this process is the most important IT governance process for their bank, but also because of the

Figure 7. COBIT domains – Deliver and support processes

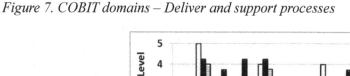

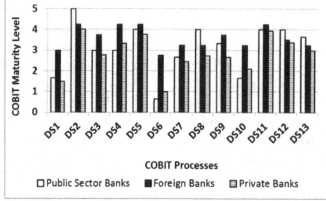

criticality of this process, a lot of focus and auditing already exist for this process and that's why this process is at "Managed" maturity level most of the time.

On cost optimization (DS6), foreign banks showed high maturity level compared to private and public sector banks, this is due the existence of operating a system which captures, allocates and reports IT costs to the users of services (see Figure 7).

Monitor and Evaluate

To guarantee continuous improvement and an effective IT governance practice, all IT processes need to be assessed on regular basis for performance and compliance with control requirements. This domain covers management issues related to performance management, monitoring of internal control, regulatory compliance and governance.

For processes in this domain, foreign banks showed a considerable higher maturity than public banks with respect ME1 and ME4. Despite the fact that performance is required to be evaluate by law, public banks concentrates mainly on workforce performance and do not cover other functional areas such as IT performance (see Figure 8).

Most of the examined banks showed low maturity level for the provide IT governance

(ME4) process, especially private and public sector banks, most of the interviewed CIOs and IT managers from the examined banks especially who reported that their organisations are not familiar with IT governance, see the value of IT governance in implementing some individual COBIT processes and not in the whole entire framework. Also from the interviewed with those CIOs they stated that implementing the IT framework in Egyptian banks will need some supervision and support from the Central Bank of Egypt (CBE).

CONCLUSION

The purpose of this research was to assess the implementation of the Control Objectives for Information and Related Technology (COBIT) domain and high-level processes in Egyptian banking sector, the results of this research will enable Egyptian banks to better understand, evaluate, implement and manage information technology governance for their businesses success. The research provides useful information for executive managers, IT managers, accountants, auditors, and academics to understand the implementation performance of the COBIT processes in Egyptian banks.

Figure 8. COBIT domains – Monitor and evaluate processes

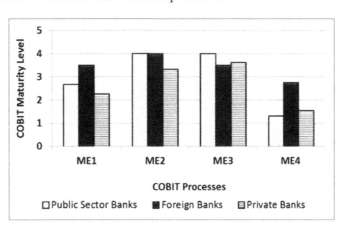

Motivation and, thus, importance of this study stems from three sources:

1. The banking sector is one of the largest sectors in Egypt in terms of contributing to Egypt GDP and in using information technology to support banking business process and requirements (Egypt State Information Service, 2009), this is why implementing a good IT governance framework is needed to align business requirements and information technology in banking sector.
2. Central bank of Egypt is preparing banks for introducing the Basel II regulations. CBE Banking Institute arranged seminars for Egyptian bankers in preparation for Basel II requirements. CBE also informed banks to start building their own internal rating systems in preparation for Basel II (Egyptian Banking Sector Reform Policy: Areas of Future Actions, 2003). This continuous focus from CBE on Basel II implementation will pave the way for implementing the IT governance regulations inside the Egyptian banks, and one of these regulations that will take place is COBIT because of the existing relations between Basel II and COBIT.
3. There was no similar published research work on the practice of IT governance in the Egyptian banking sector or in other developing countries like Egypt.

Presented results answered the four intended objectives of the research:

1. Assessment of how the importance of COBIT high-level processes are perceived.
2. Measuring the extent to which these processes are performed.
3. Examining whether any significant differences among respondent groups regarding their perception of the importance of COBIT high-level processes.

4. Examining whether any significant differences among respondent groups regarding the implementation of these processes.

In general, the study revealed that despite IT governance (COBIT high-level) processes are perceived as important an critical, the practice of these processes – defined in terms of maturity levels – is still in adequate for sector requirements.

Performance of foreign banks operating in Egypt, however, showed better performance compared to public banks on the majority of processes.

On the local level, this study recommends for actions to be taken in order to enhance IT governance practice in the Egyptian banking sector:

1. CBE should sponsor an IT governance awareness program through Federation of Egyptian Banks to raise the awareness and understating of the IT governance concepts and approaches inside the Egyptian banks especially for the management levels.
2. CBE should launch a program to start implementing the IT governance frameworks and standards inside the Egyptian banks with clear roadmap and deadlines.
3. CBE should train internal IT auditors as well as external auditors on different IT governance concepts and standards to start monitoring the IT governance performance inside the Egyptian banks.
4. IT Managers can start implementing COBIT high level processes starting from the most important processes from their organisations perspective and ending with the least.

Finally, future work would include doing the same study in other IT-intensive sectors in Egypt such as Telecommunication and Insurance.

REFERENCES

Abu-Musa, A. A. (2008). Exploring information technology governance (ITG) in developing countries: An empirical study. *The International Journal of Digital Accounting Research*, *9*, 99–126.

Bowen, P. L., Cheung, M. D., & Rohde, F. H. (2007). Enhancing IT governance practices: A model and case study of an organization's efforts. *International Journal of Accounting Information Systems*, *8*(3), 191–221.

Brown, W. (2006). *IT governance, architectural competency, and the Vasa*. Emerald Group Publishing Limited.

Cadbury, A. (1992). *The financial aspects of corporate governance*. London, UK: Gee.

Central Bank of Egypt. (2003). *Egyptian banking sector reform policy: Areas of future actions*. Retrieved September 4, 2010, from http://www. cbe.org.eg/public/Egyptian%20banking%20 reform%20policy_WB.doc

Dellit, C. (2002). Governance and the emerging salience of technology. *Software, October,* 19–24

Egypt State Information Service. (2009). The banking sector in Egypt. Retrieved August 30, 2010, from http://www.sis.gov.eg/En/Economy/ banking/bankingsector/050401000000000001. htm

El-Morshedy, R. M. (2008). *Technology transfer of information systems auditing and control standards*. Unpublished thesis, Cairo University, Faculty of Computers & Information, Information Systems Department.

Gray, H. (2004). Is there a relationship between IT governance and corporate governance? Unpublished Master's thesis, UK.

Guldentops, E. (2002). Knowing the environment: top five IT issues. *Information Systems Control Journal*, *4*, 15–16.

Hadden, L. B. (2002). *An investigation of the audit committee and its role in monitoring information technology risks*. D.B.A., Nova Southeastern University, AAT 3074875.

Hamaker, S. (2003). Spotlight on governance. *Information Systems Control Journal*, *1*, 15–19.

IT Governance Institute (ITGI). (2000). *Board briefing on IT governance*. Retrieved from www. itgi.org

Luthy, D., & Forcht, K. (2006). Laws and regulations affecting information management and frameworks for assessing compliance. *Information Management & Computer Security*, *14*(2), 155–166.

Pathak, J. (2005). *Information technology auditing*. Berlin, Germany: Springer.

Pulkkinen, M., & Hirvonen, A. P. (2005). Organizational processes in ICT management and evaluation. Experiences with large organizations. In D. Remenyi (Ed.), *Proceedings 12th European Conference on Information Technology Evaluation*, Turku, Finland, 29-30 September 2005, Trinity College Dublin, Ireland. ISBN: 1-905305-08-7

Ridley, G., Young, J., & Carol, P. (2004). COBIT and its utilization: A framework from the literature. *Proceedings of the 37th Hawaii International Conference on System Science*s – 2004. New York, NY: IEEE.

Sarvanan, D., & Kohli, R. (2000). *The IT payoff: Measuring the business value of information technology investment*. New Jersey: Prentice Hall.

Sohal, A. S., & Fitzpatrick, P. (2002). IT governance and management in large Australian organizations. *International Journal of Production Economics*, *75*(1/2), 97–112.

Son, S., Weitzel, T., & Laurent, F. (2005). Designing a process-oriented framework for IT performance management systems. *The Electronic Journal Information Systems Evaluation, 8*(3), 219–228.

Tuttle, B., & Vandervelde, S. D. (2007). An empirical examination of COBIT as an internal control framework for information technology. *International Journal of Accounting Information Systems, 8*(4), 240–263.

Weill, P., & Ross, J. W. (2004). *IT governance: How top performers manage IT decision rights for superior results*. Boston, MA: Harvard Business School Press.

Williams, P. (2006, September 19). A helping hand with IT governance. Computer Weekly, p. 26. Retrieved September 3, 2010, from http://www.computerweekly.com/Articles/2006/09/19/218517/a-helping-hand-with-it-governance.htm

KEY TERMS AND DEFINITIONS

Basel II: Basel II is the second of the Basel Committee on Bank Supervision's recommendations. It is a set of banking regulations put forth by the Basel Committee on Bank Supervision, which regulates finance and banking internationally.

Chief Information Officer: A job title commonly given to the most senior executive in an enterprise responsible for the information technology and computer systems that support enterprise goals.

Control Objectives for Information and Related Technology (COBIT): A set of best practices (framework) for information (IT) management created initially in 1992 by the Information Systems Audit and Control Association (ISACA), and the IT Governance Institute (ITGI). COBIT is an IT governance control framework that helps organizations meet today's business challenges in the areas of regulatory compliance, risk management and aligning IT strategy with organizational goals.

Information Technology Governance: The capability of organization's senior management to direct, measure and evaluate the use of IT resources to support the achievement of the organization's strategic goals.

Information Technology Maturity: A method of evaluating the organisation, so it can be rated from a maturity level of non-existent (0) to optimised (5). This provides the base for improvement and reaching the appropriate level of management and control over the information infrastructure.

Chapter 6
Adoption of ISO 27001 in Cyprus Enterprises:
Current State and Challenges

Ioanna Dionysiou
University of Nicosia, Cyprus

Skevi Magirou
University of Nicosia, Cyprus

Angelika Kokkinaki
University of Nicosia, Cyprus

Theodosios Iacovou
University of Nicosia, Cyprus

ABSTRACT

This chapter presents the findings of an investigation on current security practices in Cypriot organizations, including enterprises and public sector divisions. In order to gain knowledge on the deployed security technologies by organizations, a survey was conducted and concluded in late 2010. The survey primarily examined compliance of enterprise current security policies and procedures with ISO 27001 security guidelines. A research analysis has been performed and identified that security mechanisms and the management of information technology (IT) resources may be improved on a number of aspects. Based on the research findings, an assessment of the viability of ISO 27001 in Cyprus is given as well as recommendations on the further deployment of ISO 27001.

INTRODUCTION

Along with the benefits of the universal connectivity (wireless, broadband, 3G), comes an increased risk of security breaches. Attackers, without any specialized knowledge, could launch sophisticated attacks as they have at their disposal easily downloadable software (attack toolkits) capable of breaching computers and networks. Any networked computer is susceptible to an attack, as the majority of attackers belong to the opportunistic hacker category looking for vulnerabilities to exploit, regardless of the physical location of the computer. It only takes a click

DOI: 10.4018/978-1-4666-2083-4.ch006

on an email attachment to launch a virus or start spreading a worm. To make things even worse, if the infected computer belongs to a corporation, the entire corporate network could be contaminated, with severe financial implications.

There is an emergent need for enterprises to protect their resources and assets by taking all necessary measures to prevent, detect, and recover from security attacks (Stallings, 2010). Increased vulnerability and the threat of massive financial damage due to malicious or non-intentional security violations are augmenting the pressure to prevent damage and minimize the risk through active IT security management. However, IT security strategies are perceived to require high investment in security technology while their implementation is also considered to be demanding in terms of highly skilled human resources. In view of these, security is not usually assigned high enough priority by organizations.

Yet, the design and implementation of an effective security strategy in enterprises need not necessarily be an unrealistic goal. The main success factor is well thought out organizational procedures and reliable, informed staff who observe security requirements in a disciplined manner. ISO 27001, an Information Security Management System (ISMS) standard published by the International Organization for Standardization (ISO) provides assurance that the management system for information security is in place. To be more specific, ISO 27001 specifies "the requirements for establishing, implementing, operating, monitoring, reviewing, maintaining and improving a documented Information Security Management System within the context of the organization's overall business risks" (ISO, 2005). Compliance to ISO 27001 does not guarantee that the enterprise will never experience any security exploitations; it does though assure that the company has taken all protective measures to avert security attacks, thus lowering the risk of interruptions during business conduct.

Security attacks are on the rise, even in Cyprus, a Eurasian island country in the Eastern Mediterranean. Recent security incidents include a phishing attack targeting the online subscribers of a Cypriot Bank Corporation and the defacement of Cypriot company web sites. It has been observed that many organizations in Cyprus place at relatively low priority initiatives related to IT security. In order to substantiate this hypothesis, an investigation was launched in April 2010 to study existing IT security strategies and policies that are deployed by Cypriot enterprises, focusing on compliance with the ISO 27001 standard. The statistical analysis of the nationwide survey indeed indicated lack of awareness regarding proper security practices. The results were further exploited to unveil the underlying reasons for this situation, especially the non-compliance with the ISO 27001.

Analytically, the following objectives have been set for this chapter:

- Investigate the security policies, procedures, mechanisms, and technologies in Cyprus enterprises towards the detection of the level of compliance with ISO 27001
- Draw prescriptive conclusions on the subject of ISO 27001 compliance in Cyprus.
- Identification of the contributing factors that delay the ISO 27001 implementation in Cyprus
- Recommendations and overall directives on the use of ISO 27001 in Cyprus

The remaining of the chapter is unfolded as follows: Section 2 briefly gives an overview of the ISO 27001 standard. Section 3 describes the logistics on preparing the questionnaire on IT security strategies and policies, which is the investigation's primary research instrument. Section 4 constitutes the analysis part of the paper, where the survey findings are analyzed, followed by Section 5 that assesses the viability of ISO 27001 in Cypriot enterprises by discussing the adoption process and the factors that drive or avert enterprises to adapt the ISO 27001. Recommendations for enterprises, SME (small to medium) and Large, are given in Section 6. Section 7 outlines a framework for security governance in SME. Finally, section 8 concludes this chapter with overall observations.

OVERVIEW OF ISO 27001

One of the challenges in deploying information security in business settings is aligning the goals of two perspectives: the technical angle and the industry viewpoint. In the case there is an association between security policies and business policies, the enterprise is geared for competitive advantage producing support for supplementary expenditures (ISACA, 2009). The deliberate information security culture that focuses on the enterprise's governance needs has several important characteristics, one of them being the alignment of information security and business objectives where the information security program provides real, measurable risk reduction (Kent, 2008).

The first step that an enterprise should take towards the aforementioned goal is to plan for security by subsequent course of action for the security certification and accreditation of their information technology systems so as to comply with security standards. One of such certification standards is the ISO 27001. The International Organization for Standardization (ISO) is a consortium of national principle institutes from 157 countries and it is the largest developer of standards worldwide. The ISO 27001 is an information security management system (ISMS) standard that specifies the requirements for the establishment, implementation, monitoring and maintenance of an information management system targeting the security aspects of an enterprise. It does not dictate the implementation of specific technical solutions; for instance, it recommends the provision of backups but it does not explicitly mention what product or solution to use. Needless to say, in order for an organization to gain ISO 27001

certification it must deploy the specifications of ISO 27001.

The reasons for seeking compliance to any ISO standard may vary among companies. It could be market-related motives or motives related to upgrading of inner actions (Lipovatz et al, 1999). According to (Tsiotras &Gotzamani K, 1996), companies are motivated to be certified for four reasons: improve the image and status of the company, persuade external market requirements, facilitate and simplify procedures related to client contracts, and improve the overall quality management system. The worth of ISO 27001 series has been accredited universal recognition and acknowledgement from various institutions, companies, and quality researchers. Specifically, the British Standard Institution and the European Community strongly advocated the adoption of ISO 27001 series. Remuneration from the application of the ISO 27001 standard cannot be quantified and calculated, and this constitutes one of the main reasons that delayed its function worldwide.

Some common advantages reported by ISO 27001 compliant companies include the following (ISO 17799 News, 2007): improved Information Security, Management Assurance, Diligence, Benchmarking, Marketing, Interoperability, Security Awareness, and Business Alignment. On the other hand, the path to ISO 27001 certification is rarely pleasurable and smooth. On the contrary to the certification benefits, several manufacturers found that ISO registration is too luxurious, time overwhelming, too pompous and distant (Street & Fernie, 1993). There is also absence of top executive support and assurance, member of staff confrontation to change, lack of understanding the ISO system, unclear benefits of obtaining certification. In addition, an important barrier is the inability to define the scope of the ISMS (Kosutic, 2010) especially given that the information security is inherently complex and difficult to achieve at the optimal degree (ISO 27001 Security, 2011).

SURVEY DESIGN LOGISTICS

A nationwide investigation was launched in 2010 by researchers at University of Nicosia to uncover existing IT security strategies and policies in both private and public sectors in Cyprus. The survey relied on ISO 27001 best security practices. The investigation is part of a broader research effort that envisions the development and deployment of a web service that would assist enterprises to make an assessment of their degree of compliance with ISO 27001 and provide recommendations on the domains that need improvement. As a result, organizations that currently place at a relatively low priority any security deployment initiative will be able to harden their security defenses.

A suitable and straightforward approach to identify these current security strategies deployed in organizations was decided to be a comprehensive checklist where the respondent would simply indicate the presence or not of a security feature, technology, policy, or strategy. As a consequence, a survey questionnaire was prepared, heavily relying on checklists that addressed all factors involving security policies and procedures, including ICT Security Management, ICT Security measures, Networking and Internet Connection. The questionnaire was based on the "IT Security Guidelines" (BSI, 2007), a publication issued by the Federal Office for Information Security (BSI), which is the national security agency that promotes and provides IT security for the federal government in Germany. The document's checklists that cover 50 IT security safeguards relevant to ISO 27001 certification were extended and customized for the Cyprus market.

The final questionnaire comprised of 11 sections, as shown in Table 1. Sections B through J consisted of dichotomous questions that ask respondents to answer yes or no and are based on the security safeguard checklists outlined in the aforementioned document. The Company Profile section and section A - Network Details also included open- and closed-format questions, so as to get demographical details of the organization and its network profile respectively. Companies with an IT department were requested to supply answers to all sections, whereas enterprises without a dedicated IT department only had to provide answers to Company Profile and Network Details sections.

SURVEY FINDINGS ANALYSIS

During the period starting April 10, 2010 and ending December 10, 2010 completed responses to the survey were received from 152 organizations, in both the public and private sectors, from an original sample of 165 selected enterprises. Companies were not chosen from a specific sector, but from different divisions to obtain more general observations of the attitudes towards security. Managers, directors, or supervisors completed the questionnaire on the behalf of the organization. The response rate, which is defined as the percentage of the sample that was actually interviewed out of the original sample, was 92.12%. Callbacks formed the core mechanism for the survey's quality assurance, and were carried out by an independent quality assurance unit. Normally, at least 15-30% of all completed questionnaires are back-checked by the quality assurance unit, however in this survey, the back-check was 50%, in order to ensure higher quality standards.

A total of 55 companies had a dedicated IT department (36% of total contacts), with the remaining 97 having no IT department (64% of total contacts). On average, organizations with IT departments have 129 employees whereas companies without an IT department employ 38 people. The companies classified as Large (with 250+ employees) reached 12%, Medium (with 50-249 employees) reached 23%, and Small (with 2-49 employees) had the majority with 65%. The majority of companies support access to networks through Internet (69%), with significantly higher percentage in companies with IT department

Table 1. Questionnaire composition

Section	Questions	Topics
Company Profile	12	IT department structure (if any), business main activity, other company-related, demographical, and personal data
A : Network Details	11	Network topology and connectivity, security concerns, security technologies deployed (in-house, outsourced to third parties), current security practices, security incidents (embezzlement, fraud, theft of proprietary information, denial of service, vandalism or electronic sabotage, viruses)
B : IT Security Management	15	Objectives defined, human resources allocated, action plan documented and implemented, time intervals for security inspections, ongoing training of old and new personnel, etc.
C : Security of IT Systems	14	Protection mechanisms used, software installed, roles and profiles assigned to all users, privileges and permissions controlled, proper documentation created and updated regularly, etc.
D : Compliance with Security Requirements	6	Confidential information stored properly, confidential information handling in case of repair or maintenance of ICT equipment, security regulations monitored, security breaches properly reported and disciplined, etc.
E : Networking and Internet Connection	7	Firewall existence, configuration and functionality monitored, data visibility to outside users defined, unnecessary services disabled, etc.
F : Maintenance of IT Systems	3	Updates installed regularly, appointed personnel vigilant on required updates, test concept for software modifications, etc.
G : Passwords and Encryption	6	Types of password protection and encryption used, default passwords changed, secure passwords guidelines, safeguards on mobile ICT equipment, etc.
H : Contingency Planning	3	Contingency plan existence, adequacy of addressing all contingency situations, familiarity and accessibility of contingency plan, etc.
I : Data Backups	5	Strategy, implementation, regular control and updates, proper documentation, etc.
J : Infrastructure Security	5	Adequate protection against physical threats, sensitive areas physical protection, visitors protocol, intruders' protection, etc.

(80%). Furthermore, this category of companies support remote access (40%), and publicly accessible website without e-commerce capabilities (40%). Anti-virus software usage reached 95%, with firewalls following with 54%, and password-enabled accounts with 41%. Almost half of the companies do not outsource any computer security services. For those organizations that do outsource, the tasks most commonly assigned to a third party include the installation of computer security (24%), and the system administration of their computer security (16%). Interestingly, organizations with IT departments tend to outsource in higher rates than those without a dedicated IT department.

The focus of the analysis was to determine the level of security awareness within organizations by examining compliance to ISO 27001 recommended security practices. Sections B through J constituted the analysis' 9 attributes (labeled B, C... J). Each question in these sections was assigned a score of 1 for a positive response, and a score of 0 for a negative response. Based on this, three sets of analyses were performed:

- **Analysis 1:** Mean scores of Attributes B through J
- **Analysis 2:** Mean scores of Attributes B through J, using the size of the company as an additional parameter
- **Analysis 3:** Mean scores of Attributes B through J, using the technological knowledge and skills of the company as an additional parameter.

Table 2. Mean scores for all attributes

Attribute	Mean
B : IT Security Management	.6303
C : Security of IT Systems	.7623
D : Compliance with Security Requirements	.5909
E : Networking and Internet Connection	.8026
F : Maintenance of IT Systems	.7515
G : Passwords and Encryption	.7697
H : Contingency Planning	.4424
I : Data Backups	.7564
J : Infrastructure Security	.8182

Analysis 1: Mean Scores of Attributes B-J

Table 2 shows the mean score of all attributes. The highest mean is observed in Infrastructure Security (0.8182). The group of high average includes Networking and Internet Connection (0.8026), Passwords and Encryption (0.7697), Security of IT Systems (0.7623), Data Backups (0.7564), Maintenance of IT Systems (0.7515). The next attribute is IT Security Management with a score of 0.6303, followed by Compliance and Security Requirements (0.5909). The last place is given to the attribute Contingency Planning with a mean score of 0.4424.

Figure 1 depicts analytically the frequency of the responses per question for attribute B: IT Security Management. Only 49% of the companies

Figure 1. Response distribution per question for it security management attribute

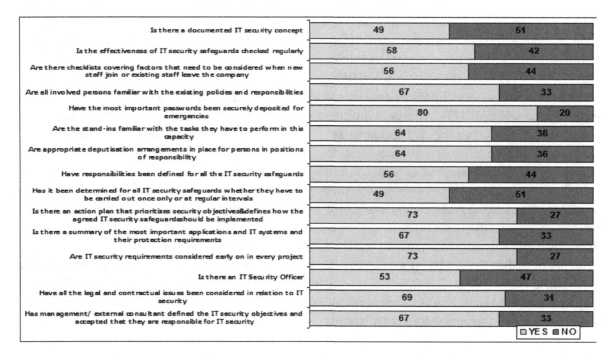

Figure 2. Response distribution per question for security of IT systems attribute

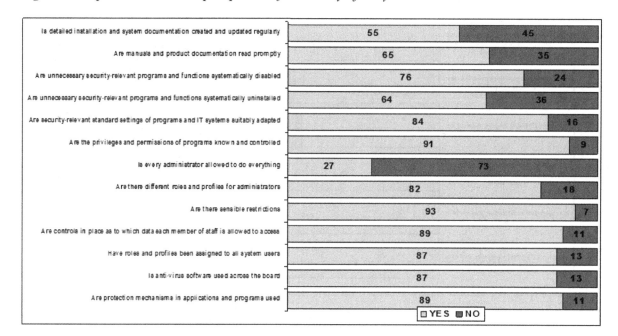

have documented their IT security policies and procedures. However, on the positive side, there are some other informal means of outlining security practices as 69% of the respondents answered positively on having their employees getting familiar with their duties concerning security practices and 73% claim to have an action plan in place for the implementation of IT security safeguards. It is alarming though that one in five companies with a dedicated IT department has not securely stored the most important passwords for emergencies. In addition, 44% does not employ check-in or checkout procedures for new and departing staff respectively.

Attribute C: Security of IT Systems is one of the high average attributes, and this is reflected in Figure 2. The vast majority of the companies deploys access control mechanisms, mostly in the form of role-based authorization, where file/applications/system privileges and permissions are assigned based on the role of the user in the overall system. In spite of having the appropriate safeguards for accessing resources by company

employees, still 13% of the interviewed enterprises do not take any precautions against malicious programs such as viruses by installing and using antivirus software.

Figure 3 illustrates the responses for attribute D: Compliance with Security Requirements, which has the second lowest average among all attributes. There is lack of promoting security best practices in the workplace: only 38% of the companies aim to promote security awareness among the employees and no more than 36% encourage training of the staff on security matters. The absence of systematic security education and training are without doubt major contributing factors in observing 51% of the organizations not deleting confidential information from their IT systems prior to maintenance. This oversight could cause leak of private information to unauthorized parties, and subsequently lead to legal actions against enterprises, not to mention financial losses.

Figure 4 depicts the response distribution for attribute E: Networking and Internet Connection Evaluation. Overall, companies are up-to-date

Figure 3. Response distribution per question for compliance with security requirements evaluation attribute

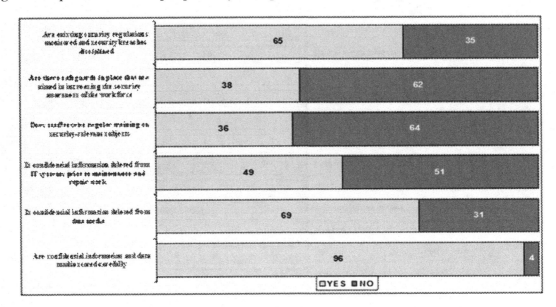

with security features for web browsers and email clients, as 89% securely configure them. In addition, 96% reports the presence of a firewall as one of their perimeter defenses and 89% monitors the activity regularly.

According to Figure 5, 84% of the companies perform regular installation of updates as part of the maintenance of their IT systems (attribute F). Interestingly, one in three companies has no appointed person that is dedicated to keep up to date

Figure 4. Response distribution per question for networking and internet connection evaluation attribute

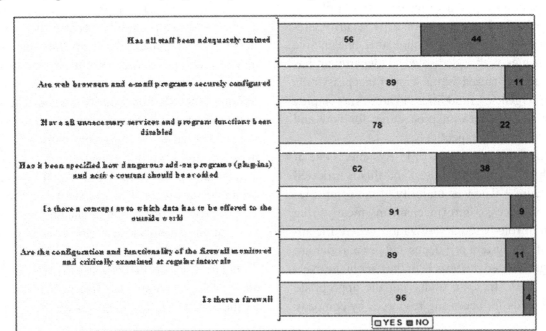

Figure 5. Response distribution per question for maintenance of IT systems attribute

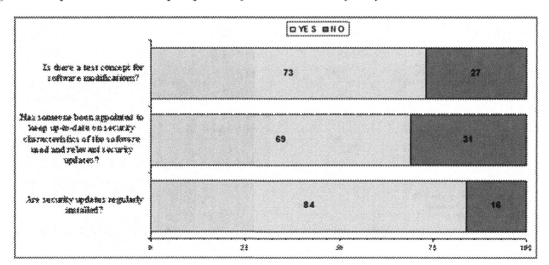

with information relating to updates or security characteristics. This implies that each employee is responsible for installing updates on their personal work computer, leaving the overall system vulnerable to attacks in case of missed updates.

Figure 6 illustrates the statistics for attribute G: Passwords and Encryption. It appears that company employees do not consider inside attackers as a realistic threat as 31% do not protect

their workstation on their absence with a password-protected screensaver. It is encouraging to observe that 84% change default and blank passwords. However, one in three companies do not provide guidelines for choosing passwords resistant to attacks and that constitutes a serious vulnerability where password weaknesses could be exploited to gain access to the business system.

Figure 6. Response distribution per question for passwords and encryption attribute

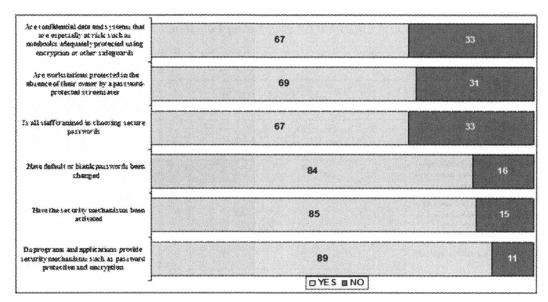

Figure 7. Response distribution per question for contingency planning attribute

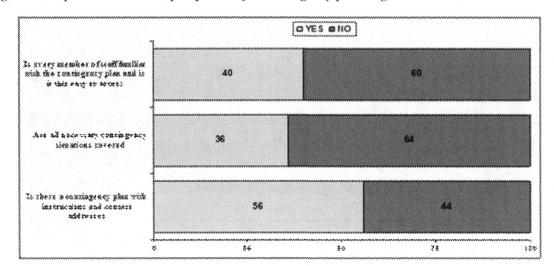

The response distribution for attribute H: Contingency Planning is given in Figure 7. Although a contingency plan exists in just over half of companies, the proportion of companies that have managed to cover all contingency situations or managed to familiarize all their staff with the plan is significantly lower.

Figure 8 illustrates the response distribution for attribute I: Data Backups. According to the responses, a backup strategy exists in almost all companies (96%) and rules have been laid down as to what needs to be backed up. However, the backup of laptops and non-networked systems is still an issue as only 45% perform such backup procedures.

Figure 9 illustrates the response distribution for attribute J: Infrastructure Security. Different aspects of infrastructure security are generally practiced by, on average, 4 in 5 companies. The weakest point appears to be unsupervised visits by non-company employees.

Figure 8. Response distribution per question for data backups attribute

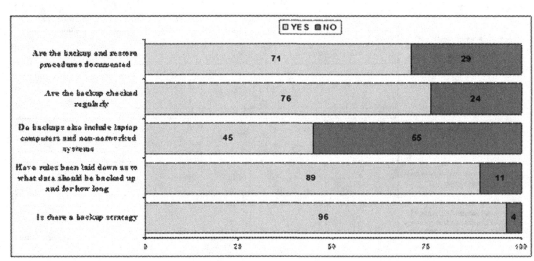

Figure 9. Response distribution per question for infrastructure security attribute

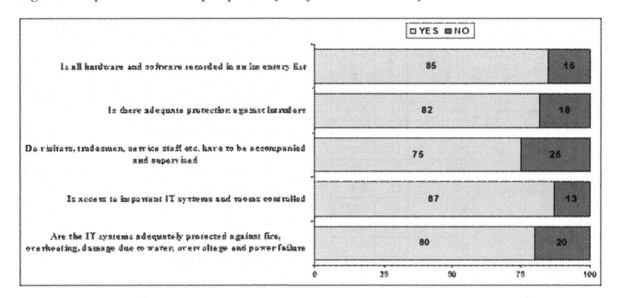

Analysis 2: Mean Scores of Attributes B-J Correlated With Company Size

This analysis focuses on examining the degree of relationship between an attribute's mean score and the company size.

The hypothesis is that the size of the company could affect the security practices in that company; the smaller the company size, the lower the security. Table 3 lists the mean scores that correspond to the company size.

The ANOVA (Analysis of Variance) test examines if there is a significant difference among the mean scores of each of the three company size categories. For example, the mean scores of IT Security Management are 0.46 for Small companies, 0.69 for Medium companies and 0.79 for Large companies. ANOVA will indicate if this difference is statistically important. If the significance is above 0.05, then there is no significant difference among the groups. In the specific case, the significance index is 0, meaning that the specific attribute is affected by the company size. As a matter of fact, all attributes exhibit a correlation with company size.

Analysis 2: Mean Scores of Attributes B-J Correlated With Company Technical Knowledge

This analysis focuses on examining the degree of relationship between the attribute's mean scores of technical Knowledge-Intensive companies and Non-Technical Knowledge-Intensive companies. Technical Knowledge-Intensive companies are the ones that are involved in Education, Government, Banking and Finance, Communication, Computer Technology/IT service. Non-Technical Knowledge-Intensive companies are the remaining. The hypothesis is that the technical knowledge of the company could affect the security practices in that company; the more knowledge a company has in terms of technical aspects, the higher the security. Table 4 lists the mean scores that correspond to the company's technical knowledge.

The ANOVA test has shown that there is significance difference for attributes IT Security Management, Security of IT Systems, Maintenance of IT Systems and Passwords/Encryption. That means, companies with technical knowledge put more importance on these attributes than companies with no technical knowledge. It is

Table 3. Mean scores for all attributes correlated with company size

ATTRIBUTE	COMPANY SIZE	Number	Mean
IT Security Management	2-49	22	.4576
	50-249	15	.6889
	250+	18	.7926
	Total	55	.6303
Security of IT Systems	2-49	22	.6786
	50-249	15	.7762
	250+	18	.8532
	Total	55	.7623
Compliance with Security Requirements	2-49	22	.5152
	50-249	15	.5556
	250+	18	.7130
	Total	55	.5909
Networking and Internet Connection	2-49	22	.6364
	50-249	15	.9143
	250+	18	.9127
	Total	55	.8026
Maintenance of IT Systems	2-49	22	.6212
	50-249	15	.7778
	250+	18	.8889
	Total	55	.7515
Passwords and Encryption	2-49	22	.5985
	50-249	15	.8333
	250+	18	.9259
	Total	55	.7697
Contingency Planning	2-49	22	.2727
	50-249	15	.4444
	250+	18	.6481
	Total	55	.4424
Data Backups	2-49	22	.6455
	50-249	15	.7867
	250+	18	.8667
	Total	55	.7564
Infrastructure Security	2-49	22	.6636
	50-249	15	.8933
	250+	18	.9444
	Total	55	.8182

interesting though that technical knowledge is not a factor when it comes to Network and Internet Connection, Data Backups, Compliance with Security Requirements, and Contingency Planning. The majority of the companies is aware of good practices when it comes to data backups. On the other hand, there is the lack of enforcing procedures that comply to with international standards and contingency planning. As a matter of fact, these two attributes received the lowest mean average scores.

ASSESSMENT OF ISO 27001 IN CYPRUS

ISO 27001 certification is still at an embryonic stage in Cyprus. In general, Cyprus businesses tend to standardize business procedures but not adhering to the ISO 27001 standardization process. This notion was created due to panCyprian business awards (e.g. excellence, innovation) and thus a free marketing exposure. Only two companies are accredited with the ISO 27001 certification, with a few being in the process of adhering the standards.

A Review on the ISO 27001 Adaptation Progress

Cyprus economy is still developing with most businesses assembling on the ground of a family-owned family-operated business model. They have grown today but hard coded in their values are the same family values. Thus, it is the matter of culture that many do not get accredited or even adhering the certification. This is the case with most small to medium enterprises in the island. A country comparison would be against Japan. Japan is the country with most accredited enterprises worldwide and this is correlative with their mentality of kaizen or continued improvement.

On the bright side, in the recent years, the Cyprus government, through a number of lectures

Table 4. Mean scores for all attributes correlated with technical knowledge

ATTRIBUTE	GROUP	Number	Mean
IT Security Management	Knowledge Intensive Companies	30	.7378
	Non Knowledge Intensive Companies	25	.5013
	Total	55	.6303
Security of IT Systems	Knowledge Intensive Companies	30	.8238
	Non Knowledge Intensive Companies	25	.6886
	Total	55	.7623
Compliance with Security Requirements	Knowledge Intensive Companies	30	.6167
	Non Knowledge Intensive Companies	25	.5600
	Total	55	.5909
Networking and Internet Connection	Knowledge Intensive Companies	30	.8333
	Non Knowledge Intensive Companies	25	.7657
	Total	55	.8026
Maintenance of IT systems	Knowledge Intensive Companies	30	.8333
	Non Knowledge Intensive Companies	25	.6533
	Total	55	.7515
Passwords and Encryption	Knowledge Intensive Companies	30	.8778
	Non Knowledge Intensive Companies	25	.6400
	Total	55	.7697
Contingency Planning	Knowledge Intensive Companies	30	.5000
	Non Knowledge Intensive Companies	25	.3733
	Total	55	.4424
Data Backups	Knowledge Intensive Companies	30	.8000
	Non Knowledge Intensive Companies	25	.7040
	Total	55	.7564
Infrastructure Security	Knowledge Intensive Companies	30	.8533
	Non Knowledge Intensive Companies	25	.7760
	Total	55	.8182

and seminars mainly delivered by the Cyprus Organization for Standardization (CYS) office, tries to promote the ISO 27001 and motivate Cypriot companies to develop and implement the information security management system. The CYS was formed by the government in 2002 to commence on the consistency actions that were under the jurisdictions of the Ministry of Commerce, Industry and Tourism. CYS is a self-directed body registered under classified law, with the Government being the solitary investor.

One of the supreme tasks of this organization is to promote the positive aspects of standardization including (but not limited to) 9000 and 27001.

In addition, following European initiatives, the Cyprus government has also formed two semi-government bodies in order to facilitate laws and jurisdictions that information should be kept confidential, intact and available. The two bodies responsible for regulating and enforcing laws are the "Office of the commissioner for personal data protection" and the "Commissioner and the

Office of the Commissioner of Electronic Communications and Postal Regulation". These two semi-government bodies issue laws that govern the assurance of quality of information.

Adopting the ISO 27001 standard is a fairly complex practice. At first, the company reports the events used for assembling its products (or delivering their services) - including those followed when things go incorrect - and evaluate them with ISO 27001 minimum requirements. An internal or external consulting group conducts the audit of this operation. Domestic teams charge less (and may also have less ISO familiarity) than outside teams (external ISO consultants can cost more than €700 a day, something that could be financially unaffordable by SME). If it is desired, the quality assurance consultants regulate policies and actions that do not meet principles, and instruct employees in keeping records of the alterations. Then the company hosts a visit from a third-party examiner (currently only the CYS has the authority to certify) that assesses whether or not the firm in fact follows the described measures. All of the actions mentioned above take from a year to eighteen months to complete. If the audit is progressing in a satisfactory manner, the auditor certifies the organization and registers the firm. Otherwise, the firm must take appropriate corrective actions, and go through a new inspection. As of today, only two organizations are registered as ISO 27001 compliant in Cyprus.

The reasons for seeking ISO 27001 in the Cyprus market are several and may vary between companies and sectors. For instance, law firms need to address strict confidentiality data exchange with other interested parties in contrast with shipping companies that need to address data organization more efficiently. Logistics is core business function and is better aligned with the implementation of standard procedures. Few start-up companies are advised in how to implement a standardization process but not ISO 27001 per se. Instead they are advised on how to proceed and follow custom made or part of the ISO 27001.

Start up companies in Cyprus have the tendency to standardize business procedures but in the process of implementing it, they either do not have the resources (human force or financial) in order to proceed or realize that such "deviation" from their perspective business function is far beyond their possibilities.

Standardization is perceived incorrectly by many small businesses. Many find it a panacea to all business aspects and others "try" it in order to modernize their companies. Once they realize the semantics and implications of the actual standard implementation, they decide that a standardization procedure is not appropriate and it does not meet their expectations. Indeed in many cases, due to the undersized market dynamics of the Cyprus economy, ISO 27001 is not appropriate. On the other hand, medium to large enterprises seem to fit more appropriately into the standardization procedures. Potential adopters have admitted that external client pressure is put on them in order to make sure their clients collaborate with suitable firms. Foreign businesses when expanding their reach in the Cyprus market, feel more secure that their investments are protected when a local firm is ISO certified. Many offshore companies even request that local financial institutions are certified since it is a requirement from the parent company in order to substantiate worldwide company standards. Recently, it has been observed that large (more than 60 employees) law firms are also interested in ISO 27001. Handling registration procedures for international companies and conducting governmental legal advice entails handling data with high levels of confidentiality, integrity and availability.

It is important to note that for the banking sector in the island, the situation is a little different. The island's banks are under the law of the Central Bank of Cyprus. They are responsible for dictating the laws that govern the banks proper functioning covering a wide spectrum of operations, ranging from financial concerns to information security matters. Regarding the information security, the directive from the Central Bank is a mixture of ISO 27001 guidelines, best security practices, and other security standards. Although the banking sector needs to follow the directives and law of the Central Bank, they most certainly adhere the ISO 27001. However, they are not certified for the ISO 27001 since the law does not oblige them to obtain such certification.

Benefits and Obstacles of ISO 27001 Implementation in the Cypriot Market

In general, adopted ISO or even adherence is a comeback to key customers' requests, or the requirement of the potential customers and the anticipation that the customers would demand the certification soon. The above provides the practical evidence that satisfaction of external demands and pressure from the market are the main drives initiating an enterprise pledge towards ISO. Another reason for seeking certification is the belief that this will serve as a competitive advantage over competitors. Furthermore, there is a claim that ISO certification would be implemented in order to improve the internal organization and efficiency and to encourage the quality management systems.

Although one may claim that ISO 27001 is unsuitable for the Cyprus marketplace due to its size and its characteristics, there are a lot of benefits to be gained from the ISO certification development. Nevertheless, if one understands the elasticity of the standard and he\she is talented to develop a simple and effectual system with minimal amount of manuscript work, then the ISO 27001 system could be confirmed successful by many organizations. The validation of the ISO adoption is in general based on the remuneration that will ensue greater competence, a first-class marketing tool, customer satisfaction, less (if any) supplier audits required and higher customer and staff morale.

Benefits perceived from the deployment of the ISO 27001 standard cannot be quantified and measured in financial terms, and this is one of the main reasons that delayed its service in Cyprus. However, those companies that obtained certification and those who attempt to follow the standard's guidelines have observed several benefits from the ISO 27001 implementation. One of them is reduced documentation. Adhering ISO certification will eventually result in a sort of documentation reduction, but in the meantime documentation prepared in order to adhere is enormous. In particular, law firms have not featured such documentation reduction but have experienced a much more organized information structure. Some other semi adopters of ISO 27001 certification in Cyprus have found that their documentation is much improved at significant cost.

Another benefit is improved customer satisfaction. An example is offshore companies. These companies maintain branches in Cyprus but are obliged by their parent companies to follow international acceptable standards as compared to local shipping companies. Offshore companies main clientele is from around the world. Since ISO 27001 is better known in the rest of the world, a better customer satisfaction is offered. Recent post audit meetings showed that, overall, firms from certain sectors believe they have made significant improvement to key areas of their business as a result of adhering ISO 27001 standards. Firm's clients have also experienced significant enhancement to the products and services supplied to them by these firms.

Despite the benefits, there is a low adaptation in Cyprus market. Some of the reasons are the ones below:

- **Strive for Excellence:** In Cyprus economy (as in Cyprus society), there is often not a tendency to procrastinate the enforcement of best practices. We have recently noticed that after the induction of Cyprus in the European Union, large construction companies offered "ISO 9000 service" in order to compete with European tenders in the field. As time goes by, entrance in the EU is affiliating Cyprus economy with standardization protocols, most popular being the ISO 9000 on quality management.

- **Law:** Under the Cyprus judicial system, there is no law that prohibits businesses processes nonconforming to standards, thus the lack of compliance with ISO 27001 is not penalized by Cyprus law. Psychologically, if a firm were not forced to comply with the law, it could perceptively interpret security and data protection in any way that would better serve its profit maximization.
- **Cost:** It is proven that the cost is rather high for implementing ISO 27001, to a point that small business cannot match it with their limited budget. Since these are harsh financial times, especially with the current unemployment rate in Cyprus, organizations focus on staying in business instead of complying with certifications, or achieving quality services.
- **Lengthy Process:** Empirically, the process from initiation to final certification is approximately 18 to 24 months. In the meantime many setbacks can occur, constituting the process as unfavorable for implementation or too sophisticated.
- **Awareness:** Most companies do not realize the benefits gained from the adaptation of ISO 27001. ISO standards were introduced after the full induction of Cyprus in the EU. Before that, awareness was really nonexistent.
- **Lack of Top Management Support:** Reviewing audits and counseling sessions have revealed lack of top administration support and indulgencing of ISO requirements as core obstacles. A commitment of the company CEO to ISO 27001 assists a more direct and faster allocation of resources to the certification process. With the influence from top management, more dedi-

cated employees are expected, enabling a better result of the ISO implementation. Many Cyprus SMEs are not exposed to EU economies and/or dynamics prevailing for quality standards. In the middle of an economic crisis, top management reviews its profit margin and not considering quality services/products.

- **Training Difficulties:** It was also noted a complexity in training of personnel. A change of attitude and documentation of scheme appeared to be the main problem during preparation of registration. It is also found that complications in altering the state of mind of people are positively correlated with time needed for preparation of registration. Some are very complicating terms/procedures and people are not comfortable in acquire new skills or training.

RECOMMENDATIONS FOR ISO 27001 ADOPTION IN CYPRUS

We recognize that organizations in Cyprus, mostly those of a smaller and medium size, are less likely to have an in house IT department, even less likely to have internal security proficiency. This section aims to assist organizations decide what approach they should take when it comes to the security of the information they have and protect it against unlawful or unauthorized use or disclosure, and accidental loss, destruction or damage. It is found that even though ISO 27001 fits into all business magnitudes, it is not an economical option in prospect of financial or human resources for a small to medium business in Cyprus.

One of the primary things any organization, regardless of size, will require to do is to review what private information they control, whether they truly process the information, or whether this is carried out by someone acting on their behalf and categorize how valuable, sensitive or confidential is the information and choose what damage or distress could be caused to clients if there was a security breach. This will help assess what security measures the business needs to have in place. A designated employee must have the daily duty for security measures, whether this is presenting to senior management what actions should be adopted, writing procedures for staff to follow, arranging training for personnel, checking whether they are following actions and that the measures work. At what extend security is desirable, will depend on the business own circumstances and good will. This will include securing the personal information it has and how is used, the premises, computer systems, how many staff are employed and what access they have to information and so on.

Since SMEs are indeed operated presumably by their owners, it is unrealistic to expect from a single person already preoccupied with various day-to-day activities, management, strategic planning and implementation to attend information security matters. In these cases, the SMEs could proceed with an emphasis on the security aspects shown below:

- **Organizational Measures:** Decide what organizational changes need to be done.
  - Has a risk appraisal been approved that takes account of what it is you need to protect, the type of security problems that could occur, the effectiveness of your current security measures?
  - Are there periodic checks done of your security arrangements to make sure that they are still appropriate and up to date?
- **Human Resources:** Training and awareness. We have also observed that security incidents show a high share of staff related issues so this is a main area to consider by making reasonable steps to ensure the dependability of employees that have access to personal information.

  - Are the employees trained in their responsibilities about the personal information being processed? Is it clear that information is confidential and the restrictions on how this should be used?
  - Are the employees aware into making disclosures of information into third parties? Do they know the proper procedures to use to categorize callers? Are they warned about possible 'phishing' scams?
- **Physical Security:** A lot of prominence is put on technological security measures to protect automated information. However, many security confrontations relate to the theft of laptops or abandoning paper based material.
  - How protected is your property? Are there high-quality doors and secure locks?
  - Do you lock up paper based personal information at night?
  - Do you control access to your premises?
  - Do you dispose paper waste containing personal information securely (i.e. shredding)?

Although large enterprises are not the majority in Cyprus economy, implementing or even adhering ISO 27001 is most appropriate due to pressure from international associates, acceptance into European competitions and minimizing local competition. A large enterprise would unavoidably operate an in-house IT department, thus a form of security of information is expected from large organizations (if anything to presume prestige and customer satisfaction). If employees assume no security expertise, then large enterprises can focus their research and development budget to adhere ISO 27001. Thus, the recommendations are as follows:

- **Plow a Security Culture:** A culture of security must be promoted, a focus on security in the development of information systems and networks among the adoption of new ways of believing and performing. Each employee is an important actor for guaranteeing security. Information technology staff should be aware of the applicable security risks and preventive measures, assume responsibility and take steps to boost the security of information systems.

- **Security Blueprint and Execution:** Information architects should fit in security as a vital element of information systems. Systems, networks, and policies need to be properly designed, implemented and harmonized to optimize security. A major focal point of this attempt is the design and adoption of appropriate fortification and solutions to avoid or limit potential harm from identified threats and vulnerabilities. Both procedural and non-procedural defenses and solutions are required and should be proportionate to the value of the information on the organization's systems. Security should be a fundamental element of all products, services, systems and networks, and an integral part of system design and architecture.

- **Security Administration:** Information security officers should assume a complete approach to security management. Security management should be based on risk assessment and should be dynamic, surrounding all levels of participants' actions and all aspects of their operations. It should include forward-looking responses to emerging threats and address prevention, detection and response to incidents, systems recovery, ongoing continuation, review and audit.

- **Risk Assessment:** Large enterprises should conduct risk assessments in order to identify threats and vulnerabilities and ought to be sufficiently broad-based to cover internal and external factors, such as technology, physical and human factors, policies and third-party services with security implications. Risk assessment will allow resolving any of the acceptable level of risk and assisting the selection of appropriate controls to manage the risk of potential harm to information systems and networks in light of the nature and importance of the information to be protected.

Security Governance in a small and medium size enterprise

Legislative regulations on sensitive information protection, security breaches, and information related crimes have increased awareness on organizational information assets. In certain cases, particularly in large organizations, the increased awareness has resulted to a structured governance approach regarding information management, protecting the organization's most critical assets—its information and the systems that handle it. Small and Medium size Enterprises lag behind in the establishment of security governance. In this section, we provide a framework for setting security governance in SMEs.

In this respect, we define and attempt to answer a set of questions:

- How is security governance defined for SMEs?
- Is it equally important to have security governance for SMEs?
- Who is responsible for the security governance within a SME?
- How can we effectively assess security governance in a SME?
- What framework could we propose for security governance within a SME?

Before the omnipresence of the Web, security governance had focused on protecting the IT systems rather than on the information stored and processed by the systems. However, this focus is too narrow and marginalizes security, as a technical concern whereas to address security challenges a more holistic approach must be sought. Information security is not only a technical issue, but also a business and governance challenge that involves adequate risk management, reporting and accountability. Effective security requires the active involvement of executives to assess emerging threats and the organization's response to them.

We argue that security governance is critical for SMEs. Information security protects information assets against the risk of loss, operational discontinuity, misuse, unauthorized disclosure, inaccessibility and damage. It also protects against the ever-increasing potential for civil or legal liability that enterprises may face as a result of information inaccuracy and loss, or the absence of due care in its protection. More than larger organizations, SMEs cannot absorb failures in security governance.

Governance may be defined as the set of responsibilities and practices exercised by the top management with the aim of providing strategic direction, ensuring that objectives are achieved, risks are managed appropriately and responsible use of the enterprise's resources. In this respect, information security governance considers as an enterprise's resource the enterprise security program. To retain an effective security governance scheme, the top management must have a clear set of guidelines to the following questions:

- What are the fundamental outcomes of information security governance?
- What information assets are to be included in the security program?
- What is the value of the security program or (viewing it from another perspective) how much should be invested?

- How the whole process should be integrated?

The essential outcomes of information security governance are:

1. Alignment between business and security strategy and definition of security performance metrics.
2. Risk mitigation, monitoring and management to maintain impact upon information resources within acceptable levels.
3. Effective informational resources management.
4. Recalculation of security performance metrics
5. Calculation of value delivery and optimization of information security investments and periodic recalibration starting from outcome 1.

The information assets to be included in the security program include information and knowledge resources within the enterprise. Data are the raw materials of information. Information can be defined as data with meaning, relevance and purpose. Combining information in ways that convey some utility creates knowledge. Information and the knowledge security must be addressed holistically within each organization level and not be marginalized as a technical issue.

The issue of investment on security governance is tightly coupled with the perceived value generated by proper security governance schemes, including:

1. Increased productivity and reduced transactional costs by lowering information security-related risks to definable and acceptable levels.
2. Protection from the increasing potential for liabilities imposed by national and EU legislation.

3. Optimized allocation of limited security resources.
4. Efficient and effective risk management.
5. Proper decision making, that is, decision making not based on faulty information
6. Accountability for safeguarding information.
7. An increase in share value for enterprises that practice good governance due to increased trust and reputation and reduced operational costs.

Security programs are usually fragmented over various business processes that render it difficult to integrate them. For this, it is critical to identify roles and responsibilities related to security governance to carefully selected top executives who should decide:

In this regard, governing boards and executive management should review:

1. The investment and return on investment.
2. The potential for technologies to restructure business practices.
3. The enterprise dependency on ICT.
4. The dependence of the enterprise beyond its direct control (i.e. cloud computing).
5. Demands on sharing information with partners, suppliers and customers.
6. Impact on reputation and enterprise value resulting from information security failures.
7. Costs from failures to bypass importance of security.

Involving top management in IT security governance is a process that needs to address multiple issues, including the intended scope of involvement (from the CEO to the managers of the business units), the development of governance structures (committees, roles and coordinators)

Table 5. IT security governance measures need to be implemented to optimize the business values and performance

IT Security Decision	Role of the Decision Maker	Consequences of Abdicating the Decision
How much should the IT Security Budget be?	Define the strategic role that IT security is envisioned to play in the organization	The company fails to reach the set IT security level, despite its spending
	Determine the level of funding available to achieve this objective	
Which business processes should receive the IT security budget?	Prioritize the IT supported business processes and select those that will receive IT security funds	A lack of focus overwhelms the IT unit with applying security measures that have little companywide value or can't be implemented well simultaneously
Which IT security capabilities need to be assigned companywide?	Decide which IT security should be supported centrally	Excessive technical and process standardization limit the flexibility of business units, or frequent exceptions to the standards increase costs and limit business synergies
	Decide which IT security should be supported at a business level	
How are the IT security services to be implemented?	Decide which IT security features are needed on the basis of their costs and benefits	The company may pay for IT security options that, given its priorities, aren't worth their costs
What security risks will be accepted?	Trade-offs between security and flexibility/convenience	An overemphasis on security may inconvenience customers, employees and suppliers; an underestimation may make data vulnerable
Who is accountable for each IT security initiative?	Assign responsibilities to business decision makers	The business values of systems is not fulfilled

and the instruments of governance (policies, procedures etc). Table 5 outlines the main IT security governance questions to optimize the business value and performance of IT security function.

CONCLUSION

To the best of the authors' knowledge, this is the first comprehensive paper that investigates the deployment of ISO 27001 in Cyprus. The survey revealed a number of interesting realities regarding the deployment of security services, which are compliant to ISO 27001, in Cypriot enterprises. In general, the presence of an IT department has a significant impact on the approach a company has towards security practices. Even though security breaches happen in all companies, their detection is higher amongst companies that have an IT department. However, it was observed that there was a hesitation to report incidents of electronic sabotage, denial of service, theft of proprietary information, fraud, and any form of embezzlement. For example, the base size for the detection of fraud question was a mere 6, meaning that only 4% of the companies detected any incidents. The non-disclosure of security violations is a practice followed by many companies, as they are concerned for the financial implications and the impact on their credibility if such incidents become public knowledge.

Companies with a dedicated IT department tend to have significantly more security procedures in place. Still, even in these companies there are unaddressed security issues and they are far from being regarded as implementing best security practices. It is indicative that some companies still lack antivirus software, firewalls and proper password management. Furthermore, many of them claim to have certain protocols in place (e.g. disaster recovery plan), but in most cases, these have never been tested or updated. Based on the survey results, it is evident that a very limited number of companies could obtain an ISO 27001

certification. As a matter of fact, only a handful companies in Cyprus are ISO 27001 compliant. IT security and its proper management are essential for any organization either in the public or private sector.

Cyprus economy is relatively sheltered from international competition, for the time being. Cyprus has an unusually high proportion of small companies, which are often family-run, and antagonism is not vigorous. This means that the need for the adoption to ISO standards is perceived as not vital. Though, with the entry of Cyprus into the EU, the interest in the implementation of ISO standards by many Cypriot companies is increasing. ISO 27001 certification may soon prove to be not only a competitive advantage, but also a requirement. Cypriot companies, in order to survive in the increasingly competitive market, must be able to produce competitive products both in price and in quality. Especially, with the entrance in the European Community, Cypriot companies will remain unprotected against the well-organized and quality-striving European competitors. In addition, ISO 27001 itself is a ticket to the European market, as the European Community strongly advocates the implementation of ISO standards. With the European Community starting to eliminate internal trade barriers, the Europeans recognized the need to adopt common standards and regulations that will harmonize the standardization process and create a common market. ISO 27001 is expected to play an important role in this harmonization.

We consider the role of the government as instrumental in the successful deployment of security standards in Cypriot enterprises. The Cyprus government should promote awareness of the need for security of information systems and force safeguards to enhance security. Awareness of the risks and available safeguards is the first line of defense for the security of information systems and networks. First and most, a law must exist in order to make businesses plan ahead for information security and data protection. Also some incentives could be given to businesses that comply with it in the form of tax reduction or excellence awards. The entire workforce should respect the legitimate interests of others. Given the pervasiveness of information systems and networks in our society, the government need to recognize that businesses actions or lack therefore may harm the Cyprus economy and insist on promoting business ethical secure code of conduct. Ethical conduct is therefore crucial and participants should strive to develop and adopt best practices and to promote conduct that recognizes security needs and respects the legitimate interests of others.

REFERENCES

Federal Office for Information Security (BSI). (2007). *IT security guidelines*. Retrieved August 12, 2011, from https://www.bsi.bund.de

International Standards Organization (ISO). (2005). *ISO/IEC 27001:2005 Information technology-security techniques- Information security management systems-Requirements*. Retrieved August 12, 2011, from www.iso.org

ISACA. (2009). An introduction to the business model for information security. Retrieved August 12, 2011, from www.isaca.org

ISO 17799 News. (2006). *ISO27000 newsletter, 14*. Retrieved August 12, 2011 from http://www.molemag.net/16.htm

ISO 27001 Security. (2011). *ISO27k FAQ quick links*. Retrieved August 12, 2011 from http://www.iso27001security.com/html/faq.html

Kent, A. (2008). A business model for information security. *Information Systems Control Journal, 3*.

Kosutic, D. (2010). *Problems with defining the scope in ISO 27001*. Retrieved August 12, 2011, from http://blog.iso27001standard.com/2010/06/29/problems-with-defining-the-scope-in-iso-27001/

Lipovatz, D., Stenos, F., & Vaka, A. (1999). Implementation of ISO 9000 quality systems in Greek enterprises. *International Journal of Quality & Reliability Management, 16*(6), 534–551.

Stallings, W. (2010). *Network security essentials applications and standards* (4th ed.). Prentice Hall.

Street, P. A., & Fernie, J. M. (1993). Costs, drawbacks and benefits : BS 5750. *Training for Quality, 1*(1), 21–24.

Tsiotras, G., & Gotzamani, K. (1996). ISO 9000 as an entry key to TQM: The case of the Greek industry. *International Journal of Quality & Reliability Management, 13*(14), 64–76.

ADDITIONAL READING

Anderson, K. (2008). A business model for information security. *Information Systems Control Journal, 3*. Retrieved August 12, 2011, from http://www.isaca.org/Journal/Past-Issues/2008/Volume-3/Documents/jpdf0803-a-business-model.pdf

Bagchi, K., & Udo, G. (2003). An analysis of the growth of computer and internet security breaches. *Communications of the AIS, 12*, 684–700.

Baskerville, R. (1993). Information systems security design methods: Implications for information systems development. *ACM Computing Surveys, 25*(4), 375–414.

Boehmer, W. (2008). Appraisal of the effectiveness and efficiency of an information security management system based on ISO 27001. *Proceedings of Second International Conference on Emerging Security Information, Systems, and Technologies*, Cao Esterel, France, (pp. 224-231).

Boehmer, W. (2009). Cost-benefit trade-off analysis of an ISMS based on ISO 27001. *Proceedings of 2009 International Conference on Availability, Reliability and Security*, Fukuoka, Japan, (pp. 392-399).

Broderick, J. S. (2006). ISMS, security standards and security regulations. *Information Security Technical Report, 11*(1), 26-31. ISSN 1363-4127

Calder, A. (2006). *Information security based on ISO 27001/ISO 17799: A management guide* (1st ed.). Van Haren Publishing.

Chew, E., Swanson, M., Stine, K., Bartol, N., Brown, A., & Robinson, W. (2008). *Performance measurement guide for information security. NIST Special Publication 800-55 Revision 1*. U.S. Department of Commerce.

Dhillon, G., & Backhouse, J. (2000). Information system security management in the new millennium. *Communications of the ACM, 43*(7), 125–128.

Dimopoulos, V., Furnell, S., Jennex, M., & Kritharas, I. (2004). Approaches to IT security in small and medium enterprises. *Proceedings of 2nd Australian Information Security Management Conference, Securing the Future*, Perth, Western Australia, (pp.73-82).

Fenz, S., Pruckner, T., & Manutscheri, A. (2009). *Ontological mapping of information security best-practice guidelines. Lecture Notes in Business Information Processing* (*Vol. 21*, pp. 49–60). Berlin, Germany: Springer.

Fomin, V., de Vries, H. J., & Barlette, Y. (2008). ISO/IEC 27001: Exploring the reasons for low adoption. *Proceedings of Third European Conference on Management of Technology* (EUROMOT 2008), Nice, France.

Freeman, E. H. (2007). Holistic information security: ISO 27001 and due care. *Information Systems Security, 15*(5), 291–294.

Gollman, D. (2011). *Computer security* (3rd ed.). Wiley.

International Standards Organization (ISO). (2005). ISO/IEC 27002:2005 Information technology-Security techniques- Code of practise for information security management. Retrieved August 12, 2011, from www.iso.org

Kissel, R., Stine, K., Scholl, M., Rossman, H., Fahlsing, J., & Gulick, J. (2008). *Security considerations in the system development life cycle. NIST Special Publication 800-64 Revision 2*. U.S. Department of Commerce.

Lee, M. C., & Chang, T. (2007). Applying ISO 17799:2005 in information security management. *International Journal of Services and Standards, 3*(3), 352–373.

Liang, H., & Xue, Y. (2009). Avoidance of information technology threats: A theoretical perspective. *Management Information Systems Quarterly, 33*(1), 71–90.

Loch, K. D., Carr, H. H., & Warkentin, M. E. (1992). Threats to information systems: Today's reality, yesterday's understanding. *Management Information Systems Quarterly, 16*(2), 173–186.

Stallings, W. (2007). Standards for information security management. *The Internet Protocol Journal, 10*(4), 10–22.

Sterne, D. (1991). On the buzzword security policy. *Proceedings of the 1991 IEEE Symposium on Security and Privacy*, Oakland, California, (pp. 219-230).

Tawileh, A., Hilton, J., & McIntosh, S. (2008). Information security status in organisations 2008. *Proceedings of Information Security Solutions Europe 2008 Conference*, Madrid, Spain, (pp. 20-29).

Verendel, V. (2009). Quantified security is a weak hypothesis: A critical survey of results and assumptions. *Proceedings of the 2009 ACM Workshop on New Security Paradigms Workshop* (NSPW09), Oxford, United Kingdom, (pp. 37-50).

KEY WORDS AND DEFINITIONS

Information Security Governance: It focuses on information security systems and their performance and risk management.

ISO: The International Organization for Standardization (ISO) is the international body that issues international standards.

ISO 27001 Standard: It belongs to the ISO 27000 family of security standards. It is a standard that specifies the requirements for the establishment, implementation, monitoring and maintenance of an information management system targeting the security aspects of an enterprise. It defines a set of requirements that must be met to obtain formal certification and allows the organization to select security practices, as listed in ISO 27002, that are tailored to its security needs.

ISO 27002 Standard: It belongs to the ISO 27000 family of security standards. It is a detailed list of best-practice information security control measures that could be integrated in an organization's information security management architecture. The control measures cover the entire spectrum of security objectives such as organizational security policies, organizational security infrastructure, asset classification/control, physical/environmental security, personnel security, communications management, access control, systems development, business continuity planning and compliance.

Standard Compliance Certification: Standard formal certification is awarded by independent third party certification bodies that conduct certification audits to check if the enterprise meets the standard's requirements.

Security Standard: It is a standard that enables an organization to practice proper security techniques.

SME: Small and medium enterprises.

Chapter 7
An Information Governance Model for Information Security Management

Matthew Nicho
University of Dubai, UAE

ABSTRACT

The purpose of this paper is to propose an IS security governance model to enhance the security of information systems in an organisation by viewing security from a holistic perspective of encompassing information security, information assurance, audit, governance, and compliance. This is achieved through the strategic integration of appropriate frameworks, models, and concepts in information governance, IS service management, and information security. This involves analysing the relevant frameworks, models, and concepts used in the above domains, extracting the best practices for implementing them from the literature and mapping these into an integrated standard. The frameworks identified are Control Objectives for Information and related Technology (COBIT), Information Technology Infrastructure Library (ITIL), ISO 27002, Risk IT, and Payment Card Industry Data Security Standard (PCI DSS). While it is evident that each of these five frameworks serve different purpose of information systems, such as information auditing and governance, facilitating the delivery of high-quality IT services, providing a model managing an Information Security Management System, providing a risk focus, and protection of cardholder data, all of these frameworks have the common objective to secure the IS assets in an organisation. Hence, extraction of the best practices in each of these framework can provide effective security of organisational IS assets rather than adequate security.

DOI: 10.4018/978-1-4666-2083-4.ch007

INTRODUCTION

IS security has become a critical concern facing modern organisations today considering the fact that organisations are fully dependent on IT for survival. This is compounded by the fact that more confidential information is stored in remote servers on the Internet. During the first half of 2011, there had been a number of high profile and persistent IS security breaches in organisations namely Sony, the data-security firm RSA, Lockheed Martin, the email wholesaler Epsilon, the Fox broadcast network, NASA, PBS, the European Space Agency, the FBI, the British and French treasuries, the banking and insurance giant Citigroup, along with dozens of other companies and government agencies (Liebowitz, 2011).An analysis of these reveal that if a few non-technical procedures were followed in most of these breaches (RSA, Sony and Epsilon see Exhibit 1) these breaches could have been avoided. The data breach at RSA, Sony

and Epsilon occurred due to spear phishing rather than highly sophisticated hacking. According to a key manager at RSA technological advances in IS security and the use of IS security controls/frameworks, and compliance on IS security regulations could have prevented the IS security breaches to a great extent. Despite these improvements over the years, there has been no reduction in the rate of attacks on information systems. According to the Identity Theft Resource Center (ITRC, 2011), hacking accounted for the largest number of breaches in the first quarter of 2011 as almost 37% of breaches were due to malicious attacks on computer systems which is more than double the amount of targeted attacks (17.1%) reflected in the 2010 ITRC Breach List. This necessitates a review of IS security controls available and employed, analyse the gaps in the IS security frameworks to propose a holistic perspective of information security governance. The high profile breaches during the first half of 2011 (see Exhibit

Exhibit 1. A case of a provider of security becoming a victim

RSA started in 1982 is a division of EMC Corp that provides security, risk, and compliance solutions for businesses and according to the company, it is chosen by more than 90% of Fortune 500 companies for managing there is security. In fact, RSA is the inventor of the public key cryptographic algorithm that enable secure transparent exchange of encrypted communications between users and enterprises on the Internet. They provide technology and business solution for managing IS security, provide strong two-way authentication, access control, data loss prevention solutions. They also provide encryption, tokenization and GRC solutions, along with a host of other security solutions.

On March 17th 2011 the company disclosed to the Securities and Exchange Commission that a data breach has occurred. Unlike other data breaches, no customer data like email addresses, usernames, credit card numbers, date of birth or social security numbers were stolen. The attackers used a common form of phishing called spear phishing. In this type of attack, the attacker sent two different phishing emails over a two-day period. The two emails were sent to two small groups of lower level employees with the email subject "2011 Recruitment Plan."The email went to the junk folder but one employee retrieved it from their Junk mail folder, and open the attached excel file. It was a spreadsheet titled "2011 Recruitment plan.xls. The spreadsheet contained a zero-day exploit that installs a backdoor through an Adobe Flash vulnerability (CVE-2011-0609). (Adobe has immediately released a patch for the zero-day, so it can no longer be used to inject malware onto patched machines).

The attacker then proceeded to install a remote administration tool that allows the attacker to control the machine. The tool used for this was a variant of Poison Ivy set in reverse-connect mode that makes it more difficult to detect. In this reverse connect mode the victim machine reaches out and connect to the command and control rather than the other way around where the attacker machine connect to the victim machine. Once this was set up,the attacker started digital shoulder surfing to establish the employee's role and their level of access. In this mode, the attacker is in a position to escalate the user privilege; they could discover valuable data sources and extract them to external rouge servers. In this case sensitive information from more than 40 million employees may have been compromised. The estimated cost to the company by various sources is $ 66 million in direct and attributable costs.

Spear phishing is a type of attack using the Advanced Persistent Threats (APT), where the attacks are targeted at individual employees rather than the organisational security defenses. One simple flaw or overlook of the employee is all needed for en entry inside these defenses. When it comes to APTs it is not about how safe, secure and good the company is, but that a totally new approach for entering the organization is selected where the attacker don't bother to hack the organization and its infrastructure, rather focus on hacking the employees.

(Source: Adapted from the 'Anatomy of an Attack' by Uri Rivner from the website http://blogs.rsa.com/rivner/anatomy-of-an-attack/*)*

1) necessitate the need for information systems security to diverge from technical information security focus to broader information technology governance incorporating security governance.

IT governance has been approached and defined from different perspectives. It had been perceived and defined as a concept, set of functions, responsibilities, processes, a system of elements, a control structure, and an area of decision making. It is such a hot and debated topic that no one seems to be sure exactly what it is or how to explain it (Broadbent, 2003). A decision making and control oriented definition of IT governance states that "IT governance is about assigning decision rights and creating an accountability framework that encourages desirable behaviour in the use of IT" (ibid, p. 1), and how those persons entrusted with governance of an entity will consider IT in their supervision, monitoring, control and direction of the entity (ITGI, 2005). IT governance from a functional and responsibility perspective "refers to the patterns of authority for key IT activities in business firms, including IT infrastructure, IT use, and project management" (Sambamurthy & Zmud, 1999, p. 261). The process nature of IT governance were indirectly implied by Parkinson and Baker (2005, p. 17) by stating that "governance has two equally important aspects – doing the right thing (driving performance) and doing things the right way (ensuring conformance)". A result oriented definition of IT governance explains it as "assessing the impact and nature of information systems, technology and communication; the development of the IS/IT skills bases; the consideration of business, legal and other IS/IT related issues" (Kakabadse & Kakabadse, 2001, p. 9).

While IT governance "refers to the patterns of authority for key IT activities in business firms, including IT infrastructure, IT use, and project management" (Sambamurthy & Zmud, 1999), "IT control frameworks are any set of processes, procedures and policies that enable an organization to measure, monitor, and evaluate their situ-

ation in relation to predefined factors, criteria or benchmarks" Webb, Pollard, & Ridley (2006, p.3). IT governance covers five major domains namely IT principles, IT architecture, IT infrastructure, business application needs, prioritization & investments decision (Weill & Ross, 2005a). Thus the definition and the domain of IT governance as well as the IT control frameworks indicate the relevance of control of IS security as a method for effective IT governance through the use of IT control frameworks.

Since the chapter focus on integrating IS security into IT governance, differentiation is made between IT governance, enterprise governance and corporate governance. Enterprise Governance of IT which goes beyond the IT-related responsibilities is an integral part of corporate governance and addresses the definition and implementation of processes, structures and relational mechanisms in the organization that enable both business and IT people to execute their responsibilities in support of business/IT alignment (Grembergen & Haes, 2009). Exhibit 1 provides a case where non-technical methods were used in hacking thus illustrating the need for a holistic approach to IS security.

Chapter Outline and Methodology

The chapter is divided into six sections:

1. Section one focus on the threat faced by organisations in the last few years (with relevant statistics) for the purpose of identifying areas of threat and the gaps in IS security.
2. Section two looks at the issues facing IS security mangers today locally and globally as well as get prescriptive suggestions on having a robust security architecture.
3. Section three analyse the IS security management methodology and models from current and past literature in IS security, IT governance and IS service management from a holistic perspective.

4. Section four evaluates frameworks that emerged from the analysis of IS security models in terms of how best to suit a holistic approach to IS security. This section map the identified models with each other (COBIT, ITIL, PCI DSS, RiskIT and ISO 27002) so as to find the common IS security controls to avoid duplication in implementation for practitioners.

5. Section five looks at IS security from a IS security culture.

6. The best practices for implementing IS security governance frameworks are evaluated in section six .

7. The final section propose an IS Security Governance model incorporating COBIT, ITIL, PCI DSS, RiskIT and ISO 27002.

The methodology used in this chapter to come up with the conceptual model of information security governance is through the critical analysis of existing concepts, models and frameworks from the information security and IT governance domain.

REVIEW OF IS SECURITY BREACHES

Cybercrime is big business as according to the written testimony to the US Senate (March 2009) by the Chief Security Officer of AT & T, cybercrime revenues are worth US $ 1 trillion. While it is difficult to verify this figure and critics have given much lower estimates on this, recent statistics on IT security breaches point out the fact that networks are witnessing more frequent and sophisticated targeted attacks. Statistics on data breaches in US that are published regularly by the Identity Theft Resource Centre, a non-profit organisation sponsored by the US Department of Justice, reveal the depth and breadth of cybercrime. According to ITRC (2011), 266 breaches had been reported with 12,823,043 records compromised

in US as on August 16, 2011 and this does not include the breaches not reported, veiled from public and unknown. A list of reported breaches in organisations (from January to August 2011) where more than 100,000 records compromised (given in Figure 1) is analysed to find out the factors behind the breaches which shed light on the issues to consider to provide a robust model of IS security (ibid).

An analysis of the type of data lost and the methodology of the above breaches are given below:

1. **Texas Comptroller:** The organisation have three agencies namely TRS, TWC and ERS which transferred data of 1.2 million, 2 million and 281,000 employees, individuals and retirees in 2010. The information contained the names and mailing addresses, and top some extend social security numbers, dates of birth or driver's license numbers. All of these numbers were embedded in a chain instead of fields. An analysis of the case revealed that many procedures were not followed.

   a. The data files transferred by those three agencies were not encrypted, as required by Texas Comptroller rules established for agencies for transfer of data.

   b. The personnel in the Comptroller's office incorrectly allowed exposure of that data.

   c. The information were being placed on a server accessible to the public.

   d. The information left in the public server was left for a long period of time without being purged as required by internal procedures.

   This is the second such breach in the same company.

2. **Health Net - IBM:** The incident involves nine server drives that went missing from the data centre from the California office of

Figure 1. Number of exposed records in data breaches in 16 organisations from January to June in 2011 (ITR, 2011)

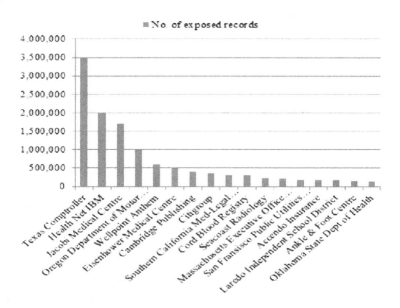

Health Net a health insurer in US. It contained the healthcare and personal information of 2 million former and current Health Net members, employees and health care providers, which may include names, addresses, health information, social security numbers and financial information. An analysis of the incident reveal that appropriate policies and procedures have not been followed by those responsible for both the physical and logical protection of critical data.

3. **Jacobi Medical Centre:** The New York City Health and Hospitals Corporation (HHC) on February 2011 announced that the personal information of 1.7 million patients, hospital staff and associated employees was stolen in late December 2010 from a van operated by GRM Information Management Services, when the driver left the van unattended and unlocked. The files (cassette tapes in a box) contained personal health records of patients, hospital staff and employees along with names, addresses, Social Security numbers and other personal information. The HHC

had experienced two file thefts in the past. In the first case, a laptop was stolen from a secured office space, and in another incident a CD shipment was lost by a private vendor.

4. **Oregon Department of Motor Vehicles:** On April 2011, detectives arrested Tim Nuss who had access to an old Oregon Department of Motor Vehicles database containing the personal information of a million Oregonians. The database that include the names, addresses, birth dates, gender and ages of people who registered with the DMV, was quite old and was once sold to marketing companies till 1990. According to the police, the data might have been bought or stolen using USB drives or CDs.

5. **WellPoint Anthem:** WellPoint an insurance provider have a company-run website that allowed applicants to track the status of their applications. The breach occurred through the site where the data belonging to more than 600,000 individual health insurance applicants can be accessed. The flaw in the website was discovered when an applicant

was able to manipulate the web address within the site to gain access to other applicants' information, including names, addresses, dates of birth, Social Security numbers and health and financial information. According to the company, an upgrade to the server caused the vulnerability, but it was revealed that security measures were not audited and validated for the system.

6. **Eisenhower Medical Centre:** On March 11 2011, the computer used to check-in patients at the Eisenhower Medical Center in Rancho Mirage was stolen from the open lobby area. It contained the names, age, dates of birth, medical record numbers, and the last four digits of their social security numbers of 514,000 patients, thus potentially compromising a half of a million records. The theft wasn't discovered until March 14 when a worker returned from the weekend and came to know of the missing computer. It was later revealed that the computer was not protected with any sort of drive encryption.

7. **Cambridge Publishing:** This is a marketing company in Long Island where the incident involved the theft of data tape from the drive. It was claimed that it contained the names, addresses, social security numbers, driver license numbers, payroll data, checking account numbers, and credit card information of 400,000 members. Apparently, the data tapes was stolen or lost by an outsourced company when the drive (with the tape inside) was sent for repair to the outsourced company.

8. **Citigroup:** In May 2011, hackers stole the information of 210,000 Citibank customers in US. The breach exposed the names of customers, account numbers and contact information, and according to the bank, key data, such as date of birth and card security codes was not compromised. The methodology of the attack is yet to be ascertained given the fact that the attack is direct and

the bank has strong defense mechanisms in place.

9. **Southern California Medical-Legal Consultants:** The breach happened in the company that represents health care providers seeking payment from patients receiving workers' compensation. In June, 2011, the company announced in their website that that electronic files containing names and social security numbers of approximately 300,000 individuals who have applied for California workers' compensation benefits had been exposed to unauthorized access. The breach came to light when a researcher from a data loss protection company discovered that personal medical data for nearly 300,000 Californians were available online in an unsecured format and could be found through Internet searches. The President of SCMLC admitted that their internal security policies and procedures were not followed (the website was not password protected).

10. **Cord Blood Registry:** The company is the world's largest and most experienced stem cell bank and is currently entrusted with storing more than 350,000 cord blood collections for individuals and their families. In December 2011, a computer along with the backup tapes containing its members name, Social Security number, driver's license number, credit card information and/or credit expiration date were stolen from an employee's locked car.

One of the most sensational, expensive and sophisticated technical data breach involve a leading US based payment processing company, Heartland Payment Systems which processes cards for 250,000 restaurants, retailers and other businesses in US and Canada. According to the company president Baldwin, the breach that occurred in 2008 was the result of a keylogging malware (planted on the company's payment processing network), which covertly captured anything typed on an infected computer, especially user names and passwords. According to the investigators, the key logger might have gone through the firewall, but ruled out insider job. It has been estimated that as many as 130 million records have been exposed (ITRC, 2009). The stolen data includes the digital information encoded onto the magnetic stripe built into the backs of credit and debit cards. This malware recorded payment card data as it was being sent for processing to Heartland, by thousands of the company's retail clients.

In all of the 11 cases mentioned, six involve theft of equipment, three cases where security procedures were not followed (1, 5 and 9) and only two involve hacking. Even in out of the two hacking cases, only one involved sophisticated technology, while the methodology of the breach in Citicorp is yet to be ascertained. It is to be noted that a large proportion of data breaches are not reported by companies for fear of losing customers, and even if reported, in most of the cases the lead time between the actual discovery of the theft and informing this to the affected parties is considerably long. (To counter this a new bill known as Personal Data Privacy and Security Act of was introduced in Congress by Sen. Patrick Leahy (D-Vt.), in 2011 that could criminalize companies concealing a cyber-attack which puts customer information at risk).

An overview of analysis of threats from various sources, reveal the extent of threat. In the year 2010 alone Symantec encountered more than 286 million unique variants of malware; 93% increase in the volume of Web-based attacks in 2010 over the volume observed in 2009 and an average of 260,000 identities exposed in each of the data breaches caused by hacking (Symantec, 2011). Symantec also reported a 42% rise in the number of reported new mobile operating system vulnerabilities (from 115 to 163), 6253 new vulnerabilities, and 14 new zero day vulnerabilities in applications such as Internet Explorer, Adobe Reader, and Adobe Flash Player.

The 2011 Verizon data breach investigation report conducted by the Verizon Risk team, the US Secret service and the Dutch High Tech Crime Unit reveals that most of the data breaches in organizations in 2010 are not the result of highly sophisticated attacks, but rather the victims are a target of opportunity rather than choice (Verizon, 2011). Moreover, according to Verizon almost all breaches are avoidable without difficult or expensive corrective action. In the year 2010 it was reported by Verizon that 83% of victims were targets of opportunity, 92% of attacks were not highly difficult, 76% of all data was compromised from servers, 86% were discovered by a third party, 96% of breaches were avoidable through simple or intermediate controls, and 89% of victims subject to PCI-DSS had not achieved compliance. This point to the need to look at IS security from a non-technical perspective as well.

Section Summary: IS security need to take into account technical as well as non technical aspects of information systems. Despite technological advances in threat detection and prevention there is no abatement of breaches into organisational networks.

ISSUES AND REQUIREMENTS IN IS SECURITY

To find out the reasons for the persistent attacks and weakness in IS security it is imperative to look at the real issues facing IS security mangers from their perspective and get recommendations/requirements for an efficient and effective security architecture.

Issues in IS Security

While data breaches and hacking have emerged as a serious and growing issue in organisations and personal computers alike it is worthwhile to look at related issues facing organisations in IS security. Two studies are taken for analysis, one

Table 1. A comparative study of IS security issues globally and in US

	Global Study (874 respondents)		US study (623 respondents)
1	Top management support	1	Top management support
2	User awareness training & education	2	Legal & regulatory issues
3	Malware	3	Malware
4	Patch management	4	User awareness training & education
5	Vulnerability & risk management	5	Protection of privileged information
6	Policy related issues (enforcement)	6	Business continuity & disaster preparation
7	Organisational culture	7	Low funding & inadequate budgets
8	Access control & identity management	8	Lack of skilled security workforce
9	Internal threats	9	Fighting spam
10	Business continuity & disaster preparation	10	Inherent insecurity of networks & information systems
11	Low funding & inadequate budgets	11	Standards issues
12	Protection of privileged information	12	Vulnerability & risk management
13	Network security architecture	13	Policy related issues (enforcement)
14	Security training for IT staff	14	Security training for IT staff
15	Justifying security expenditure	15	Governance
16	Inherent insecurity of networks & information systems	16	Patch management
17	Governance	17	Access control & identity management
18	Legal & regulatory issues	18	Justifying security expenditure
19	External connectivity to organisational networks	19	Network security architecture
20	Lack of skilled security workforce	20	Organisational culture
21	Systems development & life cycle support	21	Internal threats
22	Fighting spam	22	Systems development & life cycle support
23	Firewall & IDS configurations	23	Wireless vulnerabilities
24	Wireless vulnerabilities	24	External connectivity to organisational networks
25	Standards issues	25	Firewall & IDS configurations

a global study of 874 IS security certified professionals worldwide, and the other a study of 623 US based IS security professional who re ranked the same issues (Knapp, Marshall, Rainer & Morrow, 2008). Both the surveys came up with a ranked list of 25 information security issues (see Table 1).

An analysis of the issues based on matching the issues in the top ten in both the surveys reveal only four top four issues namely:

1. Top management support.
2. Malware attacks like viruses, Trojans and worms.
3. User awareness and training.
4. Business continuity and disaster preparation.

The above results reveal that while hacking and breaches represent a serious threat, support from the top management in IS security related issues and decisions form the most important concern for organisations. Hence this also imply that even if an organisations have the best defense technologies and resources, support from top management and user awareness & training is crucial for effective IS security This top issue is linked to eight other issues namely policy related issues (6), organisation culture (7), low funding & inadequate budgets (11), justifying security expenditure (15),

Table 2. Differentiating between technical and non-technical issues in IS security

Technical	Non-technical	Both
Malware	Top management support	Vulnerability & risk management
Patch management	User awareness training & education	Internal threats
Access control & identity mngmt	Policy related issues (enforcement)	Protection of privileged information
Network security architecture	Organisational culture	Inherent insecurity of networks & information systems
Fighting spam	Business continuity & disaster preparation	External connectivity to organisational networks
Firewall & IDS configurations	Low funding & inadequate budgets	Systems development & life cycle support
Wireless vulnerabilities	Security training for IT staff	
	Justifying security expenditure	
	Governance	
	Legal & regulatory issues	
	Lack of skilled security workforce	
	Standards issues	

governance (17), legal & regulatory issues (18), external connectivity to organisational networks (19), and the lack of skilled security workforce (20). Hence this is a serious issue in IS security.

Out of the 25 listed only three issues match the same ranking namely top management support, malware and security training for IT staff in number1, 2 and 14 respectively that reveal the cultural, legal and regulatory differences across regions in terms of IS security. Overall, the issues can be categorised into technical, non-technical, and those that are both include technical as well as non-technical in nature (Table 2) that may reveal the extent of support that IT personal have to give to technical as well as non-technical; issues in ensuring an effective IT security environment. From the table it is evident that non-technical issues are the most concern for IT security issues. This implies that for effective IS security, technical –as well as non-technical– issues in IS security, governance, and standards need to be incorporated. The evaluation of the major issues supports the need for a broader perspective of IS security incorporating IT governance (which

includes all the non-technical issues, and some technical issues given in Table 2).

It has been repeatedly emphasised by researchers, that the high incidence of security breaches in organizations could be attributed to the organization's inability to adequately focus on non-technical issues in information systems security, namely policies, procedures, practices, and strategies that, organizations put in place to minimize threats (Dhillon and Backhouse 2001; Straub and Welke 1998; and Siponen, 2005 cited in Ifendo, 2009). This is compounded by the issue of time deadlines in IS security implementations, the lack of expertise in related IS security, IT governance frameworks and standards, the enormous effort in keeping pace with the latest in IS security technologies, and the cost factor. This can result in organisations generally adopting a highly fragmented and siloed approach to IS governance, compliance and security. This necessitates an ever increasing need to manage IS security from a multidimensional, holistic and comprehensive manner for ensuring a secure IS environment (Solms, 2001). Moreover there is a need to build IS security, like a staircase of combined measures

(Hagen, Albrechtsen and Howden, 2008) since various dimensions of IS security are mutually dependent on each other (Sundt, 2006; Berghel, 2005 cited in Hagen, Albrechtsen and Howden, 2008).

Requirements for Effective IS Security

According to Elof & Elof, (2005) an integrated architectural approach to information and computer security should operate in a distributed, heterogeneous and multidisciplinary business environment. They have given five requirements for the architecture:

- **Requirement 1: Be Holistic and Encompassing:** This holistic perspective refers to the inclusion of all aspects of information security like governance, compliance, business strategy, IS security policy, ethical issues in IS, security awareness & training, administrative issues, technological issues and physical security. This is achieved through implementing frameworks on IT governance like COBIT, IT service strategy framework like ITIL, IS security standards like the ISO 27000 series, and regulatory requirement like the PCI DSS for protecting credit cardholder data (see section 4 for details).
- **Requirement 2: Make Suggestions on How Different Controls Can be Synchronised to Achieve Maximum Effect:** Organisations have to comply with numerous standards and regulations for the protection and management of information assets. Hence organizations need to implement frameworks for each of the different domains of IS. Since these standards, regulations and frameworks overlap considerably, strategic and selective integration ensures smooth implementation of the frameworks and compliance.

- **Requirement 3: Include a Comprehensive Approach to Information Security Risk Management:** A comprehensive approach takes into account utilizing risk management methodologies and taking into account the expertise of people who are involved in security planning, risk assessments, and the availability of historical data.
- **Requirement 4: Follow a Predetermined Life-Cycle Approach:** COBIT, ITIL and ISO 27 K series follow the plan-do-check-act cycle of Deming. Information systems are highly dynamic and keeping pace with the technological advances and threats enable the organizations to follow a life cycle approach. This ensures that the organisational information security system is planned, implemented, utilized, evaluated, monitored and updated in a continuous manner, creating a feedback loop for continuous improvement.
- **Requirement 5: Be Measurable:** The measurement of information systems success is critical to the understanding of the value and efficacy of information systems (DeLone & McLean, 2003). In fact IS security success should be measured through the use of specific success indicators for each IS entity to evaluate its success in preventing breaches. A simple tick box approach of 'complied', 'not complied' will not suffice to ensure secure systems.
- **Requirement 6: Security Awareness and Training:** It has been proposed and stated by numerous researchers and security practitioners that a major component of a security system is to inculcate a security culture in an organisation through awareness and technical training of all personnel. From the 10 breaches listed in section 1, breach cases 1,2,3,4,7,10 happened due to lack of procedural awareness among employees while cases 5, 6, and 9 were due

to lack of technical expertise (training). Moreover, the 2011 high profile breach in RSA, the security management firm happened when an employee opened email attachments that contained exploits which security awareness training could have prevented.

- **Requirement 7: Implement Critical Success Factors and Best Practices in Implementing the Framework and Standards:** While frameworks are in itself best practices for implementing IS security standards and complying with regulations, proper implementation is required to make the model successful. This requires following industry specific critical success factors and best practices Implementing Apart from these requirements, for an effective IS security architecture, it has been proposed and stated by numerous researchers and security practitioners that a major component of a security.

Section Summary: An effective IS security model should be holistic (include IT governance, IT service management framework and related standards). The frameworks should be mapped between them and strategically integrated; the model should follow a risk management approach; follow a life cycle pattern of iterative process; and be measurable from various perspectives. Two extra requirements that emerge are training and best practices for implementation.

HOLISTICS PERSPECTIVE OF IS SECURITY

This section address the first requirements stated in section 2. Perceiving IS security from a holistic perspective requires the analysis of the different terms of security from a multidimensional perspective. Moreover this section takes into account the different models of IS security as well as the relationship of security with compliance.

Perspectives of IS Security: Definitions

Information systems security can be viewed from a multidimensional perspective, management of IS security perspective and from the perspective of information security architecture. To understand the concept of security and information security, it is better to understand the definition of these terms. *Security* has been defined as the state of being safe from threats while *security compliance* means conformance with a given set of security requirements (Julisch, 2008, p.71). According to the US National Institute of Standards and Technology (NIST definition number 3542), the term '*information security*' means protecting information and information systems from unauthorized access, use, disclosure, disruption, modification, or destruction in order to provide integrity, confidentiality and availability (NIST, 2003, p.15). In this context integrity means guarding against improper information modification or destruction, and includes ensuring information non-repudiation and authenticity, confidentiality refers to preserving authorized restrictions on access and disclosure, including means for protecting personal privacy and proprietary information, and availability, ensures timely and reliable access to and use of information. Thus, from a regulatory point of view information security is viewed from the traditional CIA triangle (Confidentiality, Integrity and Availability). However, to maintain the CIA triangle for information system, one has to move from a pure technical perspective to a more widely organisational perspective. This does not mean that the focus should shift towards the non-technical side of IS security but rather technical focus should be widened to include non-technical domain to provide a management as well as technical focus of IS security.

The management of information security is primarily concerned with strategic, tactical, and operational issues surrounding the planning, analysis, design, implementation and maintenance of the IS security program (Choobineh, Dhillon, Grimaila & Rees, 2007). Thus Information security management is defined as "the process of administering people, policies, and programs with the objective of assuring continuity of operations while maintaining strategic alignment with the organisational mission" (Cazemer et al. 2000, cited in Choobineh, et al., p. 959). Firstly, the definition, provides a very broad meaning taking into account technical, non-technical and strategic aspects of IS security. Secondly the definition emphasize maintaining the IS operations with the objective of IS security management for strategic alignment. This strategic alignment of linking IS security mission and goals with the organizational strategic mission and goals is the prime objective of IT governance. Moreover, in a global survey of 7000 IT professionals, the importance of strategic alignment of organisational goals with the IT goals was cited by 90% of the surveyed as vital to organisation (ITGI, 2006; ITGI, 2008). Thus it can be safely assumed that the effective implementation of information security involves, using a strategic mix of the IT governance frameworks, (that aligns the IT goals with the organisational goals), IT service management framework (that maintain efficient and effective continuity of operations), along with compliance with relevant security standards (policies and programs). While it has been emphasised that governance is a key to success in setting standards, success is more likely if the governance structure includes all of the various interests in the network, and moreover the standards (ex. ISO 27 K, PCI DSS, ISO 20000) themselves need to be effective yet flexible enough to satisfy competitive interests (Sullivan, 2010).

Perspectives of IS Security: Dimensions and Models

Since, IS security is regarded as a multidisciplinary concept cutting across several related disciplines (Elof & Elof, 2005), this chapter takes a wider perspective of integrating the various security and governance frameworks with the IS security regulations and standards. In this respect Solms (2001, p. 504) have argued that "if information security is not addressed in a holistic and comprehensive way, taking all its dimensions into account, real risks exist preventing a really secure environment". With this perspective, Solms' multidimensional character of information security, which incorporate twelve dimensions focusing on governance, audit, legal, technical, human and measurement areas need to work together for creating a secure environment. Table 3 illustrates the 12 dimensions and the corresponding frameworks/models/acts. In a global survey on 834 business executives and heads of information technology (IT) covering 21 countries and 10 industries on the control frameworks used in enterprise governance of IT, 28% of those surveyed use ITIL/ISO 20000, 21.1% use ISO 27000/related security frameworks, 15.1% use six sigma, 12.9% use COBIT, 12.7% use PMI/PMBOK, and 12% use RiskIT framework of Information Systems Audit and Control Association (ISACA), along with other frameworks (ITGI, 2011). Out of these, six sigma and PMI/PMBOK are less oriented towards IT security and thus will not be discussed in this chapter. While the above controls are IT governance oriented encompassing IT security, PCI DSS is a standard focusing purely on the technical aspects of information technology.

Since IT security has a strong technical base, it is worthwhile to look at IS security from a technical view also to see the mix of technical and non-technical component. In this perspective, Elof & Elof, (2005) have proposed an information security architecture encompassing five domains of IS namely security organisation & infrastructure, security policies, standards & procedures,

Table 3. Dimensions of IS security mapped with related IS control frameworks/standards

Dimensions	Available frameworks
Strategic/corporate governance	This is high level focus of COBIT
Governance/organisational	Evident in the four domains of COBIT
Policy	IS security policy endorsed in COBIT, ISO 27002, NIST, ITIL
Best practice	33 ITG best practice; ITIL best practices;
Ethical	Extended Information Systems Secure Interconnection (ISSI) model (Leiwo & Heikkuri, 1998) address the ethical aspect of IS security
Certification	Certifications in COBIT, ITIL, ISO
Legal	Regulations like FISMA, HIPAA, SOX relate to IS security
Insurance	*(Relevant only for insurance companies)*
Personnel/human resource	Taken care of in COBIT, ITIL, ISO 27002 controls
Awareness	Information Security Culture Framework (De Veiga & Eloff, 2010)
Technical	PCI DSS 2.0 & ITIL are more technical in nature than COBIT
Measurement/metrics	Guidelines given in COBIT, ISO 27004 & ITIL
Audit	COBIT

security culture (security awareness and training), monitoring compliance, and current security program (risk management). To establish this architecture they have identified five requirements. These five requirements are mapped with the corresponding frameworks, and standards in Table 4.

The CIA triangle is a widely used benchmark for evaluation of information systems security, focusing on the three core goals of information security namely confidentiality, integrity and availability of information. NIST (NIST, 1995, p. 5) has defined *"Computer Security* as the protection afforded to an automated information system in order to attain the applicable objectives of preserving the integrity, availability and confidentiality of information system resources (includes hardware, software, firmware, information/

Table 4. IS security architecture mapped with related IS control frameworks/standards

	ISO 27 K	COBIT	ITIL	PCI DSS 2.0
Holistic and encompassing	Partly	Yes	IT service only	Cardholder data focus
Suggestions to synchronize controls to achieve maximum effect	No	Yes (COBIT, ITIL and ISO 27002 mapped with each other)	Yes (COBIT, ITIL and ISO 27002 mapped with each other)	Yes
Comprehensive approach to infosec risk management	Partly	Yes (RiskIT framework)	No	No
Follow a predetermined life cycle approach	Yes	Yes	Yes	Yes
Measurable	Guidelines in ISO 27004	Use of KPI, metrics, maturity model, compliance	Extensive use of quantifiable metrics	Compliance focus only

data, and telecommunications)". While the CIA triangle focus on the core issues in IT security, it cannot fully address the changing IS environment of today. To meet the dynamic nature of IS security Donn Parker in 2002 proposed an extended version the CIA triangle adding possession, authenticity, and utility along with confidentiality, integrity, and availability. In 1991 McCumber provided a comprehensive model for information security called the McCumber cube. It moves from a uni-dimensional view of IS security to a three-dimensional view encompassing the different perspectives and dimensions of IS security. While the cube (given in Figure 2) covers most of the aspects of IS security, the assurance/governance aspect of IS security is not evident.

Perspectives of IS Security: Compliance

Currently, security of information is enforced through mandatory compliance in the form of numerous standards, and regulations. A few commonly used ones are:

- The Payment Card Industry Data Security Standard 2.0 (PCI DSS).

Figure 2. IS security model – McCumber cube (Source: Whatman & Mattord, 2009)

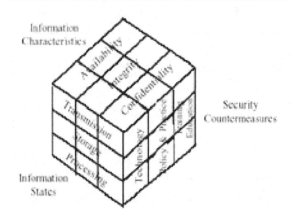

- The US Health Insurance Portability and Accountability Act of 1996 (HIPAA).
- The US Gramm-Leach-Bliley Act 1999 (GLB).
- The US Sarbanes Oxley Act 2002 (SoX).
- The US Federal Information Security Management Act 2002 (FISMA).

Thus apart from securing information systems assets organisations have the extra role of complying with mandatory and voluntary standard and regulations imposed by external entities. Hence it is worthwhile to view IS security from a compliance and assurance perspective. Moreover, a study on 500 US and multinational organisations found out that on an average it was necessary to dedicate 35% of the security budget to any compliance effort (Everett, 2009). While it seems that this percentage is a substantial proportion Exhibit 2 justifies this budget.

According to Bishop (2003) security has three components namely requirements, policy and mechanisms. Bishop defined security policy as a specific statement of what is and what not allowed in a system's security. A system is said to be secure if the system always stays in states that are allowed, and users can only perform actions that are allowed; while the system is said to be non-secure if the system can enter a disallowed state or if a user can successfully execute a disallowed action. Security mechanism has been defined by Bishop as a mechanism to enforce the policies whereby the goal is to ensure that the system never enters a disallowed state. Security assurance measures how well requirements conform to needs, policies conform to requirements, and mechanisms that implement the policy is in the realm of assurance. This reiterates that fact that enforcing IS security requires appropriate controls and controls mechanisms. Security compliance in IT systems, has been defined as the state of conformance with externally imposed functional security requirements and of providing evidence (assurance) thereof (Julisch, 2008). In this manner, Julisch

Exhibit 2. Does compliance pay?

Ponemon Institute (2011) conducted a study of 160 senior managers with a sample of 46 multinational organizations. This study used empirical data to estimate the full cost of an organization's compliance efforts, including the cost of non-compliance with laws, regulations and policies. It found out that the average cost of compliance was $3,529,570 while the cost incurred due to non-compliance was $9,368,351. This amounted to a net savings of $ 5,838,781 ($9,368,351-$3,529,570) for compliance companies. Thus, the non-compliance cost is 2.65 times the cost of compliance.

The study revealed that organizations view meeting legal and regulatory requirements (external) as more important than meeting compliance with internal policies and procedures. Regarding external compliance, the most important and difficult requirements to comply with are those of the PCI DSS, various state privacy and data protection laws, the European Union Privacy Directive, and Sarbanes-Oxley. The average cost of compliance varies from $446,000 to over $16 million, which yields a per capita compliance cost of $222 per employee. In the case of non-compliance, it range from $1.4 million to nearly $28 million with a per capita non-compliance cost of $820 per employee. The study also found that the more effective an organization's security strategy is, the lower the cost of non-compliance.

has classified IT security requirements into functional requirements, which require some functional security feature such as mandatory access control, and assurance requirements, which specify the evidence needed to establish that the functional requirements are met.

It has been repeatedly emphasized in section 2 that the most effective countermeasure is to consider a variety of controls and not only technical measures. Thus to cultivate an appropriate level of information security, organisations should ensure that a comprehensive and adequate set of information security components is implemented that aids in addressing threats on the human, process and technical levels (Veiga & Eloff, 2010). Since the field of IT and information security domain is in an evolutionary flux, more work is to be accomplished that requires the collaboration and the consensus of information security stakeholders worldwide (Gikas, 2010). Thus, IS security can be viewed from a compliance perspective involving the implementation of relevant controls, but should not be treated as a check list requirement since compliance with check lists of IS security requirements is not IS security and it is therefore only a requirement towards the goal of improving IS security.

The increasing complexity of information intensive process, and the regulations enacted in the information domain has led to the development of security frameworks, best practices and standards (collectively termed as controls) that address the technical as well as the organizational aspect of IT security. Organisations use these controls to implement IS security and as well as comply with regulations and mandatory standards. Since compliance to a variety of information security standards is mandated by regulations, organisations need to act and implement a proactive information security enforcement strategy (Madan & Madan, 2010). According to Posthumous & Solms, (2004) effective governance and management of information security requires an information security governance that enables an organization to effectively fulfill all the internal and external requirements in terms of protecting business information assets and, therefore, covers the full scope of risks faced by an organization.

The effective and efficient utilization of information technology requires the alignment of the IT strategies with the business strategies (Luftman, Lewis & Oldach, 1993; Luftman & Brier, 1999). Since alignment of IT strategies with the business strategies is the objective of IT governance, it is worthwhile to view security from an IT governance lens taking into account the internal and external issues that impact IS security. In this respect, information security should not be perceived as a technical issue alone, but as a business and governance challenge that involves adequate risk management, reporting, and accountability.

Section Summary: IS security should be regarded as a multi-dimensional and multidisciplinary concept focusing on governance, audit, legal, technical, human and measurement areas. Meanwhile the objectives of IS security have grown from preserving the integrity, availability and confidentiality of information system resources to preserving possession, authenticity, and utility. Thus to cultivate an appropriate level of information security, organisations should ensure that a comprehensive and adequate set of information security components is implemented that aids in addressing threats on the human, process and technical levels.

IT CONTROL COMPLIANCE FRAMEWORKS

This section considers requirements 1, 2, 3, and partly 4 given in section 2. Considering the fact that the current biggest challenge for IT executives is aligning activities with the business (Gartner cited in Silva and Abreu, 2009) it is worthwhile to look at security from a wider perspective taking into account the internal and external issues that can impact on IS security. Since information security should be regarded as a business and governance challenge that involves adequate risk management, reporting, and accountability, it must be addressed at the highest levels of the organization and not regarded as a technical specialty relegated to the information technology (IT) department (Abu-Musa, 2010). Information Security Governance, which is an important component of the IT governance and an integral part of the enterprise governance, could be regarded as implementing the governance concepts and principles on information security issues (ibid). IT governance is implemented through a set of internal controls embedded in frameworks like COSO and COBIT. An internal control provides reasonable assurance regarding the achievement of objectives in the area of effectiveness and efficiency of operations, reliability of financial reporting and compliance with regulations (Pathak, 2003). Internal controls are policies, procedures,

practices, and organisational structures put in place to reduce risks (Kim, et al., 2008). Moreover "a control framework is a recognised system of control categories that covers all internal controls expected in an organisation" (IIARF 2002, cited in Liu & Ridley, 2005, p. 2). Currently implementations of IS control frameworks are on the rise worldwide, due to compliance and regulatory requirements to various regulations and standards (mentioned in section 2).

Relevant Controls in ITG and IS Security

In a survey of security professionals, the Enterprise Strategy Group (ESG) discovered that 72 percent of North American organizations with 1,000 or more employees have implemented one or more formal IT best-practice control and process models (Turner et al., 2009). Among these, the study stated that the most widely used commercial IT control frameworks are ITIL, ISO 27002 and COBIT, which provide optimal security management. Furthermore, it had been stated that ISO/IEC 27002, COBIT, ISO 20000, and ITIL are the most applicable and widely used standards to manage and maintain IT services (Sahibudin, Sharifi & Ayat, 2009). IT control implementers use, ITIL to define strategies, plans and processes, COBIT for metrics, benchmarks and audits and, ISO/IEC 27002 to address security issues to mitigate the risks (ibid). Like ITIL, Microsoft Operations Framework 4.0 (MOF) released in 2008 is an approach by Microsoft to provide practical guidance for IT organizations reflecting a single, comprehensive IT service lifecycle. It helps IT professionals connect service management principles to everyday IT tasks and activities and ensures alignment between IT and the business.

In the case of securing cardholder information, the requirements set by PCI DSS are in line with the IT security best practices required by widely recognised standards such as ISO 27002, and COBIT (Laredo, 2009). Gikas (2010) did a mapping of ISO 27000 with the PCI DSS and found out 70 similar technical controls between these two standards. PCI DSS is a regulatory requirements that is mandatory for those dealing with credit cards to ensure the protection of cardholder data while the standard (also termed as best practice) while ISO 27002 is a code of practice for information security (ISO, 2011). ISO/IEC 20000, the first international standard for IT Service Management is implemented through ITIL, which is an internal requirement. On the other hand, COBIT address the business issues namely company-wide principles, goals and needs in terms of information processing through its various controls in the four domains of IS (Humphreys et al., cited in Posthumous & Solms, 2004).

Categorization of Controls

There are numerous IT security and governance frameworks and controls and attempts have been made by researchers to categorise from different perspectives. Campbell (2003) postulated three categories of control frameworks in security and governance namely:

- Business oriented controls like COSO (Committee of Sponsoring Organisation) and SAS (Statement of Auditing Standards).
- IT focused controls namely ITIL (The IT Infrastructure Library), ISO/IEC 17799:2000 (The International Organisation for Standardisation/the Electro technical Commission) and the Security Code of Conduct.
- A third category of controls that align control over IT with business goals namely, COBIT.

Posthumous & Solms (2004) postulated the IS security governance framework as containing an external and internal component. External component comprise of legal/regulatory and standards/practice domains and the internal component consist of the business issues and IT infrastructure domains. According to them legal and regulatory requirements stimulate and develop corporate information security efforts and include country specific statutes and laws while standards and best practices are used to inspire global information security principles. Likewise internal requirements that includes business issues translates requirements into organizational needs for IS security while IT infrastructure help to define relevant requirement that protect assets (ibid). Table 5 presents a mapping of the common frameworks with the categorization method of Posthumous & Solms.

The framework direct the information security governance concept towards COBIT, ITIL, ISO 27002 and PCI DSS for the purpose of this study covering the four domains of information security governance. NIST provides comprehensive set of standards for all aspects of information systems. Standards like ISO and NIST tells what to do but does not give guidelines on doing it, COBIT provides guidelines on implementation and ITIL goes deep and explains 'how' to implement IT service strategy. Since NIST has contributed to raising the quality of federal US information security by promoting operational norms and by helping agencies to find model security processes (Keblawi & Sullivan) an overview of NIST is summarized in Box 1. Here it is evident that the eight security principles and the 14 practices, support requirement 1, 2, 3, 4, 5, and 6.

Since the objective of an IS audit is to evaluate IT controls (Mahnic, et al., 2001) a list of available controls can be evaluated to select context appropriate ones. Here apart from the criteria required, the popularity and the widespread usage are looked at while selecting the IT audit framework.

Table 5. IS security governance framework

	Domains	Relevant Frameworks
External	Legal/ regulatory	PCI DSS HIPAA SoX
	Standards/ best practices	ISO 27000- series ISO 20000 NIST*
Internal	Business issues	COBIT COSO
	IT infrastructure	ITIL MOF

A Review of ITG and Security Controls

The frameworks reviewed are COBIT, ITIL, ISO

27002 and PCI DSS. While the first three can be universally applied, PCI DSS apply mostly to those companies dealing with credit cards with the objective of protecting cardholder data. However, a closer look reveals that some selected principles, requirements and testing procedures can be applied to organisations (other than dealing with credit and debit cards) to protect sensitive information (as all organisations have a proportion of sensitive information in their systems) irrespective of them storing cardholder data.

COBIT Framework

COBIT is a generic flexible framework (unlike a standard) that covers governance and management aspects of information systems across the

Box 1. Overview of NIST (source: Swanson & Guttman, 1996)

*National Institute of Standards and Technology, of the U.S. Department of Commerce (NIST) provides a set of very comprehensive standards for managing information systems security in organisations. Analysis: Published in 1996, NIST has released a collection of documents on: Audit and accountability of IS, authentication, awareness & training, biometrics, certification & accreditation, communications & wireless, contingency planning, cryptography, digital signatures, forensics, general IT security, incident response, maintenance, personal identity verification, PKI, planning, research. Risk assessment, services & acquisitions, smart cards, viruses & malware, and historical archives.

Among the set, the Generally Accepted Principles and Practices (GAPP) for Securing Information Technology Systems(NIST SP 800-14) of NIST is an accepted standard for securing information systems to use as a baseline to establish and review their IT security programs. It provides principles for the establishment of an IT security program.

NIST 800-14 defines eight generally accepted system security principles.
    1. Computer Security Supports the Mission of the Organization
    2. Computer Security is an Integral Element of Sound Management
    3. Computer Security Should Be Cost- Effective
    4. Systems Owners Have Security Responsibilities Outside Their Own Organizations
    5. Computer Security Responsibilities and Accountability Should Be Made Explicit
    6. Computer Security Requires a Comprehensive and Integrated Approach
    7. Computer Security Should Be Periodically Reassessed
    8. Computer Security is Constrained by Societal Factors

In addition to the eight principles, the framework goes on to define and describe fourteen (14) IT Security Practices. Those practices are:
    1. Policy
    2. Program Management
    3. Risk Management
    4. Life Cycle Planning
    5. Personnel/User Issues
    6. Preparing for Contingencies and Disasters
    7. Computer Security Incident Handling
    8. Awareness and Training
    9. Security Considerations in Computer Support and Operations
    10. Physical and Environmental Security
    11. Identification and Authentication
    12. Logical Access Control
    13. Audit Trails*

enterprise. Organisations that implement it normally select & customize COBIT controls to suit their compliance requirement, local regulations, organisational size, organisational culture, and business needs. COBIT was created in 1996 by the IT Governance Institute (of the Information Systems Audit and Control Association) consisting a set of controls to manage information technology resources. The mission of COBIT is to research, develop, publicize and promote an authoritative, up-to-date, international set of generally accepted information technology control objectives for day-to-day use by business managers and auditors (ibid). In due course of time, it evolved through different versions and the current version is COBIT 4.1. The COBIT set comprise of six documents namely management guidelines, implementation tool set, executive summary, framework, control objectives and audit guidelines.

Figure 3 illustrates the four domains of COBIT that is contained in the control objectives:

1. Plan and organize.
2. Acquire and implement.
3. Deliver and support.
4. Monitor and evaluate.

The cyclic nature of the figure signify the continuous management of these four domains corresponding to the Plan-Do-Check-Act of the Deming cycle (see Figure 3). Each of these domains comes with control process and detailed control processes with responsibility matrix, assessment criteria, activities to monitor and IT goals along with metrics. The organisations have the flexibility to customise any or all of these to suit their IT requirements.

COBIT is a comprehensive IT governance framework (Hojaji & Shirazi, 2010) and used by auditors to ensure that adequate control is in place for the security of the IT environment (Lin, Guan & Fang, 2010) and one control that specifically focus on security is DS 5.

COBIT is not a mandatory standard, but rather it is a generic framework that can be used by organisations to govern the information technology

Figure 3. Overview of COBIT (Source: ITGI, 2008)

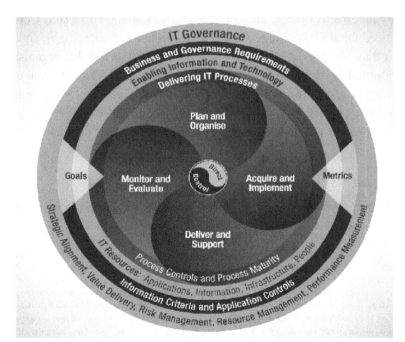

in the organisation. Hence organisations have the freedom to add, delete modify the controls, of COBIT to comply with their IT or business goals. As a guidance, COBIT have divided IT into four domains, with high level control process for each domain. The first domain – Plan and organise comes with 10 high level controls. For example, the first of the 34 controls, PO-1 (Define a Strategic IT Plan) comes with ten sub controls with detailed description of the controls. One of the sub control is given in Box 2.

Apart from the exhaustive collection of processes, COBIT focus on the fiduciary, quality and security needs of organisations by providing seven information criteria for evaluation (effectiveness, efficiency, confidentiality, integrity, availability, compliance and reliability) that defines the business needs from IT of an organisation (Hardy, 2003).

The review of COBIT from various perspectives point to the fact that it is flexible enough to be used as a governance and security framework.

The Risk IT Framework

Requirement number 3 suggests a risk based approach to IT security for effective governance of IT. ISACA has released the Risk IT Framework (ISACA, 2009) as a framework to identify, govern and manage information technology risks. This framework fills the gap between generic (non–technical) risk management frameworks and technical (security-related) IT risk management

frameworks. The framework explains IT risk, aids in making risk based decisions and enable users to:

- Integrate the management of IT risk into the overall enterprise risk management (ERM) of the organization
- Make well-informed decisions about the extent of the risk, the risk appetite and the risk tolerance of the enterprise, and
- Understand how to respond to the risk

The framework that comes with detailed guidelines, charts and templates, is divided into three domains — Risk Governance, Risk Evaluation, and Risk Response — each containing three sub processes. Risk management is an important component of IT governance such that it is the prime focus of the concept - Governance, Risk, and Compliance Management, (GRC). GRC is an integrated, holistic approach to integrate the controls and standards used in governance, risk management, IS security, and compliance with regulations and standards and IT GRC is a part of GRC that that address the role of IT in the entire GRC domain. It includes a set of IS control/ regulatory mechanisms (Ex. Sarbanes Oxley Act), IS frameworks (Ex. Control Objective for Information Technology), and IS standards (Ex. ISO 27000 series) that organisations use to audit their IS assets. Thus the goal of GRC is to "help a company efficiently put policies and controls in place to address all its compliance obligations while at the same time gathering information that

Box 2. The first of the ten sub controls of PO-1 of COBIT

PO Plan and organise
  PO-1 Define a Strategic IT Plan
   PO- 1.1 IT Value Management:
     Work with the business to ensure that the enterprise portfolio of IT-enabled investments contains programs that have solid business cases. Recognise that there are mandatory, sustaining and discretionary investments that differ in complexity and degree of freedom in allocating funds. IT processes should provide effective and efficient delivery of the IT components of programs and early warning of any deviations from plan, including cost, schedule or functionality, that might impact the expected outcomes of the programs. IT services should be executed against equitable and enforceable service level agreements (SLAs). Accountability for achieving the benefits and controlling the costs should be clearly assigned and monitored. Establish fair, transparent, repeatable and comparable evaluation of business cases, including financial worth, the risk of not delivering a capability and the risk of not realising the expected benefits.

---

helps proactively run the business" (Broady and Roland, 2008, p. 9).

ITIL Framework

ITIL is a framework of best practices for developing and deploying IT Service Management (ITSM) in an organisation. The focus is on delivering high quality IT services to support the organisational IT assets, which in turn support the business operations. It consists of seven guidances: Managers Set, Service Support, Service Delivery, Software Support, Networks, Computer Operations, and Environmental. According to OGC (2007), ITIL has grown to become the most widely accepted approach to IT Service Management in the world.

ITIL was developed by CCTA (Central Communication and Telecom Agency, now subsumed under the Office of Government Commerce, UK (OGC) in 1980s. ITIL is a method to align and comply with ISO/IEC 20000 standard. Thus, ITIL is generally equivalent to the scope of the ISO/IEC 20000 standard which means that implementation of ITIL framework generally leads to implementation of the ISO 20000 standards (ISO/IEC 20000 is an international IT Service Management standard that helps organisations benchmark the delivery of their IT services, measure the service levels and assess their performance). ITIL show the goals, general activities, inputs and outputs of the various IT service processes, which can be incorporated within IT organisations.

ITIL contains a set of books that gives detailed overview, principles, process, activities and organising, technological considerations, implementation guidelines, challenges and critical success factors along with detailed guidelines and charts linked with relevant models and frameworks. Organisations that implement ITIL can use a series of templates (checklists, tasks) and procedures, to implement it to their enterprise. ITIL is broken up into a series of processes. Each of the processes is again sub divided into sub process or guidelines to achieve a specific IT business function or discipline. The ITIL service management practices are comprised of three main sets of products and services namely ITIL service management practices – core guidance, ITIL service management practices (complementary guidance) and ITIL web support services. The core set consists of six publications:

1. Introduction to ITIL Service Management Practices.
2. Service Strategy (SS).
3. Service Design (SD).
4. Service Transition (ST).
5. Service Operation (SO).
6. Continual Service Improvement (CSI).

For example, the activity 'event detection' (Box 3) can be traced to the fifth publication namely service operation.

Since ITIL is a widely used framework and can be aligned with the higher level governance framework COBIT, mapping of these two to identify the overlap will not only reduce the effort of individual implementation but also provide a synergic effect to the governance of IT service management.

ISO 27002 Standard

The ISO 27002 (officially called the ISO/IEC 27002:2005) is a standard that establish code of practice for information security management. There are 39 control objectives and hundreds of controls. ISO 27002 controls are not mandatory but the user have the flexibility to select and implement the controls that suit them through the use of a risk-assessment process to identify the most appropriate controls for their specific requirement. They provide guidelines and general principles for initiating, implementing, maintaining, and improving information security management within an organization.

The actual controls listed in the standard are intended to address the specific requirements

Box 3. A control process of ITIL

v. Service Operation (SO)
4 Service Operations Management *4.1 Event management* *4.1.5 Process activities, methods and techniques* *4.1.5.1 Event occurs* *4.1.5.2 Event notification* *4.1.5.3 Event detection*   *Once an event notification has been generated, it will be detected by an agent running on the same system, or transmitted directly to a management tool specifically designed to read and interpret the meaning of the event.*

identified via a formal risk assessment. The standard is also intended to provide a guide for the development of "organizational security standards and effective security management practices and to help build confidence in inter-organizational activities" (ISO, 2008). It focuses on operational security, application security, computing platform security, network security and physical security. ISO 27002 control structure is demonstrated by taking a control from section 9 (see Box 4).

PCI DSS Standard

It was created for developing, managing, educating, and communicating the PCI Security Standards, including the Data Security Standard (PCI DSS), Payment Application Data Security Standard (PA-DSS), and PIN Transaction Security (PTS) Requirements to merchants, vendors and financial institutions involved in credit card transactions. The objective was to enhance the security of the cardholder through protection of cardholder data and thus help facilitate global adoption of consistent data security measures created to mitigate data breaches and prevent

payment cardholder data fraud. Compliance is enforced on those dealing with credit cards and there are penalties for non-conformance of the PCI DSS standard by PCI Security Standards Council. PCI DSS 2.0 version (released on October 2010) comprises of 6 principles, 12 major requirements, 45 sub requirements, 75 detailed requirements with corresponding testing procedures for the requirements and sub requirements. An example of the Requirement 5: Use and regularly update anti-virus software or programs is given below (Box 5).

Section Summary: COBIT, ITIL, ISO 27002 and PCI DSS follow not only uniform control structures, but they also have similar controls, the only difference being the difference in specificity. Risk IT complements this by providing a risk based approach. Whereas COBIT provides a broad set of controls with guidelines on information criteria and responsibility matrix along with measurement guidelines, PCI DSS is more specific with fewer guidelines in implementation. Meanwhile ITIL goes a step further in detailing the full methodology of implementation. All of these point to the need for integration.

Box 4. An ISO 27002 standard

Section 9: Physical and environmental security
Valuable IT equipment should be physically protected against malicious or accidental damage or loss, overheating, loss of mains power etc. *9.1 Use Secure areas* *This section describes the need for concentric layers of physical controls to protect sensitive IT facilities from unauthorized access.* *9.1.1 Use physical security perimeters to protect areas*

Box 5. A PCI DSS 2.0 principle, requirements, and corresponding testing procedures

Build and Maintain a Secure Network *(one of the six principles)*
1: Install and maintain a firewall configuration to protect cardholder data (first requirement)
1.1 Establish firewall and router configuration standards that include the following:
(Corresponding testing procedure: 1.1 Obtain and inspect the firewall and router configuration standards and other documentation specified below to verify that standards are complete)
1.1.1 A formal process for approving and testing all network connections and changes to the firewall and router configurations
(Corresponding testing procedure: 1.1.1 Verify that there is a formal process for testing and approval of all network connections and changes to firewall and router configurations.

Integrating COBIT, ITIL, ISO 27002, and PCI DSS

COBIT has been considered as high level IT governance framework combining in itself IT security, IT audit and IT assurance. Being very comprehensive covering the entire life cycle of information systems, the processes of ITIL, ISO 27002 and PCI DSS are stated as broad controls in COBIT. ITIL is strong in IT processes, but limited in security and system development while COBIT is strong in IT controls and IT metrics but does not say how and does not have a security focus; and ISO 17799 is strong in security controls but does not say how the process flows (Conradie & Hoekstra,2002). Since ISO 17799 (which is a code of practice for information security) has been renamed as ISO 27002, the statement can be true of ISO 27002 also.

From an ISO 27002 perspective the term 'information' includes all forms of data, documents, communications, conversations, messages, recordings, photographs, digital data, email, and fax communications (Praxiom Research, 2010) and since cardholder information can be transmitted in any of these forms, implementation of ISO 27002 along with PCI DSS enhances the security of cardholder data thus avoiding duplication. Quite similar to COBIT and PCI DSS, ISO 27002 has identified 11 sections (similar to the four domains or high level control areas of COBIT), 39 control objectives, and hundreds of controls.

According to Laredo (2009) the requirements set by PCI DSS are in line with the best security practices required by widely recognized standards like the ISO 27002 and COBIT. Considering the 12 principles of PCI DSS, Abu-Musa (2010) states that information security should not be regarded as a technical issue alone limited to the 12 requirements of PCI DSS, but a business and governance challenge that involves adequate risk management, reporting, and accountability. Thus integration of frameworks, standards and regulations are called for in IS security governance.

COBIT, ITIL and ISO 27002 can be aligned with each other for business benefit, and a mapping of the three frameworks in a single document have been done by ISACA and OGC that provides guidance for practitioners (see Table 6 for the COBIT control PO 2). RiskIT of ISACA is not used for comparison since it provides a risk based approach to the four selected overlapping frameworks/standards.

When ITIL is benchmarked with COBIT, it has been found that they correspond with each other to a high degree, especially, when the processes of COBIT are ITIL based as in its latest version (Sahibuddin et al., 2008). Since COBIT encompasses the controls, and processes of ITIL, ISO 27002 and PCI DSS, integration of these into COBIT provides a 360 degree view of security. Moreover, a comparison is made between COBIT and PCI DSS that provide rationale for integrating PCI DSS into COBIT for comprehensive IS security. While PCI DSS comes with 6 major 'prin-

Table 6. Mapping of COBIT with ITIL and ISO 27002 (Source: ITGI, 2008a)

CobiT 4.1 Domain: Plan and Organise (PO) *(cont.)*			
PO2 Define the Information Architecture *(cont.)*			
CobiT 4.1 Control Objective	**Key Areas**	**ITIL V3 Supporting Information**	**ISO/IEC 27002:2005 Supporting Information**
PO2.2 Enterprise data dictionary and data syntax rules	• Corporate data dictionary • Common data understanding	• *SD 5.2 Data and information management* • *SD 7 Technology considerations*	• *7.1.1.1 Inventory of assets* • *11.1.1 Access control policy*
PO2.3 Data classification scheme	• Information classes • Ownership • Retention • Access rules • Security levels for each information class	• *SD 5.2 Data and information management*	• *7.2.1 Classification guidelines* • *10.7.1 Management of removable data* • *10.8.1 Information exchange policies and procedures* • *10.8.2 Exchange agreements* • *11.1.1 Access control policy*
PO2.4 Integrity management	• Integrity and consistency of data	• *SD 5.2 Data and information management* • *ST 4.7 Knowledge management*	

ciples', 12 major requirements that follows the principles, 45 sub requirements, 75 detailed requirements, and testing procedures for the corresponding sub requirements and detailed sub requirements, COBIT comes up with 34 high level processes (corresponding to the 6 major principles of PCI DSS), and 318 detailed processes (corresponding to the 12 major requirements of PCI DSS). But, on a detailed analysis of the 318 detailed processes it can be seen that these can be segmented further to correspond to the 45 sub requirements/75 detailed requirements of the PCI DSS. COBIT further elaborates the detailed processes with 'activities' that can be equated with the 'testing procedures' of the PCI DSS.

A common theme running across all of these frameworks and standards (except RiskIT) are that they are mostly process/control based (see Table 7). While these process based frameworks/standards provides a set of controls to mitigate IT risk, Risk IT provides a framework for enterprises to identify, govern and manage IT risk thus complementing the security governance framework.

Section Summary: The IS control process of COBIT, ITIL, ISO 27002 and PCI DSS overlaps to a great extend ranging from the generic state- ments (in COBIT) to more specific statements (in PCI DSS). This aids in identifying a set of common controls and integrating it through using the best practice guidance given mainly in COBIT and ITIL for responsibility matrix, information criteria and measurement implementation using the risk based approach of RiskIT.

IS SECURITY AWARENESS, CULTURE, AND TRAINING

Information security awareness and training are both sides of the same coin where training fosters awareness which in turn create a IS security culture within the organisation (*requirement 6 in section 1*). *Culture*, from a corporate perspective have been defined as a blend of the corporate values, beliefs, symbols, and rituals that companies develop over time. In this context, an information security culture is therefore based on the interaction of employees with information assets and the security behaviour they exhibit within the context of the organisational culture in the organisation (Veiga & Elof, 2010). For the purpose of this research, an information security culture is therefore defined as the attitudes, assumptions, beliefs, values and

Table 7. Comparative evaluation of COBIT 4.1, PCI DSS 2.0, ISO 27002, and ITIL

Evaluative Criteria	COBIT 4.1	PCI DSS 2.0	ISO 27002	ITIL
Major goal/objective	Align business goals with IT goals	To encourage and enhance cardholder data security and facilitate the broad adoption of consistent data security measures globally	provide general guidance on the commonly accepted goals of information security management	Delivering and managing IT services effectively and efficiently to the users
Technical focus	Less technical, more reliant on compliance	Very much reliant on technology for compliance	Both business and technical focus	Technical focus mainly on providing IT service
Process orientation	Subdivides IT into four domains and 34 processes in line with the responsibility areas of plan, build, run and monitor, providing an end-to-end view of IT	Provides a baseline of technical and operational requirements designed to protect cardholder data based on 6 principles, 12 requirements, numerous sub requirements that are further sub divided and corresponding testing procedures.	Consists of 11 sections, 39 controls, and hundreds of sub controls.	Process based with six publications (domains of ITSM), processes' and sub processes/ activities.
Implementation guidance	Generic and need to be customized	Specific and focused, but no guidance	Specific with no guidance for implementation	Detailed guidelines given on the process and how to implement each process
Focus on	Organisational wide information audit, security and control assurance	Protection of cardholder data only	Focus on all areas of IS security including policy	Focus on IT service management only
Domain of application	Includes all IS domain	Includes only those networks, locations and flows of cardholder data	Includes all IS domain	Includes only the service part of IS domain
Target audience	Organisations who need to comply with global and country wise regulations/ requirements like SOX and who need to implement best practices in ITG	All merchants who accept credit and debit cards; credit card processors, issuers and acquirers, third party processors and gateways; developers and software providers	Security managers	
Implementation	Voluntary in most countries and organisations	Mandatory for those merchants dealing with specific credit cards	Voluntary in most countries and organisations	Voluntary in most countries and organisations
Personnel allocation	Use of the RACI chart	No evidence	No evidence	Guidance given
Measurement done by:	Benchmarking; goals and metrics; compliance – 'complaint' and 'not complaint'	Compliance – 'in place' and 'not in place'	No evidence, but guidance given in ISO 27004	Comprehensive guidance and samples given

knowledge that employees/stakeholders use to interact with the organisation's systems and procedures at any point in time (ibid). The interaction results in acceptable or unacceptable behaviour (i.e. incidents) evident in artifacts and creations that become part of the way things are done in the organisation to protect its information assets and this information security culture changes over time (ibid). To evaluate the need for a IS security culture it is imperative to answer the question "Why do organisations need a IS security culture?" A culture is a unifying mechanism that makes all concerned to act in a unified manner. From the breaches mentioned in section 1 it was evident that a very small percentage of people are responsible for security breaches in the majority of the eleven organisations due to (1) either not following or aware of the procedures and (2) unaware of the dangers of deviating from a set behaviour or unintentionally overlooking simple observations. A uniform IS security culture not only enforces uniform behaviour in terms of enforcing IS security procedures and polices but also creates IS security awareness among IS and non IS employees alike. Creating a security awareness program involves the following steps:

1. Focusing on the security objective of the organization.
2. Survey on the security awareness of employees.
3. Identifying areas of weakness and strength.
4. Categorise employee groups based on knowledge levels.
5. Create security programs to cater to all levels of employees and at different technical and non-technical levels.
6. Monitor and control the results of the program.
7. Modify and suit the dynamic nature of internal and external environment.

According to OECD (2002) there are nine principles for an IS security culture:

1. **Awareness:** Participants should be aware of the need for security of information systems and networks and what they can do to enhance security.
2. **Responsibility:** All participants are responsible for the security of information systems and networks.
3. **Response:** Participants should act in a timely and co-operative manner to prevent, detect and respond to security incidents.

4. **Ethics:** Participants should respect the legitimate interests of others.
5. **Democracy:** The security of information systems and networks should be compatible with essential values of a democratic society.
6. **Risk Assessment:** Participants should conduct risk assessments.
7. **Security Design and Implementation:** Participants should incorporate security as an essential element of information systems and networks.
8. **Security Management:** Participants should adopt a comprehensive approach to security management.
9. **Reassessment:** Participants should review and reassess the security of information systems and networks, and make appropriate modifications to security policies, practices, measures and procedures.

Section Summary: Security frameworks, standards and controls can only ensure protection to information system assets of an organization to a limited extend. Augmentation of IS security requires the creation of a robust and uniform security culture in an organization through continuous intermittent technical and non-technical awareness training at all levels to all levels of staff.

CRITICAL SUCCESS FACTORS FOR INTEGRATED IS SECURITY GOVERNANCE IMPLEMENTATION

Research have been conducted during the latter half of the 2010s to find out the 'success factors', 'critical success factors', and 'best practices' in adopting and implementing ITG, IT service management, and ISO 27001 to provide a clear roadmap to practitioners and academics alike. "Critical success factors (CSF) are those few things that must go well to ensure success for a manager or an organization and therefore they represent those managerial or enterprise areas that must be given special and continual attention to bring about high performance. CSF, thus includes issues vital to an organization's current operating activities and to its future success" (Boynton and Zmud, 1984). Although CSFs and best practices (BP) are used to denote 'success factors', BPs differ from CSFs in many respects. A 'best practice' is defined by IT Governance Institute (2007) as "a proven activity or process that has been successfully used by multiple organisations". Hence, even though both CSFs and BPs can be viewed from different perspectives, in this chapter both of these concepts are termed and perceived as 'success factors'. It should be noted here that all the selected frameworks have been termed as 'best practices' by the respective organizations that created them, but the success factors mentioned here refer to the best practices to

be followed in the process of implementing these frameworks. Hence, it may be termed as 'success factors' for implementing and maintaining IT security governance 'best practices' (COBIT/ ITIL/ISO/PCI DSS).

A review of success factors in ITG, and ITIL implementation is given below to evaluate the common themes and thus provide guidance for a holistic implementation of information security governance. While there are numerous studies on the success factors for ITIL and COBIT implementation, research on PCI DSS and ISO 27000 series is lacking. Two studies on success factors based on IT governance and ITIL are given in Tables 8 and 9 . A comprehensive study on success factors for IT governance implementation (see Table 8) was provided by Grembergen & Haes (2004). The study was more targeted at ITG

Table 8. Success factors in ITG implementation (Grembergen and Haes, 2004)

Structures	Processes	Relational Mechanisms
S1. IT strategy committee at level of board of directors	P1. Strategic information systems	R1. Job-rotation
S2. IT expertise at level of board of directors	P2. IT performance measurement (e.g. IT balanced scorecard)	R2. Co-location
S3. (IT) audit committee at level of board of directors	P3. Portfolio management (incl. business cases, information economics, ROI, payback)	R3. Cross-training
S4. CIO on executive committee	P4. Charge back arrangements – total cost of ownership (e.g. activity based costing)	R4. Knowledge management (on IT governance)
S5. CIO (Chief Information Officer) reporting to CEO (Chief Executive Officer) and/or COO (Chief Operational Officer)	P5. Service level agreements	R5. Business/IT account management
S6. IT steering committee (IT investment evaluation / prioritization at executive / senior management level)	P6. IT governance framework COBIT	R6. Executive/senior management giving the good example
S7. IT governance function / officer	P7. IT governance assurance and self-assessment	R7. Informal meetings between business and R8. IT executive/senior management
S8. Security/compliance/risk officer	P8. Project governance/management methodologies	R8. IT leadership
S9. IT project steering committee	P9. IT budget control and reporting	R9. Corporate internal communication addressing IT on a regular basis
S10. IT security steering committee	P10. Benefits management and reporting	R10. IT governance awareness campaigns
S11. Architecture steering committee	P11. COSO/ERM	
S12. Integration of governance/alignment tasks in roles & responsibilities		

implementation rather than any implementation of specific framework. An analysis of the study reveals that some of the best practices for ITG implementation are already present in COBIT controls. Examples are the COBIT controls PO 4.2 IT strategic committee, PO 4.3 IT Steering committee, PO 10 Manage projects, PO 3.5 IT Architecture board, PO 5.3 IT budgeting, PO 8.6 Quality measurement, monitoring and review, PO 10.13 Project performance measurement, reporting and monitoring, AI 7.1 Training, and DS 3.5 Monitoring and reporting. A detailed mapping of ITG best practices with COBIT can reveal more indirect linkages.

Framework specific success factors have been proposed for ITIL implementation of which two studies are given in Table 9. Even through the listed best practices are ITIL specific, considerable direct and indirect parallels can be made with the more generic ITG best practices (Table 8) like management support, training/personnel development, project champion, interdepartmental communication, strategic alignment, continuous communication of positive results, knowledge of ITIL by senior management, educating about ITIL, and standard system of measuring, analyzing, reporting on service level. This also implies that these best practices are evident in the frameworks/standards too which makes integration easier as an optimal organizational specific overlap of frameworks, standards, and best practices not only ensures greater protection against breaches, but also reduces the effort and cost of siloed implementation.

Section Summary: While COBIT, ITIL, ISO 27002, PCI DSS and RiskIT are in itself set of best practices for IT governance, IT service management, IS security, protection of cardholder data and following a risk based security approach, guidance are required in implementing these frameworks in an optimal integrated manner. Hence successful implementation requires success factors where a list of generic success factors and ITIL specific

success factors are listed which overlap with each other to a considerable extend.

IS SECURITY GOVERNANCE MODEL

IS security governance (ISSG) is defined as a comprehensive and holistic view of governing and securing information, people, hardware, software, networks and process. A comprehensive and holistic view of ISSG takes into account:

1. IT governance framework that includes IT related business as well as IT specific domains to align business goals with IT goals, using relevant processes of the framework COBIT or related homegrown ITG frameworks;
2. Viewing IT governance security from a risk based perspective using the Risk IT framework or similar approach;
3. IT service strategy in the form of ITIL and aligned with ISO 20000;
4. Following relevant standards outlined for securing the IT assets namely ISO 27002 or NIST;
5. Protecting the information in the system using selected principles, requirement, and testing procedures of PCI DSS, or similar controls;
6. Making sure that the selected frameworks and standards are integrated in an appropriate manner using success factors for optimal integrated implementation;
7. Ensuring compliance with relevant regulations and standards through the use of relevant existing frameworks; and
8. Making sure that the people involved in IT and business share a common security culture through continuous multi level optimally crafted technical and non technical training.

Figure 4 provides the positioning of the various components of the model while Figure 6 provides the process of implementing ISSG model. Training

Table 9. Overview of success factors in ITIL implementation

Success Factors	Pederson et. al., (2010);	Iden and Langeland (2010) *[Top 12]*
Quick wins	X	
Continuous improvement	X	
Management support	X	X
Training and personnel development	X	X
Virtual project team	X	
Champion for change/Project champion	X	
Plan and reinforce project objectives	X	
Careful software selection	X	
Use of consultants	X	
Interdepartmental communication and collaboration	X	X
Process priority	X	X
Strategic alignment and customer focus	X	
A contingency based approach	X	
Planned and risk driven approach	X	
Incremental implementation process	X	
High quality ITIL implementation	X	
Learning and knowledge management	X	
Change management/corporate culture		X
Manager ownership of ITIL introduction		X
Involvement of key personnel in design and improvement		X
Knowledge of ITIL by senior management		X
Educating about ITIL		X
Module based ITSM tool for process		X
Continuous communication of positive results		X
Standard system of measuring, analyzing, reporting on service level		X

and implementation success factors are a continuous process mainly due to external factors like the dynamic nature of security threats, technological advances and changes/introduction of IS related regulations. Hence, the model requires constant change and improvement to take into account the changing external and internal environment. The central focus of the security model is to manage risk through a risk- based approach (see Figure 5) riding on:

- A common set of mandatory controls.

Followed by:

- A set of heavily overlapped critical controls.
- A set of partially overlapped industry benchmarked controls.
- A set of recommended controls.
- A set of preferred controls.

Figure 4. IS security governance model (component positioning)

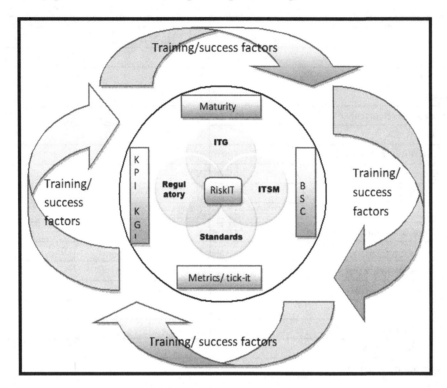

Figure 5. IS security governance model for controls prioritization

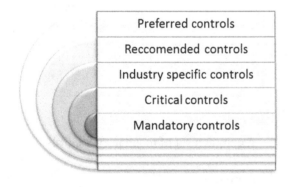

Since controls are common across frameworks and levels, these five sets of controls can again overlap with each other presenting a final set of customised controls.

IS security governance is continuous process due to the highly dynamic nature of the information technology sector and the advances made by IS security defense technologies and hackers

alike. ISO 27001 reiterates this and incorporates several Plan-Do-Check-Act (PDCA) cycles where the IS controls are regarded as a continuous activity that is reviewed and adjusted to take account of changes in the security threats, vulnerabilities and impacts of information security failures. Thus the implementation process of ISSG follows the PDCA cycle of Deming. Initially relevant frameworks/standards followed by appropriate controls are selected which in turn is followed by mapping and prioritizing the selected controls taking into account the overlap.. The implementation step takes into account the guidelines provided by the frameworks for implementation and optimal integration. Measurement being a requirement for effective security governance, COBIT provides a set of tools and techniques for measurement of controls ranging from a simple compliance (complaint and non-complaint), key performance/goal indicators (using quantitative scales), maturity model and the balance score card (BSC). Other

Figure 6. IS security governance process model

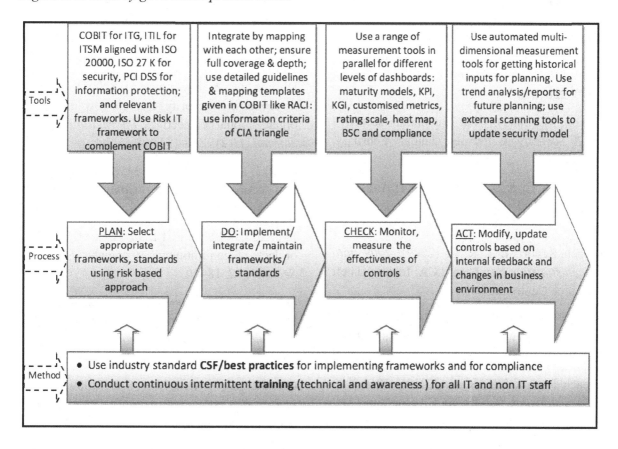

measurements used are the heat map (red-amber-green) and rating scale. A continuous approach of monitoring involves the use of automated tools to record results from measurement on a continual basis to view the trend, take corrective action and an external monitoring tool that provides suggestions on continuous improvement of the ISSG model.

The proposed model being conceptual in nature is not without its limitations. Hence the validation of the model through empirical research in different contexts and sectors is required to validate it.

SUMMARY

A successful ISSG model need to incorporate the best practices/success factors in implement-

ing relevant models, frameworks and standards; select and optimally integrate the relevant frameworks; select and map the appropriate controls from these frameworks; and integrate these in an appropriate manner for ensuring a holistic perspective of IS security governance through a risk based approach. Finally the model should ensure continuous monitoring through multi measurement tools through monitoring internal and external trends for continuous improvement of the organizational security model. Generalization of this model requires validation through empirical research in different sectors of the industry and in different geographical locations. It is hoped that further research in this domain would substantiate the model.

REFERENCES

Abu-Musa, A. (2010). Information security governance in Saudi organizations: An empirical study. *Information Management & Computer Security*, *18*(4), 226–276.

Bishop, M. (2003). What is computer security? *IEEE Security & Privacy,* January/February, 67 - 69.

Boynton, A. C., & Zmud, R. W. (1984). An assessment of critical success factors. *Sloan Management Review*, *25*(4), 17–27.

Breach Report, I. T. R. C. (2009). *2009 data breach statistics*. San Diego, CA: Identity Theft Resource Centre.

Breach Report, I. T. R. C. (2010). *2010 data breach statistics*. San Diego, CA: Identity Theft Resource Centre.

Breach Report, I. T. R. C. (2010). *2010 data breach statistics*. San Diego, CA: Identity Theft Resource Centre.

Broadbrent, M. (2003). *Deciding factors* Retrieved from http://www.cio.com.au/index. php?secid=13&id=1528039590

Broady, D. V., & Roland, H. A. (2008). *SAP GRC for dummies*. Indiana: Wiley Publishing Company.

Campbell, P. L. (2003). *An introduction to information control models* (pp. 1–88). Albuquerque, NM: Networked Systems Survivability & Assurance Department, Sandia National Laboratories.

Choobineh, J., & Dhillon, G. (2007). Management of information security: Challenges and research directions. *Communications of the Association for Information Systems*, *20*(57).

Conradie, N., & Hoekstra, A. (2002). *CobiT, ITIL and ISO17799: How to use them in conjunction*. Retrieved 5 January, 2011, from www.cccure.org/ Documents/COBIT/COBIT_ITIL_and_BS7799. pdf

DeLone, W. H., & McLean, E. R. (2003). The DeLone and McLean model of information systems success: A ten-year update. *Journal of Management Information Systems*, *19*(4), 9–30.

Dhillon, G., & Backhouse, J. (2001). Current directions in IS security research: Towards socio-organizational perspectives. *Information Systems Journal*, *11*(2), 127–154.

Eloff, J. H. P., & Eloff, M. M. (2005). Information security architecture. *Computer Fraud & Security*, (November): 10–16.

Everett, C. (2009). PCI DSS: Lack of direction or lack of commitment? *Computer Fraud & Security*, *12*, 18–20.

Gikas, C. (2010). A general comparison of FISMA, HIPAA, ISO 27000 and PCI-DSS standards. *Information Security Journal: A Global Perspective*, *19*, 132-141.

Grembergen, W. V., & Haes, S. D. (2009). *Enterprise governance of information technology*. New York, NY: Springer.

Grembergen, W. V., Haes, S. D., & Guldentops, E. (2004). Structures, processes, and relational mechanisms for information technology governance: Theories and practices. In Grembergen, W. V. (Ed.), *Strategies for information technology* (pp. 1–36). London, UK: Idea Group Inc.

Guildentops, E., Grembergen, W. v., & Haes, S. D. (2002). Control and governance maturity survey: Establishing a reference benchmark and a self-assessment tool. *Information Systems Control Journal*, *6*, 32–35.

Hagen, J. M., Albrechtsen, E., & Hovden, J. (2008). Implementation and effectiveness of organizational information security measures. *Information Management & Computer Security*, *16*(4), 377–397.

Hardy, G. (2003). *What is IT governance?* (pp. 1-19). Retrieved 7th December, 2011, from www.pinkroccade.co.uk/Images/14_38938.ppt

Hojaji, F., & Shirazi, M. R. A. (2010). *AUT SOA governance: A new SOA governance framework based on COBIT.* Paper presented at the 3rd IEEE International Conference on Computer Science and Information Technology (ICCSIT), Chengdu.

Ifinedo, P. (2009). Information technology security management concerns in global financial services institutions: Is national culture a differentiator? *Information Management & Computer Security, 17*(5), 372–387.

ISACA. (2009). *The risk IT framework.* Illinois: ISACA.

ISO. (2008). *Introduction to ISO 27002.* Retrieved from http://www.27000.org/iso-27002.htm

ITGI. (2005). *COBIT IV.* Rolling Meadows, IL: IT Governance Institute.

ITGI. (2006). *IT governance global status report - 2006.* Rolling Meadows, IL: IT Governance Institute.

ITGI. (2007). *COBIT IV.* Rolling Meadows, IL: IT Governance Institute.

ITGI. (2008a). *Aligning CobiT® 4.1, ITIL® V3 and ISO/IEC 27002 for business benefit.* Rolling Meadows, IL: IT Governance Institute.

ITGI. (2008b). *IT governance global status report.-2008.* Rolling Meadows, IL: IT Governance Institute.

ITGI. (2011). *Global status report on the governance of enterprise IT (GEIT).* Rolling Meadows, IL: ISACA & IT Governance Institute.

Julisch, K. (2009). *Security compliance: The next frontier in security research.*

Kakabadse, N. K., & Kakabadse, A. (2001). IS/IT governance: Need for an integrated model. *Corporate Governance, 1*(4), 9–11.

Keblawi, F., & Sullivan, D. (2007). The case for flexible NIST security standards. *Computer,* (June): 19–26.

Kim, N.-Y., Robles, R. J., Sung-Eon, C., Yang-Seon, L., & Tai-hoon, K. (2008). *SOX act and IT security governance.* Paper presented at the International Symposium on Ubiquitous Multimedia Computing, Hobart.

Knapp, K. J., Marshall, T. E., Rainer, K., & Morrow, D. (2006). *The top information security issues facing organisations: What can government do to help? Information Security and Risk Management.* Sept/Oct.

Laredo, V. G. (2009). PCI DSS compliance: A matter of strategy. *Card Technology Today.*

Liebowitz, M. (2011). 2011 set to be worst year ever for security breaches. *Security News.* Retrieved 7 July, 2011, from http://www.securitynewsdaily.com/2011-worst-year-ever-security-breaches-0857/

Lin, F., Guan, L., & Fang, W. (2010). Critical factors affecting the evaluation of information control systems with the COBIT framework: A study of CPA firms in Taiwan. *Emerging Markets Finance & Trade, 46*(1), 42–55.

Liu, J., & Xiao, Y. (2010). A survey of payment card industry data security standard. *IEEE Communications Surveys & Tutorials, 12*(3), 287–303.

Liu, J., Xiao, Y., Chen, H., Ozdemir, S., Dodle, S., & Singh, V. (2010). A survey of payment card industry data security standard. *IEEE Communications Surveys & Tutorials, 12*(3), 287–303.

Liu, Q., & Ridley, G. (2005). *IT control in the Australian public sector: A international comparison.* Paper presented at the Thirteenth European Conference on Information Systems, Regensburg, Germany.

Luftman, J., & Brier, T. (1999). Achieving and sustaining business-IT alignment. *California Management Review, 1*(Fall), 109–122.

Luftman, J. N., Lewis, P. R., & Oldach, S. H. (1993). Transforming the enterprise: The alignment of business and information technology strategies. *IBM Systems Journal Archive, 32*(1).

Madan, S., & Madan, S. (2010). *Security standards perspective to fortify Web database applications from code injection attacks.* Paper presented at the International Conference on Intelligent Systems, Modeling and Simulation, 2010, Liverpool.

Mahnic, V., Klepec, B., & Zabkar, N. (2001). *IS audit checklist for router management performed by third party.* Paper presented at the International Conference on trends in Communications EUROCON 2001, Bratislava.

Musa, A. (2010). Information security governance in Saudi organizations: An empirical study. *Information Management & Computer Security, 18*(4), 226–276.

NIST. (1995). *An introduction to computer security: The NIST handbook.* National Institute of Standards and Technology, Technology Administration, U.S. Department of Commerce.

NIST. (2003). *Information security (No. NIST Special Publication 800-59).* Gaithersburg, MD: NIST.

OECD. (2002). *OECD guidelines for the security of information systems and networks.*

OGC. (2007). *An introductory overview of ITIL® V3.* London, UK: itSMF Ltd.

Parker, D. B. (2002). Toward a new framework for information security. In Bosworth, S., & Kabay, M. E. (Eds.), *The computer security handbook* (4th ed.). New York.

Parkinson, M., & Baker, N. (2005). IT and enterprise governance. *Information Systems Control Journal, 3*, 17–21.

Pathak, J. (2003). Internal audit and e-commerce controls. *Internal Auditing, 18*(2), 30–34.

Ponnemon Institute. (2011). *The true cost of compliance: Benchmark study of multinational organizations.*

Posthumusa, S., & Solms, R. v. (2005). IT oversight: An important function of corporate governance. *Computer Fraud & Security,* (June): 11–17.

Praxiom Research Group Ltd. (2010). *ISO IEC 27002 2005.* Retrieved 5 January, 2011, from www.praxiom.com/iso-17799-2005

Ridley, G., Young, J., et al. (2004*). COBIT and its utilization: A framework from the literature.* 37th Hawaii International Conference on System Sciences, Hawaii, IEEE Computer Society.

Sahibudin, S., Sharifi, M., et al. (2008). *Combining ITIL, COBIT and ISO/IEC 27002 in order to design a comprehensive IT framework in organizations.* Second Asia International Conference on Modelling & Simulation, Malaysia, IEEE Computer Society.

Sambamurthy, V., & Zmud, R. W. (1999). Arrangements for information technology governance: A theory of multiple contingencies. *Management Information Systems Quarterly, 23*(2), 261–290.

Silva, L. A. F. d., & Abreu, B. E. (2009). *Exploring and overcoming major challenges in IT infrastructures faced by IT executives.* Fourth International Conference on Software Engineering Advances ICSEA '09, Porto, IEEE XPlore Digital Library.

Solms, B. V. (2001). Information security – A multidimensional discipline. *Computers & Security, 20*, 504–508.

Straub, D., & Welke, R. (1998). Coping with systems risk: Security planning models for management decision-making, Working paper version. *Management Information Systems Quarterly, 22*(4), 441–469.

Sullivan, R. J. (2010). *The changing nature of U.S. card payment fraud: Issues for industry and public policy*. Workshop on the Economics of Information Security Harvard University, Federal Reserve Bank of Kansas City.

Sullivan, R. J. (2010, May 21). *The changing nature of U.S. card payment fraud: Issues for industry and public policy*. Paper presented at the Workshop on the Economics of Information Security Harvard University.

Sundt, C. (2006). Information security and the law. *Information Security Technical Report, 11*, 2–9.

Swanson, M., & Guttman, B. (1996). *Generally accepted principles and practices for securing information technology systems*. NIST.

Symantec. (2011). *Symantec internet security threat report*, Vol. 16. Retrieved from http://www.symantec.com/business/threatreport/

Turner, M. J., Oltsik, J., et al. (2009). *ISO, ITIL, & COBIT together foster optimal security investment*. Retrieved from http://www.thecompliance-authority.com/iso-itil-a-cobit.php

Veiga, A. D., & Eloff, J. H. P. (2010). A framework and assessment instrument for information security culture. *Computers & Security, 29*, 196–207.

Verizon. (2011). *2011 data breach investigations report (No. MC14949 05/11)*. Verizon Business.

Webb, P., Pollard, C., & Ridley, G. (2006). *Attempting to define IT governance: Wisdom or folly?* Paper presented at the 39th Hawaii International Conference on Systems Sciences, Hawaii.

Weill, P., & Ross, J. W. (2005a). A matrixed approach to designing IT governance. *MIT Sloan Management Review, 46*(2), 26–34.

Whitman, M. E., & Mattord, H. J. (2009). *Principles of information security* (3rd ed.). Thompson Course Technology.

Section 3
IT Security Governance Innovations

Chapter 8
Information Security Governance Using Biometrics

Shrikant Tiwari
IT-Banaras Hindu University, India

Sanjay Kumar Singh
IT-Banaras Hindu University, India

ABSTRACT

To establish the identity of an individual is very critical with the advancement of technology in networked society. Thus, there is need for reliable user authentication technique to solve the growing demand for high level of Information Security Governance (ISG) depending on the requirement. Biometrics can be explained as the method to recognize an individual based on physical (face, fingerprint, ear, iris, etc.) or behavioral (voice, signature, gait, etc.) features to identify an individual person. Nowadays, biometric systems are being used for different purposes for information security like commercial, defense, government, and forensic applications as a means of establishing identity and to mitigate the risk which is one of the important objectives of Information Security Governance. In this chapter, an attempt has been made to explain the use and proper selection of biometric trait to help in Information Security Governance.

INTRODUCTION

According to NIST (National Institute of Standard and Technology) Information Technology (IT) governance is the process of establishing and maintaining a framework to provide assurance that information security strategies are aligned with and support business objectives, are consistent with applicable laws and regulations through adherence to policies and internal controls, and provide assignment of responsibility, all in an effort to manage risk. Information Security Governance consist of enterprise governance that provides strategic direction, ensures that objectives are achieved, manages identity and risks appropriately, uses organisational resources

DOI: 10.4018/978-1-4666-2083-4.ch008

judiciously, and monitors the success or failure of the enterprise security programme.

The concern about the Identity Management (IM) which is a subset of Information Security Governance is increasing across the public and private organisations. In private organisation it is most frequently thought of in the context of identity theft. According to FDIC figures, 10 million Americans suffered identity theft in 2003 resulted with a cost to business in excess of US$50 billion and a personal impact that is difficult to estimate[1]. As large amount as this sum is, identity theft is at the core of significantly broader economic vulnerabilities and national security concerns. Thus using biometrics to develop identity theft countermeasures has direct impact on civil infrastructure protection. Authentication and identification of people are critical to eliminating threats to organization security and public safety, and securing business transactions. As technology advances and public policy debates continue over the pros and cons of personal identity programs, the identity management industry continues to grow and change. Information and the knowledge based on it have increasingly become recognised as information assets, i.e., a business-critical asset, without which most organisations would simply cease to function. It is a business enabler, requiring organisations to provide adequate protection for this vital resource.

Organizations depend heavily on Information Technology to run their daily operations and deliver products and services efficiently. With an increasing reliability on IT, a growing complexity of organization IT infrastructure, and a constantly changing information security threat and risk environment, Information Security has become a mission-essential function. In order to ensure the organization ability to do business, security must be manage and govern to mitigate the risk to organization. To support their mission organization ensure that agencies are actively implementing appropriate information security control in a cost effective manner to reduce the risk at the required level.

Information Security Governance is a subset of Information Technology Governance and both come under the purview of Corporate Governance. Information Security Governance has recently expanded so much that organisations employ a specific person to handle only Information Security issues (Von Solms, S. H., 2005) Figure 1

Figure 1. Information security governance consisting of a number of disciplines

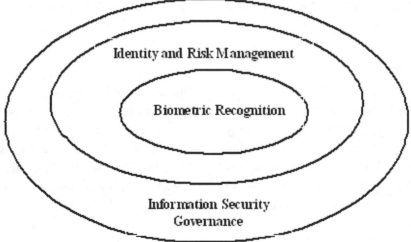

presents the relationship between the disciplines, and positions Information Security Governance with biometric recognition. Biometrics is the science of establishing the identity of an individual based on the physical, chemical or behavioral attributes of the person. The relevance of biometrics in modern society has been reinforced by the need for large-scale identity management systems whose functionality relies on the accurate determination of an individual's identity in the context of several different applications. All three governance types are crucial to a successfully implemented Information Security Governance structure, since all three governance types have some impact on the discipline.

The overall outline of this book chapter is as follows: The Section 2 reviews need for information security governance. Section 3 explains the objective of information security governance. Section 4 introduces the challenges of information security governance. Identity management requirement and Authentication methods are explained in the section 5. Biometrics and its system technology are explained in section 6. Section 7 explains the information security governance using biometrics and its application. Biometrics traits and its application are explained in detail in the section 8. Introduction to multibiometrics is explained in section 9. Solutions and recommendations of information security and use of cancelable biometrics are explained in section 10. Finally section 11 and 12 present future research direction and conclusion.

NEED FOR INFORMATION SECURITY GOVERNANCE

The key objective of information security governance is that the information must be protected from threats leading to loss, non availability, alteration and wrongful disclosure to reduce adverse impacts on the organisation to an acceptable level of risk. The risk includes errors, omissions, fraud, accidents and intentional changes and the role of information security is protecting the interest of those relying on information and systems from the harm resulting from failure of availability, confidentiality and integrity. Information security protects information assets against the risk of loss, operational discontinuity, misuse, unauthorised disclosure, inaccessibility and damage. It also protects against the ever-increasing potential for civil or legal liability that organisations face as a result of information inaccuracy and loss, or the absence of due care in its protection.

The dramatic rise of information crimes, including phishing and other cyber attacks, few today would contend that improved security is not a requirement. With new worms/malware and the increase in reported losses of confidential customer information and intellectual property theft, senior management is left with little choice but to address these issues. Information security requires a balance between sound management and applied technology. With the widespread use of networks, individuals and organisations are concerned with other risks pertaining to privacy of personal information and the organisation's need to protect the confidentiality of information, whilst encouraging electronic business.

The systems and processes that handle information have become pervasive throughout enterprises. Organisations may survive the loss of other assets, including facilities, equipment and people, but few can continue with the loss of their critical information (i.e., accounting and financial reporting information and operations and process knowledge and information) or customer data. The risks, benefits and opportunities these resources present have made information security governance a critical facet of overall governance. Information security should be an integral part of enterprise governance, aligned with IT governance and integrated into strategy, concept, design, implementation and operation. Protecting critical information must constitute one of the major risks to be considered in management strategies and should also be recognised as a crucial contributor to success.

Content owners, such as authors and authorized distributors, are losing billions of dollars annually in revenue due to the illegal copying and sharing of digital media.

Following are the advantages of Information Security Governance[2]:

- Good governance increases predictability and minimizes uncertainty by mitigating security risk to desired level.
- Share value and confidence is increased by good governance.
- Civil and legal liability is reduced caused by inaccuracy or negligence.
- The structure and framework to optimise allocation of limited security resources.
- Allocations of limited security resources are optimized.
- Persons involved are assured regarding information security policy.
- There is significant improvement in efficient and effective risk management, process improvement, and quick rapid incident response.
- Decisions are not based on faulty information.
- Important business activities, such as mergers and acquisitions of organizations, business process recovery and regulation are safeguarded and accountable.

OBJECTIVE OF INFORMATION SECURITY GOVERNANCE

The objective of information security is to secure information recorded, processed, stored, and communicated which is considered to be valuable asset for any organization. Information security governance also has a defining role in identifying key information security roles and responsibilities, and it influences information security policy development and oversight and ongoing monitoring activities. To ensure an appropriate level of support of agency missions and the proper implementation of current and future information security requirements, each agency should establish a formal Information Security Governance structure.

One of the main Information security governance objective is also the protection of relevant information (e.g., multimedia data) thereby ensuring that only genuine person are able to access the contents available in organization. Thus an organization must have an effective security governance strategy and information must be treated like any other asset essential to the survival and success of the organization.

The objective of Information Security Governance consists of following subtask[3]:

1. Strategic alignment of business strategy with information security to achieve organisational objectives.
2. Appropriate measures should be taken to manage and mitigate risks and reduce potential impacts on information resources to an acceptable level.
3. In order to achieve organisational objectives performance measurement by measuring, monitoring and reporting information security governance metrics to ensure that risk is optimized to acceptable level.
4. Information security knowledge and infrastructure should be used efficiently and effectively.
5. Optimise information security investments in support of organisational objectives to achieve better return on investment.

CHALLENGES OF INFORMATION SECURITY GOVERNANCE

Listed below are challenges of ineffective governance (Allen, 2007). These challenges can be very useful in presenting rationale to leadership and increased security for implementing an effective institution security governance model.

1. Understand the implications of ubiquitous access and distribution of information with reference to security of information.
2. Focusing the institution-wide nature of the security problem.
3. Overcoming the lack of a game plan at implementation level.
4. Distributing the proper organizational structure and segregation of duties at various levels.
5. Understanding complex global legal compliance requirements and liability risks.
6. Assessing security risks and the magnitude of harm to the organization.
7. Determining and justifying appropriate levels of resources and investment.
8. Dealing with the intangible nature of security.
9. Reconciling inconsistent deployment of security best practices and standards.
10. Overcoming difficulties in creating and sustaining a security-aware culture.
11. Assessment of various information security tools and deployment of security tool according to requirement.

IDENTITY MANAGEMENT REQUIREMENT

Identity Management is an important component of Information Security Governance and establishing a user's identity and determining where he is allowed to venture and what he might be entitled to do when he has reached his destination is a multipronged process. Authentication, authorization, and accounting address these fundamental issues:

- **Authentication Asks:** Who are you?
- **Authorization Asks:** What are you allowed to do, and when?
- **Accounting Asks:** When, where, and how long were you there?

Authentication

Authentication is the process of verifying that someone, or something, is really who or what he says he is. Following are important methods for authentication:

- Passwords and access cards.
- Strong authentication and biometrics.

The existing authentication methods use a generic cryptographic system and the user authentication method is possession based. It means the possession of the decrypting key is sufficient to establish the authenticity of the user. Since cryptographic keys are long and random they are difficult to member. So, these keys are stored and released based on some alternative authentication mechanism i.e. password. As shown in Figure 2 if internet users use simple password then it is easy to guess, and they compromise security and complex password which are difficult to remember, and are costly to maintain. Most internet users use the same password across different application, as hacker or impostor after getting a single password can now access multiple applications. So in a multiuser account case, passwords are unable to provide no repudiation.

Password Survey (Nov. 2006)

- 26%- use common words, dates, phone, address numbers.
- 38%- recycle old passwords.
- 62%- change password only if perceiving a security threat.
- 17%- keep password list on monitor, keyboard or desk drawer.

Figure 2. Different methods to remember the password

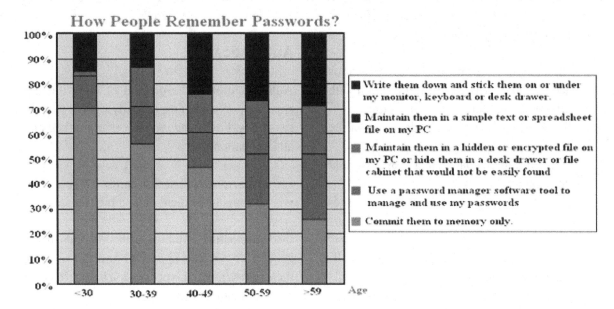

Authorization

Authorization consists of rules for an organization that specify who is allowed access, and where and when they are allowed to go. When a user signs on, he provides his identity to identification devices, which in turn check his access level with the authorization server. Any new attempt to perform an action results in the rules being consulted prior to granting said access. The process is efficient, because authentication and authorization often reside on the same server. Computers that act as Access Control Servers (ACSs) running mission-specific software are usually responsible for the authentication process, the accounting process, and some aspects of the authorization process.

Accounting

Accounting is the process of gathering data to determine the following items:

- What resource access did a user occupy or which networks did he visit, and when did it happen?
- What was the consumption the length of time the user was there and the amount of data that was downloaded?

The data is used to determine tracking (of users), auditing, trends analysis, capacity planning, billing, and cost allocation.

Authentication Methods

There are three main ways to authenticate an identity of a person: (Reid, 2003).

Something We Know: This refers to anything that needs to be remembered to prove our identity. The information remembered could be of the following types:

- Passwords.
- Pass phrases.
- Personal Identification Numbers(PIN).
- Secret handshakes.

Passwords are the most frequently used method to authenticate a person that only he is required to know. However passwords have many limitations: They can be stolen, written down in easily accessible locations, shared, or guessed. To strengthen passwords, they are normally implemented with a supporting policy and guidelines. Sharing passwords, writing them down, or not changing them frequently violates most password policies and should be avoided. Automated methods can be used to enforce a password policy to help users.

Something We Have: This refers to anything that the user is required to possess which can be used as an authenticating token. A token or card is generally issued to one user uniquely and it should be with the user to authenticate himself when required. A token is registered to a user, and when it is presented for authentication, that unique token is verified as being genuine or imposter. If the token is matched, the user is authenticated; otherwise the authentication request is rejected and the user may be an imposter. Tokens are categorised into two types:

- Storage tokens
- Dynamic tokens

Currently the most popular way to protect data or information on a network or computing device is the use of password. But password has its own limitation and this has already been explained in the previous section.

Something We Are: Any physiological (static) or behavioural (dynamic) trait or characteristics that can be reliably measured can be used to authenticate a person is called Biometric. Physiological characteristics are static in nature and change very little which include fingerprints, iris and hand geometry, ECG signals, retina, facial characteristics, thermal images etc. and behavioural characteristics are dynamic which include signature, voice, keystroke, gait etc. Soft Biometrics are the features such as age, gender, height, weight, ethnicity, hair color, and clothing color can be used to describe a person in some limited contexts. Individually they have little discriminatory power, but when several are combined they begin to approximate a biometric system (see Figure 3).

The performance of different authentication method is shown in Figure 4. The parameters for performance evaluation are security, convenience and cost. As can be seen from the figure biometrics is having highest security and cost compare to other authentication methods.

BIOMETRICS

A biometric system is essentially a pattern recognition system that recognizes a person by comparing the binary code of a uniquely specific biological or physical characteristic to the binary code of the stored characteristic. Samples are taken from individuals to see if there is a similarity to biometric references previously taken from known individuals.

Why Biometrics?

The objective of Biometrics is to mitigate the security risk and to facilitate convenient transactions which can be used as an important information security tool. Thus we can say the biometric can be a very effective tool of information security governance. Identity management is a subset of information security governance and it includes regulating and controlling the places where information about identity is used or processed. It is our assertion that a biometric system alone will never add security to a system that does not have good identity controls around the beginning, or subsequent, enrolment of individuals. Any individual can self-enrol a biometric with no check or audit, system spoofing is easy, regardless of the strength of the biometric control. The strength of biometric can be enhanced by authenticating the supporting documentation, such as birth certificates or passports.

Figure 3. Different biometric traits

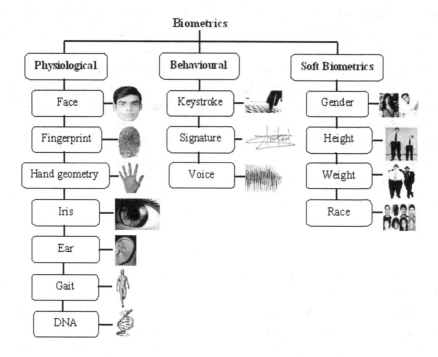

Biometrics is not an overnight development and it took years of development of the technology to mature, which we are having now is in the fourth decade. With the advancement of time as in many other areas, advances in computer technology also accelerated the capabilities and quality of biomet-

ric technology. Before application of biometrics it is important to study its potential and considering specific applications for use, it is more important to appreciate its substantive qualities and inherent limitations. There is no equivalent substitute for biometrics in the automated subject identification,

Figure 4. Authentication element positioning

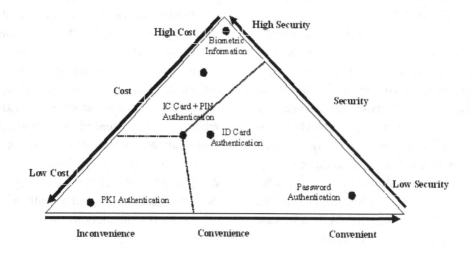

and any claim to the contrary, including those who assert we can rely on "something we have" or "something we know" without biometrics, must be treated with great scepticism.

Biometrics offers certain advantages such as negative recognition and no repudiation that cannot be provided by tokens and passwords (Prabhakar, Pankanti, and Jain, 2003). Negative recognition can be explained as the method by which a biometric system determines that a certain individual is enrolled in the system although the individual might deny intentionally. Care should be taken especially in case of critical applications such as welfare disbursement scheme where an impostor may attempt to claim to be genuine where multiple benefits are to be provided under different names. Biometrics can be used as non-repudiation in such a way to guarantee that an individual who accesses a certain facility cannot later deny using it.

Biometric systems make use of variety of physical or behavioural characteristics, which consist of fingerprint, face, hand/finger geometry, iris, retina, signature, gait, palm print, voice pattern, ear, hand vein, odour or the DNA information to identify an individual. (Jain, Bolle and Pankanti, 1999, Wayman, Jain, Maltoni, and Maio, 2005). These characteristics are known as traits, indicators, identifiers or modalities in different biometric literature,. Although biometric systems have their own shortcomings (O'Gorman, 2002) but they have an advantage over existing security methods where they cannot be easily shared or stolen. Apart from enhancing security, biometric systems also enhance user convenience by alleviating the requirement to design and remember passwords which is difficult to recall correctly.

The primary use of Biometric security will be to replace the current password system as maintaining password security can be a tedious task for even a small organization. According to policy and guidelines passwords have to be changed very regularly and most of the time people forget their password or lock themselves out of the system by incorrectly typing their password repeatedly. Very often people write their password down and keep it near their computer and this completely defeats the purpose of security.

Thus we can assert that biometric identifiers are difficult to share copy and exchange because in case of biometrics the person being authenticated is required to be present at the time and place of authentication. In this way it is very difficult for hackers or impostor to forge Biometrics (as it requires more experience, time, memory and access privileges). Finally a biometrics based security scheme is a better alternative to traditional authentication schemes. Biometrics can also be used in conjunction with password (or tokens) to increase the level of internet security.

Biometric System Technology

A biometric system is basically a pattern recognition system which identifies an individual based on their physiological and behavioral characteristic. As shown in Figure 5 a biometric system consists of five main modules: a sensor module; a quality assessment and feature extraction module; a matching module; and a database module. Each of these modules is described below.

Sensor Module: In order to acquire the raw biometric data of an individual a suitable biometric reader or scanner is required and this is the interface between user and biometric system. Thus to capture fingerprint images, for example, an optical fingerprint sensor may be used to image the friction ridge structure of the fingertip. Sensor module is interface between user and biometric system and therefore, the performance of the biometric system depends on the quality of the sensor module and the capture data. The quality of the raw data is also impacted by the characteristics of the camera that is used to capture the images.

Quality Assessment and Feature Extraction Module: The function of quality assessment and feature extraction module is to check the quality

Figure 5. Biometric system technology

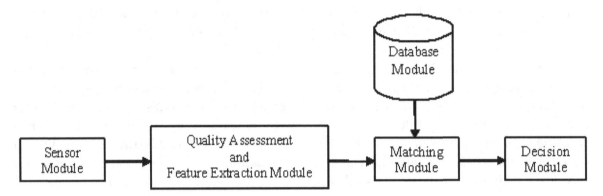

of enrolled data in order to determine its applicability for further processing. In order to improve the quality the capture data is subjected a signal enhancement algorithm.

Thus if quality of data is very poor then the user is asked to present the biometric data again. After this the biometric data is processed and unique features are extracted for next processing step. This unique feature is stored in the database at the time of enrollment and it is called template.

Matching Module: The function of matching module is to match the unique features extracted from the previous module to the stored template and generate match scores. For example in a fingerprint-based biometric system, the number of matching minutiae between the enrolled and stored features is calculated. These match scores are used to authenticate an individual biometric user.

Database Module: Database of biometric system consist of the feature set obtained from the raw biometric data i.e. template. This is the repository of biometric information that is templates and is stored in the database along with biographic information such as Name, Address, Personal Identification Number (PIN), etc. to distinguish the biometric user. Depending on the application requirement the data acquired during the enrolment process may or may not be

supervised by an operator. For example a biometric user a biometric-enabled ATM, will have to register their biometric features in the presence of the bank authority, after presenting their non biometric details while creating a new computer account user may proceed to enroll their biometrics feature without any supervision.

The template (extracted feature) of a user can be extracted from a single biometric sample, or generated by processing multiple samples. Thus, the minutiae template of a finger may be extracted after mosaicing multiple samples of the same finger. Some biometric systems store multiple templates in order to account for the intra-class variations associated with a user. Face recognition systems, for instance, may store multiple templates of an individual, with each template corresponding to a different facial pose with respect to the camera. Depending on the application, the template can be stored in the central database of the biometric system or be recorded on a token (e.g., smart card) issued to the individual.

The raw biometric images stored in the database are often referred to as gallery images while those acquired during authentication are known as probe images. These are synonymous with the terms stored images and query or input images, respectively.

Types of Biometrics

The biometrics treats can be characterized in to three categories: Physiological, Behavioral and Soft Biometrics. Following is the brief description about the types of biometrics.

Physiological

Physiological methods try to identify the user by some sort of physical trait that is typical to the user. Example includes fingerprint, face, iris, ear and retina etc. The physical trait is analysed, measured and digitally stored. Physiological biometrics is much harder to mask or alter, and can be collected without user compliance.

Behavioral

Behavioral biometrics deals with the identification or verification of individuals based on the behavioural characteristics e.g. voice, signature, gait etc. Behavioural biometrics are much less likely to be deployed in a privacy-invasive fashion

Soft Biometrics

Less powerful biometrics is called soft biometrics. Unlike the face, ear, or fingerprint, these soft biometrics are not expected to stay constant over time, or to uniquely identify a subject. Features such as age, gender, height, weight, ethnicity, hair color, and clothing color can be used to describe a person in some limited contexts. Individually they have little discriminatory power, but when several are combined they begin to approximate a biometric system.

Soft biometrics has been used not only to supplement hard biometrics, but have been used on their own for recognition. Soft biometric traits are those characteristics that provide some information about the individual, but lack the distinctiveness and permanence to sufficiently differentiate any two individuals. Soft biometric traits are physical, behavioral or adhered human characteristics, classifiable in pre–defined human compliant categories. These categories are, unlike in the classical biometric case, established and time–proven by humans with the aim of differentiating individuals. In other words the soft biometric traits instances are created in a natural way, used by humans to distinguish their peers. We note that the human compliant labeling is referred to as semantic annotation in (Sina, Nixon, and Guo, 2008).

Soft biometrics have gained more and more interest of the biometry and other communities for various reasons, like the need for higher reliability in biometric systems and the great number of advantages coming along with the integration of soft biometric traits in systems.

INFORMATION SECURITY GOVERNANCE USING BIOMETRICS

We propose a framework for Information Security Governance using biometrics and this framework in turn provides the basis for the development of a cost effective information security programme that supports the organisation's goals and provides an acceptable level of predictability for operations by limiting the impacts of adverse events. The proposed framework generates a set of activities that supports fulfilment of Information Security Governance objective. Figure 6 indicates the necessary people components in developing a security strategy aligned with business objectives. To promote alignment, the business strategy provides one of the inputs into risk management and information security strategy development. Other inputs are the business processes, risk assessments, business input analyses and the information resources critical for their success. Regulatory requirements must also be considered in developing the security strategy. Security requirements are the output of the risk management activity and are input to the planning activity together with the current state

Figure 6. Conceptual information security governance

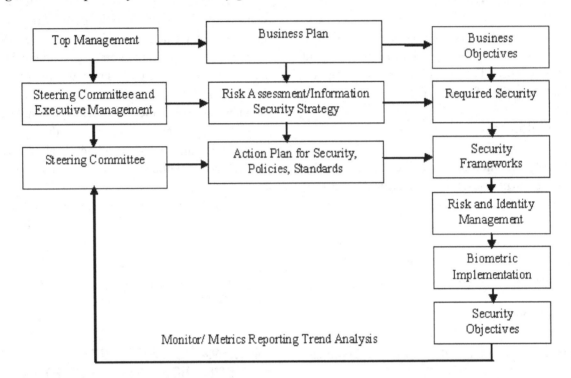

of the enterprise relative to these security requirements. Other inputs to the planning stage are the available resources and applicable constraints for achieving the desired state of security.

As shown in block diagram biometric implementation is part of Risk and Identity management, the selection of biometric trait and detail configuration of the selected biometric trait is done at the implementation level. After implementation security objective is evaluated and analysis is done, and the analysis report is submitted to the steering committee.

Given the scenario and goals of a commercial application, there are a number of trade-offs that the decision makers must take into account during design. This trade-off may include recognition reliability, system integrity, complexity, cost, privacy, government standards, liveness detection, ease of integration, durability, modality of usage, etc. For example, a commercial application that requires the biometric system to work for all the people

all the time demands a high recognition reliability which may come at an expense of requiring high computation/memory power or specialized capture equipment. In another example, compliance with certain government standards may facilitate inter-operability but may decrease recognition reliability.

The strategy provides the basis for an action plan comprised of one or more security programmes that, as implemented, achieve the security objectives. The strategy and action plans must contain provisions for monitoring as well as defined metrics to determine the level of success. This provides feedback to the chief information security officer (CISO) and steering committee to allow for mid-course correction and ensure that security initiatives are on track to meet defined objectives. Once managers and directors know what information resources need what level of protection, information security baselines can be developed and implemented. Information security baselines are the minimum acceptable security that should be provided to protect information resources. Baselines vary depending on the sensitivity and criticality of the asset. Baselines can be expressed as technical, procedural and personnel standards throughout the enterprise.

As explained earlier one of the main objective of Information Security Governance is to provide high level of information security and minimize the risk to achieve business objectives. Since Identity Management (IM) is the subset of Information Security Governance or part of Information Security Governance and authentication or authorization is an important component of IM, we can use Biometrics for Identification Management or Information Security Governance. Identity refers to the packaging of subject information. Identity is made up of elements such as identifiers assigned to subjects, subjects credentials and different attributes related to subjects. Attributes can be separated into two categories: static attributes,

which are modified frequently, and dynamic attributes which are modified infrequently. Static attributes include names, address, departments and job titles. Dynamic attributes include user's current locations. The collections of all of these attributes are also called profiles.

The proposed model for Information Security Governance is shown in the Figure 7 through block diagram.

Synchronization of master ID management repositories and ID management ledgers for managed subjects/objects is called ID provisioning. ID provisioning provides integrated management of administrator and end user ID information and attributes information (access rights, administrator rights, etc.), and provides central creation, modification and deletion functions. An integrated identity management structure must be deployed in order to carry out ID provisioning. Integrated identity management covers a wide range of systems, including physical security

Figure 7. Integrating identity management model

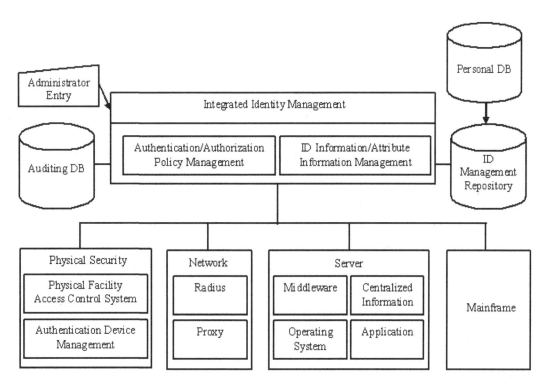

systems, networks, server operating systems, middleware, applications and legacy systems with ID information management structures.

The enrolment, verification, and identification processes involved in user recognition make use of the following system modules:

- **Capture:** A digital representation of biometric characteristic needs to be sensed and captured. A biometric sensor, such as a digital camera or fingerprint scanner, is one of the central pieces of a biometric capture module. The captured digital representation of the biometric characteristic is often known as a sample; for example, in the case of a fingerprint system, the raw digital fingerprint image captured by the fingerprint scanner is the sample. The data capture module may also contain other components (e.g., a keyboard and screen) to capture other (non-biometric) data.

- **Feature Extraction:** In order to facilitate matching or comparison, the raw digital representation (sample) is usually further processed by a feature extractor to generate a compact but expressive representation, called a feature set.

- **Template Creation:** The template creation module organizes one or more feature sets into an enrolment template that will be saved in some persistent storage. The enrolment template is sometimes also referred to as a reference.

- **Pre-selection and Matching:** The pre-selection (or filtering) stage is primarily used in an identification system when the number of enrolled templates is large. Its role is to reduce the effective size of the template database so that the input needs to be matched to a relatively small number of templates. The matching (or comparison) stage (also known as a matcher) takes a feature set and an enrolment template as inputs and computes the similarity between them in terms of a matching score, also known as similarity score. The matching score is compared to a system threshold to make the final decision; if the match score is higher than the threshold, the person is recognized, otherwise not.

- **Data Storage:** Is devoted to storing templates and other demographic information about the user. Depending on the application, the template may be stored in internal or external storage devices or be recorded on a smart card issued to the individual. Using these five modules, three main processes can be performed, namely, enrolment, verification, and identification.

A verification system uses the enrolment and verification processes while an identification system uses the enrolment and identification processes. The three processes are:

- **Enrolment:** User enrolment is a process that is responsible for registering individuals in the biometric system storage. During the enrolment process, the biometric characteristic of a subject is first captured by a biometric scanner to produce a sample (see Figure 8). A quality check is often performed to ensure that the acquired sample can be reliably processed by successive stages. A feature extraction module is then used to produce a feature set. The template creation module uses the feature set to produce an enrolment template. Some systems collect multiple samples of a user and then either select the best image (or feature set) or fuse multiple images (or feature sets) to create a composite template. The enrolment process then takes the enrolment template and stores it in the system storage together with the demographic information about the user (such as an identifier, name, gender, height, etc.).

Figure 8. Biometric enrolment & authentication system

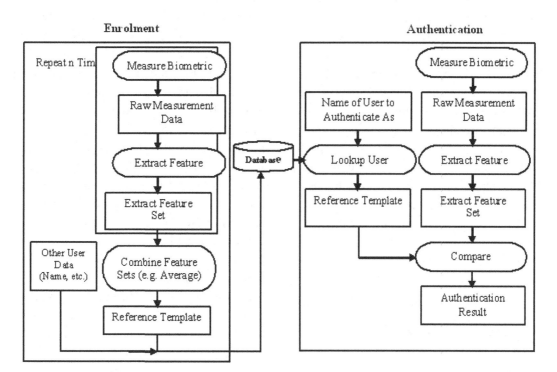

- **Verification:** The verification process is responsible for confirming the claim of identity of the subject. During the recognition phase, an identifier of the subject (such as username or PIN [Personal Identification Number]) is provided (e.g., through a keyboard or a keypad or a proximity card) to claim an identity; the biometric scanner captures the characteristic of the subject and converts it to a sample, which is further processed by the feature extraction module to produce a feature set. The resulting feature set is fed to the matcher, where it is compared against the enrolment template(s) of that subject (retrieved from the system storage based on the subject's identifier). The verification process produces a match/non-match decision.
- **Identification:** In the identification process, the subject does not explicitly claim an identity and the system compares the

feature set (extracted from the captured biometric sample) against the templates of all (or a subset of) the subjects in the system storage; the output is a candidate list that may be empty (if no match is found) or contain one (or more) identifier(s) of matching enrolment templates. Because identification in large databases is computationally expensive, a pre-selection stage is often used to filter the number of enrolment templates that have to be matched against the input feature set. Depending on the application domain, a biometric system could operate either as an online system or an off-line system. In case if the recognition is to be performed quickly and immediate response is required then online system is used otherwise off-line system is used. Online systems are often fully automatic and require that the biometric characteristic be captured using a live-scan scanner, the enrolment process be unattended, there be no (manual) quality control, and the matching and decision making be fully automatic. Off-line systems, however, are often semi-automatic, where the biometric acquisition could be through an offline scanner (e.g., scanning a fingerprint image from a latent or inked fingerprint card), the enrolment may be supervised (e.g., when a suspect is "booked," a police officer guides the fingerprint acquisition process), a manual quality check may be performed to ensure good quality acquisition, and the matcher may return a list of candidates which are then manually examined by a forensic expert to arrive at a final decision.

Application of Biometrics

According to Wayman the application context of a biometric recognition system can be understood by examining the following characteristics of the user:

- Cooperative versus non-cooperative user.
- Habituated versus non-habituated user.
- Attended versus non-attended user.
- Standard versus non-standard operating environment.
- Public versus private user.
- Open versus closed user.
- Overt versus covert user.

Cooperative user versus non-cooperative user refers to the behavior of the genuine or impostor in interacting with the fingerprint recognition application. In a positive recognition application i.e., an application that assumes a positive claim of identity; it is in the best interest of an impostor to cooperate with the system to be accepted as a valid user. On the other hand, in a negative recognition application i.e., an application that assumes a negative claim of identity; it is in the best interest of the impostor not to cooperate with the system

so that the system does not find their matching to any of the subjects in the watch list. For example electronic banking is a cooperative application whereas an airport application to catch terrorists is an example of a non-cooperative application.

If a subject is aware that they are being recognized by biometrics, the application is categorized as overt and if the subject is unaware, the application is covert. Face recognition can be used in a covert application by surveillance cameras, while fingerprint recognition cannot be used in this mode except for forensic identification of criminals based on latent fingerprints. Most of the commercial applications of biometrics are overt, whereas some government and law enforcement applications are covert. Thus overt applications need only verification whereas covert applications typically require identification of an individual.

The category, habituated versus non-habituated use of a biometric system refers to how often the users in that application interact with the biometric recognition system. For example, a computer network logon application typically has habituated users after an initial habituation period due to their use of the system on a regular basis. However, in a driver's license application, the users are non-habituated since a driver's license is renewed only once in 5 years or so. This is an important consideration when designing a biometric system because the familiarity of users with the system affects its recognition accuracy.

Attended versus non-attended classification refers to whether the process of biometric data acquisition in an application is observed, guided, or supervised by a human e.g., a security officer. Depending upon the requirement, an application may have an attended enrolment but non-attended recognition. For example, a banking application may have a supervised enrolment when an ATM card is issued to a user but the subsequent uses of the biometric system for ATM transactions will be non-attended. Non-cooperative applications generally require attended operation.

The category standard versus non-standard environment refers to whether the application is being operated in a controlled environment such as temperature, pressure, moisture, illumination conditions, etc. Indoor applications such as computer network logon operate in a controlled environment whereas outdoor applications such as parking lot surveillance operate in a nonstandard environment. This classification is also important for the system designer as a more rugged biometric scanner is needed for a non-standard environment. Similarly, infrared face recognition may be preferred over visible-band face recognition for outdoor surveillance at night. The classification Public or private refers to whether the users of the application are customers or employees of the organization deploying the biometric system. For example, a network logon application is used by the employees and managed by the information technology manager of that company is a private application. The use of biometric data in conjunction with electronic identity cards is an example of a public application.

Closed versus open application refers to whether a person's biometric template is used for a single or multiple applications. For example, a user may use a fingerprint-based recognition system to enter secure facilities, for computer network logon, electronic banking, and ATM. Should all these applications use separate template storage for each application, or should they all access the same central template storage? A closed application may be based on a proprietary template whereas an open system may need standard biometric data format and compression method to exchange and compare information among different systems most likely developed by different vendors.

Biometric recognition applications are classified as horizontal categorization and vertical categorization. Horizontal categorization results in the following main categories of biometric applications:

- **Physical Access Control:** Access is restricted to facilities such as nuclear plants, bank vaults, corporate board rooms, and even health-clubs, amusement parks, and lockers.
- **Logical Access Control:** Access to desktop computers or remote servers and databases is restricted to authorized users. Increasingly, access to software applications is also being restricted to only authorize users.
- **Transaction Authentication (or Consumer Identification):** Transactions may be executed at ATM site or from remote locations for on-line banking or between banks (e.g., in high-value transactions). Fingerprint recognition systems are used for security of the transaction as well as accountability (so the parties involved in the transaction cannot later deny it).
- **Device Access Control:** Laptops, PDAs, cell phones, and other electronic devices often contain personal and sensitive data. To protect such data, fingerprint recognition systems are used to conduct recognition on the stand-alone device.
- **Time and Attendance:** Time and attendance systems are used to keep track of employee working hours and to compute payrolls. Use of fingerprint recognition systems in these applications is fairly well received to improve efficiency for employees and also for preventing various types of payroll frauds (e.g., buddy-punching).
- **Civil Identification:** In civilian identification application, the most important objective is to prevent multiple enrolments and to find duplicates (e.g., duplicate passport, driver license, national identification card). The size of the database can be of the order of millions (e.g., the entire population of a country). In some applications (such as border control to prevent suspected ter-

rorists or expellees from entering the country), the identification is not needed to be conducted against the entire population but rather against a "watch-list" database.

- **Forensic Identification:** In forensic identification, latent fingerprints lifted from the crime scenes are matched against a criminal database to identify the suspect (and sometimes the victims).

Vertical categorization results in the following main industries that benefit the most from the use of fingerprint systems:

- Health care.
- Financial.
- Gaming and hospitality (casinos, hotels, etc.).
- Retail.
- Education.
- Manufacturing.
- High technology and telecommunications.
- Travel and transport.
- Federal, state, municipal, or other governments.
- Military.
- Law enforcement.

Each vertical market may have a need for a number of different horizontal applications (see Table 1). For example, while the most widespread almost ubiquitous use of fingerprint recognition systems in law enforcement departments is for criminal investigations, these departments also use computers that contain sensitive data. So, this sector needs solutions for fingerprint-based logical access control. Further, law enforcement departments have laboratories and other restricted physical areas, so they can benefit from fingerprint-based physical access control solutions. Fingerprint-based time and attendance solutions can also be used to manage payroll of law enforcement officers and other employees of the department (see Figure 9).

Table 1. Biometric recognition applications are divided here into three categories

Forensic	Government (Civil)	Commercial
Corpse Identification Criminal Investigation Missing Children	Social Security Welfare Disbursement Border Control Passport Control National ID card Driver License Credentialing	Computer Network Logon Electronic Data Security e-Commerce Internet Access ATM, Credit Card Physical Access Control Cellular Phones Personal Digital Assistant Medical Records Management Distance Learning

BIOMETRIC TRAITS

A number of biometric characteristics are being used in various applications and each biometric has its own advantages or disadvantages and, therefore, the choice of a biometric trait for a particular application depends on a variety of issues besides its matching performance (see Table 2). Jain et al. (Jain, Bolle, and Pankanti, 1999) have identified seven factors that determine the suitability of a physical or a behavioral trait to be used in a biometric application:

- **Universality:** All biometric users should have that particular trait to be recognized otherwise the biometric system will fail.
- **Uniqueness:** The biometric feature of the selected biometric trait should be unique i.e. interclass difference should be there.
- **Permanence:** The selected biometric trait for recognition should be permanent or invariant over a period of time or age, otherwise biometric system may fail.
- **Measurability:** The acquired raw data should be amenable to processing in order to extract representative feature sets. The biometric trait to be used for recognition

Figure 9. Various applications involving electronic access or transaction that require reliable automatic user recognition

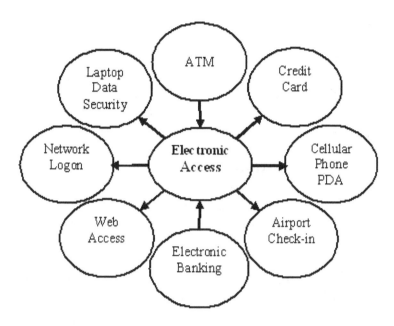

should be possible to acquire and digitize the biometric feature using suitable devices that do not cause undue inconvenience to the individual.

- **Performance:** The accuracy of biometric recognition system should meet the requirement imposed by the application.

Table 2. Comparison of biometrics technology (Ross, Nandakumar, and Jain, 2006)

Biometrics	Universality	Uniqueness	Permanence	Collectability	Performance	Acceptability	Circumvention
Face	High	Low	Medium	High	Low	High	Low
Fingerprint	Medium	High	High	Medium	High	Medium	High
Hand Geometry	Medium	Medium	Medium	High	Medium	Medium	Medium
Keystrokes	-	-	Low	Medium	Low	Medium	Medium
Hand Vein	Medium	Medium	Medium	Medium	Medium	Medium	High
Iris	High	High	High	Medium	High	Low	High
Retinal Scan	High	High	Medium	Low	High	Low	High
Signature	Low	Low	Low	High	Low	High	Low
Voice Print	Medium	Low	Low	Medium	Low	High	Low
F.Thermograms	High	High	Low	High	Medium	High	High
Odor	High	High	High	Low	Low	Medium	Low
DNA	High	High	High	Low	High	Low	Low
Gait	Medium	Low	Low	High	Low	High	Medium
Ear	Medium	Medium	High	Medium	Medium	High	Medium

- **Acceptability:** Users of biometric system should be willing to present their biometric trait to the system for recognition.
- **Circumvention:** Spoofing the biometric system should not be an easy task e.g., fake fingers, in the case of physical traits, and mimicry, in the case of behavioral traits.

The choice of biometric traits depends on applications where it is to be applied as each biometric trait has its own strengths and weaknesses. According to literature available, no single trait is expected to effectively meet the requirements of all the applications. The matching between a biometric trait and an application is determined depending upon the characteristics of the application and the properties of that particular trait. The important issues that need to be addressed in selecting a biometric trait for a particular application are: (Maio, Jain and Prabhakar, 2009)

- What is the requirement, a verification or identification? If database size is large then there is requirement of very distinctive biometric trait e.g., fingerprints or iris.
- What are the implementation characteristics? The characteristics include: automatic or semiautomatic, users are trained or un-

trained, users cooperative or non-cooperative and required application is covert or overt.
- What is the memory size required? An application that performs the recognition on a smart card may require a small template size.
- How much accuracy is required? Distinctive biometric trait is more appropriate for hogh accuracy applications.
- What is the acceptability rate? Acceptability depends on the cultural, ethical, social, religious, different demographic regions and hygienic standards.

Figure 10 displays several biometric traits that have been either used in commercial systems or are being explored.

According to literature available no single biometric is expected to effectively meet all the requirements (e.g., accuracy, practicality, cost) imposed by all applications (e.g., Digital Rights Management (DRM), access control, welfare distribution). Thus we can say that no biometric trait is sufficient to all applications. The usefulness of a particular biometric to a specific application is established depending upon the nature and requirements of the application, and the properties

Figure 10. Examples of biometrics traits: a) ear, b) face, c) facial thermogram, d) hand thermogram, e) hand vein, f) hand geometry, g) fingerprint, h) iris, i) retina, j) signature, and k) voice

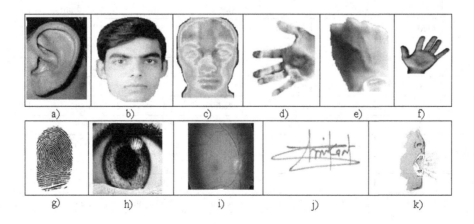

of the biometric trait. A brief description to some of the commonly used biometric characteristics is given below:

Face

Face recognition is a non-intrusive method, and facial attributes are probably the most common biometric features used by humans to recognize an individual. Facial imaging or recognition identifies people by comparison of sample images to stored templates using extracted features and mathematical analysis of the groups of acquired pixels.

Biometric system using face recognition technology capture facial images using digital cameras, and like other biometric trait generate templates for comparing a live face to a stored enrolment template. Face recognition is mostly used in the verification mode. Although the authentication performance of the face recognition systems that are commercially available is justified but they impose a number of restrictions on how the facial images are captured, often requiring a fixed and simple background with controlled lightning condition. Face recognition systems also have difficulty in matching face images captured from two different views or pose, under different illumination conditions, and at different interval of time. In order for a facial recognition system to work well in practical situation, it should automatically (i) detect whether a face is present in the captured image; (ii) locate face recognition range from a static, controlled "mug-shot" authentication to dynamic, uncontrolled face identification in a cluttered background. Most popular approaches to face recognition (Li and Jain, 2005) are based on either (i) the location and shape of facial attributes, such as the eyes, eyebrows, nose, lips, and chin and their spatial relationships, or (ii) the overall (global) analysis of the face image that represents a face as a weighted combination of a number of canonical faces. It is interesting to note that face recognition not based on common facial features such as cheeks, nose, chin, and mouth, which

cannot be found reliably by the face recognition algorithms. However it must find the eye centres for the purpose of detecting the face (iii) recognize the face from a general viewpoint i.e., from any pose under different ambient conditions.

Applications

Implementing a face recognition system has its own set of challenges that other trait may not experience. For example, other biometric traits might work in different kinds of application environments and, to a certain degree, may not be affected as much by external variables. With face recognition, performance can be greatly influenced by the type of application being used.

Application environments for face recognition systems can be categorized as "controlled" and "random." In a controlled environment, most of the parameters are under control and there is not much variation in the background conditions, pose, expression or illumination. The user will look into the camera and good quality enrolment and verification templates will be created. A typical example of a controlled environment is of a physical access entry at a location or site.

There is more variation in a random environment, and typical example of a random setting is in surveillance. Facial recognition systems have not been successfully used at for such purposes. Results are poor because the facial recognition system has to identify and filter faces from different lighting environments, angles, poses, and different locations with varying background distractions. Face recognition has been successful in access control, whether to a location, building, room, or for computer access. Face recognition has been successfully applied as a tool for screening individuals to see if they are already known to the system. This is used for fraud prevention when individuals apply for visas or driver's licenses. The same technique is used in some law enforcement jurisdictions during the criminal booking process to get an immediate indication of the identity of an arrestee well before a FBI fingerprint check is conducted.

Fingerprint

Fingerprints for personal identification has been used for many years. The matching (i.e., identification) accuracy using fingerprints has been shown to be very high (Wilson, Hicklin, Bone, Korves, Grother, lery, Micheals, Zoepfl, Otto, and Watson, 2004). A fingerprint is the pattern of ridges and valleys on the surface of a fingertip whose formation is determined during the first seven months of neonatal development of newborn. Even the fingerprints of identical twins are different and so are the prints on each finger of the same person (Maltoni, Maio, Jain, and Prabhakar, 2003). Presently most fingerprint scanners cost less than US $50 when ordered in large quantities and the low cost of embedding a fingerprint-based biometric in a system e.g., laptop computer has become very cheap in a large number of applications. Fingerprint recognition systems are adequate for authentication systems in several applications, particularly forensics. Multiple fingerprints of a person (e.g., ten-prints) provide additional information to allow for large-scale identification involving millions of identities. One problem with large-scale fingerprint recognition systems is that they require a huge amount of computational resources, especially when operating in the identification mode.

Applications

Fingerprint biometrics have four main application areas: large-scale Automated Fingerprint Imaging Systems (AFIS) that are generally used by law enforcement, for fraud prevention in entitlement programs, physical access control (doors) and "logical" access to computer systems. Workstation access applications seem to be based almost exclusively around fingerprints, due to the relatively low cost, small size easily integrated into keyboards, mice, and laptops and ease of integration.

Ear

Ears have gained attention in biometrics due to the robustness of their shape. This shape does not change due to emotion as the face does, and the ear is relatively constant over most of a person's life. It has been found that the shape of the ear and the structure of the cartilaginous tissue of the pinna are distinctive. The ear recognition approaches are based on matching the distance of salient points on the pinna from a landmark location on the ear. The ear of human being is a good biometric characteristic since it is full of features. It is a stable structure, which varies little with age, and it does not change its shape. Furthermore, ear is larger in size compared to fingerprints but smaller as compared to face and it can be easily captured without a fully cooperative subject.

Ears have several advantages over complete faces: reduced spatial resolution, a more uniform distribution of color, and less variability with expressions and orientation of the face. In face recognition there can be problems with e.g. changing lightning, and different head positions of the person.

Application

Ear biometrics can be used as a supplementary source of evidence in identification and recognition systems, for example a system designed for face recognition already includes all the necessary hardware for capturing and computing ear biometrics. An Application Scenarios Ear biometrics can be used as a supplementary source of evidence in identification and recognition systems, for example a system designed for face recognition already includes all the necessary hardware for capturing and computing ear biometrics.

Hand Geometry

Biometric Recognition using Hand geometry is based on the measurement of shape, size of palm, and the lengths and widths of the fingers (Jain, Bolle and Pankanti, 1999). It has some advantages over other biometric trait because the technique is very simple, relatively easy to use, and inexpensive and environmental factors such as dry weather or individual anomalies such as dry skin do not appear to adversely affect the authentication accuracy of hand geometry-based systems. But the geometry of the hand is not very distinctive and hand geometry-based recognition systems cannot be scaled up for systems requiring identification of an individual from a large database. In addition to that hand geometry information may not be distinguishing during the growth period of children. With the advancement in sensor technology commercial hand geometry-based authentication systems have been installed at various locations around the world for authentication.

Applications

Hand geometry can be suitable for one-to-one applications where there are larger user databases and/or where users may access the system infrequently and, therefore, be less disciplined in their approach to the system. As mentioned earlier, hand geometry systems are most commonly used in access control and/or time and attendance applications.

Palmprint

Palmprint for personal recognition is much like the fingerprints because similar to fingerprint palms of the human hands contain pattern of ridges and valleys. According to study Palmprints are distinctive than the fingerprints because the area of the palm is much larger than the area of a fingerprint (Zhang, Kong, You, and Wong, 2003). Since the surface area of palmprint is larger, they require

bulkier and comparatively expensive sensor than the fingerprint sensors. Palmprint also contain additional distinguishing features such as principal lines and wrinkles that can be captured even with a lower resolution scanner, which would be cheaper. If a high-resolution palmprint scanner is used then all the features of the hand such as geometry, ridge and valley features e.g., minutiae and singular points such as deltas, principal lines, and wrinkles may be combined to build a highly accurate biometric system.

Interest in palmprints applications is motivated by the latent palmprints found at crime scenes, which can be just as useful as latent fingerprints for crime solving and can be useful for law enforcement agencies. For example in United States places such as California, Connecticut, Virginia, and Wisconsin are among those adopting palmprint recognition in their law enforcement activities. Palmprint technology is also appropriate for the access control market and adding palmprint recognition to fingerprint systems can improve the identity verification provided by fingerprints in cases where fingerprint images cannot be properly acquired e.g., due to dry skin. Similarly, palmprint biometrics could be symbiotic with hand geometry systems, providing a higher degree of accuracy in identification when the two technologies are combined into a single system.

Iris

The texture of the iris is formed after the birth of the child and stabilizes during the first two years of life the pigmentation, however, continues changing over an extended period of time. The iris texture carries has distinguishing characteristic useful for personal recognition (Daugman, 2004). Iris recognition has a very high accuracy and speed and support the feasibility of large-scale identification systems based on iris information. Each iris of an individual is distinctive and even the irises of identical twins are different from one another. It is possible to detect contact lenses printed with a fake iris (Jain, Bolle, and Pankanti, 1999). Earlier iris-based recognition systems required considerable user participation and were expensive but the new systems have become more user-friendly and cost-effective (Negin, Chmielewski, Salganicoff, Camus, Seelan, Venetianer, and Zhang, 2000, Fancourt, Bogoni, Hanna, Guo, Wildes, Takahashi, and Jain, 2005). While iris systems have a very low False Accept Rate (FAR) compared to other biometric traits, the False Reject Rate (FRR) of these systems can be rather high[4].

Some programs and applications include: Airline passenger screening, border security, facility access control, computer login, ATMs, inmate identification in correctional facilities, and grocery stores (for automated checkout). The Charlotte-Douglas International Airport uses iris recognition for physical access of workers when entering non-public areas of the airport. During the Winter Olympics in Nagano, Japan, an iris recognition system controlled access to the rifles used in the biathlon. The United Arab Emirates has used an iris recognition biometric screening system for over two years to screen all arriving visa holders at their points of entry to detect previously deported persons. The United Nations has also successfully used the system in refugee control applications.

Keystroke

Keystroke comes under the category of behavioral biometrics and it is hypothesized that each person types on a keyboard in a characteristic way. keystroke biometric is not expected to be unique to each individual but it has been found to offer sufficient discriminatory information to permit identity verification (Monrose and Rubin, 1997). The keystrokes of a person could be monitored unobtrusively as that person is keying in information. One may expect to observe large intra-class variations in a person's typing patterns due to changes in emotional state, position of the user

with respect to the keyboard, type of keyboard used, etc. This biometric permits "continuous verification" of an individual's identity over a session after the person logs in using a stronger biometric such as fingerprint or iris.

Applications

An useful application of keystroke biometric is computer access, where this biometric could be used to verify the computer user's identity continuously. Monitoring of the interaction of users while accessing highly restricted documents or executing tasks in environments where the user must be "alert" at all times for example, air traffic control is an ideal scenario for the application of a keystroke authentication system. Keystroke dynamics may be used to detect uncharacteristic typing rhythms such as those brought on by drowsiness, fatigue, etc., and alarm a third party.

Signature

Signature biometrics comes under the category of behavioral biometric trait. It depends on the way a person sign their name is known to be a characteristic of that individual (Nalwa, 1997, Lee, Berger and Aviczer, 1996). Although signatures require contact with the writing instrument and an effort on the part of the user, they have been accepted in government, legal, and commercial transactions as a method of authentication. With the proliferation of PDAs and Tablet PCs, on-line signature may emerge as the biometric of choice in these devices. Signature is a behavioral biometric that changes over a period of time and is influenced by the physical and emotional conditions of the signatories. Signatures of some people vary substantially: even successive impressions of their signature are significantly different. Further, professional forgers may be able to reproduce signatures that fool the signature verification system (Harrison, 1981).

Voice

Voice biometric is a combination of physical and behavioral characteristics which is considered to be unique for every individual (Campbell, 1997). Physical characteristics of human speech are invariant for an individual, but the behavioral aspect of the speech changes over time due to age, medical conditions such as common cold, emotional state, etc. Voice biometric is not very distinctive and may not be appropriate for large-scale identification. The physical features of subject voice are based on the shape and size of the appendages e.g., vocal tracts, mouth, nasal cavities, and lips that are used in the synthesis of the sound. A text-independent voice recognition system recognizes the speaker independent of what she speaks while a text dependent voice recognition system is based on the utterance of a fixed predetermined text. A text-dependent system offers more protection against fraud compared to text-independent system as it is more difficult to design. The disadvantage of voice-based recognition is that speech features are sensitive to a number of factors such as background noise. Thus speaker recognition is most appropriate in telephone-based applications but the voice signal is typically degraded in quality by the communication channel.

Text-dependent speaker verification systems have been used in logical access control applications and where remote identity verification is required. A major example of this is call centre automation, where transaction processing is automated via telephone or computer. Popular uses include financial transactions (account access, funds transfer, bill-payment, trading of financial instruments) and credit card processing (address changes, balance transfers, loss prevention). Speaker verification/recognition has also made an impact in the penal system where it is used to monitor and control inmate phone privileges and identity verification of parolees, juvenile inmates, and those under house arrest.

Although speaker verification technology has not been as widely adopted and utilized as other biometric technologies, there are indications that speaker verification could be adopted on a larger scale in the future for a number of reasons.

- Telephone is the primary means by which consumers conduct financial transactions and access financial account information.
- Consumers know about the problem of identity theft.
- Many consumers feel that PINs and passwords are not secure enough.
- Consumers have a strong level of concern when communicating confidential information over the telephone. Because of these fears of identity theft and other forms of fraud, consumers might be more willing to participate in a speaker verification system.

Gait

Gait is an example of behavior biometric and it depends on the manner in which a person walks, and is one of the few biometric traits that can be used to recognize people at a distance. Gait biometric is considered to be very appropriate in surveillance scenarios where the identity of subject can be surreptitiously established. Some algorithms use the optic flow associated with a set of dynamically extracted moving points on the human body to describe the gait of an individual (Jain, Bolle, and Pankanti, 1999). Most gait recognition algorithms attempt to extract the human silhouette in order to derive the spatio-temporal attributes of a moving subject. Thus the selection of a good model to represent the human body is pivotal to the efficient functioning of a gait recognition system. Gait-based systems also offer the possibility of tracking an individual over an extended period of time. However, the gait of an individual is affected by several factors including the choice of footwear, nature of clothing,

Table 3. The false accept and false reject error rates associated with the fingerprint, face, voice, and iris modalities. The accuracy estimates of biometric systems depend on a number of test conditions including the sensor employed, acquisition protocol used, subject disposition, number of subjects, number of biometric samples per subject, demographic profile of test subjects, subject habituation, time lapse between data acquisition, et cetera.

Biometric Trait	Test	Test Conditions	False Reject Rate	False Accept Rate
Fingerprint	FVC 2004 (Maio, Maltoni, Cappelli, 2004)	Exaggerated skin distortion, rotation	2%	2%
Fingerprint	FpVTE 2003 (Wilson, Hicklin, Bone, Korves, Groth-er, Ulery, Micheals, Zoepfl, Otto, and Watson., 2004)	US Government operational data	0.1%	1%
Face	FRVT 2002 (Phillips, Grother, Micheals, Blackburn, Tabassi, and Bone, 2003)	Varied lighting, out-door/indoor. time	10%	1%
Voice	NIST 2004 (Przybocki and Martin, 2004)	Text independent, multi-lingual	5-10%	2-5%
Iris	ITIRT 2005[5]	Indoor environment, multiple visits	0.99%	0.94%

affliction of the legs, walking surface, etc (see Tables 3 and 4).

WHY MULTIBIOMETRICS?

When more than one Biometric feature is used to identify an individual then we call it multibiometric system and systems that are presently in use, typically use a single biometric trait to establish identity i.e., they are unibiometric systems. With the increasing use of biometric identification, it is important that the vulnerabilities and shortcomings of these systems are clearly analysed. The main

challenges commonly encountered by biometric systems are given below:

- **Noisy Data:** The biometric data being presented to the biometric system may be contaminated by noise due to imperfect acquisition conditions or variations in the biometric sensor. For example, a cut or scar can change a individual's fingerprint while the cough and cold can alter the voice feature characteristics of a speaker. In similar way unfavorable lightning conditions may affect the face and iris images captured from subject. Due to noisy it can result

Table 4. Biometric trait along representation scheme and matching algorithms

Modality	Representation of Scheme	Matching Algorithms
Fingerprints	Minutiae distribution, Ridge and Valleys analysis	String Matching, Correlation techniques, Hough Transfo- rmation
Face	Principal Component Analysis (PCA), Linear Discrimi-nant Analysis(LDA), Eigenfaces	Euclidian Distance, Elastic Bunch graph, Neural Networks, Support Vector Machine SVM
Iris	Texture analysis, Key point extraction, Contour enhance-ment	Hamming Distance
Voice	Linguistic and acoustic acquisition	Hidden markov Model, Phonotactic recognition
Ear	Helix and lobe analysis, PCA, Force Field Transform	Euclidean distance, Local Surface patch(LSP), ICP

in subject being incorrectly recognized as an impostor thereby increasing the False Reject Rate (FRR) of the biometric system.

- **Non-Universality:** Sometimes the biometric system may not be able to capture required biometric data from a subset of individuals which result in a failure to enroll (FTE) error of the system. For example, a fingerprint system may fail to image the friction ridge structure of some subjects due to the poor quality of their fingerprints. Similarly, an iris with long eyelashes, drooping eyelids or certain pathological conditions of the eye recognition system may be unable to obtain the iris information of a subject. In order to accommodate such users into the authentication system exception processing will be necessary.

- **Limitation of Identification Accuracy:** There is limitation of matching performance of a unibiometric system and it cannot be continuously improved by tuning the feature extraction and matching modules. The number of distinct biometric feature sets that can be represented using a template uniquely is limited. Variations observed in the feature set of each subject i.e., intra-class variations and the variations between feature sets of different subjects i.e., inter-class variations is limited.

- **Spoof Attacks:** Behavioral traits such as voice (Eriksson and Wretling., 1997) and signature (Harrison, 1981) are vulnerable to spoof attacks by an impostor attempting to mimic the traits corresponding to legitimately enrolled subjects. Physiological traits such as fingerprints can also be spoofed by inscribing ridge-like structures on synthetic material such as gelatine and play-doh (Matsumoto, Matsumoto, Yamada and Hoshino, 2002, Putte and Keuning, 2000). Targeted spoof attacks can undermine the security afforded by the biometric system and, consequently, miti-

Figure 11. Multimodal biometrics

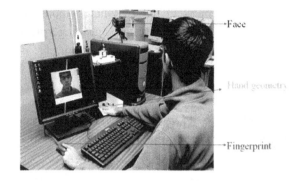

gate its benefits (Ratha, Connell and Bolle, 2001).

Limitations of a unibiometric system can be minimized by designing a biometric system that uses multiple sources of biometric information. Thus in order to increase the identification accuracy fusion or combination of multiple traits of an individual, or multiple feature extraction and matching algorithms operating on the same biometric can be used. (Ross, Nandakumar and Jain, 2006, Jain and Ross, 2004., Hong, Jain and Pankanti, 1999) can improve the matching accuracy of a biometric system while increasing population coverage and deterring spoof attacks.

Multimodal Biometric System is a system that uses more than one independent or weakly correlated biometric trait taken from the subject e.g., Fingerprint and Face of the same person, or Fingerprints from two different fingers of an individual. A typical Multimodal system is shown in Figure 11. which uses face, fingerprint and hand geometry. Following are the advantages of Multimodal Biometrics.

- Multimodal Biometrics systems improve performance of system.
- A combination in a verification system improves system accuracy.
- A combination in an identification system improves system speed as well as accuracy.

- The performance of multimodal biometric system is increased when fusions of uncorrelated modalities e.g. fingerprint and face, two fingers of a person, etc. is implemented.

SOLUTIONS AND RECOMMENDATIONS

Information Security should be an integral part of enterprise governance, aligned with IT governance and integrated into strategy, concept, design, implementation and operation. Protecting critical information must constitute one of the major risks to be considered in management strategies and should also be recognised as a crucial contributor to success.

While biometric technology appears to be well suited to provide a user-convenient component of secure person-identity linkage, there may be cultural, societal, and religious resistance toward acceptance of this technology. On the other hand, the hyperbole underlying biometric technology has created the expectation that biometric is the panacea for all of our security and identity theft problems and not merely one of the several complementary technologies (e.g., RFID, conventional security, process engineering) that need to be integrated in a way that remains to be well defined. For example, one of the fundamental sources of identity theft problem is the critical reliance on the linkages to and information in legacy identity management systems. While biometric technology can mitigate some of the enrolment problems (e.g., multiple identities), it cannot solve the problem of having to rely on imperfect legacy identity management systems. Much remains to be accomplished in terms of general education of the end users, system administrators, integrators, and most important, public policy makers. The limitations of the current state of the biometric technology should not be construed to imply that it is not currently useful in many applications. In

fact, there are a large number of biometric solutions that have been successfully deployed to provide useful value in practical applications.

Following are the recommendation for successful Information Security Governance:

- Information security responsibilities must be assigned and carried out by appropriately trained persons. Establishing information security governance framework and the act of governing the agency's implementation of information security should be done at the top level management.
- Using available tools and information, Information security managers should continuously monitor the performance of the security program/effort for which they are responsible.
- Person responsible for information security within the agency should be held accountable for their actions or lack of actions and information security activities should be governed based on relevant requirements, including laws, regulations, and organizational policies.
- In order to ensure a successful implementation of an information security program, the information security priorities should be communicated to stakeholders of all levels within an organization.
- Integration of information security activities must be with other management activities of the enterprise, including strategic planning, capital planning, and enterprise architecture.
- If the organization undergoes change then information security organization structure should be appropriate for the organization it supports and should evolve with the organization objectives.
- The improvement of security posture and the overall performance of the organization, information found through monitor-

ing should be used as an input into management decisions.

- Management needs to have regular contact with the users of their business processes that deal with operations and/or use IT, in order to make sure the right actions are being undertaken to achieve the right balance.

Cancelable Biometrics

Cancelable biometrics offers a solution for preserving user privacy since the user's true biometric is never revealed in the authentication process. The concept of cancelable biometrics is introduced to make a biometric template can be cancelled and be revoked like a password, as well as being unique to every application (Maltoni, Maio, Jain and Prabhakar, 2003). Cancelable biometrics requires storage of the distorted version of the biometric template which provides high privacy level by allowing multiple templates to be associated with the same biometric data. This helps to promote non-linkability of user's biometric data stored across various databases.

Four objectives of designing a cancelable biometric scheme are as followed:

- **Diversity:** No same cancelable features can be used across various applications; therefore a large number of protected templates from same biometric feature is required.
- **Reusability/Revocability:** Straightforward revocation and reissue in the event of compromise.
- **Non-Invertibility:** Non-invertibility of template computation to prevent recovery of original biometric data.
- **Performance:** The formulation should not deteriorate the recognition performance.

It ensures that template protection is achieved at the feature level with the assistance of the auxiliary data/non-invertible transforms. On the other hand, cancellable biometrics has certain limitations that need to be taken into account. For instance in biometric salting design, the template may not longer secure when the auxiliary data is compromised. For non-invertible transforms, non-invertibility enhances the security of the template space by employing a transformation process to reset the order or position of the feature set. However, this weakens the discriminatory power (performance) of the transformed features due to the enlargement of intra-class variation in the biometrics. In this context, if performance is the main concern in the design of a biometric system, then the system is expected to be lacking in randomness as required for the design of a secure and unpredictable template space. Hence, it is very challenging to design a non-invertible function that satisfies both performance and non-invertibility requirements.

Cancelable biometrics refers to the intentional and systematically repeatable distortion of biometric features in order to protect sensitive user-specific data. If a cancelable feature is compromised, the distortion characteristics are changed, and the same biometrics is mapped to a new template, which is used subsequently. Cancelable biometrics is one of the major categories for biometric template protection purpose besides biometric cryptosystem.

FUTURE RESEARCH DIRECTIONS

With the advancement of technology and cut throat completion among organization it has become imperative to implement effective information security governance using latest technologies. Although biometric has matured to certain level but lots of research is still in progress. We have tried to summarize the future research directions in form of Table 5.

Table 5. Information security governance function, contribution and future direction

ISG Function	Contributions		Inter disciplines	Future Research
	Organizational	**Technical**		
Access	Biometric authentication, Non- Biometric methods, cognitive passwords, maximizing users' intent to comply with security policy (through deterrence and motivation means).	Authentication methods (passwords, token-based authentication), access control and information-flow control models, memory protection of operating systems, anti-virus techniques, watermarking, image security, audit/intrusion detection, firewalls	Computer Vision, Artificial Intelligence, Mathematics and philosophical logic, biosciences, psychology, criminology, philosophy	Information Fusion, Feature extraction, Mathematical approaches (mathematical modelling), theory-testing research, Pattern Recognition, Classification, conceptual analysis.
Communication	Virtual private networks, Intranet security	Bio-encryption Cryptographic techniques, including message encryption, digital signatures, steganography, watermarking, hash, virtual private networks, electronic cash, Intranet security, anonymity techniques	Mathematics (in particular cryptology), law	Mathematical approaches, Signal Processing (mathematical modelling), conceptual analysis.
Security Management	Template and Key management, creation of organizational security policies and guidelines, backup and contingency management, security checklist and management standards, security management methods, security of outsourcing	Template management, Key management, management of security policies, virtual private networks	Mathematics, law, criminology, philosophy	Mathematical approaches (mathematical modelling), conceptual analysis, empirical theory-testing research and theory-creating research.
Implementation	Risk management, security methods for developing secure IS, testing methods and methodologies.	Programming and programming language security	Computer Science, Mathematics, philosophy	Algorithm development, Mathematical approaches (mathematical modelling), conceptual analysis, artifact building and evaluating research, empirical theory testing research and theory creating research.

CONCLUSION

According to literature available on Information Security Governance it is concluded that the use of a single best practice document in the realisation of Information Security Governance is inadequate, the methodology requires holistic approach and an in-depth inter-disciplinary research analysis to allow for the comprehensive implementation of biometrics to improve Information Security Governance. The aim is to identify a number of key elements from various best practice and related documents that can add value to an Information Security Governance model using biometrics. This proposed model is applicable to all organisations, irrespective of size, culture or domain. It combines aspects of Information Technology Governance, Information Security Governance and Identity Management to contribute to the successful and secured use of Information Security Governance by any organisation.

We can conclude that the biometric technologies that are available today can be used in security systems to help in identity management and minimise the risk. Biometrics presents important technical, policy, and system challenges that must be solved because there is no substitute for this technology for addressing many critical information security problems. Considering the recent government mandates for national and international use of biometrics in delivering crucial societal functions, there is urgency to further develop basic biometric capabilities, and to integrate them into practical applications. Because biometrics cannot be easily shared, misplaced, or forged, the resultant security is more reliable than current password systems and does not encumber the end user with remembering long cryptographically strong passwords. Biometric-based system administrator access to sensitive user information affords effective accountability.

However, it is important to bear in mind that effective security cannot be achieved by relying on technology alone. Technology and people must work together as part of an overall security process. As we have pointed out, weaknesses in any of these areas diminishes the effectiveness of the security process. We have found that three key considerations need to be addressed before a decision is made to design, develop, and implement biometrics into a security system:

1. Decisions on how the biometric technology will be used must be taken.
2. Determine the benefits gained by a detailed cost-benefit analysis.
3. A trade-off analysis must be conducted between the increased security, and convenience which the biometric would provide.

Balance between security concerns with practical cost and operational considerations as well as political and economic interests are necessary.

REFERENCES

Allen, J. (2007). *All characteristics of effective security governance*, 2007.

Campbell, J. P. (1997). Speaker recognition: A tutorial. *Proceedings of the IEEE, 85*(9), 1437–1462.

Daugman, J. (2004). How iris recognition works? *IEEE Transactions on Circuits and Systems for Video Technology, 14*(1), 21–30.

Eriksson, A., & Wretling, P. (1997). How flexible is the human voice? A case study of mimicry. In *Proceedings of the European Conference on Speech Technology,* (pp. 1043–1046). Rhodes, 1997.

Fancourt, C. L., Bogoni, L., Hanna, J., Guo, Y., Wildes, R. P., Takahashi, N., & Jain, U. (2005). Iris recognition at a distance. In *Fifth International Conference on Audio- and Video-based Biometric Person Authentication* (AVBPA), (pp. 1–13). Rye Brook, USA, July 2005.

Harrison, W. R. (1981). *Suspect documents, their scientific examination*. Nelson-Hall Publishers.

Hong, L., Jain, A. K., & Pankanti, S. (1999). Can multibiometrics improve performance? In *Proceedings of IEEE Workshop on Automatic Identification Advanced Technologies* (AutoID), (pp. 59–64). New Jersey, USA, October 1999.

International Biometric Group. (2005). Independent testing of iris recognition technology: Final report. Retrieved from http://www.biometric-group.com/reports/ public/ITIRT.html

Jain, A. K., Bolle, R., & Pankanti, S. (Eds.). (1999). *Biometrics: Personal identification in networked society* (pp. 87–102). London, UK: Kluwer Academic Publishers.

Jain, A. K., Flynn, P., & Ross, A. A. (2008). *Handbook of biometrics*. New York, NY: Springer.

Jain, A. K., & Ross, A. (2004). Multibiometric systems. *Communications of the ACM. Special Issue on Multimodal Interfaces, 47*(1), 34–40.

Lee, L., Berger, T., & Aviczer, E. (1996). Reliable on-line human signature verification systems. *IEEE Transactions on Pattern Analysis and Machine Intelligence, 18*(6), 643–647.

Li, S. Z., & Jain, A. K. (Eds.). (2005). *Handbook of face recognition*. Springer-Verlag.

Maio, D., Maltoni, D., Cappelli, R., Wayman, J. L., & Jain, A. K. (2004). FVC2004: Third fingerprint verification competition. In *Proceedings of International Conference on Biometric Authentication (ICBA)*, (pp. 1–7). Hong Kong, China, July 2004.

Maltoni, D., Maoi, D., Jain, A. K., & Prabhakar, S. (2009). *Handbook of fingerprint recognition*. New York, NY: Springer.

Matsumoto, T., Matsumoto, H., Yamada, K., & Hoshino, S. (2002). Impact of artificial gummy fingers on fingerprint systems. In *Optical Security and Counterfeit Deterrence Techniques IV, Proceedings of SPIE*, volume 4677, (pp. 275–289). San Jose, USA, January 2002.

Monrose, F., & Rubin, A. (1997). Authentication via keystroke dynamics. In *Proceedings of Fourth ACM Conference on Computer and Communications Security*, (pp. 48–56). Zurich, Switzerland, April 1997.

Nalwa, V. S. (1997). Automatic on-line signature verification. *Proceedings of the IEEE, 85*(2), 215–239.

Negin, M., Chmielewski, T. A., Salganicoff, M., Camus, T. A., Seelan, U. M. C., Venetianer, P. L., & Zhang, G. G. (2000). An iris biometric system for public and personal use. *IEEE Computer, 33*(2), 70–75.

O'Gorman, L. (2002). Seven issues with human authentication technologies. In *Proceedings of Workshop on Automatic Identification Advanced Technologies* (AutoID), (pp. 185–186). Tarrytown, USA, March 2002.

Phillips, P. J., Grother, P., Micheals, R. J., Blackburn, D. M., Tabassi, E., & Bone, J. M. (2003). *FRVT 2002: Overview and SUMMARY*. Retrieved from http://www.frvt.org/FRVT2002

Prabhakar, S., Pankanti, S., & Jain, A. K. (2003). Biometric recognition: Security and privacy concerns. *IEEE Security and Privacy Magazine, 1*(2), 33–42.

Przybocki, M., & Martin, A. (2004). NIST speaker recognition evaluation chronicles. In *Odyssey: The Speaker and Language Recognition Workshop*, (pp. 12–22). Toledo, Spain, May 2004.

Putte, T., & Keuning, J. (2000). Biometrical fingerprint recognition: Don't get your fingers burned. In *Proceedings of IFIP TC8/WG8.8 Fourth Working Conference on Smart Card Research and Advanced Applications*, (pp. 289–303).

Ratha, N. K., Connell, J. H., & Bolle, R. M. (2001). An analysis of minutiae matching strength. In *Proceedings of Third International Conference on Audio- and Video-Based Biometric Person Authentication* (AVBPA), (pp. 223–228). Halmstad, Sweden, June 2001.

Reid, P. (2003). *Biometrics for network security*. Prentice Hall PTR.

Ross, A. A., Nandakumar, K., & Jain, A. K. (2006). *Handbook of multibiometrics*. New York, NY: Springer.

Samangooei, S., Nixon, M., & Guo, B. (2008). The use of semantic human description as a soft biometric. In *Proceedings of BTAS*, 2008.

Singer, G., & Sundararajan, A. (2004). Are digital rights valuable? Theory and evidence from the e-book industry. In *Proceedings 25th International Conference on Information Systems,* Washington, DC, (pp. 533–545).

Von Solms, S. H. (2005). Information security governance. Compliance management vs operational management. *Computers & Security, 24*(6), 443–447.

Wayman, J. L., Jain, A. K., Maltoni, D., & Maio, D. (Eds.). (2005). *Biometric systems: Technology, design and performance evaluation*. Springer.

Wilson, C., Hicklin, A. R., Bone, M., Korves, H., Grother, P., & Ulery, B. … Watson, C. (2004). *Fingerprint vendor technology evaluation 2003: Summary of results and analysis report*. NIST Technical Report NISTIR 7123, National Institute of Standards and Technology, June 2004.

Zhang, D., Kong, A. W.-K., You, J., & Wong, M. (2003). Online palmprint identification. *IEEE Transactions on Pattern Analysis and Machine Intelligence, 25*(9), 1041–1050.

KEY TERMS AND DEFINITIONS

Biometrics: A field of science that uses computer technology to identify people based on physical or behavioral characteristics, such as fingerprints or voice scans. "Bio" in the name refers to the physiological traits that are measured, while "metrics" refers to the quantitative analysis that provides a positive identification of a unique individual.

Identification: The process of trying to find out a person's identity by comparing the person who is present against a biometric pattern/template database.

Information Security Governance: A subset of enterprise governance that provides strategic direction, ensures objectives are achieved, manages risk appropriately, uses organizational resources responsibility, and monitors the success or failure of the enterprise security programme."

Multimodal Biometric: Multimodal Biometric System is a system that uses more than one independent or weakly correlated biometric identifier taken from an individual (e.g., fingerprint and face of the same person, or fingerprints from two different fingers of a person).

Recognition: The process of recognizing something or someone by remembering; "a politician whose recall of names was as remarkable as his recognition of faces"; "experimental psychologists measure the elapsed time from the onset of the stimulus to its recognition by the observer".

Template: A biometric template (also called *template*) is a digital reference of distinct characteristics that have been extracted from a biometric sample. Templates are used during the biometric authentication process.

Verification: A person's identity is known and therefore claimed a priority to search against. The pattern that is being verified is compared with the person's individual template only. Similar to identification, it is checked whether the similarity between pattern and template is sufficient enough to provide access to the secured system or area.

ENDNOTES

[1]   Biometric Technology Application Manual Volume 1 Published by National Biometric Security (2008).

[2]   Information Security Governance: Guidance for Boards of Directors and Executive Man-

agement, 2nd Edition Printed in the United States of America.

3   Information Security Governance: Guidance for Boards of Directors and Executive Management, 2nd Edition Printed in the United States of America.

4   http://www.biometricgroup.com/reports/public/ITIRT.html

5   http://www.biometricgroup.com/reports/public/ITIRT.html,

Chapter 9
Ontology Based Multi Agent Modelling for Information Security Measurement

Partha Saha
Indian Institute of Management Calcutta, India

Ambuj Mahanti
Indian Institute of Management Calcutta, India

ABSTRACT

IT security governance bridges the gap between corporate governance and information security which is defined as the protection of information and other valuable assets in the organization from a wide range of threats in order to maximize ROI (Return On Investment) and minimize risk. These risks emanate from multiple sources like espionage, sabotage, malicious code, computer hacking, sophisticated denial of service attacks, vandalism, fire, flood, and other natural or manmade calamities. Information security in an organization is achieved by implementing suitable sets of safeguards or controls, including policies, processes, procedures etc. These controls need to be established, monitored, and suitably implemented across organization to ensure smooth functioning of business. There are existing sets of internationally recognized standards like CobiT, ISO17799, and others available, which are country and industry specific. These standards include a set of specific controls. Organizations operating in a particular country should be compliant of these standards, and as often these are legal obligations. Stakeholders and auditors are concerned with discrepancies that accrue in the implementation phases of implementation of these standards in any organization. Compliance Auditing (CA) is the process that identifies and analyses any misalignment of the organization's rules and policies with respect to government regulations/industry best practices, which they are supposed to implement. A distinct challenge in compliance auditing is the measurement of discrepancies between company policies, controls, and industry standards vis-a-vis actual organizational practices.

DOI: 10.4018/978-1-4666-2083-4.ch009

INTRODUCTION

In this chapter we discuss a framework for building a multi agent information model that captures the notion of compliance semantics and present it using event ontology. We also present a methodology for computing the compliance measure of organizational practice with regulatory/standards requirements capturing the relevance of the ontological concepts using fuzzy weights towards estimating the compliance. Without any loss of generality we demonstrate our technique in some particular cases of Information Technology - Security Techniques (AS/NZS ISO/IEC 17799:2006 & CobiT4.1) where we present an ontology, construct semantic model, and derive compliance rules from the information security controls. Finally we compare the two standards and discuss how the model can be used as a decision support system tool at the hands of auditors in the chosen domain.

In this book chapter we endeavour to establish a direct linkage between corporate governance and information security via internal controls. Corporate security governance is a part and parcel of wider corporate governance framework which is meant to be the signpost for strategic guidance of the company. It is a symbol of board of director's commitment towards the stakeholders. Corporate security governance is expected to provide transparent and authentic reports of financial and accounting system of the organization. Higher echelon of management is legally held responsible for its veracity. The whole exercise is achieved through existence of appropriate framework of internal control which is essential part of corporate governance. Top management are held responsible for the consequence of failure of internal control in the organization. This internal control is critically dependent on information security which is based on particular information security standard, the organization adheres to. Often stakeholders, legal entities, partners, legislators demand multifarious requirements which are often difficult to satisfy si-

multaneously. To satisfy regulatory requirements, which are often conflicting by nature, information security standards and various industry best practices are deployed by respective organizations to quantitatively measure adherence to numerous industry and country specific regulations. Thus we get the linkage between corporate security governance (which is part of wider gamut of corporate governance), based on internal controls, which in turn exclusively depends on information security for its very existence. Auditing is done to scrutinize the whole process. Auditors are professionals who are legally empowered to critically examine the performance of the organization to make an opinion thereof whether the performance of organization is consistent with the security standards it is supposed to follow. Compliance Auditing (CA) is a process employed by auditors which critically examines and measures any discrepancies between organization's actual practice and guidelines prescribed in information security standards which the organization is supposed to follow. Hence information security based on organizational internal controls proves to be the vital link for the very existence of corporate governance edifice. Our endeavour in this chapter is to provide a methodology to automatize the compliance auditing process and measure discrepancies between actual performance and security guidelines.

Information security is a direct corporate governance responsibility and lies squarely on the shoulders of the Board of the company.

The chapter is composed of four parts. Part 1 introduces corporate security governance and risk management problems associated with any organization, in a particular domain and in a specific country. Part 1 consists of two sections A &B. Section A defines what is asset (tangible and intangible assets) for an organization and how the security of the asset, which is subject to multiple threats from various sources, is a fiduciary responsibility on the part of management. This section defines how the risk factor is mitigated by introducing procedures, guidelines and regulations in what is commonly known as controls in corporate security governance. It illustrates some government regulations like SOX, HIPAA as well as some information security standards like BSI, CobiT, ISO /IEC 17799:2005 etc. as part of corporate security governance framework. These regulations are legally enforceable in respective countries and strictest compliances are mandatory for organizations operating in those countries. Section B defines risk in greater detail and introduces the concept of risk containment strategy and measurement of risk compliance metric as part of management of information security in an organization.

Part 2 defines information auditing as a practical tool employed by the auditors to quantitatively but manually measure the discrepancies between guidelines in regulatory standards and actual organizational practices. Part 2 consists of three sections A, B and C. While section A introduces information auditing and section B specifically talks of auditing an organization in an IT environment, section C discusses information auditing practices in the industrial environment. Part 2 is important as far as the practical/industrial aspect of compliance auditing is concerned albeit in a manual regulatory environment.

Part 3 describes repository of our knowledge management toolkit. Here ontology and semantic modelling issues including designing of robust reasoning framework and semantic compliance rules are illustrated. Part 3 acts as a bridge between manual auditing process described in Part 2 and automated compliance auditing described in Part 4. This part is also intended to give a sound technical foundation for part 4 where we derive the ontology based automated framework for compliance auditing. Part 4 consists of four sections A, B, C and D. Section A defines ontology as "formal specification of shared conceptualization" and depicts a partial ontology model of an

organization while section B narrates concept of semantic modelling with semantic web layer. Section C describes semantic based robust reasoning framework & section D describes compliance rules for semantic production system.

Part 4 culminates in designing a methodology for automated agent based compliance auditing framework that we have been talking so far. It contains two sections A &B. Section A describes knowledge acquisition and expert system while section B describes ontology based framework for compliance auditing. The last section introduces fuzzy weight while measuring the discrepancies between recommendations/interpretation of different experts on regulatory standards and actual organizational practices. There is much subjectivity involved in this process due to existence of different viewpoints and there is lot of scope for conflicting professional interpretation. It also quantifies relationship between two regulatory standards viz. ISO/IEC 17799 and CobiT4.1 while measuring performance of an organization using these two metrics.

PART 1: CORPORATE SECURITY GOVERNANCE AND RISK MANAGEMENT

Nowadays the overall economy is getting digitized and IT is moving away from being only one of the several peripheral issues concerning organization towards occupying its very core business strategic goal. At the same time information security and risk management has long ceased to be only organization's finance & engineering department's concern and become a broader management issue in general. Information security, as part of organization's corporate security governance, is entrusted with the responsibility of keeping integrity, confidentiality and availability of information and valuable electronic assets from various security threats. Day by day these security threats are becoming increasingly sophisticated in nature leading to catastrophic consequence for security failure. In the following sections we will discuss these issues in greater detail. In section A corporate security governance is discussed while in section B risk assessment in any organization with all its intricacies are deliberated in detail. We will see that these issues are becoming extremely important in the strategic management of any organization in every domain.

Corporate Security Governance

In IT parlance people, information, application (application software, procedures), system (system software), methods, service, processing facilities, infrastructure (hardware, network, software), intellectual properties (patents, trademarks, copyrights) etc. may be defined as assets. Asset may exist in either tangible (hardware, network, application, infrastructure, personnel etc.) or intangible (information, intellectual property, patent, trademark, methods, procedures etc.) form. Sometimes value of intangible assets outweighs that of tangible assets even though the former may not find any mention in the balance sheet of the organization. The assets are subject to multiple levels of threats due to weaknesses or vulnerabilities in access control.

The weaknesses are exploited by numerous threats like theft, hacking, sabotage, malicious code, espionage etc. The threats to assets in turn disrupt controls and safeguards, cause breach of security policy of the organization or bring forth hitherto unknown situations which may cause serious security breakdown. Thus safeguarding assets become an inescapable fiduciary obligation on the part of management to retain the intrinsic value of the asset, safeguard stakeholder interests as well to strengthen corporate governance.

IT governance may be formally defined as the set of procedures, formal processes, customs, prevalent policies, laws, regulations, legislations, management practices and governing institutions

affecting the way IT assets in an enterprise or organization is being controlled and managed. IT governance as a part of corporate governance strategy constitute a high level framework encompassing top leadership, management, processes, roles and responsibilities of the individuals concerned and information requirement at each level of the organization.

Increasing corporate governance regulations strengthen compliance with risk-management standards defined by various regulatory agencies and best practices. Multinational companies doing business globally are subject to plethora of different rules and regulations. The different stakeholders on their parts may demand greater compliance of organizational practices with industry regulations and standards.

Global corporations while simultaneously being active in multiple countries for its production, distribution, logistic and marketing activities are faced with two formidable challenges. On the one hand they are subject to a plethora of strict rules and regulations (SOX, Basel II, HIPAA, GLB etc.) which are country & industry specific. Compliance to these rules is absolutely mandatory. On the other hand organizations are increasingly relying on conformity of numerous standards (COBIT, ISO17799, ITIL, BSI etc.) to maintain sanctity of corporate governance as well as protection of assets or valuable resources.

In this chapter we are building a framework for a multi-agent information model that captures the notion of compliance semantics and present it using event ontology. The methodology is efficient in computing the compliance measure of organizational practices with regulatory/standard requirements capturing the relevance of the ontological concepts towards the computation of compliance using fuzzy weights.

In the next two subsections below we will try to describe government regulations as well as some prevalent information security standards which are applicable in various countries.

Government Regulations

We present in this section several prominent regulations that contribute to the importance of compliance management.

1. **Sarbanes Oxley Act (SOX):** Sarbanes-Oxley Act is "the most far reaching reforms of American business practices since Franklin Roosevelt was president" (President George W. Bush). These laws are by-product of massive corporate frauds (Adelphia, Enron, MCI, Global Crossing, WorldCom etc.) in US which led to tremendous erosion of public confidence in financial numbers in corporate reports. While the explicit focus of SOX is narrow "to protect investors by improving the accuracy and by reliability of corporate governance (Zhang, 2005)", the implicit focus is much broader viz. "to restore public confidence in U.S. capital markets and US institutions.(Zhang, 2005)" SOX clearly aimed at "enhancing public corporate governance, management & board responsibility and transparency" (Zhang, 2005). SOX defines safeguard in annual report by fixing: (a) "management's responsibility for establishing and maintaining adequate internal control over financial reporting", (b) "framework used by management to conduct evaluation of effectiveness of internal control over financial reporting", (c) "management's conclusions about effectiveness of internal control over financial reporting as of yearend, based on management's evaluation" (US Securities Exchanges Commission, 2004). Thus SOX holds topmost echelons of senior management directly responsible for the true and fair view of financial health of the corporation as expressed in the annual reports. Violation of the provisions attract severe penalty including delisting from stock exchange and prison term for top management. The major provisions of the SOX Act tried to address certain issues by establishing the Public Company Accounting Oversight Board (PCAOB). Further, Section 404 of the Act requires that top echelons of the board strengthen internal controls of their respective organization. Audit firms are also made to compulsorily report on the internal controls of their clients. "By requiring deeper oversight, imposing greater penalties for misconduct, and dealing with potential conflicts of interest, the Act aims to prevent deceptive accounting and management misbehaviour" (Zhang, 2005).

2. **Health Insurance Portability and Accountability Act (HIPAA):** HIPAA was introduced to "reform the insurance market, simplify health care administrative processes and to protect the privacy of an individual's medical information"(US Department of Health and Human Services, 1996).HIPAA aims to "reduce administrative costs and burdens in the health care industry by means of standardized, electronic transmission of administrative and financial data." HIPAA requires the Department of Health and Human Services (DHHS) to: (a) adopt national uniform standards for the electronic transmission of certain health information, (b) increase use/efficiency of computer-to-computer methods of exchanging standard health care information (US Department of Health and Human Services, 1996). Medical information being highly confidential in nature is also prone to manipulation, data corruption and potential abuse by vendors. Hospitals, insurance providers, healthcare service providers and clearing houses are principally affected by HIPAA. These standards also must address the security of electronic health information systems.

Information Security Standards

In this subsection we describe some important industry standards and best practices prevalent in the information security domain. Organizations follow these guidelines for complying with the relevant rules and regulations.

1. **ISO/IEC17799:2005**: ISO 17799:2005 is an internationally recognized information security management standard. ISO 17799 is a direct descendant of the British Standard Institute's (BSI) information security management standard BS 7799ISO. ISO 17799:2005 is a high level standard, which is broad in scope and conceptual in nature. ISO 17799:2005 is broad based, technology and product neutral, domain independent and hence suitable for applications across multiple types of enterprises (International Organization for Standardization, 2005). ISO 17799 defines information as an asset that may exist in many forms and has value to an organization. The goal of information security as defined by ISO17799 is to suitably protect this particular asset. Preservation and careful cultivation of this powerful asset ensures business continuity, enterprise risk mitigation and maximizing return on investments (International Organization for Standardization, 2005). As defined by ISO 17799, information security is characterized as the preservation of (a) confidentiality (ensuring that information is accessible to authorized users only) (b) Integrity (preserving and safeguarding the accuracy and completeness of information and processing facilities and eliminating possible data loss/corruption), (c) availability (on time service delivery and prompt and hassle free access of business assets to authorized user). Variation and up-gradation of the ISO 17799:2005 standard exists in the form of ISO31000, AS/NZS ISO/IEC 17799:2006,

    AS/NZS 4360 etc. The information security process has traditionally been based on sound best practices and guidelines, accumulated through years of hands on experiences in industry. ISO 17799 is a comprehensive information security process that affords enterprises the following benefits: (a) an internationally recognized, structured sound methodology (b) a well defined process to evaluate, implement, maintain, and manage information security infrastructure (c) a set of tailored policies, standards, procedures and guidelines for implementation purpose (d) certification allows organizations to demonstrate their own and evaluate their trading partners' information security status to the stakeholders, lawmakers and consumers and (e) certification shows "due diligence" on the part of organizations(International Organization for Standardization, 2005).

2. **Control Objectives for Information and related Technology (COBIT):** Control Objectives for Information and related Technology (COBIT) stands for industry good practices. It also provides process framework across a specific domain. COBIT presents activities in a manageable and logical structure which is very useful for managers, users, and information security practitioners in general. COBIT fulfils a gap for management's necessity for appropriate measurable control. Value, risk and control constitute the core of IT governance. IT governance is the responsibility of executives and the board of directors. Furthermore, IT governance integrates and institutionalises good practices to ensure that the enterprise's IT supports the business objectives. To discharge these responsibilities, as well as to achieve its objectives, management should understand the status of its enterprise architecture for IT and decide what governance and control it should provide. Control Objectives for Information and

related Technology (COBIT) provides good practices across a domain and process framework and presents activities in a manageable and logical structure. For IT to be successful in delivering against business requirements, management should put an internal control system or framework in place. The COBIT control framework contributes to these needs by "(a) Making a link to the business requirements (b) Organising IT activities into a generally accepted process model (c) Identifying the major IT resources to be leveraged (d) Defining the management control objectives to be considered"(IT Governance Institute, 2005). The process focus of COBIT is illustrated by a process model, which subdivides IT into 34 processes in line with the responsibility areas of plan, build, run and monitor, providing an end-to-end view of IT. Enterprise architecture concepts help identifies those resources essential for process success, i.e., applications, information, infrastructure and people. COBIT's good practices represent the consensus of industry experts. COBIT best practices are strongly focused on safeguards and control and less on execution in a specific domain. These practices will help optimise IT-enabled investments, ensure agile service delivery and provide a benchmark which will serve as a standard when things do go wrong which is often the case. (IT Governance Institute, 2005)

3. **BSI – IT Baseline Protection Manual:** The IT Baseline Protection Manual was brainchild of the BSI group. It aims to help organization achieve and maintain normal security requirements. The BSI (www.bsi-global.com) has long been proactive in the evolving arena of information security. The BS7799 standard now consists of *Part 1: Code of Practice*, and *Part 2: Specification of Information Security Management Systems*. Part 1 is an implementation guide, based on

suggestions. It is used as a means to evaluate and build sound and comprehensive information security infrastructure. It details information security concepts an organization "should" do. BS7799 Part 2 is an auditing guide based on requirements. To be certified as BS7799 compliant, organizations are audited against Part 2. It details information security concepts an organization "shall" do. This rigidity precluded widespread acceptance and support. BS7799 is therefore a model guideline for IT systems and applications which automatically requires a high degree of information security as well as effective risk mitigation. With suitable use of infrastructural, technical, managerial, organizational and personnel controls and safeguards standard security parameters are achieved and maintained which ensure security (Bundesamt fr Sicherheit in der Informationstechnik, n.d.).

Risk Management

An organization in its lifecycle is confronted with various risks which emanate from multiple sources.

Information Security (IS) concerns itself with the protection of information and asset from a wide range of threats that an organization has to endure. Risk is inherent in any business venture.

Risk is defined as an event. A business risk is a threat that an event or action will adversely affect an enterprise's ability to maximize return on investment (ROI) or diminish stakeholder value and may cause severe financial damage by way of incurring additional costs.

Mathematically risk may be defined as the product of probability of occurrence of an event and the financial impact of such occurrence to an enterprise. Minimising either of the two terms in the right hand side of the equation (probability of occurrence or financial impact) minimises risk.

Risk may be broadly classified into four types (i) strategic risk (ii) operational risk (iii) financial risk and (iv) knowledge related risks. Strategic risks are associated with the purpose of existence of the organization. It is associated with the reason why the organization is operating in the particular industry in the first place viz. organization's primary long-term purpose, objectives and direction of the business. Operational risks are associated with the day-to-day operations of running the enterprise. Financial risks are related specifically to the processes, techniques and instruments related with financial health of enterprise as well as concerned with economic interactions with stakeholders and third parties e.g. bank and other financial institutions. Knowledge risks are associated with the custody and upkeep of knowledge and protection of vital information asset within the organization (The Institute of Chartered Accountants of India, n.d.).

Security requirements are identified by methodical assessments of security risks inherent in the business environment and particular domain in which the organization is operating. Organizations in pursuant of creating opportunities for its stakeholders must have to cope up with the risk factor as an unavoidable by-product of value management.

The total risk factors of an organization change more during the dynamic, turbulent phases (proliferation of business, merger and acquisition of newer enterprises, launching of different products) of organization's existence rather than during relatively stable operating phases. A good understanding of the information security requirements, risk assessment and risk management are imperative for successful establishment of information security conditionality.

Visible support, funding and commitment from all levels of management and appropriate awareness, training and marketing of the security parameters to all stakeholders are recipe for success. A proper methodical balance between expenditure accrued on establishing security controls against the erosion of business value likely to result from security breaches is helpful.

Establishing an effective information security incident management process, implementation of a measurement system that is used to evaluate the performance in information security management and introduction of suggestion and improvement in the form of a feedback loop are some other essential ingredient for a successful information security regime.

The basic purpose of internal auditing is to establish standards & provide guidance regarding an entity's risk management system and provide firm assurance regarding effectiveness of the system as sought by the company's management. Auditing an enterprise risk management system serves four fold specific goals. The first one effectively deals with risk. The second one associates uncertainty with each of the process. The third one enhances capacity to build value to the enterprise and fourth one monitors the overall system for risk identified.

Risk management within an organization is about setting up a structured framework which monitors consistently and continuously organizational processes associated with risk and developing strategies to manage risk within the risk appetite of the organization. Risk appetite differs for different organizations. Risk mitigation strategy involves five step process viz. (i) identification, assessment and prioritization of risk (ii) implementation of risk containment steps (iii) risk reporting (iv) developing an appropriate risk response policy (v) continuous risk monitoring and risk assurance (International Organization for Standardization, 2005). Management is responsible for establishing and operating the risk containment framework, and assurance phase provided by internal audit is the key part of lifecycle of risk management. In this respect the internal auditor is expected to adopt independence and neutrality. The auditor's work include (a) assessing the risk maturity level within the organization (b) determining compliance metrics with the risk management policy and framework and (c) assessing the efficiency and/or effectiveness of the risk response and (d) assessing relative risk tolerance vis a vis residual risk faced by organization.

While information security in general encompasses all facets of securing information and its protection, in this chapter we present a framework for measuring the compliance of information (data) against a specified standard. Our framework comprises the following two phases: The first phase involves preparation of input in which information to be checked for compliance against the standards document is classified and saved in ontology. The second phase is to produce an output which consists of compliance measurement. The whole process is broken down into the following parts.

- Derive an event based semantic model from the view point of compliance.
- Represent the concepts from the model in event based ontology.
- Derive (composite) semantic models from controls.
- Derive semantic rules and express them in SWRL.
- Load given data into the ontology, and apply SWRL rules.
- Derive strategies for handling partial/missing/incomplete data and new concepts encountered in the data, but which is not defined in the ontology.
- Determine the relevance or each concept using fuzzy weights for the computation of compliance.
- Compute the compliance measure.

PART 2: AUDITING AN ORGANIZATION

Auditing of an organization is a highly complex operation and it has intricate financial, legal, economic and ethical implications for the organization and society as a whole. The auditors check and report on the fidelity of the information related

to the organization, to verify if the procedures of the organization is conducted according to the procedures set by auditing standards. Information auditing is discussed in section A. We specially discuss the auditing in an information security domain in section B and methodology used in this case and also the special security control. Section C discusses information auditing practices in general.

Information Auditing

Auditing is defined as a systematic and independent examination of data, statements, records, operations and performances (financial or otherwise) of an enterprise for a stated purpose. In any auditing situation, the auditor perceives and recognises the propositions before him for examinations, collects evidences, evaluates the same and on this basis formulates his judgement which is communicated through the audit report. Audit is an independent examination of financial and other information of any entity, whether profit oriented or not, and irrespective of its size or legal form, when such an examination is conducted with a view to expressing an opinion thereon. (The Institute of Chartered Accountants of India, n.d.)

Thus the whole process of auditing encompasses reviewing financial statements to reflect a true and fair view of state of affairs and working result or it may measure the cost effectiveness or management performance of an enterprise. In a broader framework auditing basically measures whether the transaction of an enterprise have been executed in compliance within the framework of certain standard reference parameters. Thus the questions of compliance or conformity to regulations, obligations & standards become paramount as far as auditing is concerned.

Compliance is a multi-faceted concept that encompasses the capability of an organization to monitor and meet impinging obligations. In an IT centric environment catering to multifarious and often conflicting and competing regulatory requirements & demands imposed by customers, legal entities, business partners and likes there are various best practices and standards which are employed to benchmark organizational adherence to different regulations.

In a heterogeneous, multi-regulated, multi-disciplined and global environment, organizations starting from Global Multinationals, Public Sector Undertakings (PSU), Non Government Organization (NGO), Military Industrial Complex (MIC), Private Sector etc. find it difficult to deal with the process of checking the organization practices with the regulatory policies and guidelines of the business as they are often required to comply with multiple business standards and regulations. Information audit is a systematic process through which a firm's information system is analysed and evaluated and important records are managed. Through information audit organizations understand its own information needs, perform gap analysis, and stop dissipation and pilferage of valuable knowledge and draws necessary inference. Auditing records are systematically arranged, organized and retained for necessary purpose. The objective of this whole process is to "improve accuracy, relevance, security and timeliness of the recorded information (The Institute of Chartered Accountants of India, n.d.)." Information auditing involves a ten stage process: (i) identifying information need, types of the organization (ii) scrutinizing organization task (business process, activities, transactions) (iii) identifying existing record keeping systems (iv) reviewing the internal/external information resources (v) performing gap analysis of performance and information requirement of organization (vi) mapping the information flows and current bottlenecks within those flows (vii) developing an knowledge and information map of the organization (viii) designing and improving new record management system which ensure fulfilment of existing and/or new requirements (ix) developing some quick fixes which may be required in exigencies and (x) developing

comprehensive information management system within the organisation.

In a large organization, since it may not be possible to assess all events and resources in all aspects in their entirety, company auditors use Pareto Analysis (more popularly known as 80/20 rule) which is a statistical decision making technique. This tool is used to select limited number of significant events (20%) which may potentially produce maximum overall problems (80%) for organization. Auditors commit to a strategy of analysing finer level of details in 20% of Pareto significant activities. Another terminology used by professional auditors is CEAVOP. CEAVOP stands for Completeness, Existence, Accuracy, Valuation, Ownership, and Presentation. It is an acronym used to represent assertions of a control in auditing. In information security audit parlance CEAV is mostly looked into by the auditors.

Information audit primarily concerns with important information or data (electronic /non-electronic format) pertaining to commercial activities cutting across functional boundaries of the enterprise or organization. These information/data are strategically significant from organizational perspective and are shared by multiple persons & departments. The practical methods of auditing will be composed of following interlinked phases: (i) it will investigate different business processes, their information need & information generation in the process. Depending upon the particular situation a top-down and/or a bottom up approach may be preferable which will scrutinize barriers, and inefficiencies in the information flows (ii) an information compliance management team in the form of independent information auditors is often preferable bringing confidentiality, fairness and perspicaciousness to the whole process. The team may question/ contact the concerned persons in the department for records (iii) identifying records (iv) classify records according to importance (v) investigate the staffs most responsible for records & information (vi) inspection and sampling of records (vii) for the benefit of auditing process a mixtures of interviews, questionnaires, discussion groups and focus groups methodology may be used (viii) top echelons of management may be interviewed for understanding of the overall process

The output from the whole auditing process will comprise of a report summarising the gist of investigation and salient discrepancies between information requirements and existing information keeping systems. The information thus arrived at & categorization may be integrated & register maintained for business continuity and strategic planning. Finally a retention period & disposition schedule and methodology of information may be undertaken. Periodic review, update and implementations should be a regular feature of information audit. Information needs & flow change with changes of business dynamic and environment. Hence information audit should be a regular feature of organizations keen on maintaining and updating information. Thus information auditing becomes a cornerstone of knowledge management and information security governance. Following benefits accrue to organizations who perform regular audit and possess robust knowledge management system (i) deliver value and service at competitive price (ii) improved knowledge and information resources (iii) better understanding and efficient use of core strategic asset called knowledge (internal and external) (iv) better information access and efficient storage (v) identification of critical information records (vi) retention of vital information (vii) avoid information overload (viii) avoid inefficiencies and duplication of records (ix) improved record management and (x) satisfying legal & regulatory compliances.

Auditing in an Information Technology System Environment

Special considerations are needed and definitive procedures are to be followed when an internal audit is performed in an information technology

(IT) environment. An information technology environment exists when processing of financial information, including quantitative data, and other types of information processing facilities are operated internally or by third party entity using IT. IT system uses technology to capture, classify, summarize and report data in a meaningful manner to interested users, stakeholders, consumer protection groups etc. The relevant data may be stored in capacity storage including an enterprise resource planning (ERP) system. Even though the overall objective and scope of an internal audit remains unchanged in an IT environment, the use of ICT (Information and Communication Technology) changes the nomenclature and rule of the procedures including processing, storage, retrieval and communication of relevant information and the interplay of processes, systems and control procedures. This may affect the internal control systems employed by the entity or the third party. The internal auditor must be careful in employing procedure in obtaining a sufficient understanding of the processes, systems and internal control system of the enterprise it evaluates. ICT environment also impacts the auditor's review of the entity's risk management and continuity systems. The following considerations on the effect of an ICT environment on the internal audit work may be undertaken by a competent auditor viz. (i) the extent to which the ICT environment's involvement is used to record, compile, process and analyse audit information (ii) the flow of authorised, correct and complete data to the storage media (iii) the processing, analysis and reporting tasks undertaken in the installation (iv) the impact of ICT based accounting system on the audit trail (The Institute of Chartered Accountants of India, n.d.).

On its own competency the internal auditor should have sufficient knowledge of the information technology systems to plan, direct, supervise, control and review the work performed. The internal auditor should consider whether any specialised IT skills are needed in the conduct of the audit. Specialised skills e.g. operating system of ERP or specialised financial packages are needed to obtain sufficient understanding of the effect of the ICT environment on systems, processes, internal control and risk management systems. It is also used to design and perform appropriate tests of control and to determine the effect of the IT environment on assessment of overall audit risk. If specialized skills are needed, technical experts from internal staff or outside professional may be approached.

The internal auditor should obtain a thorough understanding of the ICT systems, processes, control environment, risk-response activities and internal control systems. The auditor should be sufficiently technically competent to plan the internal audit in an ICT environment and to determine the nature, timing and extent of the audit procedures. In planning the portions of the internal audit which may be affected by the ICT environment, the internal auditor should obtain an understanding of the significance and complexity of the IT activities and the availability of the data for use in the internal audit. Source documents, computer files, and other evidential matter that may be required by the internal auditor may exist for only a short period or only in machine-readable form. Information Technology systems may generate reports that might be useful in performing substantive tests (particularly analytical procedures). The potential for use of computer-assisted audit techniques may permit increased efficiency in the performance of internal audit procedures, or may enable the auditor to economically apply certain procedures to the entire population of transactions.

Information Auditing Practices

The objective of information audit is to enable the auditor to express an opinion regarding preparation of audit statement in accordance with identified reporting framework and criteria to give a "true and fair view". Information auditor's satisfaction

regarding reliability of the assertion of the entity the auditor is auditing stems from the sufficient procedural evidences and subsequent conclusions drawn.

In an audit engagement the auditor provides a high but not absolute assertion while in review auditing the assurance given is moderate regarding material/informational mismanagement. A review comprises enquiry and analytical procedure to attest reliability of information audit. Procedure followed and result thereof form level of satisfaction for the information auditor and subsequent attested assurance for compliance by him. Agreed upon procedures of an auditor, an entity and any appropriate third parties culminate in factual findings. In compilation a specialized information auditor collects, classifies and summarizes detailed information to a manageable form with professional skill and perfection. Integrity, objectivity, interdependence, confidentiality and impartiality are hallmarks of professional auditing. The entire business is expected to be performed by people with due professional competence, training and experience. The auditor should obtain sufficient appropriate audit evidence through the performance of compliance and substantive procedures to enable him to draw reasonable conclusion there from on which to base his opinion. Compliance procedures are tests designed to obtain reasonable assurances that those internal controls on which audit reliance is to be placed are in effect. Auditing framework with all its requisite steps is depicted in Figure 1.

The management is responsible for maintaining an adequate information system incorporating various internal controls to the extent appropriate to the size and nature of the business, maintenance of adequate record, selection of application of accounting policies and safeguarding of enterprise assets etc. The information audit does not relieve the management of their basic responsibilities. The auditor should therefore be genuinely satisfied about the adequacy of the auditing system and sufficiency of recorded information. An adequate

Figure 1. Framework for auditing and related services

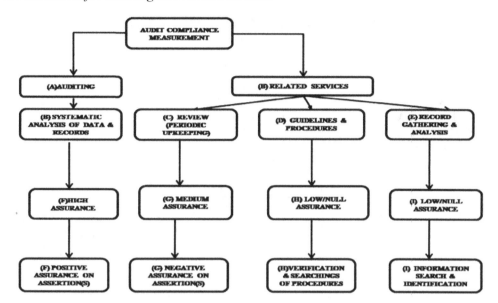

information system and insight of internal controls are sine qua non for an auditor, as upon these controls nature, timing and extent of the audit procedures exclusively rely. The auditor carries out tests, enquiries and other verification procedures of transactions whatsoever (s) he deems fit. The auditor determines whether the relevant information is properly disclosed or not. The authenticity of these internal controls reduces the burden of substantive procedures. The information audit report should contain a clear written expression of opinion on the information system concerned. If any statute, legislation or agreement prescribes particular formation of report the auditor should comply. When an opinion expressed by the auditor contains qualifier, adverse remark or disclaimer the report should clearly state the reasons thereof. Evaluation for information system auditing control with various steps is explained in Figure 2.

PART 3: ONTOLOGY BASED SEMANTIC MODELLING

After identifying our goal in Part 1 as mitigating risk which is an integral part of corporate security governance of an organization and again selecting our manual auditing procedure in Part 2 as effective means at the hands of auditors to quantitatively measure discrepancies between organization practice and principles laid down at information security standards, we gather our knowledge management toolkit in this Part 3 as we will require them most in Part 4 to succinctly present automated compliance auditing prototype in information security domain. We start with definition of ontology in section A and present partial ontology model of an organization. In section B we define semantic modelling and then combine the knowledge of these two sections in section C in semantic based robust reasoning framework (SemRRF) and in section D as compliance rules using semantic production system.

Figure 2. Evaluation of information system accounting and security control

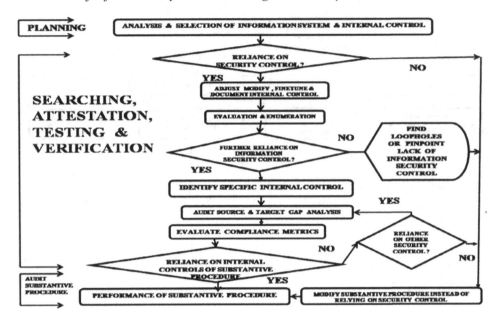

Ontology

Ontology is the branch of metaphysics that studies the nature of existence or being as such. Ontology which claimed its origin in philosophy as systematic and structural nomenclature of being is nowadays used in such diverse branches as medicine, computer science, health care, law, natural language processing(NLP), knowledge management, e-commerce, semantic web etc. It represents computational logic and uses uncertain and imprecise knowledge for more robust inference and exact conclusion by statistical confidence measurement. "Ontology defines the basic terms and relations comprising the vocabulary of a topic area as well as the rules for combining terms and relations to define extensions to the vocabulary"(Neches et al., 1991). Later more succinctly it was defined "An Ontology is an explicit specification of a conceptualization"(Gruber, 1993).The most popular definition of ontology runs like this "Ontologies are defined as a formal specification of a shared conceptualization"(Borst, 1997). A further improvisation of Gruber's and Borst's definition was provided by Studer et. el as:

"Ontology is a formal, explicit specification of a shared conceptualization. Conceptualization refers to an abstract model of some phenomenon in the world by having identified the relevant concepts of that phenomenon. Explicit means that the type of concepts used, and the constraints on their use are explicitly defined. Formal refers to the fact that the ontology should be machine-readable. Shared reflects the notion that an ontology captures consensual knowledge, that is, it is not private of some individual, but accepted by a group"(Studer, Benjamins, & Fensel, 1998).

Ontology contains a quadruple set of concepts, relations, axioms and instances. It may also be graphically represented as a directed graph with tuple (nodes, nodes contents and arrows) representing (concepts, instances and relationships) respectively. Partial ontology model of an organization on its information security risk is depicted in Figure 3 below.

Semantic Modelling

Semantic Web Technologies (SWT) are now having important real world commercial applications

Figure 3. A partial ontology model on information security risk of an organization

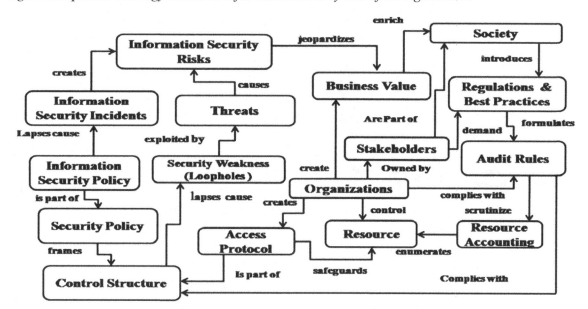

across different domains of industry like healthcare, financial engineering, commerce, economic forecasting, insurance, mobile technologies etc. along with a growing body of standards, nomenclatures and recommendations supporting them. Here we are mostly concerned with regulatory auditing domain as a new emerging field in which tools and techniques of semantic web technologies like ontologies, semantic based rules, fuzzy production logic can be used to smoothen out semantic ambiguities and incongruities in information systems. As of now interconnected web pages in hypertext mark up language or HTML are not amenable to machine language interpretation. The ultimate aims of semantic web engineering along with its rules, regulations, services and ontologies are to create machine-machine and machine-human interpretable and interoperable dynamic formats of web pages. SWT facilitates this machine-machine and machine-human semi automatic or automatic processing of information and its subsequent integration in standard languages like Web Ontology Language (OWL), Resource Description Framework (RDF) etc.

For modelling complex systems (including multi role, multi platform and multi system aspects) we use event models. The central concepts needed for compliance checking are modelled as multi agent events in which we hypothesize that events have several attributes, of which two are most important: physical events corresponding to physical state changes, and mental events corresponding to agent's mental state changes, and these events occur over a time interval. Further, events can be primitive, composite, or abstract. The different classes of event models are then used to construct event ontology. Security requirements are identified from three sources: (i) possible risks to the organization while taking overall business strategy and objectives into account; (ii) the set of principles, objectives and business requirements; and (iii) the legal, statutory, contractual requirements that all stakeholders viz. trading partners, contractors and service providers have to follow. We model an organization by identifying the relationship between its various business activities. Semantic web is made up of several components and the enabling standards and technologies can be depicted as a "layer cake" as shown in Figure

Figure 4. Semantic web layer cake (Yip, 2011)

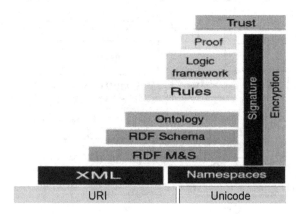

4 (Yip, 2011). Each layer below extends to the layer one up

The logic and proof layer checks inconsistency of data set while proof layer enriches logic based reasoning. The trust layer authenticates veracity of agents, data and services.

Semantic-Based Robust Reasoning Framework (SemRRF)

We propose Semantic-based Robust Reasoning Framework (SemRRF) to layout the components required in building semantic-based solutions for real world applications that require robust automated reasoning. The framework emphasises requirement of approximate decision support system. The SWT and AI techniques used in SemRRF framework are presented in which we denote them as framework enablers.

The Semantic-based Robust Reasoning Framework (SemRRF) is composed of four basic components viz. (i)Interface (tightly coupled domain expert knowledgebase and external database) (ii) Reference Knowledge Base (iii) Inference Engine and (iv) Target Knowledgebase.

The first component i.e. Interface component serves as a linkage between humans/domain expert and external knowledge bases. The second component i.e. Reference Knowledgebase (RefKB) component combines domain knowledge

(i.e. metadata and semantics of the domain) and application logic. This application logic part 1s constructed as set of specific rules to be fired at the time when definite conditions are satisfied. The third part 1.e. Reasoning Engine component is composed of a Reasoner and the associated working memory for facilitating the reasoning process that is used under uncertain and imprecise reasoning environment. It also provides a solution implementation roadmap for applications that require approximate decision support. Each component contributes and provides guidance to the solution implementation. While each component outlines the scope of functionalities and characteristics, it does not mandate any particular implementation or technology choice. The SemRRF framework is depicted in Figure 5 (Yip, 2011). Target Knowledgebase (Target) refers to the actual knowledge and instances in which rules are executed. Now let us discuss each one of the four components in detail.

Interface

Interface is the first component of SemRRF. It is an intermediate block between "agents" (the entities that provides external input and output (I/O) of data and knowledge to the RefKB and TargetKB of the framework) and knowledge bases which is provided by domain expert(s). Software agents acting on behalf of semantically enabled software are examples of agents in the Interface component block. The software agents use domain knowledge stored in the knowledge bases (i.e. ontologies and semantic-based rules). These software agents are example of intelligent artificial agents mimicking human agents.

Human domain experts constitute another category of intelligent agents. Domain experts possess plethora of knowledge modelling tools and editors (Protégé Ontology Editor) at their disposal to model new knowledge. Also these domain experts amend and delete existing redundant/spurious knowledge from the KB. A common activity

Figure 5. Semantic-based robust reasoning framework (SemRRF) modules (Yip, 2011)

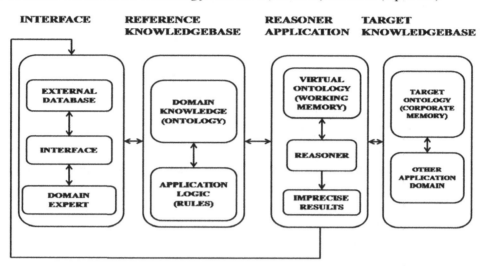

usually performed by domain experts is to add, remove and amend rules in rule bases of the KB. They are also empowered to modify the domain knowledge definitions in domain ontologies when the existing rules fired fail to resolve a problem.

External data sources in any form such as SQL database, file systems, XML data sources are considered as data and knowledge providers and interface to the knowledgebase within the framework. External data sources can synchronize with knowledge in the reference and target KB using techniques such as natural language processing, data mining, XSL transforms, macros, scripts etc.

Reference Knowledgebase

The Reference Knowledgebase (RefKB) in SemRRF is a semantic-based KB that is composed of two sub-components: (a) Domain Knowledge; and (b) Application Logic.

1. **Domain Knowledge (DK):** This sub-component houses the knowledge of the given domain. The closest analogy that can be given is the specific dictionary type which contains knowledge of particular subject (legal dictionary, dictionary of medicine,

sports dictionary etc.). Therefore, the DK sub-component acts as a taxonomy definition for machines to understand and interpret the domain concepts, relations and axioms for a given application domain.

2. **Application Logic (AL):** Once the DK sub-component becomes fully functional, another subcomponent is needed that complements the DK sub-component for capturing operation, execution and business logic of a domain. The AL sub-component enquires from the knowledge captured in the DK knowledge base for reference.

Reasoner Application

A virtual ontology as the working memory (WM) and a semantic-enabled Reasoner together constitute the reasoning engine (RE) part of SemRRF. The working memory is structured so as to support robust and automated reasoning process. The Reasoner processes RefKB's Application Logic rules. It executes the RefKB's rules against Target Ontology in Target Knowledgebase (TargetKB). The WM works as a runtime memory and placeholder that contains the correlations between

RefKB's Domain Knowledge and TargetKB's Target Ontology.

Target Knowledgebase

The Target Knowledgebase (TargetKB) is composed of information and knowledge against which RefKB's Application Logic is executed. The execution infers additional knowledge and produces decision results. In an organizational context, TargetKB represents the Corporate Memory of an organization that contains knowledge and data instances representing the state of the organization and its processes that are required to be verified for their compliance against government regulations.

Compliance Rules Using Semantic Production System

A Production System (PS) or sometimes called rule-based system is a computer program typically used to provide some form of Artificial Intelligence (AI) functionality in an application, which consists primarily of a working memory and a set of rules that describe behaviours. These rules are also called "production rules" and are one of the basic representational formalisms found useful in the field of knowledge representation, AI planning, expert systems and action selection. The popularity of production systems is mostly driven by the increased amount of knowledge and data that humans need to process today. These production systems are able to represent to some extent experts' problem-solving logic (application logic) and techniques in terms of a set of situation-action rules.

While traditional production systems greatly assist humans in processing information and in making decisions, they are distant from solving problems and providing results in a way that is highly automated and with little human interventions. These systems inherit several limitations and are challenged in solving real world and pragmatic use case scenarios in a natural and straightforward

way. Automated systems that work independently from human interventions are still a major challenge at large and have been an on-going active research topic in the AI communities.

The controls in the standards documents are modelled using production system rules. Production System (PS) is a forward chaining reasoning system that provides the artificial intelligence found useful in information and decision support systems. An automated and robust reasoning process is achieved by leveraging the semantics modelled in ontologies and semantic-based rules called "Robust Rules'. PS addresses the need for processing formally represented knowledge and logic captured from human. Consequently, it provides a practical means and foundation for building automated (information) systems that is otherwise performed by humans. PS is suitable in modelling the "rules of thumbs" used by domain experts in carrying out tasks (Brachman & Levesque, 2004). Systems that use PS architecture can model explicitly both the application knowledge and the reasoning logic those experts use when performing tasks. In general, human experts solve problems in a heuristic fashion from symptoms to cause which resemble those of PS's in handling such diverse problems as medical diagnosis, credit checking, compliance auditing, etc. Existing production system formalisms do not support semantic approximations. In order to support approximate decision support and implement a robust automated reasoning, an enhanced version of production system is required.

Conventional PS suffers from the lack of ability to reason with vague or imprecise values. In comparison, human is able to reason, process and make conclusions based on vague, incomplete and imprecise information with the sacrifice of result accuracy. The limitation of traditional PS hinders the process to represent experts' knowledge into machine readable form that closely resembles of humans'. It also poses the challenge for knowledge engineers to precisely extract and represent experts' knowledge into the knowledgebase of the production systems. To address these limitations, some form of approximated representation and reasoning techniques are needed to support vague and uncertain information processing. Fuzzy logic and fuzzy reasoning introduced by Zadeh (Zadeh, 1965) in the early 1960s as a solution to allow computer to support approximated reasoning are not directly semantic driven.

PART 4: EXPERT SYSTEM AND COMPLIANCE AUDITING

Once identifying our goal about automated compliance auditing, at the concluding part of our chapter we define common structure of expert system and knowledge acquisition system in section A and in section B we talk about ontology based semantic framework for compliance auditing. It is the transition from manual auditing described in part 2 with the help of our knowledge management toolkit in part 3 that the final framework for automated compliance system is constructed.

Knowledge Acquisition and Expert System

Production System (PS) otherwise known as rule based system tries to impart 1ntelligence to the artificial entities by a set of rules which are highly knowledge encoded. This knowledge can be expressed as a body of rules for problem solving. The body of knowledge is a part of expert system which tries to mimic the "human expert" in a given domain who in exigency often uses heuristics or rule of thumb to arrive at a decision in shortest possible time. The whole procedures of expert system is a four step processes (a) exactly specifying the problem(s) in the given domain (b)an efficiently built up repository of domain knowledge base and its exact representation format (c) one or more reasoning mechanism to interpret the domain knowledge to the specific problem (d) a robust mechanism for interpretation and

explanation of the result to the intended user for his proper conviction & reliance upon the system. The reasoning process & interaction of the expert system needs to be crystal clear for the user before its proper use. This meta-knowledge or knowledge for the reasoning process for the creation of the expert system is therefore essential for the benefit of user of the system. The robustness of the system stems from cumulative repository of multiple experts knowledge bases accumulated over a long period of time. A number of iterative cycles need to be executed along with feedback loop between experts and system while experts go on transferring their years of accumulated knowledge to the system under different scenarios.

Expert system normally acts erratically with commonsense application and the ideal borderline is hard to define or specify accurately. Amount of knowledge to be transferred and the rules to be formulated depend on task at hand. Choice of control structure for a particular system depends on specific characteristics of system. It is possible to extract the non-domain specific parts from existing expert systems and use them as tools for building new system in the new domains. An expert system is as strong as the power of its knowledge bases and hence complete and accurate knowledge repository with periodic up-gradation and modification is what is pertinently required. For this purpose the expert system needs to be capable of extracting knowledge from raw data and/or interaction with human experts in the specific fields. The whole procedures are composed of following steps (a) knowledge acquisition from raw data (b) maintaining and up-keeping integrity of knowledge base (c) systematic periodic review and up-gradation of knowledge base. Overall knowledge based expert system structure is depicted in Figure 6.

Expert systems suffer from multiple deficiencies. One using an expert system should be critically aware of the defects of the expert system which needs careful remedy and rectification: (a) expert systems lack common sense or general knowledge which is amply possessed by human

Figure 6. Knowledge based expert system structure

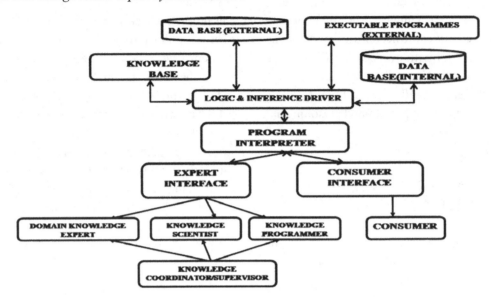

experts as it depends too much on highly specific domain knowledge; (b) insufficient meta knowledge (knowledge of the expert system on its own procedures, methods and structures) prevents expert systems from appreciating about their own scope and limitations and highly challenging task of auto correction and speedy recovery from an error loop; (c) knowledge acquisition remains a principal impediment towards application of expert system into new domains; (d) performance measurement and validation of expert systems remain a challenging area as formal validation remains difficult and only indirect methods like benchmarking the performance of expert systems against human experts on some real world problem may be cited as its performance metrics.

A knowledge-based expert system is composed of five components: (i) the knowledge base; (ii) the database (both external and internal database); (iii) the logic and inference driver; (iv) the program interpreter; and (v) the interface (both for producer and consumer). Let us enumerate them one by one.

The first of the five components is knowledge base which is the heart of expert system. The expert system is normally modelled using a specific set of rules for solving problems. Each rule is formed using *IF (condition) THEN (action)* structure. Condition part (IF) specifies certain relations which require satisfaction whereas action part (THEN) contains certain recommendation, directive, strategy or heuristic algorithms. When the condition part of a rule is fulfilled, the rule is said to fire and the action part 1s executed. The result of this rule firing is the transition of state, *viz.* the system undergoes transformation from one state to another. The second is the database component. The database includes a set of facts used to match against the IF (condition) parts of rules stored in the knowledge base. Here both external and internal databases are considered. The third part *viz.* logic and inference driver concerns with the reasoning part whereby the expert system tries to find a solution. It is a linking bridge between the knowledge base rule and the database. The fourth component *viz.* program interpreter helps explain to the user how to reach a particular conclusion or need for a particular fact. A user who is conversant with the expert system must be satisfied with the ability of the expert system to explain its reasoning and justify its advice, analysis or conclusion. The fifth component i.e.

interfaces between expert system and its users may be of two types: (i) expert interface; and (ii) user interface. The expert interface is broken down into three parts - each one belonging to domain knowledge expert, knowledge engineer, and programmers. Activities of all three are coordinated by a knowledge coordinator/supervisor. The expert interface usually includes knowledge base editors, debugging aids and input/output facilities, and a simple text editor to input and modify rules to check their correct format and spelling. Debugging aids usually consist of tracing facilities and break packages. Tracing provides a list of all rules fired during the program's execution, and a break package makes it possible to tell the expert system in advance where to stop so that the knowledge engineer or the expert can examine the current values in the database. The user interface between a user and an expert system should be as concise, meaningful and as user friendly as possible so that even a layman will find no difficulty in accessing the system. A design of smart interface is what a system designer will strive for.

Expert system is endowed with capability of self-reviewing its reasoning process and explaining its own decisions. Its self explanation capability stems from its ability to trace the rules fired during problem solving time. But the expert system lacks the "human insight" as it is unable to have basic domain knowledge or mimic a domain expert. Each high level rule stored in the rule base is accompanied by appropriate domain knowledge and a basic rule tracing capability. Expert systems built for decision support system should be accompanied with complete and thoughtful explanations, as the cost of a wrong decision may be very high. Expert system unlike conventional programming may employ inexact reasoning and capable of dealing with incomplete, uncertain, imprecise and fuzzy data.

Methodology: Ontology Based Semantic Framework for Compliance Auditing

Ontology as explained is "an explicit specification of a shared conceptualization of a domain". It is constructed to capture implicit, explicit and commonsense-knowledge of a domain such that the knowledge can be shared, reused and consumed by humans and autonomous computer agents. They have been used successfully in the fields of artificial intelligence, information retrieval, natural language processing and knowledge engineering. In the context of Multi Agent System (MAS), ontology has been acknowledged as being beneficial to various MAS development activities in addition to operational aspects of MAS. Ontological modelling of agent knowledge is regarded as essential to operations of MAS, particularly to the communication between system components and reasoning of agents. Ontology brings both a degree of interoperability and reusability of system design for MAS. The growing popularity of agent-based technologies leads traditional software engineering methodologies to evolve into a set of Agent Oriented Software Engineering methodologies (AOSE). The role of the AOSE methodologies is to assist in all the phases of the life cycle of an agent-based application, including its management and make the application robust, reusable, autonomous and dependable.

Some of the benefits and limitations of ontology and multi-agent systems are explained below:

1. Exploration of AOSE methodologies and their usefulness in designing multi-agent based systems.
2. Limited awareness for ontology in these methodologies and lower runtime support.
3. Inadequacies in detailing on architecture specific implementation as a part of the methodology.

In this section, we will present the methodology as a framework for compliance auditing in an ontology based environment. We are specifically working on ontology based multi agent system called MOMASD (The Methodology for Ontology-Based Multi-Agent System Design) with event based representation. One difficulty with development of methodology in any system that incorporates domain expertise is the accompanying need for intricate agent development knowledge for its functionality. MOMASD attempts to circumvent this difficulty by incorporating in ontology as much domain knowledge and business logic as possible to address inadequacies and limitations in the existing methodologies in the following possible ways:

1. Providing a structured meta-model for the development of ontology for agent application development.
2. Ontological models defining agent behaviour there by bringing forth business logic from agent implementation to abstract conceptual level.
3. Facilitating software tools to drive development, conceptual testing and implementation of ontology for agent systems.
4. Using modularity and structural independence process to facilitate reuse and sharing.
5. Decoupling roles of domain expert and agent developer in the MOMASD development phase assuming their mutual operating independence. Domain experts should be able to handle the system without unnecessarily depending upon agent developer.

MOMASD development life cycle is shown below in Figure 7.

The process of compliance auditing involves the following three pre-requisites:

1. Domain knowledge modelling.
2. Application logic modelling.
3. Application logic extension modelling.

These pre-requisite steps are not within the scope of our present discussion, but we are mainly concerned with the knowledge representation and construction process to codify the domain knowledge.

Our ontology based framework for compliance in information security is shown in Figure 8.

At the heart of our framework are two ontologies: a Reference Ontology (RO) and a Target Ontology (TO). Briefly, RO is an ontology of the particular information security standard being verified at the audit domain (CobiT, ISO17799 etc.) and TO is the ontology used by the organization. The data in the TO are checked for compliance using a set of compliance rules (written in SWRL). Compliance calculation strategy should be used in the whole process.

Reference Ontology (RO) – Representing Domain Using Multi-Agent Information Model

The reference ontology (RO) is the source of concepts that are obtained from the information models derived from the following sources:

- Information Security standards and best practices (e.g. ISO17799, CobiT).
- Information Security dictionaries (e.g. Glossary for Information Security).
- Domain Experts knowledge (e.g. Compliance Officer).
- Compliance handbooks (e.g. Australian Standard: AS3806-2006).

Auditing process for an organization being staggered over a time period (normally one year), it is our intuition that for compliance auditing purposes, information must be stored and reasoned with as events where agents have participated. Thus, in our information model, almost all facts and rules in the domain use event models. Events are formalized using event calculus. In an organization the activities are performed by a hierarchy

Figure 7. MOMASD development life cycle

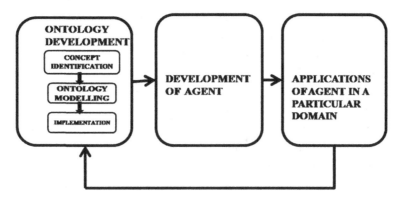

of individuals in a coordinated and systematic manner and thus activities can be viewed as multi-agent events.

Target Ontology (TO) – Target Domain Model

TO is the *Corporate Memory* of the organization. It contains the facts and knowledge about the organization in a systematic format. The knowledge can come from the following sources:

- Document management systems (e.g. knowledge and metadata stored in existing information systems of the organization).
- File systems (e.g. instances of documents stored in network drives).
- Employee Management System (e.g. knowledge of organization entities).
- Infrastructure (e.g. intrusion detection logs, access control list).

Compliance auditing involves executing compliance audit rules (written in SWRL) on

Figure 8. An ontology based framework for compliance auditing

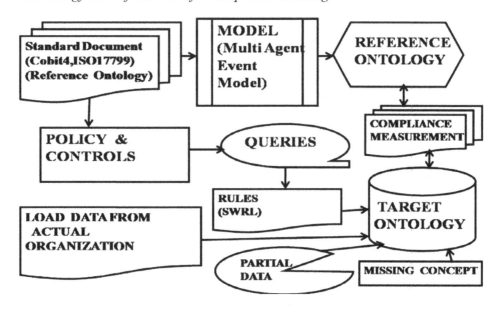

the target ontology TO, which is populated with the data of the organization. The audit rules are originally meant to be used on the reference ontology (RO), which was formulated according to the controls of the standards like ISO17799 or CobiT etc. This means, quite likely the SWRL would not successfully match against at least some of the concepts in RO since not all source ontology concepts may be present in the target ontology and vice versa. In such situations, a measure of deviation is computed using ontology mapping techniques, and this deviation becomes the source of fuzziness in our framework.

Automated Compliance Auditing

In an ideal world, all compliance knowledge and facts are properly captured and stored in an ontology in which machines can confidently reason and infer results based on the precise and complete data. However, in the real world, not all information is complete, precise, and properly captured. This fact was first proposed in the previous section in knowledge acquisition of expert system. Even for compliance experts, they often can only rely on partial and imprecise knowledge or refer to personal experience to infer approximated judgments in the absence of clear cut, precise knowledge or evidence. The opinions of experts may vary widely and sometimes contradictorily (one popular example in this regard is the verdict of a lower court being upturned in the higher court even though all the judges involved in two courts, cite the same rule books. Also any evidence cited in the lower court cannot be tampered with in the higher court). Therefore, compliance is generally considered as a biased and subjective process. In such situations, it is thus necessary to quantify the contribution made by available data and the missing data towards the compliance measure. A human auditor typically uses his intuition (extracted from his experience) to estimate the relative contribution each piece of information could make towards the compliance calculation.

Most conventional checklist or static rule-base compliance software are generally designed as a computer assisted auditing tool requiring a high level of human interaction and prompts for human inputs whenever ambiguous situations arise. This characteristic exists mainly due to the static nature of the check-list approach and the complexity in modelling abstract and non-system related rules that can be interpretable by software agents.

Fuzzy Compliance Rules Based on Similarity Measures

The consistency of compliance results cannot be guaranteed and is dependent on the compliance auditor and the compliance data that are sampled. To capture the imprecise and uncertainty of compliance knowledge, we make use of weighted fuzzy production rules (WFPRs) as a mechanism to represent our compliance requirements.

Consider the following example where we assume that the doors are digital lock with logs retrievable for subsequent inspection.

R1: Doors to the rooms that contain confidential information should be locked at all times.

R2: The locks on the doors should be biometric locks.

Rules R1 and R2 can be represented by the following logical statements respectively:

```
Rule R1
IF
    room(?a) & door(?b) & has(?a, ?b)
    & confidential_information(?c)
    & contains(?a, ?c) & lock(?d)
    & has(?b, ?d) & isLocked(?d)
THEN
    compliant(R1);
Rule R2
IF
    door(?b)
    & lock(?d)
    & has(?b,?d)
    & biometric(?d)
```

```
THEN
     compliant(R2);
```

In the above example, we have a simple rule set that mandates that rooms that contain confidential information must be locked by a biometric key. This rule is written using the concepts from the RO (Reference Ontology). However, the concept Biometric Key may be missing from the organization's TO (Target Ontology). In a classical rule-base system, *R2* would fail to fire, and no conclusions would be inferred. On the contrary, the concept of adaptive rules exploits the semantics of the reference ontology and identifies and makes use of alternate facts and knowledge to prove compliance automatically within a controlled deviation. This is done by mapping the concept Biometric Key onto TO, and finding a concept C that is most similar to the concept Biometric Key with a similarity measure μ where $0 \leq \mu \leq 1$. The rule R2 is then rewritten as R2□ where the concept Biometric Key from RO is replaced by the concept C from TO and R2□ is now associated with the similarity measure μ which is then interpreted as a fuzzy quantity and the rule R2□ is viewed as a fuzzy rule. From now on, whenever R2□ is involved in any reasoning, the consequence of the fuzzy factor μ is also associated with all the inferred facts. Thus, the challenge in our approach is to estimate the overall compliance using the fuzzy quantities in the overall calculations. In this context, we have identified the following challenges that we plan to address in this proposed research:

1. Given a set of compliance rules R1 written for the source ontology, how do we translate them and obtain a new set of rules R2 so that they can be interpreted with the target ontology? We propose to address this problem by using ontology mapping techniques. There are several ontology mapping techniques available and it is necessary for us to find the one(s) that is appropriate for our domain and application (one technique is illustrated in B.5). The similarity measure between the concepts in the reference ontology RO and the target ontology TO will be associated with every pair of concepts <C1,C2> where concept is from ontology RO, and C2 is from TO, to rewrite the compliance rules R1 to produce the rules R2.

2. Using the new set of rules R2 above how do we assign a measure of confidence to each inferred fact and how do finally compute an overall compliance measure? We propose to address this problem by associating a weight w with each concept C in the reference ontology RO, and use it to estimate the confidence measure c of each derived conclusion, and thus finally estimate the compliance. A simple strategy to arrive at a compliance measure will be to use the weighted average of confidence measures associated with all facts provided by the organization and the inferred facts.

Calculating Compliance Ratio between Two Information Security Ontologies (Ontology Mapping between ISO17799 & COBIT4.1)

In the preceding sections we identified discrepancies between actual organizational practices and theoretical recommendations of information security standards as our area of concern which may cause security risk for the organization. We introduced audit tools in Part 2 as a yardstick to manually calculate the discrepancies. In this section we will try to describe automated process using agent based systems and quantify the gap between organization practices with respect to two popular information security standards and also the relationship between these two measuring standards.

We will show how risk assessment metric can be calculated for both CobiT (Figure 9) and ISO17799 (Figure 10) separately and finally calculate the ratio between the two metrics to arrive at the relative compliance measurement between the two important standards. Basic idea is that both CobiT and ISO17799 can be compared to two different measuring units (like centimetre and inch scale) which are used to measure the length of a particular distance. If we do not know the relationship between two measuring units' viz. centimetre and inch what we can do is simply measure the distance by both measuring units, note down the numbers and takes the ratio between the two numbers which will give us the relationship between two units. The same strategy is followed in this case. Figures 9 & 10 are constructed from control structures governing risk assessment in CobiT4.1 & ISO/IEC 17799 respectively. In this tree structure each node represents weight w_i which measures relative contribution of each child node/sub-event to the overall parent node/event viz. assessing risk. Now specific weight distribution is beyond the scope of this chapter but nominally they are proportional to fraction of total man-hour an auditor spends in auditing each task[1]. The auditor may award partial marks to each of the node /event depending on how the performance of the organization is compliant vis. a vis. individual performance of child node/sub-event in the tree. The marking of the parent node is calculated by adding up marks of children nodes in a bottom-up manner. Now one auditor may, while checking for an organization claiming to be CobiT compliant, first want to verify whether risk assessment is done or not.

In this respect while evaluating Figure 9 goes to the bottom nodes of the tree and after thorough evaluation award identification of strategic and tactical risk to be .2 out of .25 and .05 out of .1 respectively making risk portfolio to be .25 out of .35. The auditor also may give historical risk trends and events to be .1 out of .15, making categorizing risk to be .35 out of possible .5. the auditor also gives identification of internal/external context of risk assessment a value equal to .15 out of .2, selecting risk criteria to be .05 out of .07 and goals of risk assessment to be .01 out

of .03 making establishing risk context to be .21 out of possible .3 . It also selects critical IT objectives to be .15 out of .2. It makes assessing risk to be .71 (.35+.21+.15).

By identical analysis the auditor may evaluate for an organization aiming for compliance in ISO/IEC 17799 risk management framework in Figure 10 and identify sources of risk as .25 out of .35 and estimating risk category as .15 out of .2 making analyzing risk to be .4 out of .55 . Similarly measuring risk criteria to be .2 out of .25 and prioritizing risk significance to be .15 out of .2 as evaluating risk turns out to be .35 out of possible .45. It makes performing risk analysis to be .75 (.4+.35) out of possible 1.0 for Figure 10.

The ratio of CobiT to ISO/IEC 17799 compliance metric for an organization turns out to be .9467(.71/.75). It means that if an organization is 100% ISO/IEC 17799 compliant it will be 94.67% compliant on CobiT.

Experimenting with a number of organizations we can come out with upper and lower bound of ratios (RU & RL) of compliance. We conclude that if an organization is X% compliant with CobiT then it will be highly likely that the organization will be within this compliance boundary of ISO17799 [RU*X, RL*X]. The cluster of ratio or ratio band rather a single ratio is justified because the multidimensionality of the measuring standards involved as well as the size, financial status or domain of the organizations being considered make unique ratio for compliance mapping between two standards an unlikely event. This framework may be implemented using a hierarchy of software agents as indicated in the tree structure of Figures 9 & 10.

CONCLUSION

Here we take time to summarize what has been achieved so far. We started with a link between corporate governance and information security and presented a number of information security stan-

Figure 9. Assessing risks (CobiT)

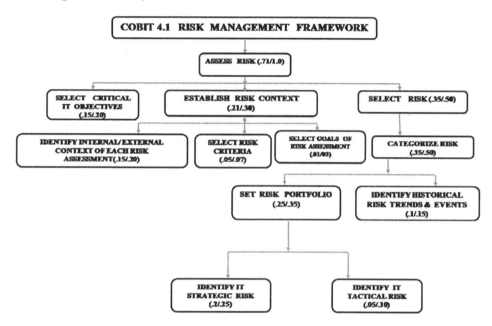

dards. We introduced auditing as practical tool for measuring discrepancies between organizational practices and guidelines embedded in standards and presented some knowledge management tools which may be used for automated compliance auditing framework. Finally we presented a methodology for computing the compliance measure of organizational practice with regulatory/ standards requirements capturing the relevance of the ontological concepts using fuzzy weights towards estimating the compliance. We also demonstrated our technique in two particular cases of information security standards (AS/NZS ISO/IEC 17799:2006 & CobiT 4.1) and calculate the ratio between standards. Given compliance metric for one standard this ratio if multiplied/divided will give compliance metric of the organization for the other standard. So our chapter basically tries

Figure 10. Assessing risks (ISO/IEC 17799)

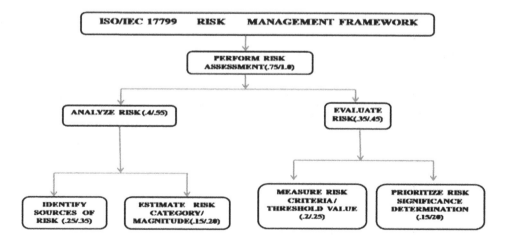

to narrow the gap between corporate governance issues concerning integrity, confidentiality and availability of valuable electronic assets and information towards knowledge management concern of consistency, completeness and redundancy of the same knowledge assets.

Now we will discuss some future research challenges. Computer assisted auditing tools are currently available which concern mostly with the lower end spectrum of configuration compliance, change management, software patch & licensing management issues and their functionality is technology and vendor specific. They try to mostly solve small, lower level problems and never addresses the knowledge management level problems. There are major issues to address in the compliance mapping viz. how to construct ontologies usable by software agents, designing of logical inference driver in intelligent processing and reasoning and problems associated with knowledge entries representations. In case of regulatory requirements there are representational issues of approximate/incomplete/partial knowledge processing /reasoning associated with fuzzy logic, weighted fuzzy production rules. Finally compliance auditing as a gateway to corporate governance is a subset of complex knowledge management issue in which identification, clustering, classification, processing, representation of knowledge as well as consistency, completeness, non-redundancy of knowledge base pose formidable challenges in future research direction.

ACKNOWLEDGMENT

This work was partially supported by the collaborative research project "Supporting Information Exchange across Organizations for e-Business" led by academics in the University of New South Wales (UNSW) and the Indian Institute of Management Calcutta, hosted at the Asia Pacific ubiquitous Healthcare research Centre (APuHC), UNSW and funded by the Australia India Institute grant2011.

REFERENCES

Borst, W. N. (1997). *Construction of engineering ontologies for knowledge sharing and reuse.* Thesis, University of Twente.

Brachman, R. J., & Levesque, H. J. (2004). *Knowledge representation and reasoning.* San Francisco, CA: Morgan Kaufmann Publishers Inc.

Bundesamt fr Sicherheit in der Informationstechnik (BSI). (n.d.). *IT baseline protection manual standard security safeguards.* Retrieved from http://www.bsi.bund.de

Gruber, T. (1993). A translation approach to portable ontology specifications. *Knowledge Acquisition, 5*(2), 199–220.

International Organization for Standardization. (2005). *ISO17799:2005.* Retrieved from http://www.iso.org

IT Governance Institute. (2005). *Control objectives for information and related technologies* (COBIT). Retrieved from http://www.isaca.org/KnowledgeCenter/COBIT/Pages/Overview.aspx

Studer, R., Benjamins, V. R., & Fensel, D. (1998). Knowledge engineering: Principles and methods. *IEEE Transactions on Data and Knowledge Engineering, 25,* 161–197.

The Institute of Chartered Accountant of India. (n.d.). *Auditing.* Retrieved from www.icai.org

US Department of Health and Human Services. (1996). *Health Insurance Portability and Accountability Act* (HIPAA), 1996. Retrieved from http://www.hhs.gov/ocr/privacy

US Securities Exchanges Commission. (2004). *Performance and accountability report.* Retrieved from www.sec.gov/about/secpar.shtml

Yip, F. (2011). *A framework for semantic enabled applications: A case study in regulatory compliance*. Ph D Thesis, School of Computer Science and Engineering, University of New South Wales, Sydney.

Zadeh, L. (1965). Fuzzy sets. *Information and Control*, *8*, 338–353.

Zhang, I. X. (2005, February). *Economic consequences of the Sarbanes-Oxley Act of 2002*.

ADDITIONAL READING

ISO. (2006). *AS/NZS ISO/IEC 17799: 2006 Information technology-Security techniques-Code of practice for information security management.*

ISO. (2009). *ISO/IECGuide73:2009*. Retrieved from http://www.iso.org/iso/iso_catalogue/catalogue_ics/catalogue_detail_ics.htm

Logan, N. (2002). *Pareto analysis operation management*. Retrieved from http://www.freequality.org/documents/knowledge/Pareto%20 Analysis.pdf

Neches, R., Fikes, R. E., Gruber, T. R., Senator, T., & Swartout, W. R. (1991). Enabling technology for knowledge sharing. *AI Magazine*.

Saha, P., Parameswaran, N., Ray, P., & Mahanti, A. (n.d.). Ontology based modelling for information security management. *DASC '11 Proceedings of the 2011 IEEE Ninth International Conference on Dependable, Autonomic and Secure Computing*, (pp. 73-80).

KEY TERMS AND DEFINITIONS

Compliance Management: It quantifies similarities/discrepancies between company policies, controls or industry standards against actual organizational practices. The compliance management process is a key component of any regulatory standard. A compliance management reveals whether a designed and specified control is employed and used correctly in an organization. This function assesses the organization's level of adherence to the applicable laws and regulations of the country by legally binding senior management to monitor and reveal the effectiveness or deficiencies of the employed controls and corporate compliance program with respect to standard regulatory practices.

Fuzzy Logic: The term "fuzzy logic" is associated with development of the theory of fuzzy sets by Zadeh(Zadeh, 1965). A fuzzy subset A of a (crisp) set X is denoted by assigning to each element x of X the degree of membership of x in A (e.g., X is a group of people, A the fuzzy set of young people in X). On one hand Fuzzy logic is characterized by applications in fuzzy control, analysis of vagueness in natural language and several other domains. On the other hand Fuzzy logic connotes symbolic logic with a comparative notion of truth developed fully in the spirit of classical logic (syntax, semantics, truth-preserving deduction, completeness, both propositional and predicate logic). It is a branch of many-valued logic based on the paradigm of inference under vagueness which has wide variety of applications in designing of smart appliances, robotics and control theory and in multitudes of other interrelated emerging disciplines (Zadeh, 1965).

Information Auditing: It is a generic term used to denote a systematic process through which an organization estimates its knowledge requirements, information flows and gap analysis. It builds the knowledge management strategic framework as well as lays the foundation for corporate governance. Information Auditing involves a ten stage process (i) identifying information needs of the organization (ii) scrutinizing organization task (business process, activities, transactions) (iii) examining and identifying existing archives and record keeping systems (iv) reviewing and verifying the internal/external information resources and storages (v) undertaking gap analysis of performance measurement and information requirement of target organization (vi)mapping information flows and its bottlenecks (vii)developing an information/ knowledge map of the audited organization (viii) designing and improving new record management system (ix)developing some quick fixes which may be required in exigencies (x) developing comprehensive information management system(The Institute of Chartered Accountants of India, n.d.).

Information Security: It is the process of maintaining an acceptable level of perceived risk. It is all about protecting and preserving information and information processing in every format by preserving the confidentiality, integrity, authenticity, availability and reliability of information and other information related asset(International Organization for Standardization, 2005).

IT Governance: It is actually a part and parcel of the broader corporate governance framework of an organisation. It primarily focuses on information technology systems, their performance and risk management processes. IT Governance adjusts structural relationships and organizational processes to direct and control the enterprise to achieve the enterprise's goals. It adds value in the organization while balancing risk versus return over IT and its processes. IT Governance is formally defined as a set of procedures, formal processes, customs, prevalent policies, laws, regulations, legislations, management practices etc. regulating the networked environment within which the organization has to function. It specifies the decision rights and accountability framework within the organization to encourage desirable behaviours in the use of IT .The primary goals of IT Governance are to assure that the investments in IT generate business value, and to mitigate the risks that are associated with IT. This can be done by implementing an organisational structure with well-defined roles of stakeholders for the responsibility of information, business processes, applications and infrastructure.

Multi Agent Based System (MAS): A multi-agent system (MAS) is a loosely coupled network of software agents that interact among themselves to solve complex problems beyond the capabilities/ knowledge of individual agent. Multiple agents working together are used to solve a growing number of increasingly complicated problems which are too difficult for monolithic systems. MAS is a decentralized system and hence relatively immune from critical single point failure of individual agent and resource bottleneck. Autonomy of individual agents justifies better system performance, efficiency, reliability and extensibility. Modularity of individual agents ensures robustness, maintainability, responsiveness, flexibility, and reuse in situations where individual resource is spatially and temporally distributed.

Ontology: It is defined as formal specification of a shared conceptualization in a particular domain (Neches et al., 1991). It is defined as a set of representational primitives (classes, properties or attributes and relationships among classes and class members) with which to model domain knowledge in a systematic manner. The definitions of representational primitives define their constraints on logically consistent manner. In the context of database design ontology may be viewed as modeling knowledge on a level of abstraction away from design and implementation details(Gruber, 1993).

Risk Management: It is a process that includes four activities (i) risk assessment (ii) risk acceptance (iii) risk treatment and (iv) risk communication. Risk assessment combines two sub-processes viz. risk analysis (identifying possible sources of risk) and risk evaluation (comparing estimated risk with a set of risk criteria to determine significance of risk).Risk acceptance is a part of risk treatment decision making process whereby organizations determine the acceptable level of risk .Risk treatment is a decision making process whereby risks are treated by selecting and implementing measures designed to mitigate risks. Risk communication normally occurs when risk treatment strategy proves inadequate and need for escalation arises as final recourse. Through risk communication remedial action and preventive maintenance strategy for the organization is encoded for future reference. Overall risk management may be accomplished by developing a risk containment strategy, whereby threats and vulnerabilities affecting organizational assets are identified and the commensurate risk is quantified. Countermeasures or safeguards then can be carefully chosen to accept, avoid, transfer, or mitigate risk to an admissible level, whichever is applicable (International Organization for Standardization, 2005).

ENDNOTE

[1] Arrived after extensive consultation with information security auditors regarding relative weight distribution in risk management of an enterprise undergoing Information Security Compliance

Chapter 10
Using Indicators to Monitor Security Risk in Systems of Systems:
How to Capture and Measure the Impact of Service Dependencies on the Security of Provided Services

Olav Skjelkvåle Ligaarden
SINTEF ICT & University of Oslo, Norway

Atle Refsdal
SINTEF ICT, Norway

Ketil Stølen
SINTEF ICT & University of Oslo, Norway

ABSTRACT

Systems of systems are collections of systems interconnected through the exchange of services. Their often complex service dependencies and very dynamic nature make them hard to analyze and predict with respect to quality in general, and security in particular. In this chapter, the authors put forward a method for the capture and monitoring of impact of service dependencies on the security of provided services. The method is divided into four main steps focusing on documenting the system of systems and IT service dependencies, establishing the impact of service dependencies on risk to security of provided services, identifying measureable indicators for dynamic monitoring, and specifying their design and deployment, respectively. The authors illustrate the method in an example-driven fashion based on a case within power supply.

DOI: 10.4018/978-1-4666-2083-4.ch010

INTRODUCTION

In today's business environment, companies (businesses, enterprises, organizations) co-operate with other parties by providing and/or requiring information and communication technology (ICT) supported services. The ICT-systems facilitating such co-operation are often so-called system of systems (SoS). An SoS may be thought of as a kind of "super system" comprising a set of inter-connected systems that work together towards some common goal.

(Allen, 2005) defines governance as *"setting clear expectations for the conduct (behaviors and actions) of the entity being governed, and directing, controlling, and strongly influencing the entity to achieve these expectations."* In an SoS setting, a company is often expected to provide services fulfilling requirements to security. If the services are not provided according to their security requirements, then it may have severe consequences for the company providing them. Thus, the company needs to govern the security of the provided services. Risk assessment is a necessity for ensuring that risks to security of provided services are at an acceptable level. However, it is not straight-forward to assess risk to security of provided services in an SoS. Firstly, the exchanged services may require other services in order to function. Such requirements result in so-called service dependencies. Change in the security attributes of one service may easily cause the security attributes of its dependent services to change as well. Secondly, the different systems may be under different managerial control and within different jurisdictions. For the systems that are outside our control, we have limited knowledge of their security risks, structure, and behavior. Thirdly, such a large number of systems, controlled and operated by different parties, evolve rapidly in a manner that may be difficult to predict.

To cope with this situation we propose the use of detailed dependency models to capture the impact of services dependencies, trust relations as a basis for analysis in the case of insufficient documentation, and monitoring to cope with evolution. Our main result is a method facilitating the set-up of such monitoring. This method can be used in security governance for the purpose of assessing to what extent the security expectations to the provided services are achieved.

The method is divided into four steps. Service dependencies and trust relations are identified and documented in the first step. In the second step we conduct a security risk analysis to capture the impact of service dependencies on risk to security of provided services. The identified trust relations are used when analyzing service dependencies involving systems of which we have insufficient documentation. In the third step we identify the security risks to be monitored, as well as measureable indicators for monitoring their risk values. In the fourth and final step we specify how these indicators should be designed, i.e., how they should be calculated, and deployed in the SoS, i.e., how data needed in the calculations should be extracted and transmitted within the SoS in question. The result of applying the method is a security risk picture parameterized by indicators, each defined by design and deployment specifications.

The rest of the chapter is organized as follows: in the next section (Section 2) we introduce basic terminology and definitions. Section 3 presents the methodological approach, while the four steps of the approach are demonstrated on an example case within power supply in Sections 4 – 7. In Section 8 we present related work, while we conclude and indicate further research in Section 9.

BASIC TERMINOLOGY AND DEFINITIONS

In this section we provide basic terminology, definitions, and conceptual models for system of systems, risk, and related concepts.

Figure 1. Conceptual model relating system, system of systems, and other concepts

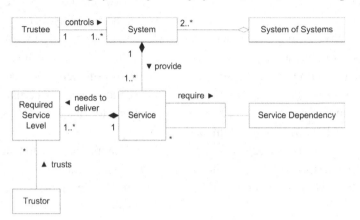

System of Systems and Related Concepts

Our definition of SoS is based on the definitions of (Office of the Under Secretary of Defense for Acquisition, Technology, and Logistics, 2002) and (Jamshidi, 2008): "A system of systems (SoS) is a set or arrangement of systems that are related or connected to fulfill common goals. The different systems may be controlled, operated, and maintained by different parties and within different jurisdictions. The loss of any system may seriously impact the other systems and the process of fulfilling the common goals."

An SoS may arise naturally from the interconnection of individual systems, or it may be built specifically for the purpose of achieving goals that the individual systems cannot achieve alone. An example of the former is the interconnection of critical infrastructures, while a sensor network, constructed for the purpose of gathering low-level data to be aggregated, is an example of the latter.

We focus on SoS where the systems are interconnected through the exchange of services. In Figure 1 is a conceptual model, in the form of a UML (OMG, 2004) class diagram, relating system, system of systems, and other concepts. The associations between the different concepts have cardinalities that specify how many instances of

one concept that may be associated to an instance of another concept. The filled diamond specifies composition, while the hollow diamond, used in Figure 2, specifies aggregation.

As shown in Figure 1, a *System of Systems* consists of at least two *Systems*. The different systems may be controlled and operated by different *Trustees*. A system needs to provide at least one *Service*, in order to be recognized as a system. Typically, a service will have a required level of service defined for each area of service scope. These required service levels may for instance be specified in a service-level agreement. Thus, one or more *Required Service Levels* are associated with each service. For each required service level, a *Trustor* may have a certain amount of trust in that the service delivers the required level of service. A service provided by one system may require other services in order to function. Such requirements result in *Service Dependencies*, shown by an association class in Figure 1. These dependencies help us to better understand the importance of the individual services exchanged between the systems.

Risk and Related Concepts

Figure 2 shows a conceptual model for risk and closely related concepts. A *Risk* involves an

Figure 2. Conceptual model for risk and closely related concepts

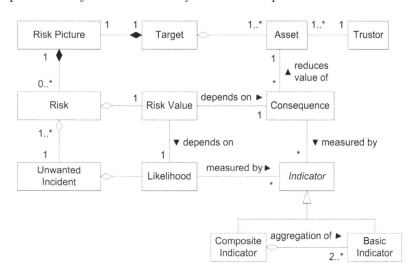

Unwanted Incident, such as "System operator is unable to control and operate the power plant." The unwanted incident may occur with a certain *Likelihood*. When the incident occurs, an *Asset* will be damaged (and its value reduced). This is the *Consequence* of the risk. An asset is owned by a *Trustor* and it is something of value that the trustor seeks to protect. It can be a physical thing, e.g., "Power plant," or conceptual, e.g., "Reputation of trustor." Since the consequence of an incident depends on the particular asset in question, the same incident may have different consequences for different assets.

By conducting a risk analysis we obtain a *Risk Picture*, consisting of zero or more risks, for the *Target* of analysis. The target characterizes the focus and scope of the analysis. In order to choose and prioritize between treatments, we assign a *Risk Value* to each risk. A risk function calculates the risk value by taking the likelihood of the unwanted incident and its consequence for the asset in question as input. Typically, likelihood is measured in terms of frequency or probability, while the measure of consequence depends on the asset in question.

Zero or more *Indicators* may be used to measure likelihood and consequence values. An indicator is either basic or composite. Thus, an abstract class (name in italic) is used to represent *Indicator* in the conceptual model. By *Basic Indicator* we mean a measure such as the number of times a specific event generated by the ICT infrastructure has been observed within a given time interval, the average time between each generation of a specific event, the load on the network at a particular point in time, or similar. A *Composite Indicator* is the aggregation of two or more basic indicators.

METHODOLOGICAL APPROACH

An overview of the methodological approach is presented in Figure 3. In the following we describe each of the four main steps as well as their substeps in terms of a detailed guideline.

Our intended client enterprise corresponds to the trustor in Figure 2. The trustor controls a fragment of the SoS which we refer to as the target. The target depends on the rest of the SoS that is controlled by other enterprises that may be thought of as trustees of our client enterprise. Our task is to establish a dynamic security risk picture that captures the impact of service dependencies on

Figure 3. Overview of the methodological approach

Step 1 – Document system of systems
1.1 – Model system of systems
1.2 – Capture service dependencies
1.3 – Capture trust relations

Step 2 – Analyze the impact of service dependencies on risk to security of provided services
2.1 – Identify security assets
2.2 – Construct high-level threat diagrams of the impact of service dependencies on identified security assets
2.3 – Construct detailed threat diagrams of the impact of service dependencies on identified security assets

Step 3 – Identify indicators for system of systems
3.1 – Identify security risks to be monitored
3.2 – Identify relevant indicators for the security risks to be monitored

Step 4 – Specify design and deployment of identified indicators for system of systems
4.1 – Specify design of indicators for monitoring security risks
4.2 – Specify deployment of indicators for monitoring security risks

risk to the security of the client's provided services.

Step 1: Document System of Systems

Step 1.1: Model System of Systems

- **Objective:** Model the SoS.
- **Rationale:** To capture the impact of service dependencies on risk to security of provided services, we need to document the services exchanged between the different systems in the SoS. In particular, it is essential to understand the dependencies between the target and the target's environment, i.e., the rest of the SoS. We also need to document the requirements to the different services, since we are only concerned with the impact of services on risk when they are not delivered according to requirements.
- **How Conducted:** A system model is created by the analysis team based on input

documentation provided by the trustor. The system model describes the systems of the target as well as the systems of the target's environment. It also captures system interactions in the form of service exchanges, and the required service levels. Each required service level is specified for one area of service scope. We can for instance specify the required level of availability, integrity, etc., for a service.

- **Input Documentation:** The trustor provides information on the SoS, their interactions in the form of service exchanges, and the requirements, in the form of required levels of service, for each service exchanged.
- **Output Documentation:** A system model documenting:
  - The systems of the target and environment.
  - The interactions between the systems in the form of service exchanges.
  - The required service levels for each service.

- **Modeling Guideline:** The SoS is modeled in the form of a graph, as illustrated by Figure 4. The system elements (vertices) in the graph represent systems, while service relations (edges) represent exchanges of services. The bold rectangular container with rounded corners separates the target from its environment. Each system element is annotated with the trustor/trustee controlling and operating the system represented by the element, while each service relation is annotated with the service exchanged and its required levels of service. In Figure 4 this has only been shown for two service relations, in order to save space. For one of the service relations, a required service level has been specified for one area of service scope, while required service levels have been specified for two areas of service scope for the other ser-

vice. Here, *A* stands for availability, while *I* stands for integrity.

The source of a service relation represents the provider of the service, while the target of the relation represents the consumer of the service. A system may need to consume services in order to provide other services. If one system provides two or more services to another system, then the model is a multigraph, i.e., a graph which allows multiple edges, meaning edges with the same pair of source and target vertices.

Step 1.2: Capture Service Dependencies

- **Objective:** Identify and document service dependencies within the SoS.
- **Rationale:** In Step 1.1 we documented the services exchanged between the different systems. In this step we identify the service

Figure 4. System model

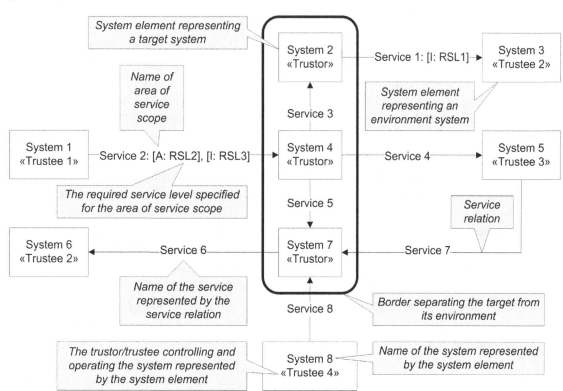

Figure 5. System model annotated with service dependencies

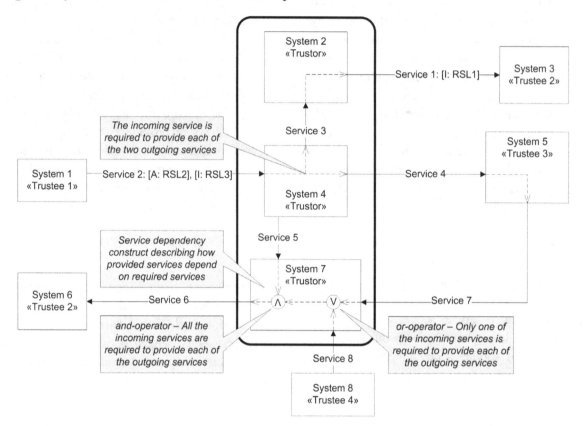

dependencies resulting from the exchange of these services. This enables us to analyze the impact of service dependencies on risk to security of provided services.

- **How Conducted:** The system model, from Step 1.1, is annotated with service dependencies, based on input documentation provided by the trustor. The annotated model shows how provided services depend on required services.
- **Input Documentation:**
  - The system model from Step 1.1.
  - The trustor provides information on the relationships between required and provided services for the different systems documented in the system model.

- **Output Documentation:** The system model, from Step 1.1, annotated with service dependencies.
- **Modeling Guideline:** Figure 5 shows the system model in Figure 4 annotated with service dependency constructs. The constructs describe dependencies between provided and required services. Dependencies between required and provided services are combined with "and" (∧) or "or" (∨) operators. The meaning of the and-operator is that all the incoming services are required to provide each of the outgoing services, while the meaning of the or-operator is that only one of the incoming services is required to provide each of the outgoing services. As seen in Figure 5, operators may be combined to express dependencies that cannot be expressed by a single operator alone.

Step 1.3: Capture Trust Relations

- **Objective:** Document the trustor's trust in the required levels of services being delivered by its trustees.
- **Rationale:** A trustor will normally not have detailed knowledge of the interior of systems owned by its trustees. Moreover, they may be changed and updated in a manner not controlled by the trustor. Hence, services provided by environment systems are difficult to analyze due to lack of documentation as well as control. To cope with this lack of knowledge we use trust levels to reason about the failure of environment systems to provide their services to target systems according to required service levels. Each trust level states the degree to which the trustor trusts the required service level to be delivered.

- **How Conducted:** The system model, from Step 1.2, is annotated with trust relations. Each trust relation relates a trust level (in the interval [0,1]) determined by the trustor to a required service level of a service provided by an environment system to a target system.
- **Input Documentation:** The system model from Step 1.2.
- **Output Documentation:** The system model, from Step 1.2, annotated with trust relations.
- **Modeling Guideline:** Figure 6 shows the system model in Figure 5 annotated with trust relations. The trust relations are shown with dotted clouds. Each cloud is assigned to a required service level of a service provided by an environment system to a target system.

Figure 6. System model annotated with trust relations

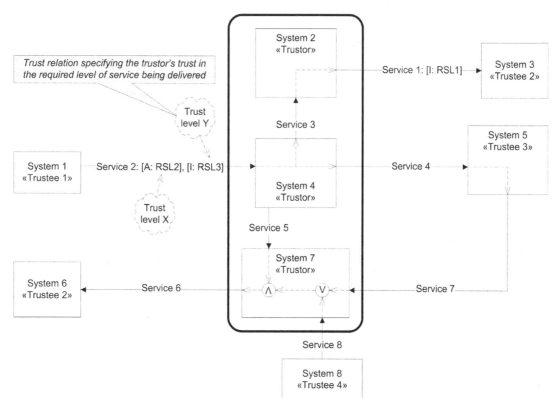

Step 2: Analyze the Impact of Service Dependencies on Risk to Security of Provided Services

Step 2.1: Identify Security Assets

- **Objective:** Identify the security assets for which impact of service dependencies should be analyzed.
- **Rationale:** By identifying the security assets we restrict the identification of risks caused by service dependencies to only those risks that may harm the security assets of the trustor, i.e., reduce their values. By doing so, we ensure that the available time and resources are spent identifying the most critical and important security risks for the trustor in question.
- **How Conducted:** For each provided service, the trustor identifies the security assets for which protection is required. Zero or more security assets may be identified for each provided service. The value of the security asset is reduced if the service level is less than the required service level.
- **Input Documentation:** None.
- **Output Documentation:** Zero or more security assets for each provided service.

Step 2.2: Construct High-Level Threat Diagrams of the Impact of Service Dependencies on Identified Security Assets

- **Objective:** Achieve an initial high-level understanding of the impact of service dependencies on the identified security assets by schematically constructing threat diagrams from the system model.
- **Rationale:** In order to conduct a detailed analysis of the impact of service dependencies on risk to security of provided services, we first establish an initial high-level understanding of how the failure of individual systems to deliver their services according to requirements may lead to the failure of other individual systems to deliver their services according to requirements, as a result of the service dependencies. Moreover, we establish how this eventually may lead to unwanted incidents that harm the identified security assets if they occur. Such an initial high-level understanding is achieved by schematically constructing a threat diagram for each provided service with security assets.

- **How Conducted:** Figure 7 shows the schematic construction of a threat diagram from an excerpt of the system model in Figure 6. The threat diagram provides an initial overview of how the security asset "Integrity of Service 1 delivered to System 3" may be harmed if the systems represented by the referring threat scenarios fail to deliver their services according to their required service levels.

We use CORAS (Lund, Solhaug, & Stølen, 2010), which is a model-driven approach to asset-oriented risk analysis, for the modeling and analysis of risk. The threat diagram is expressed in the CORAS language. Examples of the semantics (as defined in (Lund et al., 2010)) of elements and relations are given in Step 2.3 of the demonstration of the methodological approach on the example case. As can be seen in the diagram, referring threat scenarios, vulnerabilities, and the referring unwanted incident have been given names following the conventions "Services not delivered by System X according to requirements," "System Y depends on Service Z," and "Incident with impact on the A," (where A is the name of the asset) respectively.

A threat diagram is constructed from the system model resulting from Step 1.3 for each provided service where security assets were identified in Step 2.1 by using the following schematic procedure[1]:

1. Create an excerpt of the system model by removing model elements in the following order:
   a) All service relations representing services that are different from the provided service in question and that:
      i. Are provided by target systems to environment systems.
      ii. Are both provided and required by environment systems.
      iii. The provided service in question does not depend directly or indirectly on.
         Modify/remove the service dependency constructs of system elements representing target systems that were connected to the removed service relations.
   b) All system elements that are no longer connected to other system elements through service relations.
   c) The system element representing the environment system that requires the provided service in question, unless the environment system provides services that the provided service in question depends directly or indirectly on.
   d) All trust relations that are no longer associated with service relations, and all service dependency constructs of system elements representing environment systems.
   e) The border separating the system elements representing the target systems from the system elements representing the environment systems.
2. Replace each system element with a referring threat scenario. This scenario represents the failure of the system to provide its services according to their required service levels.
3. Insert the security assets of the provided service into the excerpt, and insert a referring unwanted incident for each security asset. Insert an impacts relation between the referring unwanted incident and its security asset.
4. Replace the service relation representing the provided service with as many leads-to relations as there are referring unwanted incidents. Let the source of each leads-to relation be the referring threat scenario representing the system delivering the provided service and let the target of each leads-to relation be one of the referring unwanted incidents.
5. Replace each service relation between two referring threat scenarios with a leads-to relation, and assign a vulnerability to each relation. The vulnerability denotes that the system represented by the target scenario depends on the service represented by the replaced service relation.

For all leads-to relations in the threat diagram, the source and target of the relation is an out-gate and in-gate, respectively. The gates are connected to referring threat scenarios and unwanted incidents. Moreover, the source of each impacts relation is an out-gate, where the out-gate is connected to a referring unwanted incident. In-gates and out-gates are explained in more detail in Step 2.3 of the demonstration of the methodological approach on the example case.

- **Input Documentation:**
  ○ The system model from Step 1.3.
  ○ The identified security assets from Step 2.1.
- **Output Documentation:** One high-level threat diagram outlining the impact of service dependencies on the security assets for each provided service where security assets were identified in Step 2.1.

Step 2.3: Construct Detailed Threat Diagrams of the Impact of Service Dependencies on Identified Security Assets

- **Objective:** Achieve a detailed understanding of the impact of service dependencies on the identified security assets.
- **Rationale:** The threat diagrams from Step 2.2 provide only a high-level outline of the impact of service dependencies on the identified security assets. To establish a security risk picture that can be monitored, we need to detail those diagrams.
- **How conducted:** In Figure 8 is a threat diagram (where some of the details have been suppressed) that shows part of the result of detailing the threat diagram in Figure 7. The referring threat scenarios have been decomposed by creating referenced threat scenarios. Each referenced threat scenario describes the internal threat behavior of the system represented by a referring threat scenario. Moreover, the referring unwanted incident has been decomposed by creating a referenced unwanted incident. The referenced unwanted incident documents the different unwanted incidents that may arise due to the service dependencies. Examples of referenced threat scenarios and unwanted incidents are given in Step 2.3 of the demonstration of the methodological approach on the example case. The two vulnerabilities "V1" and "V2" are the results of the decomposition of the high-level vulnerability "System 2 depends on Service 3," documented in Figure 7. Symbolic names have been used for the two vulnerabilities in Figure 8. By describing the internal threat behavior of "Services not delivered by System 4 according to requirements," these symbolic names can be replaced by names of real vulnerabilities. For each of these two vulnerabilities, a con-

ditional likelihood has been assigned to the same leads-to relation as the vulnerability is assigned. We can also see that the vulnerability "System 4 depends on Service 2" has been decomposed into the two vulnerabilities "System 4 depends on availability of Service 2" and "System 4 depends on integrity of Service 2"; one for each of the required service levels associated with "Service 2." As a result of the decomposition of the high-level vulnerabilities, the referring threat scenarios, and the referring unwanted incident, the high-level in-gates and out-gates and the impacts relation have been decomposed, and likelihood values and consequences values have been assigned to the gates and impacts relations, respectively.

In the following we provide a more detailed description of how to detail the high-level threat diagrams resulting from Step 2.2. Each high-level threat diagram is detailed by:

- Decomposing each referring threat scenario and its high-level in-gates and out-gates by creating a referenced threat scenario. The referenced threat scenario describes the internal threat behavior of the system represented by the referring threat scenario.

  For target systems the internal threat behavior describes how the failures of other systems to deliver their services according to requirements may affect the ability of the target system to deliver its services according to requirements. It also describes how internal failures of the target system may affect its ability to deliver services according to requirements, if the referring threat scenario may lead to other referring threat scenarios. The decomposition also results in likelihood values being assigned to the in-gates and out-gates of the referring and referenced threat scenario.

Figure 7. Threat diagram, constructed schematically from an excerpt of the system model in Figure 6, which provides a high-level outline of the impact of service dependencies on the security asset "Integrity of Service 1 delivered to System 3"

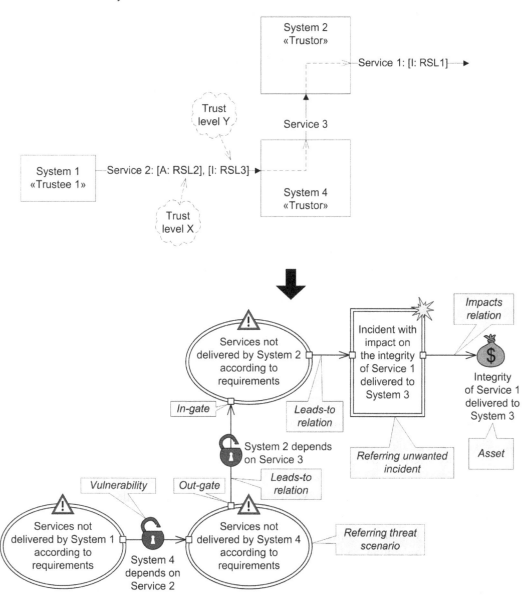

For an environment system we only provide a high-level description of its internal behavior. One or two threat scenarios are used to describe this behavior. Two scenarios are used if the environment system is not explicitly required to fulfill all the requirements associated with its provided services. The first threat scenario represents the failure of the system to deliver its services according to requirements that it needs to fulfill, while the second represents the failure of the system to deliver its services according to

Figure 8. Threat diagram that shows part of the result of detailing the threat diagram in Figure 7

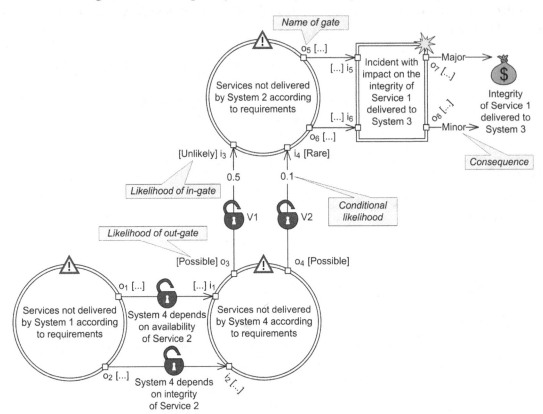

requirements that the system are not explicitly required to fulfill. For the latter we are referring to requirements to services that are not part of the contract, e.g., service-level agreement, between the environment system and the target systems, but that are of importance to the trustor controlling and operating the target systems.

○ Decomposing each referring unwanted incident and its high-level in-gates and out-gates by creating a referenced unwanted incident. Each referenced unwanted incident documents different unwanted incidents that may arise due to the service dependencies. The decomposition also results in likelihood values being assigned to the in-gates and out-gates of the re-

ferring and referenced unwanted incident. We also decompose the impacts relation of the referring unwanted incident, and we assign consequence values to the new impacts relations.

○ Decomposing high-level vulnerabilities assigned to leads-to relations between referring threat scenarios representing target systems. A conditional likelihood is assigned to each leads-to relation for which a vulnerability resulting from the decomposition of a high-level vulnerability has been assigned.

○ Decomposing high-level vulnerabilities assigned to leads-to relations where the source of the relation is a referring threat scenario representing an environment system, while the target is a referring threat scenario representing a target system. The high-level vulnerability is decomposed into as many vulnerabilities as there are required service levels associated with the service represented by the high-level vulnerability. Each of the vulnerabilities resulting from the decomposition specifies that the target system depends on the particular area of service scope associated with the required service level. To estimate the likelihood of the required service level not being delivered, we first calculate the worst-case service level of the particular area of service scope. The worst-case service level specifies our minimum expectation to the particular area of service scope. It is calculated based on the required service level and the trust level calculated in Step 1.3. The likelihood is then estimated based on the difference between the required service level and the worst case service level. The estimated likelihood values are assigned to out-gates of the referring and referenced threat scenarios representing the environment systems.

As part of this step, we also specify scales for measuring likelihood and consequence, and functions for calculating risk values. The risk functions are used after we have created the detailed threat diagrams to determine the risk values of the different risks to security of provided services. A risk value is determined based on the likelihood of an unwanted incident and its consequence with respect to a security asset.

- **Input Documentation:** The high-level threat diagrams from Step 2.2.
- **Output Documentation:**

  - Detailed threat diagrams documenting the impact of service dependencies on the security assets.
  - Worst-case service levels.
  - Scales for measuring likelihood and consequence.
  - Risk functions for calculating risk values.
  - A list of risks to security of provided services.

Step 3: Identify Indicators for System of Systems

Step 3.1: Identify Security Risks to be Monitored

- **Objective:** Identify the risks to security of provided services that should be monitored.
- **Rationale:** A risk analysis will often result in a number of identified risks to security of provided services. We need to identify the security risks that should be monitored, since it is often not in the trustor's interest to monitor all the security risks. Moreover, there may be security risks for which monitoring is not feasible.
- **How Conducted:** For each security risk resulting from Step 2.3, we must decide whether it should be monitored. Typically, a risk to security of provided services is selected for monitoring if it is believed that the likelihood and/or consequence value determining its risk value is likely to change in a manner that will considerably harm the trustor. A security risk may also be selected for monitoring if we are uncertain about the risk value.
- **Input Documentation:**
  - The detailed threat diagrams from Step 2.3.
  - The list of risks to security of provided services from Step 2.3.

- **Output Documentation:** A list of risks to security of provided services to be monitored.

Step 3.2: Identify Relevant Indicators for the Security Risks to be Monitored

- **Objective:** Identify relevant indicators for monitoring the risk values of the security risks to be monitored.
- **Rationale:** To monitor changes in risk values we need to identify indicators. The indicators are calculated from measurable properties of the SoS.
- **How Conducted:** For the security risks identified to be monitored in Step 3.1, we identify relevant indicators. Indicators for monitoring consequence are related to impacts relations between unwanted incidents and security assets. On the other hand, indicators for monitoring likelihood may not only be related to unwanted incidents, but also to vulnerabilities and threat scenarios leading up to an incident, since the likelihoods of vulnerabilities being exploited and threat scenarios occurring will affect the likelihood of the unwanted incident occurring.
  Basic indicators are identified for the different likelihood and consequence values to be monitored. If more than one basic indicator is needed for monitoring a consequence or likelihood value, then a composite indicator, aggregating the basic indicators, is also identified.
- **Input Documentation:**
  ○ The list of risks to security of provided services to be monitored from Step 3.1.
  ○ The detailed threat diagrams from Step 2.3.
- **Output Documentation:** A set of relevant basic and composite indicators for monitoring likelihood and consequence.

Step 4: Specify Design and Deployment of Identified Indicators for System of Systems

Step 4.1: Specify Design of Indicators for Monitoring Security Risks

- **Objective:** Specify how basic and composite indicators for monitoring likelihood and consequence values should be designed.
- **Rationale:** We need to specify how the identified basic and composite indicators from Step 3.2 should be designed, i.e., how they should be calculated, in order to be useful for monitoring.
- **How conducted:** A design specification, in the form of an algorithm, is provided for each indicator identified in Step 3.2. It specifies the data needed for calculating the indicator, how the indicator should be calculated, and the output from the calculation. Assuming the likelihood and consequence intervals obtained in Step 2.3 are correct, the algorithm should yield likelihoods and consequences in these intervals when applied to the basic indicator values at the time these intervals were determined.
- **Input Documentation:**
  ○ The list of risks to security of provided services to be monitored from Step 3.1.
  ○ The relevant indicators identified in Step 3.2.
  ○ The detailed threat diagrams from Step 2.3.
  ○ Basic indicator values from the time when the detailed threat diagrams were constructed.
- **Output documentation:** A design specification for each indicator identified in Step 3.2.

Step 4.2: Specify Deployment of Indicators for Monitoring Security Risks

- **Objective:** Specify how basic and composite indicators for monitoring likelihood and consequence values should be deployed in the SoS.
- **Rationale:** We need to specify how the identified basic and composite indicators from Step 3.2 should be deployed in the SoS, i.e., how the data needed to calculate the different indicators is extracted and transmitted within the SoS, in order to be useful for monitoring.
- **How Conducted:** A deployment specification is provided for each indicator identified in Step 3.2. It specifies how the data used by the design specification is extracted and transmitted within the SoS.
- **Input Documentation:** The design specifications from Step 4.1.
- **Output Documentation:** A deployment specification for each indicator.

DEMONSTRATION OF STEP 1: DOCUMENT SYSTEM OF SYSTEMS

We consider an SoS consisting of an electrical power production infrastructure (EPP), a public telecom infrastructure (PTI), and an electrical power grid (EPG). In the following we assume that we have been hired by the company in charge of the electrical power production infrastructure, Client EPP, to help capture and monitor the impact of service dependencies on the security of its provided services.

Step 1.1: Model System of Systems

Figure 9 documents the electrical power production infrastructure and its environment. The different systems provide and/or require electricity

(*elec*), control instructions (*cintr*), and sensor data (*sdata*). All the services with the exception of electricity service are data services. The required service levels for the electricity services state the amount of electricity that needs to be delivered (availability) in the period of one year. For the data services, the required service levels (also for the period of one year) state the percentages of sensor data/control instructions messages that needs to be delivered (availability), be confidential, and have integrity.

In the electrical power production infrastructure there is a "Large hydro power plant." The electrical power produced by this plant is transmitted on a high-voltage "Transmission line" to a "Power substation." Here, the power is transformed to low-voltage power by a transformer, before being distributed to its end-users by distribution lines. "Distribution line 1" provides electrical power to the "Public telecom system." The infrastructure also consists of a "Small hydro power plant." This power plant distributes power directly to its end-users by the use of "Distribution line 2" and "Distribution line 3." "Private telecom system" and "Control system," both located within the electrical power production infrastructure, are two of the end-users that receive electrical power from these two distribution lines. These two systems share a "Backup power system," which is used when the electrical power grid fails to provide electricity to one or both systems.

The "Control system" is used to operate the "Large hydro power plant." By the use of the "Private telecom system" it sends control instructions to the plant, while sensors at the plant send data to the "Control system" through the same telecom system. The "Control system" responds to errors arising at the plant. If it cannot resolve the errors, it will shut down the plant to protect equipment. If the connection to the "Control system" is lost, the plant will automatically shut down if it cannot resolve errors by itself. The required service level with respect to availability is 99% for all the data services exchanged between the "Control system"

Figure 9. System model for electrical power production infrastructure and its environment

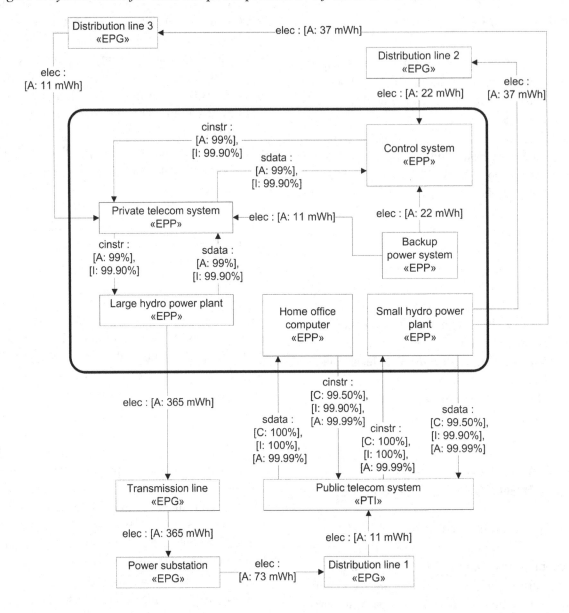

and the "Large hydro power plant," since the plant has some ability of operating independently of the "Control system." Moreover, the required service level with respect to integrity is 99.90% for all the data services.

Due to its size, the "Small hydro power plant" is operated by a system operator from his "Home office computer." The operator uses a computer that is dedicated to this task. He sends encrypted control instructions to the plant through the "Public

telecom system," while the sensors at the plant sends encrypted data to the operator through the same telecom system. The system operator responds to errors arising at the plant. If he cannot resolve the errors, he will shut down the plant to protect equipment. If the connection to the "Public telecom system" is lost, the plant will automatically shut down to protect equipment. This is done as a precautionary step, since the plant is not able to resolve errors by itself. Since the availability of the data services exchanged between the "Small hydro power plant" and the "Home office computer" are crucial for the operation of the "Small hydro power plant," the required service level for all the data services with respect to availability is 99.99%. It should be noticed that the required service levels for integrity and confidentiality for data services provided by "Public telecom system"

Figure 10. System model annotated with service dependencies

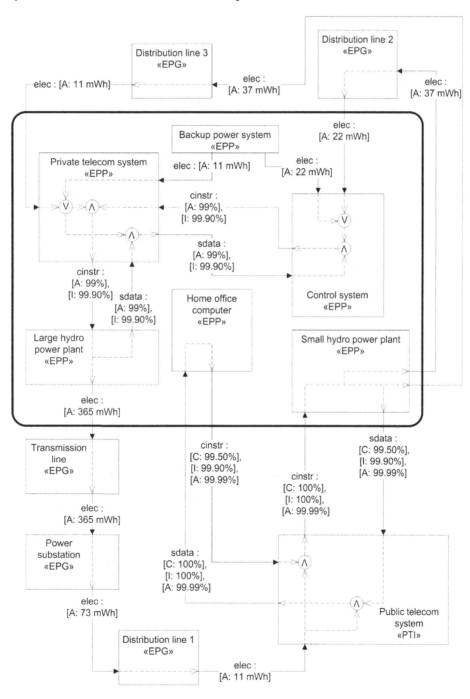

to "Home office computer" and "Small hydro power plant" do not specify explicit requirements that "Public telecom system" needs to fulfill when providing the data services. It is more correct to say that these requirements are to the data messages themselves. As can be seen in Figure 9, Client EPP requires that the confidentiality and integrity of data messages should not be changed while at "Public telecom system" or during transmission to its destinations.

Step 1.2: Capture Service Dependencies

In Figure 10, the system model in Figure 9 is annotated with the service dependencies. Most of the service dependencies are self-explanatory, but note especially that "Small hydro power plant" depends on the availability of control instructions, provided by "Home office computer," to produce electricity. The "Large hydro power plant" is less dependent on control instructions than the "Small hydro power plant," but since it depends on control instructions in situations where it cannot resolve errors, there is a dependency between the required control instructions service and the electricity service provided to "Transmission line." It should also be noticed that both "Private telecom system" and "Control system" can require electricity from the "Backup power system" if the electrical power grid fails to provide electricity, and that incoming sensor data messages may affect the outgoing control instructions messages, and vice versa. The dependencies between incoming and outgoing messages are a result of control instructions messages often being created based on the incoming sensor data messages, and that control instructions messages affect the operation of "Small hydro power plant" and its data sensors, which again affect the outgoing sensor data messages.

Step 1.3: Capture Trust Relations

In Figure 11, the system model in Figure 10 is annotated with trust relations. As can be seen in the figure, trust levels have been assigned to the required service levels for those services that are provided by systems of the environment to systems of the target.

All the services for which trust levels should be assigned are considered very reliable by Client EPP. Thus, it is expected that they should achieve their required service levels. Even so, Client EPP is aware that the services can fail. After having considered both the high reliability of the services and the possibility of service failures, Client EPP assigns high trust levels to the different required service levels.

For the control instructions services provided by "Public telecom system" to "Small hydro power plant," Client EPP has a trust of:

- 0.95 in that the control instructions messages are delivered according to the confidentiality requirement;
- 0.90 in that the control instructions messages are delivered according to the integrity requirement; and
- 0.99 in that the control instructions messages are delivered according to the availability requirement.

DEMONSTRATION OF STEP 2: ANALYZE THE IMPACT OF SERVICE DEPENDENCIES ON RISK TO SECURITY OF PROVIDED SERVICES

Step 2.1: Identify Security Assets

For the sake of simplicity, we demonstrate the method by only identifying security assets for one of the provided services. In an industrial case we would consider all the provided services when identifying security assets.

Figure 11. System model annotated with trust relations

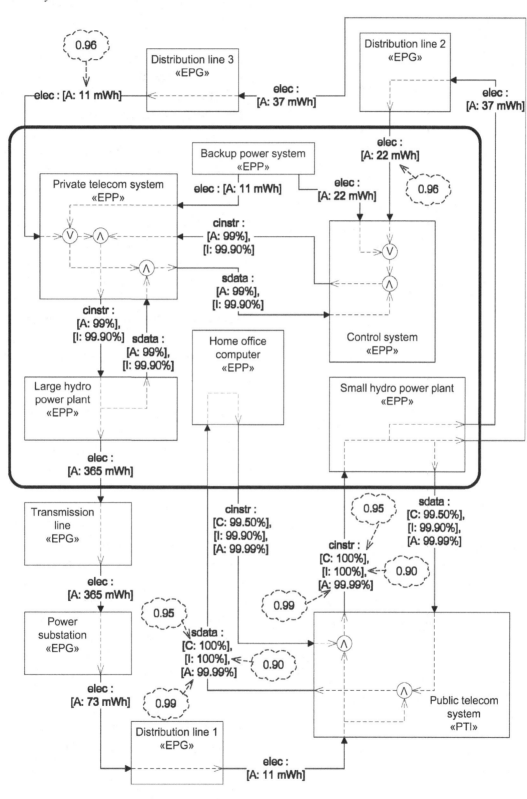

Figure 12. Excerpt, from the system model in Figure 11, for schematic construction of the threat diagram for the sensor data service provided to "Public telecom system"

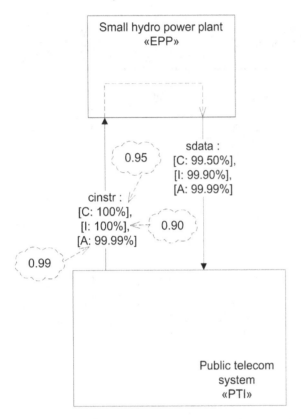

A concern of Client EPP is that services dependencies in the SoS may affect the ability of "Small hydro power plant" to provide the sensor data service according to the security requirements associated with the service. If this service is affected, then the ability of "Home office computer" to control and operate the "Small hydro power plant" may be affected as well, which again may impact the electricity services provided to "Distribution line 2" and "Distribution line 3." Client EPP therefore seeks to protect the security assets "Confidentiality of sensor data delivered to Public telecom system," "Integrity of sensor data delivered to Public telecom system," and "Availability of sensor data delivered to Public telecom system," and wants to identify the service dependencies' impact on these security assets.

Step 2.2: Construct High-level Threat Diagrams of the Impact of Service Dependencies on Identified Security Assets

For the sensor data service provided to "Public telecom system," the excerpt in Figure 12 of the system model in Figure 11 and the threat diagram in Figure 13 have been created by following the schematic procedure. The threat diagram provides a high-level description of the impact of service dependencies on the security of the sensor data service provided to "Public telecom system."

Step 2.3: Construct Detailed Threat Diagrams of the Impact of Service Dependencies on Identified Security Assets

Before we perform the detailed security risk analysis of how target systems may fail to provide services according to requirements, we need to establish how to measure likelihood and consequence, as well as defining the risk function. Table 1 shows how likelihood is measured, while Table 2 shows how consequence is measured for the different security assets. To calculate the number of sensor data messages not sent, sent with lack of confidentiality, or sent with lack of integrity, it is helpful to have an estimate of the number of sensor data messages sent from "Small hydro power plant" in the period of one year. Client EPP estimates this number to be 5000.

For all risks, the risk is classified as acceptable or unacceptable as shown in Exhibit 1.

Here, the *Maximum service level* is the highest achievable service level for the area of service scope associated with the security asset in question. For example, the highest achievable service level for the integrity of the sensor data service is 5000. This means that all the 5000 sensor data

Figure 13. Threat diagram constructed schematically from the excerpt in Figure 12

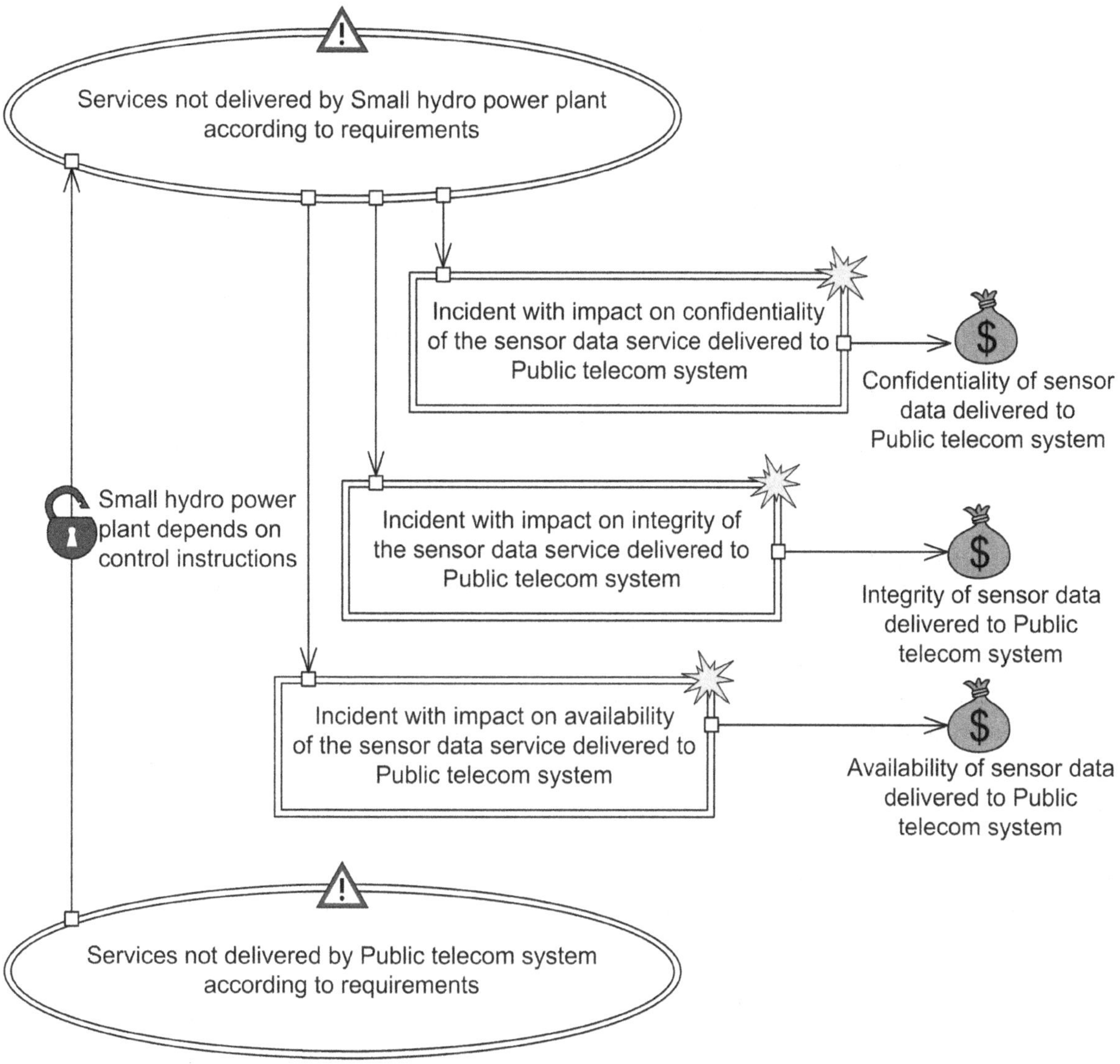

Table 1. Likelihood scale

Likelihood	Description
Certain	Fifty times or more per year [500, ∞>: 10 years
Very likely	Ten to fifty times per year [100, 499]: 10 years
Likely	Five times to ten times per year [50, 99]: 10 years
Possible	Two to five times per year [20, 49]: 10 years
Unlikely	Once a year [6, 19]: 10 years
Very unlikely	Less than once per year [2, 5]: 10 years
Rare	Less than once per ten years [0, 1]: 10 years

Table 2. How consequence is measured for the three security assets

Availability of sensor data delivered to Public telecom system
Number of sensor data messages not sent
Confidentiality of sensor data delivered to Public telecom system
Number of sensor data messages sent with lack of confidentiality
Integrity of sensor data delivered to Public telecom system
Number of sensor data messages sent with lack of integrity

Exhibit 1.

```
Expected service level = Maximum service level - (Likelihood · Consequence)        (1)


if Expected service level ≥ Required service level then                             (2)
    Risk value = Acceptable
else
    Risk value = Unacceptable
endif
```

messages sent during the period of one year have integrity. A risk associated with a security asset is *Unacceptable* if the *Expected service level* is less than the *Required service level*.

In Figure 14 is the detailed version of the high-level threat diagram in Figure 13. The referring elements in the diagram refer to the referenced threat scenarios provided in Figures 15 and 16, and the referenced unwanted incidents provided in Figure 20. Moreover, the referenced threat scenario in Figure 16 contains three referring threat scenarios, which refer to the referenced threat scenarios provided in Figures 17-19. Client EPP has estimated all the likelihood and consequence values in the different figures.

We refer to i_x and o_y of the referring threat scenarios and unwanted incidents as in-gate and out-gate, respectively. Relations to an element inside a referenced threat scenario must go through an in-gate, while relations to an element outside the referenced threat scenario must go through an out-gate. The likelihood value of an in-gate i_x documents the contribution of an element outside the referenced threat scenario via gate i_x to the likelihood of an element inside the referenced threat scenario, while the likelihood of the out-gate o_y documents the contribution of the likelihood of an element inside the referenced threat scenario via gate o_y to the likelihood of an element outside the referenced threat scenario.

Below we provide some examples of the semantics of elements and relations in the different figures. For more information on the semantics of the CORAS language, see (Lund et al., 2010).

- **Threat Scenario:** Threat scenario "Control instructions message is not delivered" occurs with likelihood "Very likely" (Figure 17).

- **Leads-To Relation (with Conditional Likelihood):** "Control instructions message is not delivered" leads to "Missing control instructions are needed for correcting a serious error" with conditional likelihood "0.5" (Figure 17).

- **Leads-To Relation (with Vulnerability):** "Control instructions message with lack of integrity is delivered" leads to "Retransmission of control instructions message is not requested" with undefined conditional likelihood, due to vulnerability "Possible that checksum algorithm fails to detect integrity violations" (Figure 18).

- **In-Gate (with Likelihood):** i_1 is an in-gate with likelihood "Very likely" (Figure 14).

- **Out-Gate (with Likelihood):** o_1 is an out-gate with likelihood "Very likely" (Figure 14).

- **Leads-to Relations (Between Elements of Referenced Threat Scenarios):** "Services not delivered by Public telecom system according to requirements that Public telecom system are required to fulfill" leads to "Control instructions message is not delivered" via gates o_1, i_1, and i_{10}, due to vulnerability "Small hydro power plant depends on availability of control instructions" (Figures 14, 15, 16, and 17).

- **Unwanted Incident:** Unwanted incident "Confidential sensor data is sent in

Figure 14. Detailed version of the high-level threat diagram in Figure 13

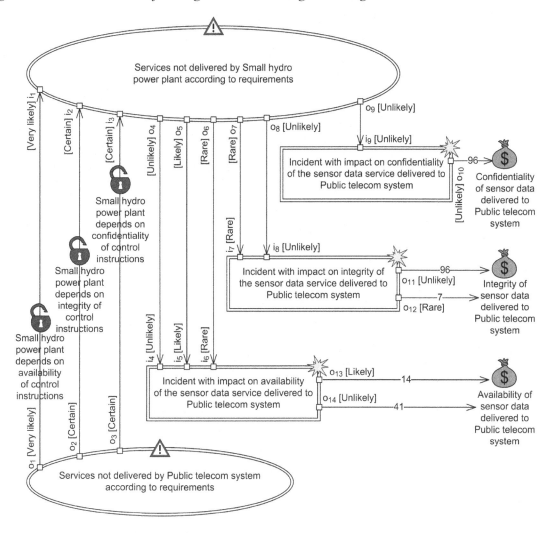

plain text from Small hydro power plant to an outsider" occurs with likelihood "Unlikely" (Figure 20).

- **Impacts Relation (Between Element of Referenced Unwanted Incident and Asset):** "Confidential sensor data is sent in plain text from Small hydro power plant to an outsider" impacts "Confidentiality of sensor data delivered to Public telecom system" via gate o_{10} with consequence "96" (Figures 14 and 20).

As can be seen in Figure 14, the vulnerability "Small hydro power plant depends on control instructions" in Figure 13 has been decomposed into three vulnerabilities. "Public telecom system" is only required to deliver the control instructions service according to the availability requirement. The referenced threat scenario in Figure 15 is therefore made up of two threat scenarios, since "Public telecom system" is not explicitly required to fulfill the confidentiality and integrity requirements of the control instructions service.

Client EPP estimates the number of control instructions messages delivered each year to

Figure 15. The referenced threat scenario "Services not delivered by Public telecom system according to requirements," referred to in Figure 14

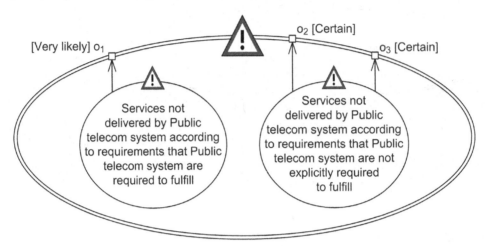

Services not delivered by Public telecom system according to requirements

Figure 16. The referenced threat scenario "Services not delivered by Small hydro power plant according to requirements," referred to in Figure 14

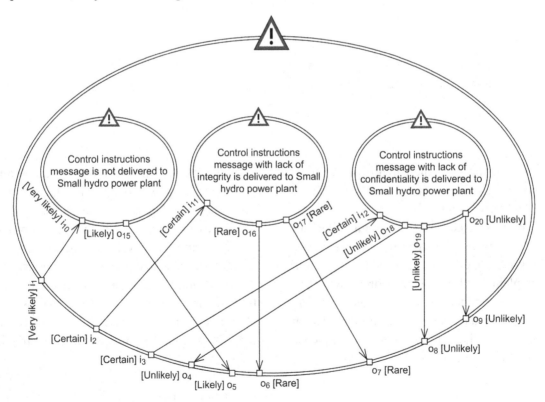

Services not delivered by Small hydro power plant according to requirements

Figure 17. The referenced threat scenario "Control instructions message is not delivered to Small hydro power plant," referred to in Figure 16

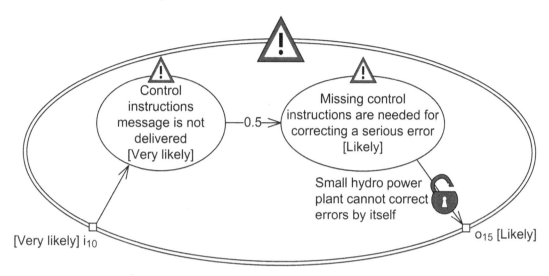

Control instructions message is not delivered to Small hydro power plant

Figure 18. The referenced threat scenario "Control instructions message with lack of integrity is delivered to Small hydro power plant," referred to in Figure 16

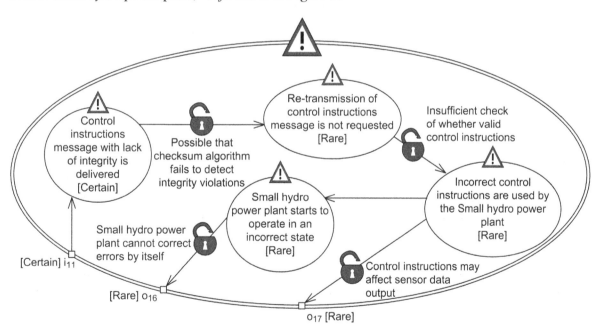

Control instructions message with lack of integrity is delivered to Small hydro power plant

Figure 19. The referenced threat scenario "Control instructions message with lack of confidentiality is delivered to Small hydro power plant," referred to in Figure 16

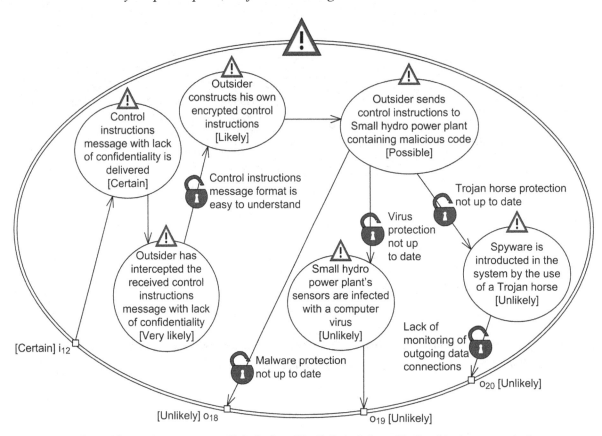

Control instructions message with lack of confidentiality is delivered to Small hydro power plant

"Small hydro power plant" to be 1000. Before we can estimate the likelihoods of the control instructions service not being delivered according to the confidentiality, integrity, and availability requirements, we need to calculate the worst-case service levels of the control instructions service delivered by "Public telecom system." These are as follows:

- 95% (100% · 0.95) of the delivered control instructions messages are confidential.
- 90% (100% · 0.90) of the delivered control instructions messages have integrity.
- 98.99% (99.99% · 0.99) of the control instructions messages are delivered.

To estimate the likelihoods we use the estimated number of control instructions messages sent each year in combination with the required and worst-case service levels of the control instructions service delivered by "Public telecom system." According to the required service levels, 999.9 (99.99% of 1000), 1000 (100% of 1000), and 1000 (100% of 1000) of the control instructions messages should be delivered, should be confidential, and should have integrity, respectively. On the other hand, our expectations according to the worst-case service levels are: that 990 (999.9 · 0.9899) out of the 999.9 required control instructions messages are delivered; that 950 (1000 · 0.95) out of the 1000 required control instructions messages are confidential; and that 900 (1000 ·

Figure 20. The referenced unwanted incidents "Incident with impact on confidentiality of the sensor data service delivered to Public telecom system," "Incident with impact on integrity of the sensor data service delivered to Public telecom system," and "Incident with impact on availability of the sensor data service delivered to Public telecom system," referred to in Figure 14

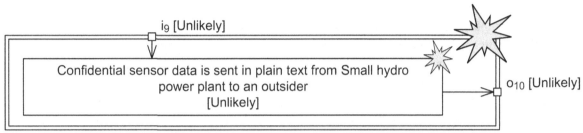

Incident with impact on confidentiality of the sensor data service delivered to Public telecom system

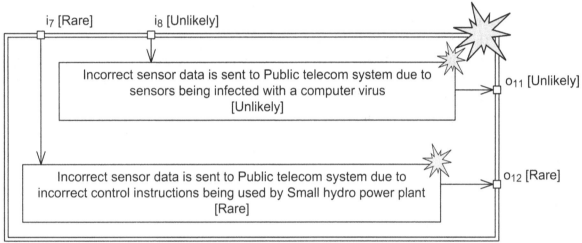

Incident with impact on integrity of the sensor data service delivered to Public telecom system

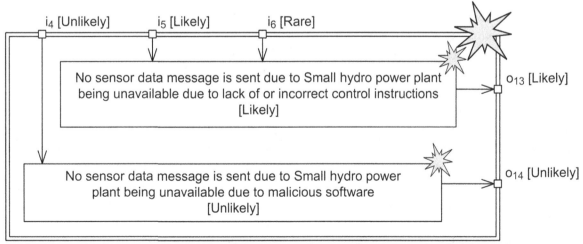

Incident with impact on availability of the sensor data service delivered to Public telecom system

0.90) out of the 1000 required control instructions messages have integrity. Thus, the likelihood of control instructions messages not being delivered according to the availability requirement is "Very likely" (999.9 − 990 ≈ 10 per year), while the likelihoods of control instructions messages not being delivered according to the confidentiality and integrity requirements are "Certain" (1000 − 950 = 50 per year) and "Certain" (1000 − 900 = 100 per year), respectively.

The referenced threat scenario "Services not delivered by Small hydro power plant according to requirements" is given in Figure 16. The internal threat behavior of "Small hydro power plant" is described by the referenced threat scenarios in Figures 17-19. The different referenced threat scenarios describe how "Small hydro power plant" may fail to provide the sensor data service according to its requirements as a result of "Public telecom system" failing to provide the control instructions service according to requirements.

Figure 20 contains the referenced unwanted incidents referred to in Figure 14. For each of the unwanted incidents, Client EPP believes that more than one sensor data message is affected by the incident. For the incident "No sensor data message is sent due to Small hydro power plant being unavailable due to lack of or incorrect control instructions," Client EPP estimates a down time of one day, while a down time of 3 days is estimated for the incident "No sensor data message is sent due to Small hydro power plant being unavailable due to malicious software." For the incident "Incorrect sensor data is sent to Public telecom system due to incorrect control instructions being used by Small hydro power plant," Client EPP estimates that "Small hydro power plant" sends incorrect sensor data messages for a period of 12 hours as a result of using incorrect control instructions. For the incident "Confidential sensor data is sent in plain text from Small hydro power plant to an outsider," Client EPP believes that this can go on

undetected for at much as seven days. The same is believed for the incident "Incorrect sensor data is sent to Public telecom system due to sensors being infected with a computer virus." With an average number of 13.7 sensor data messages being sent each day, we get the consequence values documented in Figure 14.

The result of the detailed analysis is five security risks, where each risk consists of an unwanted incident, its likelihood of occurring, and the consequence of the unwanted incident with respect to a security asset. Based on the risk function, defined in eq. (1) and eq. (2), the estimated number of sensor data messages sent each year (5000), and the required service levels for the sensor data service, we can calculate the risk values of the five security risks. All the security risks, with the exception of "Incorrect sensor data is sent to Public telecom system due to incorrect control instructions being used by Small hydro power plant," are unacceptable. For the acceptable risk the expected service level (4999.3 of the sent sensor data messages have integrity) is higher than the required service level (4995 of the sent sensor data messages have integrity).

DEMONSTRATION OF STEP 3: IDENTIFY INDICATORS FOR SYSTEM OF SYSTEMS

Step 3.1: Identify Security Risks to be Monitored

Client EPP believes that the likelihood values used to calculate the risk values of the risks "Incorrect sensor data is sent to Public telecom system due to sensors being infected with a computer virus" and "Confidential sensor data is sent in plain text from Small hydro power plant to an outsider" may be subject to change. We therefore decide to monitor these security risks.

Figure 21. Relevant indicators, assigned to leads-to relations in the referenced threat scenario in Figure 19, for monitoring the risks "Incorrect sensor data is sent to Public telecom system due to sensors being infected with a computer virus" and "Confidential sensor data is sent in plain text from Small hydro power plant to an outsider"

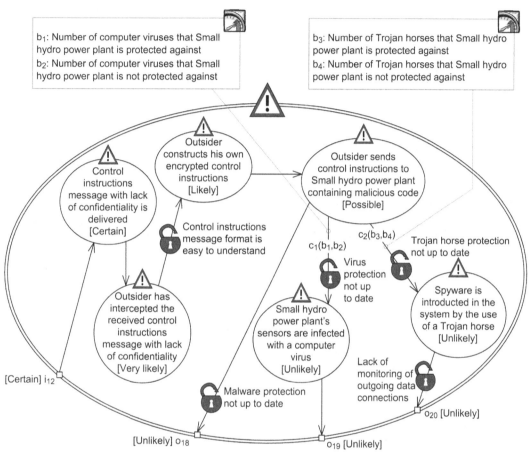

Control instructions message with lack of confidentiality is delivered to Small hydro power plant

Step 3.2: Identify Relevant Indicators for the Security Risks to be Monitored

Indicators should be used to monitor likelihood values, since the likelihood values used to calculate the risk values of the two risks may be subject to change. Client EPP does not find it feasible to directly monitor the likelihoods of the unwanted incidents occurring, and has therefore decided to monitor the conditional likelihoods of two leads-to relations in the referenced threat scenario in

Figure 19 that affect the likelihoods of the two unwanted incidents occurring. The relevant indicators for the two leads-to relations are presented in Figure 21. Note that in order to save space we only demonstrate how the conditional likelihoods of these two leads-to relations are monitored based on indicators. In a real-life case we would of course also monitor the resulting likelihoods for the risks identified for monitoring in Step 3.1, which depend on the conditional likelihoods we now address, as well as other factors.

One composite indicator c_1, which aggregates the two basic indicators b_1 and b_2, has been identified for one leads-to relation. c_1 makes a prediction about the percentage of computer viruses that "Small hydro power plant" is not protected against. For the other leads-to relation, we have identified the composite indicator c_2, which aggregates the two basic indicators b_3 and b_4. c_2 makes a prediction about the percentage of Trojan horses that "Small hydro power plant" is not protected against.

To calculate the indicators, Client EPP relies on data from the security vendor that delivers the security solutions and patches that are used in the control system of "Small hydro power plant." At the "Small hydro power plant" it may take some time between each upgrade of the security solutions and patching of the control system. This is due to that the updates and patches need to be inspected and tested before they can be introduced into the control system in order to ensure the stability of the control system of "Small hydro power plant." The consequence is that "Small hydro power plant" may be unprotected for some time against well-known computer viruses and Trojan horses.

DEMONSTRATION OF STEP 4: SPECIFY DESIGN AND DEPLOYMENT OF IDENTIFIED INDICATORS FOR SYSTEM OF SYSTEMS

Step 4.1: Specify Design of Indicators for Monitoring Security Risks

In Figure 21 the composite indicators c_1 and c_2 are associated to one leads-to relation each. No conditional likelihoods were assigned to these leads-to relations during the detailed analysis in Step 2.3. Thus, values are not obtained for the basic indicators from the time when the referenced threat scenario in Figure 19 was constructed.

Table 3. Design specifications, in the form of algorithms, for the basic indicators b_1 and b_2 and the composite indicator c_1

Algorithm for b_1
Input: $list_1$: "List of names of computer viruses that Small hydro power plant is protected against" $b_1 := 0$ **for each** $name_1$ **in** $list_1$ **do** $\quad b_1 := b_1 + 1$ **end for each**   **Output:** b_1

Algorithm for b_2

Input: $list_1$: "List of names of computer viruses that Small hydro power plant is protected against," $list_2$: "List of names of all computer viruses that the security vendor delivering security solutions and patches to Small hydro power plant offers protection against," $list_3$: "List of names of computer viruses that the security vendor delivering security solutions and patches to Small hydro power plant is aware of but does not yet offer protection against"
 	
 $b_2 := 0$
 for each $name_2$ **in** $list_2$ **do**
 $\quad$ **if** $name_2$ **not in** $list_1$ **then**
 $\quad\quad b_2 := b_2 + 1$
 $\quad$ **end if**
 end for each
 for each $name_3$ **in** $list_3$ **do**
 $\quad b_2 := b_2 + 1$
 end for each
 	
 Output: b_2

Algorithm for c_1
Input: b_1, b_2 $var_1 := b_2 + ((b_1 + b_2) \cdot [0.001, 0.005])$ $var_2 := b_1 + var_1$ $c_3 := var_1 / var_2$ **Output:** c_1

In Tables 3 and 4 are the design specifications for the different basic and composite indicators. All the specifications have been given in the form of algorithms. The six algorithms are to be used by a risk monitor within the electrical power production infrastructure.

To calculate the two composite indicators, Client EPP takes into account that there may be

Table 4. Design specifications, in the form of algorithms, for the basic indicators b_3 and b_4 and the composite indicator c_2

Algorithm for b_3
Input: $list_4$: "List of names of Trojan horses that Small hydro power plant is protected against" $b_3 := 0$ **for each** $name_4$ in $list_4$ **do** $b_3 := b_3 + 1$ **end for each** **Output:** b_3

Algorithm for b_4

Input: $list_4$: "List of names of Trojan horses that Small hydro power plant is protected against," $list_5$: "List of names of all Trojan horses that the security vendor delivering security solutions and patches to Small hydro power plant offers protection against," $list_6$: "List of names of Trojan horses that the security vendor delivering security solutions and patches to Small hydro power plant is aware of but does not yet offer protection against"
 	
$b_4 := 0$
for each $name_5$ in $list_5$ **do**
   if $name_5$ not in $list_4$ **then**
      $b_4 := b_4 + 1$
   end if
end for each
for each $name_6$ in $list_6$ **do**
   $b_4 := b_4 + 1$
end for each
 	
Output: b_4

Algorithm for c_2
Input: b_3, b_4 $var_3 := b_4 + ((b_3 + b_4) \cdot [0.001, 0.003])$ $var_4 := b_3 + var_3$ $c_4 := var_3 / var_4$ **Output:** c_2

Table 5. Deployment specifications for the basic indicators b_1 and b_2 and the composite indicator c_1

Deployment specification for b_1
Extraction and transmission of $list_1$: At the start of each week, an automated ICT process creates the list $list_1$. The list $list_1$ is created by extracting the names of all computer viruses that "Small hydro power plant" is protected against from the information security database in the electrical power production infrastructure. The process transmits $list_1$ to the risk monitor by using the internal data network of the electrical power production infrastructure.

Deployment specification for b_2
Extraction and transmission of $list_2$: At the start of each week, an automated ICT process updates the information security database in the electrical power production infrastructure. The database is updated by retrieving the names of all new computer viruses that the security vendor of Client EPP offers protection against from the security vendor's database. After having updated the database, the process creates the list $list_2$ by extracting the names of all computer viruses that the security vendor offers protection against from the information security database. The process transmits $list_2$ to the risk monitor by using the internal data network of the electrical power production infrastructure. **Extraction and transmission of $list_3$:** At the start of each week, an automated ICT process updates the information security database in the electrical power production infrastructure. The database is updated by retrieving the names of all new computer viruses that the security vendor of Client EPP is aware of but does not yet offer protection against from the security vendor's database. After having updated the database, the process creates the list $list_3$ by extracting the names of all computer viruses that the security vendor is aware of but does not yet offer protection against from the information security database. The process transmits $list_3$ to the risk monitor by using the internal data network of the electrical power production infrastructure.

Deployment specification for c_1
Extraction of b_1 and b_2: The risk monitor calculates the two basic indicators b_1 and b_2 each week. After having calculated the two basic indicators, the risk monitor uses them to calculate the composite indicator c_1.

computer viruses and Trojan horses that the security vendor is not aware of. Client EPP thinks it is reasonable to assume that the total number of computer viruses is $0.1 - 0.5\%$ higher than the sum $b_1 + b_2$, and that the total number of Trojan horses is $0.1 - 0.3\%$ higher than the sum $b_3 + b_4$. For both composite indicators we end up with an interval.

Step 4.2: Specify Deployment of Indicators for Monitoring Security Risks

In Tables 5 and 6 are the deployment specifications for the basic and composite indicators. The six specifications specify how data needed in the calculations of the indicators should be extracted and transmitted within the SoS. As we can see from the specifications, the security risk picture is updated on a weekly basis.

Table 6. Deployment specifications for the basic indicators b_3 and b_4 and the composite indicator c_2

Deployment specification for b_3
Extraction and transmission of $list_4$: At the start of each week, an automated ICT process creates the list $list_4$. The list $list_4$ is created by extracting the names of all Trojan horses that "Small hydro power plant" is protected against from the information security database in the electrical power production infrastructure. The process transmits $list_4$ to the risk monitor by using the internal data network of the electrical power production infrastructure.
Deployment specification for b_4
Extraction and transmission of $list_5$: At the start of each week, an automated ICT process updates the information security database in the electrical power production infrastructure. The database is updated by retrieving the names of all new Trojan horses that the security vendor of Client EPP offers protection against from the security vendor's database. After having updated the database, the process creates the list $list_5$ by extracting the names of all Trojan horses that the security vendor offers protection against from the information security database. The process transmits $list_2$ to the risk monitor by using the internal data network of the electrical power production infrastructure.   **Extraction and transmission of $list_6$:** At the start of each week, an automated ICT process updates the information security database in the electrical power production infrastructure. The database is updated by retrieving the names of all new Trojan horses that the security vendor of Client EPP is aware of but does not yet offer protection against from the security vendor's database. After having updated the database, the process creates the list $list_6$ by extracting the names of all Trojan horses that the security vendor is aware of but does not yet offer protection against from the information security database. The process transmits $list_6$ to the risk monitor by using the internal data network of the electrical power production infrastructure.
Deployment specification for c_2
Extraction of b_3 and b_4: The risk monitor calculates the two basic indicators b_3 and b_4 each week. After having calculated the two basic indicators, the risk monitor uses them to calculate the composite indicator c_2.

RELATED WORK

The methodological approach presented in this chapter is a specialization of the approach presented in (Refsdal & Stølen, 2009). The approach in (Refsdal & Stølen, 2009) is general in the sense that it only restricts the risk identification to the identified assets and nothing else. In our approach, the risk identification focuses entirely on risks to security of provided services that have been caused by service dependencies. The approach in

(Refsdal & Stølen, 2009) can of course be used to identify indicators for the purpose of measuring the impact of service dependencies on risk to security of provided services, because of its generality. Compared to our approach, however, it is inferior. The approach in (Refsdal & Stølen, 2009) does not offer any support for dealing with SoS or service dependencies. In addition, it focuses to a much lesser extent on the calculations of indicators, and it cannot be used to specify how the indicator calculations should be embedded in the systems to be monitored.

We are not aware of other approaches targeting the capture and measure of impact of service dependencies on risks to the security of provided services. In (Debar, Kheir, Cuppens-Boulahia, & Cuppens, 2010), which is an approach for constructing formal models of services dependencies in information systems, the dependency models are used in security policy-based management. The dependency models are used to find enforcement points for security rules, which then support countermeasure deployment, and for computing the impact of attacks and countermeasures that propagate over the information system.

Service dependencies are also used in fault analysis (Gruschke, 1998) and dependability analysis (Rugina, Kanoun, & Kaâniche, 2007), as well as in analyses targeting critical infrastructures. A number of the approaches addressing service dependencies within critical infrastructures focus primarily on the consequences of infrastructure services not being provided. One such approach is (Svendsen, 2008). This approach is used to create models of infrastructure systems and their interactions. The models are used in computer simulations where the main purpose is to investigate how the functionality of infrastructure systems and interconnections react to different attack scenarios ("what if" scenarios where one or two systems are removed), and how mechanisms for strengthening the underlying dependency graph can be used. Svendsen's approach differs, in particular, from our approach in that the likelihoods of incidents (systems failing to provide services according to requirements) are not considered.

Even though a lot of work has been done within the SoS field, there is still no single accepted definition of what an SoS is. Examples of different definitions may be found in (Jamshidi, 2008). With different understandings of what an SoS is, we also get different understandings of what should be addressed with respect to risk and security. For instance, some definitions state that an SoS only consists of systems that operate independently of each other, i.e., that the different systems do not rely on services from other systems in order in to function. This is quite different from our understanding of an SoS. In the literature, SoS has received relatively little coverage when it comes to security and risk analysis. Papers like (Waller & Craddock, 2011), (Gandhi, Gorod, & Sauser, 2011), (Bodeau, 1994), and (Sage, 2003), focus primarily on the challenges and relatively little on actual approaches.

Dependent CORAS (Lund et al., 2010) is is an approach for modular risk modeling, which can be used to document and reason about risk in SoS. It extends the CORAS risk modeling language with facilities for documenting and reasoning about risk analysis assumptions. It was motivated by the need to deal with mutual dependencies in risk analysis of SoS. By employing dependent CORAS we may document risk separately for the individual systems in an SoS. In addition, we document the risk analysis assumptions for the different systems, i.e., how threat scenarios and unwanted incidents, documented for other systems, may lead to threat scenarios and unwanted incidents, documented for the system in question. These assumptions are due to some form of dependencies, not necessarily service dependencies, between the different systems. Thus, dependent CORAS deal with dependencies in a general way compared to our approach, which only focus on service dependencies. The different risk models may be combined in the end, if the dependencies between them are well-founded, i.e., not circular.

There exist a number of approaches for measuring information security. One of those is the NIST Performance Measurement Guide for Information Security (Chew et al., 2008). This approach aims to assist in the development, selection, and implementation of suitable measures. It also provides a number of candidate measures. Unlike our approach, it is not specialized towards using these measures for the purpose of calculating explicit likelihood and consequence values.

CONCLUSION

In this chapter we have addressed the issue of how to capture and measure the impact of service dependencies on risk to security of provided services by the use of measureable indicators. To this end we have put forward a method consisting of four steps, which can be used in security governance for the purpose of assessing to what extent the security expectations to the provided services are achieved. To the best of our knowledge, there exists no similar approach. The applicability of the approach has been demonstrated on an example case within power supply.

In Step 1 of the approach, dependencies due to service exchange between different systems are captured. Their impact on risk to security of provided services is established in Step 2. In Step 3 we identify relevant indicators for monitoring the security risks arising from service dependencies, while in Step 4 we specify how likelihood and consequence values associated with the security risks should be calculated from sets of indicators and how these calculations should be embedded in the SoS. The result of applying the method is a security risk picture capturing the impact of service dependencies on security of provided services that can be dynamically monitored via the specified indicators.

An interesting topic for further research is the use of leading indicators (Jansen, 2010) to monitor the impact of service dependencies on security risk. Many security indicators can be viewed as lagging indicators (Jansen, 2010). These indicators reflect security conditions that exist after a shift in security, e.g., occurrence of unwanted incidents. Leading indicators, on the other hand, reflect security conditions that exist before a shift in security. In the case of service dependencies, the leading indicators may be used to predict their future impact on security risk. By employing leading indicators, countermeasures may be implemented prior to security risks occurring.

ACKNOWLEDGEMENT

The research on which this chapter reports has been carried out within the DIGIT project (180052/S10), funded by the Research Council of Norway, and the MASTER and NESSoS projects, both funded from the European Community's Seventh Framework Programme (FP7/2007-2013) under grant agreements FP7-216917 and FP7-256980, respectively.

REFERENCES

Allen, J. (2005). *Governing for enterprise security* (Tech. Rep.). Pittsburgh, PA: Carnegie Mellon University. (CMU/SEI-2005-TN-023)

Bodeau, D. (1994). System-of-systems security engineering. In *Proceedings of 10th Annual Computer Security Applications Conference* (pp. 228–235). Los Alamitos, CA: IEEE Computer Society.

Chew, E., Swanson, M., Stine, K., Bartol, N., Brown, A., & Robinson, W. (2008). *Performance measurement guide for information security* (Tech. Rep.). Gaithersburg, MD: National Institute of Standards and Technology. (NIST Special Publication 800-55 Revision 1)

Debar, H., Kheir, N., Cuppens-Boulahia, N., & Cuppens, F. (2010). Service dependencies in information systems security. In *Proceedings of the 5th International Conference on Mathematical Methods, Models and Architectures for Computer Network Security (MMM-ACNS'10)* (pp. 1–20). Berlin, Germany: Springer-Verlag.

Gandhi, S., Gorod, A., & Sauser, B. (2011). A systemic approach to managing risks of SoS. In *Proceedings of 2011 IEEE International Systems Conference (SysCon'11)* (pp. 412–416). Piscataway, NJ: IEEE.

Gruschke, B. (1998). Integrated event management: Event correlation using dependency graphs. In *Proceedings of Ninth Annual IFIP/IEEE International Workshop on Distributed Systems: Operations and Management (DSOM'98)*. Retrieved February 9, 2012, from http://www.nm.ifi.lmu.de/pub/ Publikationen/grus98a/PDF-Version/grus98a.pdf

Hammond, A., Adriaanse, A., Rodenburg, E., Bryant, D., & Woodward, R. (1995). *Environmental indicators: A systematic approach to measuring and reporting on environmental policy performance in the context of sustainable development*. Washington, DC: World Resources Institute.

ISO (International Organization for Standardization), & IEC (International Electrotechnical Commission). (2005). *ISO/IEC 17799:2005 Information technology – Security techniques – Code of practice for information security management*.

Jamshidi, M. (2008). System of systems engineering – New challenges for the 21st century. *IEEE Aerospace and Electronic Systems Magazine*, *23*(5), 4–19.

Jansen, W. (2010). *Directions in security metrics research*. Darby, PA: DIANE Publishing Company.

Ligaarden, O. S., Refsdal, A., & Stølen, K. (2012). *Using indicators to monitor security risk in systems of systems: How to capture and measure the impact of service dependencies on the security of provided services* (Tech. Rep.). Oslo, Norway: SINTEF. (SINTEF A22301)

Lund, M. S., Solhaug, B., & Stølen, K. (2010). *Model-driven risk analysis: The CORAS approach* (1st ed.). Berlin, Germany: Springer-Verlag.

Lysemose, T., Mahler, T., Solhaug, B., Bing, J., Elgesem, D., & Stølen, K. (2007). *ENFORCE conceptual framework* (Tech. Rep.). Oslo, Norway: SINTEF. (SINTEF A1209)

Office of the Under Secretary of Defense for Acquisition, Technology, and Logistics. (2002). *SoS and FoS FAQ*. Retrieved February 9, 2012, from http://www.acq.osd.mil/dpap/Docs/FAQs -- SoS & FoS.doc

OMG (Object Management Group). (2004). *Unified modeling language specification, Version 2.0*.

Refsdal, A., & Stølen, K. (2009). Employing key indicators to provide a dynamic risk picture with a notion of confidence. In *Proceedings of Third IFIP WG 11.11 International Conference (IFIPTM'09)* (pp. 215–233). Berlin, Germany: Springer-Verlag.

Rugina, A., Kanoun, K., & Kaâniche, M. (2007). A system dependability modeling framework using AADL and GSPNs. In de Lemos, R., Gacek, C., & Romanovsky, A. (Eds.), *Architecting Dependable Systems IV* (pp. 14–38). Berlin, Germany: Springer-Verlag.

Sage, A. (2003). Conflict and risk management in complex system of systems issues. In *Proceedings of 2003 IEEE International Conference on Systems, Man and Cybernetics* (pp. 3296–3301). Piscataway, NJ: IEEE.

Svendsen, N. K. (2008). *Interdependencies in critical infrastructures: A qualitative approach to model physical, logical, and geographical interdependencies*. Doctoral dissertation, University of Oslo, Oslo. (In series of dissertations submitted to the Faculty of Mathematics and Natural Sciences, University of Oslo, No. 748)

Waller, A., & Craddock, R. (2011). Managing runtime re-engineering of a system-of-systems for cyber security. In *Proceedings of 6th International Conference on System of Systems Engineering (SoSE'11)* (pp. 13–18). Piscataway, NJ: IEEE.

KEY TERMS AND DEFINITIONS

Indicator: An indicator is something that provides a clue to a matter of larger significance or makes perceptible a trend or phenomenon that is not immediately detectable (Hammond, Adriaanse, Rodenburg, Bryant, & Woodward, 1995). For example, an unexpected rise in the traffic load of a web server may signal a denial of service attack in progress. Thus, the significance of an indicator extends beyond what is actually measured to a larger phenomenon of interest.

Required Service Level: A service has one or more required service levels. Each required service level describes a requirement to one area of service scope. Availability, integrity, etc., are all examples of areas of service scope.

Security Asset: A security asset is something of value to security that a party seeks to protect.

Security Risk: A security risk is defined by the likelihood of an unwanted incident, and its consequence with respect to a security asset.

Security: Security is the preservation of confidentiality, integrity, and availability of information; in addition, other properties such as authenticity, accountability, non-repudiation, and reliability can also be involved (ISO & IEC, 2005).

Service Dependency: A service dependency describes a relationship between a service provided by a system and services required by the system. A service depends on other services if it requires the other services in order to be provided.

Service: A service is provided by a system and consumed by a system. It represents the exchange of some commodity or the exchange of information.

System of Systems: A system of systems (SoS) is a set or arrangement of systems that are related or connected to fulfill common goals. The different systems may be controlled, operated, and maintained by different parties and within different jurisdictions. The loss of any system

may seriously impact the other systems and the process of fulfilling the common goals.

Trust: Trust is the subjective probability by which an actor (the trustor) expects that another entity (the trustee) performs a given transition on which its welfare depends (Lysemose et al., 2007). The level of trust may vary from 0 (complete distrust) to 1 (complete trust).

ENDNOTE

[1]   This procedure is only valid if there are no mutual dependencies. We refer to the full technical report (Ligaarden, Refsdal, & Stølen, 2012) for the general procedure.

Chapter 11
Information Security Governance:
The Art of Detecting Hidden Malware

Mamoun Alazab
Australian National University, Australia

Paul Watters
University of Ballarat, Australia

Sitalakshmi Venkatraman
University of Ballarat, Australia

Moutaz Alazab
Deakin University, Australia

ABSTRACT

Detecting malicious software or malware is one of the major concerns in information security governance as malware authors pose a major challenge to digital forensics by using a variety of highly sophisticated stealth techniques to hide malicious code in computing systems, including smartphones. The current detection techniques are futile, as forensic analysis of infected devices is unable to identify all the hidden malware, thereby resulting in zero day attacks. This chapter takes a key step forward to address this issue and lays foundation for deeper investigations in digital forensics. The goal of this chapter is, firstly, to unearth the recent obfuscation strategies employed to hide malware. Secondly, this chapter proposes innovative techniques that are implemented as a fully-automated tool, and experimentally tested to exhaustively detect hidden malware that leverage on system vulnerabilities. Based on these research investigations, the chapter also arrives at an information security governance plan that would aid in addressing the current and future cybercrime situations.

INTRODUCTION

A number of criminal justice agencies and organisations are increasing rapidly (Khan, Wiil, & Memon, 2010) and they share responsibility for detecting and stopping digital crime (Kruse

& Heiser, 2001). The Regional Computer Forensics Laboratory (RCFL) of the Federal Bureau of Investigation (FBI), in their annual report (RCFL, 2008), stated that 1,756 TBs of data was processed in USA for computer forensic analysis in the year 2008 alone. It was only one year

DOI: 10.4018/978-1-4666-2083-4.ch011

earlier (RCFL, 2007), they had announced that the amount of data to be examined per criminal case would increase by 35% annually, which was immediately surpassed in the subsequent year. In addition, according to recent reports (RSA, 2011) 2010 has witnessed new threats with increased level of sophistication in the attacks, targeting employees in enterprises globally. Only recently there has been a high rise in smartphone malware that warrant further forensic investigations. With online crime escalating to great heights in the form of hidden malware, both in quantity as well as in sophistication of stealth techniques being adopted to inflict computing devices, digital forensics and information security governance have become a major challenge worldwide (Stolfo, Wang, & Li, 2007; Venkatraman, 2010).

Digital forensics is the science of preserving, identifying, extracting, analysing and documenting evidence found in computing devices at crime scenes so that this evidence may be used in a court of law (Vacca, 2005). It also answers questions and attempts to provide full descriptions of a digital crime scene. In computing systems, the primary goals of digital forensic analysis are fivefold: i) to identify all the unwanted events that took place, ii) to ascertain their effect on the system, iii) to acquire the necessary evidence to confirm malicious activity, iv) to prevent future incidents by detecting the malicious techniques used and v) to recognize the incitement reasons and intention of the attacker for future predictions. The focus of this research is on the third goal, to acquire the necessary digital electronic evidence to confirm malicious events that may have occurred on computing devices. Also in this chapter we will illustrate the variety of stealth strategies adopted by malware authors to hide the maliciousness in the devices including smartphones. Based on our experimental investigations performed successfully, we propose detection techniques to identify hidden malware in a systematic method that facilitates in arriving at an information security governance plan that would help in developing,

implementing and continuously reforming malware forensic techniques.

Overall, this chapter aims to investigate two main questions with regard to research in digital forensics. Firstly, we need to identify what are the infection strategies undertaken by malicious authors, since that forms the basis of any further investigation that could be fruitful in digital forensics. Secondly, we need to adopt innovative techniques and examine how they could detect hidden malware. Therefore, this chapter is focused on an important research study of the current issues in digital forensics.

The organisation of the remainder of the chapter is as follows. Section 2 provides the trends in malware attacks and the escalated infections due to the recent emergence of smartphones. Section 3 describes current techniques used in data analysis following which previous research work conducted in digital forensics is described in section 4. Our main contributions in this chapter are two-fold: i) to unearth and report the various new strategies employed by malicious authors through our experimental investigations, described in section 5, and ii) to present our proposed innovative techniques that we have implemented as a fully-automated tool to successfully detect unknown and hidden malware, as explained in section 6. In section 7, we provide an information security governance plan derived based on the research study conducted, and finally, a brief summary and conclusions are provided in section 8.

MALWARE ATTACK TRENDS

The continued growth and diversification of the Internet has resulted in the increasing sophistication of tools and methods used to conduct computer system attacks and intrusions (Venkatraman, 2010). Among these attacks, Malware or malicious software is one of the biggest threats posing the digital world (Alperovitch, 2011; RSA, 2011). With more and more use of computers, portable devices and the Internet in everyday life, identification of new or unknown malware has become the biggest challenge in digital forensics (Vassil, 2009). Of late, malwares are being designed more for financial gains (RSA, 2011) leading to a huge impact against individuals, organisations and business assets. Recent trends in malware for such financial fraud purposes indicate their increasing complexity and that they are evolving rapidly, as information systems provide more opportunities for automated online financial activities (Venkatraman, 2009). As a result, the damages caused by malware to individuals and businesses have dramatically increased in the past few years.

Malware contains code that is designed to perform illegal activities, to cause damage, and to affect the integrity and the functionality of the digital system. Malware attackers are taking advantage of our increased reliance on digital systems, available digital resources, and increased connectivity and activity through Internet. On one hand, technology advancements have resulted in home computers featuring Terabyte (TB) of storage that are now available for purchase at very low cost. On the other hand, sophistication in malware has risen to great heights offering new class of criminal activity that has created new challenges for law and forensic examiners (Alazab, Venkatraman, & Watters, 2009a; Alazab, Venkatraman, Watters & Alazab, 2011). As the number of cybercrime and computer attacks have increased exponentially, there is a need for developing standards in evidence collection and conducting malware analysis effectively as part of both the incident response and forensic analysis processes (Alazab, Venkatraman & Watters, 2009b; RSA, 2011).

Recent predictions are that mobile devices are expected to become seriously targeted by malware as they become the most common computing platform (Felt, Finifter, Chin, Hanna, & Wagner, 2011). Also, the explosive growth of mobile devices as a general purpose computer has made them an attractive target for cybercriminals to exploit.

In addition, mobile application downloads are increasing at an alarming rate and malware has become more and more sophisticated in recent years. Today, consumers are using their mobile devices more than ever before, and in 21 century there is barely anyone having no mobile devices. Recently, mobile technology is being used for online banking and payments. But it is not just consumers and their banks that must consider the risks of mobile malware. Mobile is also used for checking e-mail, accessing online accounts, performing work related functions, Instant Massages (IM) and storing personal data. All these features are opening up a backdoor for malware to make its way onto the corporate network and create an alternate means of threat for data.

A smartphone is a mobile phone that can be used to send/receive calls and messages, but offers more advanced computing ability and connectivity such as run applications, allows the user to run and multi task applications, run complete operating system software, powerful processors, abundant memory, larger screens, has functions such as camera phone, and a personal digital assistant (PDA). The recent development is that cell phones evolved to smartphones can be used to work similar to computers, such as download program through the internet, share files and software in close distance like Bluetooth connections, and for large distance like Multimedia Message Service (MMS), and can also exchange memory cards in few devices unlike computers. Also, most of smartphones use WiFi.for connecting to the internet.

Since smartphones of today can do functions just as the computers, they are being targeted by hackers. Malware writers never grow tired of finding new ways to compromise computers, and now they venture on attacking through smartphones and vice versa. Soon the situation would become such that smartphone malware overtakes the history of PC malware. However, PC malware offers lessons that we need to study so that we could anticipate some of the techniques that malware authors would undertake for attacking through smartphones, and to take necessary countermeasures to thwart them. Smartphone malware can cause many problems in the device, such as completely disable phone, cause harm by leaking user's private data, cause extra service charges by automatically sending expensive multimedia messages or by making long-distance calls, delete the data on it or result in financial losses by automatically initiating the device to send costly messages to premium-priced numbers, transfer credit card information to other accounts, and even drain away the phone's battery.

Beyond the threat of mobile malware, cyber-criminals are involved in other exploits of mobile devices in general. The number of vulnerabilities witnessed in smartphone is being increased. Synchronization is needed for updates, transferring contact information, and even for backup purposes, and it would be possible to launch the attack during the synchronization process. For example, they could use ligament process to infect mobile devices such as by using Sync softwares that make transferring data easier and faster. Since such software can be used for exchanging contact information, messages, songs, photos, email and all important files, they provide a good platform for injecting attacks. The disadvantage of synchronization is that it can be used to infect smartphones through PCs, or vice versa. Malware attackers use this facility to infect synchronisation data with malicious code so that they could attack both devices.

Smartphone malware and PC malware are both written by malicious writers with the same objective and purpose, but different in the devices being targeted and the propagation methods. Hence, smartphone malware is similar to PC malware but can additionally spread via non-traditional modes such as SMS, MMS, and Bluetooth. Smartphone malware can affect smartphones through features such as, call premium telephone numbers, send messages, spy on calls, steal sensitive information like, passwords, confidential information, credit card numbers, bank account details, contacts, mes-

sages and emails. Not all malware that infect PC can infect smartphones, and such an example is W32.Downadup, a worm categorised as PC malware that infect the following Windows Operating Systems: Windows 98, Windows 95, Windows XP, Windows Me, Windows Vista, Windows NT, Windows Server 2003, and Windows 2000. W32. downadup aims to delete registry entries in order to disable any access to Safe Mode, and to disable Windows Security Alert notifications. However, it has not been reported to infect the smartphone.

Countermeasure such as Anti-virus engines are using signature based detection to detect and identify smartphone malware as well as computer malware. Malware writers are using obfuscation methods to evade the scanning process by disguising the code to another variant which the antivirus cannot detect. As a result, current detection engines do not provide enough opportunity to learn and understand malware threats that can be used in implementing security prevention mechanisms and to detect unknown or zero day malwares.

NEED FOR NEW FORENSIC TECHNIQUES

Digital electronic evidence is the data and information that has an investigative value confirming their existence in electronic device (Scanlon & Kechadi, 2010; Riley, Dampier, & Vaughn, 2008). There is no single universal procedure to conduct the investigation of a digital crime scene (Keane, 2008) to confirm a malicious event which is the prime motivation of this research. Many situations have adopted three major phases for investigative process, which are, acquisition, preservation, and analysis (Carrier, 2005; Casey, 2004). In particular, the proposed research aims to assist investigates to improve the digital forensic techniques by providing better understanding of the infection strategies used by malware authors and thereby such techniques could be adopted to analyse digital data and acquire evidences more effectively.

Digital investigation is a process to answer questions about the compromised digital data; this involves two stages of analysis: static and live analysis techniques. This research focuses on a static analysis technique, where the hard disk would be isolated to perform analysis in a lab for the identification of hidden malware. Hence, this research work would form a major initial step towards addressing the open problem of identifying any unseen or new malware that could evade detection in the form of hidden or obfuscated malicious code.

The data collected for analysis can be classified as volatile and nonvolatile data (Carrier, 2006). The volatile data is information we might lose if we turn off the system or yank out the power core, such as the current network connection, open TCP or UDP ports, cached NetBIOS name table, users currently logged on, internal routing table, running processes, running services, scheduled jobs, open files, process memory dumps and others. To analyse volatile data (also called Live Analysis) the system needs to be online during the investigation. On the other hand, the nonvolatile data is the information that is not lost if we turn off the system, such as register data, file system date and time stamps, system version and patch level. In any computing device, information such as file system MD5 checksum values, user accounts, IIS logs, stored file data, etc., are collected to detect malware, which is the main goal of this research. Such an analysis of nonvolatile data is also called Static Analysis.

The malware signature is a byte sequence that uniquely identifies a specific malware as shown in Table 1. Typically, a malware detector uses the malware signature to identify the malware like a fingerprint. Most countermeasures such as anti-malware engines are supplied with a database containing information of existing malware in order to identify maliciousness by looking for code signatures or byte sequences while scanning the system. A malware detector scans the system in various locations for characteristic byte sequences or signature that match with the one in the database and declares existence of malware to subsequently block user access to the system. The signature matching process is called signature-based detection and most traditional AV engines use this method. It is a very efficient and effective method to detect known malware. But, the major drawback is the inability to detect new or unknown malicious code and zero day attacks (Alazab, Layton, Venkatraman, & Watters, 2010; Alazab, Venkatraman, & Watters, 2010; Alazab, Watters, Venkatraman, Alazab, & Alazab, 2011). Therefore, updating the detection engine or AV software daily with latest malware signatures is essential so as to protect the computer system against all known malware. Hence, the more malware signatures are fed into the AV engine, the more effective it is in detecting latest known malwares. Since hidden and obfuscated malware apply sophisticated evasion techniques, signature-based AV engines fail to detect them.

The new threat for computers is that the malware writers are recycling existing malware such as w32.Parite with different signatures ('byte sequence'), by using obfuscation techniques such

Table 1. Signature of original code of Virus.Win32. Bolzano.2122

Original Code	
B8 F2070000	MOV EAX,7F2
03C5	ADD EAX,EBP
E8 0D000000	CALL 0041158D
B8 07080000	MOV EAX,807
03C5	ADD EAX,EBP
E8 01000000	CALL 0041158D
C3	RETN
Signature	
B8F2 0700 0003 C5E8 0D00 0000	
B807 0800 0003 C5E8 0100 0000 C3	

as packing, polymorphic transformations and metamorphic obfuscations, instead of creating an entirely new malware. This means that the AV scanners will not be able to detect these new malware due to the non-existence of their finger-prints in the signature database. The present malware detection systems usually rely on exist-ing malware signatures with limited heuristics and are unable to detect those malware that can hide themselves during the scanning process in online systems (Skoudis & Zeltser, 2003; Venka-traman, 2010; Alperovitch, 2011; RSA, 2011).

Current live malware detection tools such as anti-virus (AV) software that analyse volatile data are able to identify known malware, therefore, at-tackers are continually developing new techniques for creating malware that are not detectable by anti-virus (AV) engines. Once new malware is released, the AV engines will reactively update their signatures to combat the new malware. However, recent methods adopted by computer intruders, attackers and malware writers are to target hidden and deleted data so that they could evade from virus scanners. As a result, some malwares adopt circumvention techniques such as polymorphic, metamorphic, obfuscation, etc. so that they cannot be detected through current live analysis techniques.

Although signature based detection is one of the well-established methods by AV engines, it suffers from the following drawbacks:

- **High False Positive:** This occurs by iden-tifying benign files as malware. In May, 2007, Symantec updated their malware sig-natures and crippled thousands of Chinese PCs by mistakenly identifying two core Windows.dll files as Trojan horse that Symantec dubbed the virus, "Backdoor. Haxdoor" (Keizer, 2007).
- **High False Negative:** This is due to the in-ability to detect unknown or new malware (Paul, 2008).

Even though the quality of malware detectors used in popular AV software and anti-forensic methods is improving in their techniques from signature-based detection towards heuristic-based detection, the malware cyber criminals are one step ahead of them (Ghosh & Turrini, 2010). The present malware detection systems usually rely on existing malware signatures with limited heuristics and are unable to detect those malware that can hide itself during the scanning process in online systems (García-Teodoro, Díaz-Verdejo, Maciá-Fernández, & Vázquez, 2009).

Countermeasure such as detection engines are failing to detect such hidden malware and are identifying benign file as malware resulting in high false alarm rate (FAR) and false positives. Recently, David Stang (Stang, 2011) tested 41 updated scanners on 54,016 malware files, and report that only 1 among these files were detected by less than half the scanners used. On an average the overall malware detection has been only 62% with a maximum of about 80% in some studies. However, sophistication in malware through code obfuscation has created another challenge for digital forensic examiners, namely the detection rate of new and unknown malware is very low (Alazab, Venkatraman, Watters, & Alazab, 2011; Stang, 2011) and identifying benign code as mali-cious (false alarm rate) is quite high.

Our goal is to conduct static analysis rather than live analysis as it helps in capturing evi-dence during forensic investigations to a certain extent, and more importantly the false negatives rate in live analysis rate is high. Another reason is that malware such as rootkits can hide and change itself without being seen and the existing forensic tools are unable to detect all malware, in particular, hidden malware. Moreover, the attack-ers target a hidden area on the system structure to hide the malware, and to conduct live analysis is extremely hard. Hence, in this research static analysis is adopted rather than live analysis so that all the hidden information can be captured and the information cannot be modified to produce false data as in live analysis techniques. Static analysis has the advantage that it can reveal how a program would behave under unusual conditions, because we can examine parts of a program that normally do not execute. In real life, static analysis gives an approximate picture at best.

PREVIOUS WORK

In the Digital Forensics Research Workshop, Brian Carrier defined Digital Forensic Science (Carrie, 2003) as: "The use of scientifically derived and proven methods toward the preservation, collection, validation, identification, analysis, interpretation, documentation and presentation of digital evidence derived from digital sources for the purpose of facilitating or furthering the reconstruction of events found to be criminal, or helping to anticipate unauthorized actions shown to be disruptive to planned operations". Every investigation is unique, and it is the responsibility of the investigator to analyze each situation to determine the appropriate investigative approach. However, typically a malware investigator starts the data analysis process after acquiring a potentially malicious infection system, usually an image taken from infected system and brought into the isolated laboratory. Since the physical medium such as hard drive is the fingerprint of both legal and illegal activities and contains evidence that is vital to digital forensic investigations, it is very important to analyse the physical medium for any malware presence.

Currently there is lack of consistent or standardized procedure for accomplishing digital forensics (Jones, Bejtlich & Rose, 2005). There is no standard methodology and approach for conducting a digital forensic investigation (Palmer, 2001), in spite of the fact that digital crimes are on the rise and less than 2% of the reported cases result in conviction (Baryamureeba & Tushabe, 2006). The literature surveys conducted in the last few years on digital forensics were more focused on the

technical aspects without any consideration for a generalized model. Instead of having a genalalised model or framework, literature provides many different models and frameworks suggested by many organisations, agencies and researchers such as, Farmer and Venema (Farmer & Venema, 2005), Brian Carrier (Carrier, 2005), Eoghan Casey (Casey, 2004), Kruse and Heiser (Kruse & Heiser, 2001), the Integrated Digital Investigation Process by Carries and Spafford (Carrier & Spafford, 2003), A Ten Step Process for Forensic Readiness by Robert Rowlingson (Rowlingson, 2004), An Examination of Digital Forensic Models (Reith, Carr, & Gunsch, 2002). The Enhanced Digital Investigation Process Model (Baryamureeba & Tushabe, 2006), New Digital Forensics Investigation Procedure Model (Shin, 2008) and many others adopt varying digital forensic techniques and procedures. While some road maps indicate steps to collect image copy of physical devices, the main challenge is that "analytical procedures and protocols are not standardized nor do practitioners and researchers use standard terminology" (Palmer, 2001) or give recent references (Riley, Dampier, & Vaughn, 2008). This has resulted in a variety of forensic analysis tools that provide different ways to search for the digital evidence of malware and most of these tools adopt different techniques for different kind of information (Alazab, Venkatraman & Watters, 2009a).

With all the data being stored on medium devices, malware capitalises on the weakness of the disk structure to store itself without being recognized from the AV engines, and hence the necessity emerges to start analysis from the physical storage media. Analysis of the physical storage media could provide useful information leading towards malware detection and presentation of digital evidence for the court of law. For example, since NTFS stores all events that take place on a computer system, there is a huge amount of data analysis required while scanning the entire NTFS disk image for forensic purposes. From a preliminary experimental investigation conducted on the hidden data of the $Boot file, it is observed that a variety of tools and utilities have to be adopted along with manual inspections to identify unseen malware. It takes an enormous amount of time to analyse the data derived with such tools and most of the existing tools are complex and not easy to use.

Smartphones are becoming more complicated every day since the virtual memory and scheduling is different between platforms, and even between versions of the same type of smartphone (Felt, Finifter, Chin, Hanna, & Wagner, 2011). Also the executable file format and spreading mechanism adopted by the malware are different between the different platforms. Hackers that target for infecting the operating systems, such as Cardtrap and Mobler malware, can affect across any platform. However, for this type of malware functionality to deliver executable to the targeted operating system, a connection mechanism is required for the propagation, such as synchronization, exchange memory card, Bluetooth and MMS. Clearly, the expectation for malware writers in the next generation will be more sophisticated, and advance techniques that are not only energy and resource efficient, but also appropriate for each smartphone platforms such as windows mobile, Android, Symbian will soon prevail. According to (Schmidt & Albayrak, 2008), majority of attackers target Symbian device and great amount of attention focus the vulnerabilities of Symbian operating system because Symbian has lower level application security, as it allows any system application to install and overwrite without requiring user consent. However, this has been overcome in later versions such as Symbian OS version 9. Previous research studies discuss on reverse engineering techniques similar to computer forensic tools. However, many of those tools and techniques investigated and reported are seldom applicable to new models or phones, such as iPhones or Android. Also, most of the literature focuses on discovering vulnerabilities in smartphones rather than forensic strategies to cope with the latest trend in hidden malware.

Hence, in this research we investigate the recent strategies adopted by hidden malware.

RECENT MALWARE INFECTION STRATEGIES

The primary goal of malicious writers is to execute the malicious program silently without interrupting the user's device and no clue given through error messages. This is very dangerous, as a malware is allowed to execute fully, without the expressed permission of the user, or indirect feedback from the computing device. In this section, through our experimental investigations, we have identified the main evasion techniques and strategies adopted in the recent malware infections taking place in the IT world of today.

Malware authors use a variety of methods in order to avoid detection, and some authors use different kinds of tricks and techniques to exploit device vulnerabilities. From the recent literature studies, we have identified patterns in malware trends (Skoudis & Zeltser, 2003) (Szor, 2005) (Rathgeber, Ludovica, & Solis, 2009), and by conducting further experimental investigations of recent malware threats, we have grouped the malware infection strategies under nine main categories as follows:

Overwriting Infection

This is accomplished by inserting malicious code into an area of the original file (such as XLS, DOC or PDF) in the host computer. Some types of malware using this strategy would completely overwrite a file which destroys the original file, rendering an entire program useless. Consequently, when the users run the executable, the system will execute the malicious code instead. However, the advanced malware do not try to destroy the file so as to trick the user or the scanner. This is accomplished by adding the malicious code in the head or the tail of the host file, so that

Figure 1. Companion infection example

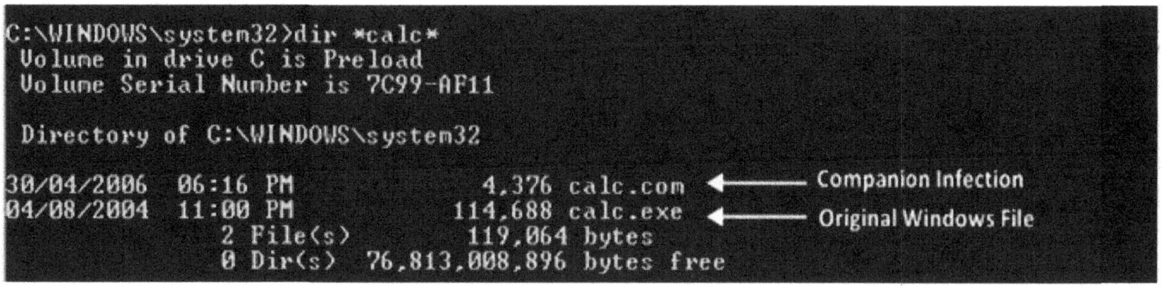

the functionality of the host file is preserved. The steps below explain how such infections work: i) Find file. ii) Open the file (read/write). iii) Destroy the original data and write the malicious code instead with the functionality preserved. v) Close the file. iv) Finally, exit. For instance, the VBS/LoveLetter.A@mm uses this infection method, and the TDL3 rootkit also overwrites the master boot record with its own code.

Companion Infection

This strategy is different from overwritten malware as it does not required a host file to insert the malicious code, instead it exists as a companion file to the EXE host file. We did a simple experiment here by injecting the windows XP professional SP2 system with a malware that we named similar to original windows file, namely 'calc' but with the file name extension as COM (calc.COM), and we saved it in the same path of the original file of calc.EXE as shown in Figure 1. Usually, users type the name of the file at the run command without typing in the file extension to launch an EXE program. As a result, we found that Microsoft DOS will look for .COM files before it looks for .EXE files. Therefore, malware authors need to only save or copy malware file as .COM in the same directory as the original .EXE with the same name. Malware authors are taking this advantage and they save the malicious file with .COM at the same path as the .EXE (Skoudis & Zeltser, 2003). Such use of companion infection

method is adopted by Win2K.Stream companion virus, which was found in 2000, and Trilisa virus/worm in 2002 (see Figure 1).

Appending Infection

It is also called hooking infection, and this method is well known based on the kind of rootkit used, such as Import Address Table (IAT) hooks, inline function hooks, System Service Descriptor Table SSDT hooks, etc. It uses operand commands instructions, such as jump (JMP) and CALL), by modifying the first few instructions in the file function itself so that the execution jumps the pointer to the malicious function code, usually inserted at the end of the file where it does not affect the functionality and sequence of the original code. This way, it does not raise any suspicioun, and an example of such appending virus is 'Vienna', and many other rootkits. The infection technique can be used in all types of portable executables (PE), such as executable files (EXEs), Extensible Linking Format (ELF), etc. For instance, in 2002 the W32.Appix.Worm (Symantec Enterprise Security, 2002) infected PHP and PHTML files by appending code that is designed to infect other PHTML, HTM, PHP, and HTML files.

Rootkit has infected smartphones by exposing voice, GPS or even running down the phone's battery. Malware writers install the rootkit in smartphones, after they get the first root level access by obtaining password through exploiting a known vulnerability or social engineering. Once the rootkit is installed in the victim's device it allows the attackers to mask and maintain privileged access of the device by giving them normal authorization, after they can easily hide applications and steal password without any knowledge from the victim about being attacked. Also, it targets firmware, kernel, or most commonly adopted user-mode applications.

Prepending Infection

This is similar to appending infection, except that the malware inserts itself at the start of a file. Malware authors have implemented this type of infection on various operating systems (Daoud, Jebril, & Zaqaibeh, 2008). Since the malicious code is allocated at the start, and the operating system usually runs beginning of the executable first, it makes the malicious prepending code run before the original code. An example of the use of this technique is the Hungarian virus Polimer.512.A, which prepending itself with 512 bytes long, at the beginning of the executable and shifts the content to follow itself.

Cavity or Space Fill Infection

This kind of infection attempts to enclose the malicious code in an empty space while not affecting the actual program itself and nor increase the length of the program. Malware authors infect files without increasing their sizes or damaging the files. They accomplish this by overwriting unused areas of executable files. These are called cavity malware. For example, the CIH virus, or chernoby1 virus, infects portable Executable files. Also, in the Microsoft NTFS file system, viruses make use of the Master File Table (MFT), which is the core of NTFS since it contains details of every file and folder on the volume. NTFS stores both user data and internal management data, in the form of files. The most important of these are a set of special system files, which are also called metadata files. Metadata files contain internal information about the data in NTFS Volume. These metadata files are automatically formed when the NTFS partition is formatted, and is placed at the top of the partition. The MFT is actually one of these metadata files, but it also contains descriptions of other metadata files. The metafiles are in the NTFS disk root directory, and they start with

Table 2. NTFS Metadata files information

Metadata Name	Metadata	#	Description
Master File Table	$MFT	0	Itself MFT
Master File Table Mirror	$MFTmirr	1	Copy of the first 16 MFT records placed in the middle of the disk or the end of the partition.
Log File	$LogFile	2	Transaction logging file for the volume.
Volume Decription Table	$Volume	3	Contains information about the volume label (partitions), file system version, time, etc.
Attributate Definition Table	$AttrDef	4	List of standard file attributes on the volume
Root Directory	$.	5	Root directory
Cluster Allocation Bitmap	$Bitmap	6	Volume free space bitmap
Volume Boot Code	$Boot	7	Boot sector (bootable partition)
Quota Table	$Quota	9	Containing information if disk quota are being used on the volume. (only for NTFS)
Upper Case Table	$Upcase	10	Table containing information for converting file names to the Unicode 16 bit file naming system for international.

a name character "$", and it is difficult to get any information about them by standard means. By looking at $MFT file size, it is possible to find out useful information such as, time spent by the operating system in cataloguing all the disk. In fact, the first 16 records of the MFT are reserved for metadata files. Table 2 provides the important information about the metadata files, including their names, file names, MFT record numbers and a brief description.

Each MFT entry has a fixed sized which is 1 KB containing two attributes; an attribute header and attribute content. The attribute header is used to identify the size, name and the flag value. The attribute content can reside in the MFT followed by the attribute header if the size is less than 700 bytes (known as a resident attribute), otherwise it will store the attribute content in an external cluster called cluster run (known as a non-resident attribute). This is because; the MFT entry is 1KB in size and hence cannot fit anything that occupies more than 700 bytes. The Lehigh virus is an example of this infection.

Compressing/ Packing

Packers are commonly used today for code obfuscation or compression. Packers are software programs that are able to be used to compress and encrypt the PE in secondary memory and restore the original executable image, when loaded into main memory (RAM). Recently, malware authors have used packers to avoid detection and to run malware faster. This is mainly used for changing any byte sequence in the PE resulting in a new different byte sequence in the new produced packed PE. Packing the malware makes the obfuscation method difficult to understand and the malware authors only need to change a small number of lines of code in order to change the malware signature. Malware authors are continually developing new techniques for creating malware that cannot be detected by AV engines, and their level of sophistication is continuing to grow.

Encryption Malware / Polymorphic Malware

This technique enables a malicious program to mutate at byte level when the program creates a copy of itself, where every new copy of the malware is encrypted with a unique key, which also contains more or less unique byte sequence. It also uses encryption and data appending/ data prepending in order to change the body of the malware as shown in Figure 2, and further, it changes decryption routines from infection to infection as long as the encryption keys change. Such examples are P2P-Worm.Win32.Polip, Virus.DOS.Chameleon, w32.Polip and w32.Detnat.

Boot Sector Malware

This type of malware infects the boot sector in order to affect the system every time the machine boots up. The boot sector placed in the beginning of each partition is appropriately called the partition boot sector (PBS) and the Master Boot Record (MBR) allocated in the first sector of the hard drive that contains the boot code. Hence, when the system starts, it locates the first sector on the hard drive, and executes MBR. Boot sector malware infects the Master Boot Sector of the hard drive and attacks the system every time it boots up.

Michelangelo virus is an example of a Boot sector malware. Another example of boot sector malware is Cabir.G (Aubrey-Derrick Schmidt & Albayrak, 2008) and it has infected the mobile devices. It uses Bluetooth to look for other phones to infect. When a suitable phone is found, Cabir adds infected hostile file as auto start program in order to start in every boot operation of the device. The virus sends.SIS file, and if the target user accepts the file, the malware will disable the "select" button on that mobile. Mabir (Aubrey-Derrick Schmidt & Albayrak, 2008) is another variant of Cabir, and is aimed to spread through Bluetooth as well as via MMS, SMS by waiting for the incoming message.

Figure 2. The polymorphic code example of P2P-Worm.Win32.Polip

```
  seg004:00419AC0 sub_419AC0     proc near              ; CODE XREF: .text:0040652D↑p
  seg004:00419AC0                                       ; sub_407600+5↑p
* seg004:00419AC0                push    ebp
* seg004:00419AC1                mov     ebp, esp
* seg004:00419AC3                sub     esp, 14h
* seg004:00419AC6                pusha
* seg004:00419AC7                mov     edx, (offset dword_40FCC2+2)
* seg004:00419ACC                neg     byte ptr [edx+0]
* seg004:00419ACF                mov     ebx, eax
* seg004:00419AD1                push    eax
* seg004:00419AD2                and     edi, eax
* seg004:00419AD4                push    dword ptr [edx]
* seg004:00419AD6                push    38F27789h
* seg004:00419ADB                bts     ecx, edx
* seg004:00419ADE                push    dword_40FA6C+3
* seg004:00419AE4                call    sub_41CD90
* seg004:00419AE9                add     esp, 10h
* seg004:00419AEC                mov     byte ptr word_40FC6E, 3Ah
* seg004:00419AF3                shr     byte ptr dword_40FCD0+3, 1
* seg004:00419AF9                and     byte ptr [edx], 0BFh
* seg004:00419AFC                jnz     loc_419BFD
* seg004:00419B02                sbb     al, 5Bh
* seg004:00419B04                dec     ebx
* seg004:00419B05                dec     bx
* seg004:00419B07                push    dword_40FB16+2
* seg004:00419B0D                push    dword_40FCA5+1
* seg004:00419B13                push    dword ptr [edx+0]
* seg004:00419B16                cmp     dword_40FBE7+2, eax
* seg004:00419B1C                jl      loc_419BB9
* seg004:00419B22                mov     ecx, 0Fh
* seg004:00419B27                dec     dword_40FD32+3[ecx*4]
* seg004:00419B2E                add     edi, dword_40F76C[ecx*4]
* seg004:00419B35                inc     dword_40FA7E+2[ecx*4]
* seg004:00419B3C                or      dword ptr [edx+ecx*4], 5DEBF5E2h
* seg004:00419B43                call    sub_41BEDF
* seg004:00419B48                push    dword_40FE17
* seg004:00419B4E                push    1AF958ADh
* seg004:00419B53                inc     word ptr dword_40FAD5+2
* seg004:00419B5A                call    sub_40C24C
* seg004:00419B5F                add     esp, 8
```

In our experimental investigation, we had extracted the MFT from the boot sector and had analyzed the MFT using hexeditor tools such as WinHex and used NTFSINO to check the number of sectors allocated to the NTFS file system. Next, we extracted $Boot file and the backup boot sector. The $Boot file is extracted to investigate hidden data. The hidden data was then analyzed in the $Boot metadata file system using WinHex, TSK and Autopsy tools. The analyzer should start by making a comparison between the boot sector and the backup boot sector. The image with the boot sector and backup boot sector are supposed to be identical; otherwise there is some data hidden in the $Boot data structure. One method is to check the integrity of the backup boot sector and the boot sector by calculating the MD5 for both of them. A difference in checksum indicates that there is some hidden data. This comparison is done using the following commands on the $Boot image file and the backup boot image:

```
dd if=image.dd bs=512 count=1
skip=61949 of=c:\backupbootsector.dd
-md5sum -verifymd5 -md5out=c:\hash1.
md5
dd if=image.dd bs=512 count=1 of=c:\
bootsector.dd -md5sum -verifymd5 -
md5out=c:\hash2.md5
```

The boot sector of the NTFS file system could be used as a vehicle to hide data by computer attackers as there is a potential weakness. Our main observations are that hidden data in the $Boot data structure could not be detected directly by the currently available popular existing forensic tools and laborious manual inspections are required to be performed alongside these tools. In other words, existing forensic software tools are not competent enough to comprehensively detect all hidden data in boot sectors.

Macro Malware

Macro malware embeds itself in a data file. The term macro means a series of command steps and character strings saved in a single location that is assigned a name. Malware authors are using macro to infect applications that make use of the command in applications such as word processor and spreadsheet. Usually, when the name of the macro is found in a document file the macro would get expanded. The set of commands could perform the series of steps automatically for manipulating and creating files or changing menu settings. A macro virus is often spread as an e-mail virus. A well-known example is the Melissa virus in March, 1999. Another example of a smartphone worm malware, Letum which was discovered in 2006 (Tudor, 2006), spreads via email and Usenet technology, and infects windows mobile platform. Letum copies itself in the directory, and adds itself to the registry with a path

In our experimental investigations, we checked if there are any unknown macros inside files such as word processing and spread sheet files. Though some office packages have hotkeys to check for valid macros, some macro viruses tend to hide themselves from users by making the text invisible to the default view pane. Then it requires efficient use of the backup template files, such as normal.dot for MS Word files and XLStart backup directory for MS Excel files, and adopts techniques such as comparing file sizes and turning on the Macro Virus Protection

PROPOSED DETECTION OF HIDDEN MALWARE

Indeed, a review of the history of malware shows a continuous growth thriven in sophistication over the years and traditional malware detections appear insufficient to tackle increasingly sophisticated malware. Scanning engines have major problems as listed below:

1. They are only good in detecting known malware. However, the threat here is that in real life, some malware variants within the same family could reach ten thousands in number and the scanning engines are not good at detecting such evolutionary malware.

2. Currently, systems with one or two terabytes of storage can be purchased for under $1,000 in the market. This has raised an issue to the antivirus engines in terms of the time required in scanning the entire system for signature or patterns.
3. Maintaining day-to-day virus signature updates to the detection engine to ensure the effectiveness has become difficult.

The focus in this section is in applying the proposed detection techniques, which we have implemented as a fully-automated tool to identify hidden malware embedded in the NTFS file system. Since the NTFS is the file system of most computers in use today, attackers and malware creators try to target NTFS to infect more computers worldwide. They are capitalizing on the vulnerabilities of NTFS to hide the malware from AV engines and further exploit the weaknesses of the present digital forensic techniques from being detected. An in-depth forensic examination of NTFS system can answer questions about a malware incident, including how malware was placed on the system and what actions were performed. Similar approach could be adopted to other platforms. This section provides the techniques that can be adopted to detect hidden malware using forensic analysis of deleted files, hidden/ deleted partitions, alternate data streams (ADS), slack space and bad sectors. Similar to such nomenclatures used in NTFS, file systems in other platforms, including smartphones, have terms that require attention, when it comes to detecting hidden malware. Hence, the proposed techniques could be applied to those platforms also. In some cases, the vulnerability could have been addressed in the newer version of the operating system. However, every system has a set of vulnerabilities that malware attackers try to exploit. The first and foremost task is to identify the vulnerabilities present in the platform. In NTFS, we have identified five main vulnerabilities that malware attackers exploit for hiding their new attacks. Once these are discovered, we have experimentally shown that all the hidden malware in a computing device could be unearthed with least human intervention, using our fully-automated system.

Deleted Files

Usually when files are deleted, their information is not removed from the storage device and the actual file contents still remain available. Microsoft Windows, for both file systems NTFS and FAT, simply marks the hard drive space as being available for use by changing one character in the file table so that the file entry will not be displayed. Cybercriminals are taking advantage of this and they are trying to hide their malicious code as a deleted file. One of the digital forensic tasks that we propose is to find and recover the files that have been deleted from the system to check if they contain malicious code.

Hidden/Deleted Partitions

Partitioning is dependent on the OS and not the type of interface on the hard disk [7], Windows OS uses the same partition system, whether the disk uses an AT Attachment interface (ATA/IDE) or Small Computer System Interface (SCSI). This research project is not focusing on the hard disks and types but their basic structures are explored to see how the malware can hide itself as hid-

den data. Many existing techniques have failed to identify malicious code in hidden data of the disk structure. Therefore, it is very important to analyse the volume system, so first we need to investigate the data structure that describes the volumes. When analysing a volume system it is important to check the consistency of partition by checking the start and end sectors.

A volume is a collection of addressable sectors that the users can use for data storage (read and write) and is responsible for the creation of partitions that could be defined as a set of consecutive sectors; Figure 3 provides an example of HDD partition and volume. Volume analysis involves looking at the data structure with partitioning and assembling data in digital storage media devices that are stored when installing Microsoft Windows operating system.

Windows operating system marks a partition as hidden or deleted, but does not delete the actual contents. Hidden partitions are almost useless when hiding information for criminal purposes. However, Master Boot Record (MBR) located in the first block on the drive contains all file systems. The MBR also contains a partition table for each partition that has information about the partition on the drive. Examples of such information are, the primary or logical partitions on the hard disk, and in the windows system, each partition has one or more tables to describe the starting, the ending sector (the length) and also the partition-

Figure 3. Hard disk volume and partition

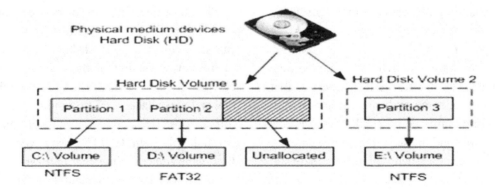

type descriptor. Hence, it is possible for a user to delete the partition table, or modify the partition table. The deleted partitions still remain on the disk just as deleted files/folders do, so it may be possible to recover or reconstruct these partitions to check for malicious code. We propose this technique to detect malware in hidden or deleted partitions.

Alternate Data Streams

Alternate Data Streams (ADS) are a method of hiding information in the Windows NT operating system. In NTFS the primary data stream called $DATA or unnamed data stream, each file has an associated $DATA attribute that describes the content of the file. Alternate Data Streams (ADSs) is more than one $DATA attribute that is associated with a file. In 2005, Symantec reports that there is a marked increase in the use of these streams by cybercriminals in storing their malicious code. It is important to note that the current major countermeasures including detection operations and forensic tools are able to detect and view ADS. Also, data stream attached does not support copying. In other words, the action of moving a file into another file system that does not support ADS will automatically remove any ADS, such as thumb drives or email attachments. Any binary such as malicious code, executables, passwords and secret information can effectively become ADS. However, it is impossible to protect computer against ADS hidden files. Therefore, the investigator has to be aware that ADS may exist on a NTFS image and that ADS may contain hidden information.

We illustrate this ADS feature of hiding information as follows. We created a file, Test.txt of 1 KB in size, after injecting a message 'You can't see me in this Script' in another hidden file, secret.exe and noticed that the file size of sample. txt did not increase. Moreover, this file was not visible with command prompt like DIR, or Task Manager, or even by using the Windows Explorer.

```
C:\>echo You can't see me in this
Script>sample.txt:secret.txt
```

ADS not only works with files, but also with directories. In the example below we created a new folder by name FolderTest with 0KB in size:

```
C:\>md FolderTest
C:\>cd FolderTest C:\ FolderTest>echo
Hide in FolderTest>:secret.txt
```

Same as the first example, the folder size was still 0KB and did not increase at all. In order to view the hidden part in both examples above, since we had previous knowledge of the names of the hidden file and directory, the following commands were used:

```
C:\>notepad sample.txt:secret.txt
C:\FolderTest> notepad:secret.txt
```

In addition to the above hiding techniques of ADS, streams can be executed or be used to hide executables behind another file, as shown in the example below:

```
C:\WINDOWS>echo Test>File.txt
```

Next we attached an EXE behind notepad. exe as follows:

```
C:\WINDOWS> type notepad.exe> File.
txt:Script.exe
```

Again, the Windows executable file notepad. exe did not increase the size of File.txt. Now to run our Script.exe

```
C:\WINDOWS> start .\File.txt: Script.
exe
```

Since novice computer users are not aware of NTFS streams and the hiding techniques illustrated above, this NTFS stream feature is being misused by cybercriminals to hide malicious code in the $DATA attributes. Furthermore, the size of the file does not increase, no matter how large is the stream. Just as we had an executable file attached or hooked to a harmless file, a malicious file could be attached using this technique. This provides a stealthy way for malware to hide itself in a computer system. Hence, it has been reported that the Malware using streams to infect computer machines are commonly used executables such as W2k.stream. Hence, a combination of modern countermeasures such as anti-virus engines and forensic tools are required to scan for malware in all Windows data streams (Berghel & Brajkovska, 2004).

Slack Space

Master File Table (MFT) entry in NTFS is 1KB in size. Slack space is the area of the cluster that was not fully overwritten by a recent file. The content can reside in the MFT if the size is less than 700 bytes, otherwise it will store the content in an external cluster. In addition, since the Windows operating system does not zero the slack space, it becomes a vehicle to hide data, especially in $Boot file. Such limitations in NTFS have led to attackers using different techniques such as disguising file names, hiding attributes and deleting files to intrude the system.

Since NTFS stores all events that take place on a computer system, there is a huge amount of data analysis required while scanning the entire NTFS disk image for forensic purposes. From a preliminary study, any information hidden in the slack space will be revealed once the image is examined by modern tool kits. However, it takes an enormous amount of time to analyse the data in the entire hard disk image.

Bad Clusters

MFT entry $BadClus contains a list of bad clusters on the drive to ensure the exclusion of a cluster

that may cause data loss. When there is a read or write error on a drive, NTFS makes a notification in $BadClus metafile of the cluster number containing the failed sector. NTFS flags each sector in the cluster as 'bad' when corrupted data is found on a cluster of sectors. Also, NTFS flags each sector in the cluster as 'in use' within the $Bitmap metadata file. This stores 1 bit indicating whether a cluster is free or in use, so that the bad sector does not get reused.

We performed an experiment to image a drive that contains bad clusters into another new drive. We found that the bad cluster file $BadClus also gets copied into the new drive. Hence, clusters on the new drive are marked as bad when in fact they are not. Since there is no documentation from Microsoft about metadata files, most modern tools aid users in identifying bad clusters and even allow users to edit metadata file system. Cybercriminals exploit this to hide malicious code by marking it as bad cluster and this is important for forensic analysis.

INFORMATION SECURITY GOVERNANCE PLAN

In this section, we describe a plan for developing, implementing and continuously reforming malware forensic techniques based on the investigations conducted in this research and reported in earlier sections of the chapter. Such a plan would serve as a guideline for information security governance, with a view to address the recent trends in hidden malware attacks witnessed globally.

Based on our proposed techniques for the digital forensic investigation described earlier, we have derived the following steps that form an information security governance plan.

- **Step 1: Policy and Procedure Development:** In this step, suitable tools that are needed in the digital scene are determined as part of administrative considerations. All aspects of policy and procedure development are considered to determine the mission statement, skills and knowledge, funding, personal requirement, evidence handling and support from management.

- **Step 2: Hard Disk Acquisition:** This step involves forensic duplication that could be achieved by obtaining NTFS image of the original disk using DD tool command. This step is for obtaining sector-by-sector mirror image of the disk and the output of the image file is created as Image.dd.

- **Step 3: Check the Data Integrity:** This step ensures the integrity of data acquired through reporting of a hash function. We used MD5 tool to guarantee the integrity of the original media and the resulting image file.

- **Step 4: Perform the Digital Forensic Techniques Proposed in Section 6 on the Following Items:**
  - Deleted Files
  - Hidden/Deleted Partitions:
  - Alternate Data Streams
  - Slack Space
  - Bad Clusters

- **Step 5: Physical Presentation:** In this step, all the findings from the forensic investigation are documented. It involves presenting the digital evidence through documentation and reporting procedures.

- **Step 6: Review and Reform of Policy and Procedure:** This step involves performing a review of the results achieved and documented in Step 5 that leads to incremental improvements in the tools and techniques used for computer forensics. Based on the findings of the review, suggestions to reform the policies and procedures are arrived at. Steps 1 to 6 are then carried out again as the next cycle of the information security governance plan.

The above six steps would facilitate towards achieving continuous improvements in the information security governance plan that would be able to address the ever-changing trends in the new malware attacks from time to time.

CONCLUSION

Information hiding is a strategy adopted by malware authors to evade from current commercially available virus scanners, and making computer forensic investigation tedious. Most modern toolkits provide methods for detecting, recovering, and viewing common types of information hiding. However, as these toolkits make detecting the common methods of information hiding more trivial, malware authors employ new and sophisticated obfuscated ways of information hiding to circumvent the current methods and thwart the toolkits' capabilities. They are able to come up with new strategies for exploiting the vulnerabilities in a system. This research work has successfully unearthed and reported these new strategies adopted by malware authors in the context of NTFS platforms. We have grouped these strategies under nine main categories and have identified five specific vulnerabilities or weaknesses in NTFS that are being exploited by malware attackers. Based on our experimental investigations of these weak spots of NTFS, we have proposed and implemented innovative techniques to detect unknown and hidden malware so as to address the zero-day malware problem. These techniques have been developed in a fully-automated system so as to ease the burden of forensic analysis of the systems for detecting hidden malware. Finally, the information security governance plan derived in this chapter serves as a guideline to continuously improve digital forensic policies and procedures to address the ever-changing trends in new malware attacks witnessed now and the future.

ACKNOWLEDGMENT

This work was supported in part by the Australian Federal Police, Westpac Banking Corporation, IBM, the State Government of Victoria and the University of Ballarat.

REFERENCES

Alazab, M., Layton, R., Venkatraman, S., & Watters, P. (2010). *Malware detection based on structural and behavioural features of API calls.* Paper presented at the 1st International Cyber Resilience Conference, Perth Western Australia.

Alazab, M., Venkatraman, S., & Watters, P. (2009a). Effective digital forensic analysis of the NTFS disk image. *Ubiquitous Computing and Communication Journal*, *4*(1), 551–558.

Alazab, M., Venkatraman, S., & Watters, P. (2009b). Digital forensic techniques for static analysis of NTFS images. *Proceedings of International Conference on Information Technology* (ICIT2009), 3-5 June, Jordan. IEEE Computer Society.

Alazab, M., Venkatraman, S., & Watters, P. (2010). *Towards understanding malware behaviour by the extraction of API calls.* Paper presented at the Cybercrime and Trustworthy Computing, Workshop, Ballarat.

Alazab, M., Venkatraman, S., Watters, P., & Alazab, M. (2011). *Zero-day malware detection based on supervised learning algorithms of API call signatures.* Paper presented at the Ninth Australasian Data Mining Conference, Ballarat, VIC.

Alazab, M., Watters, P., Venkatraman, S., Alazab, A., & Alazab, M. (2011). *Cybercrime: Current trends of malware threats.* Paper presented at the International Conference in Global Security Safety and Sustainability / International Conference on e-Democracy, Thessaloniki, Greece.

Alperovitch, D. D. T., Greve, P., Kashyap, R., Marcus, D., Masiello, S., Paget, F., & Schmugar, C. (2011). *McAfee Labs - 2011 threats predictions.* McAfee, Inc.

Baryamureeba, V., & Tushabe, F. (2006). The enhanced digital investigation process model. *Asian Journal of Information Technology*, *5*(7), 790–794.

Berghel, H., & Brajkovska, N. (2004). Digital village: Wading into alternate data streams. *Communications of the ACM*, *47*(4), 21–27.

Carrie, B. (2003). Defining digital forensic examination and analysis tools using abstraction layer. *International Journal of Digital Evidence*, *1*(4), 1–12.

Carrier, B. (2005). *File system forensic analysis* (1st ed.). Addison-Wesley Professional.

Carrier, B. (2006). Risk of live digital forensic analysis. *Communications of the ACM*, *49*(2), 56–61.

Carrier, B., & Spafford, E. (2003). Getting physical with the digital investigation process. *International Journal of Digital Evidence*, *2*(2), 1–20.

Casey, E. (2004). *Digital evidence and computer crime: Forensic science, computers and the Internet* (2nd ed.). London, UK: Academic Press.

Daoud, E. A., Jebril, I., & Zaqaibeh, B. (2008). Computer virus strategies and detection methods. *International Journal of Open Problems in Computer Science and Mathematics*, *1*(2).

Farmer, D., & Venema, W. (2005). *Forensic discovery* (*Vol. 6*). Addison-Wesley Professional.

Felt, A. P., Finifter, M., Chin, E., Hanna, S., & Wagner, D. (2011). A survey of mobile malware in the wild. *Proceedings of the 1st ACM Workshop on Security and Privacy in Smartphones and Mobile Devices*, Chicago, Illinois, USA.

García-Teodoro, P., Díaz-Verdejo, J. E., Maciá-Fernández, G., & Vázquez, E. (2009). Anomaly-based network intrusion detection: Techniques, systems and challenges. *Computers & Security*, *28*(1-2), 18–28.

Ghosh, S., & Turrini, E. (2010). *Cybercrimes: A multidisciplinary analysis*. Springer Verlag.

Golden, G., Richard, I., & Roussev, V. (2006). Next-generation digital forensics. *Communications of the ACM*, *49*(2), 76–80.

Jones, K., Bejtlich, R., & Rose, C. (2005). *Real digital forensics: Computer security and incident response*. Addison-Wesley Professional.

Keane, A. (2008). *The modern law of evidence* (6th ed.). Oxford University Press.

Keizer, G. (2007). *Symantec false positive cripples thousands of Chinese PCs*. Retrieved 3 March, 2010, from http://www.computerworld.com/action/article.do?command=viewArticleBasic&articl-eId=9019958&intsrc=hm_list.

Khan, A., Wiil, U. K., & Memon, N. (2010, 20-20 May). *Digital forensics and crime investigation: Legal issues in prosecution at national level*. Paper presented at the Fifth IEEE International Workshop on Systematic Approaches to Digital Forensic Engineering.

Kruse, W., & Heiser, J. (2001). *Computer forensics: Incident response essentials* (1st ed.). Addison-Wesley Professional.

Palmer, G. (2001). *A road map for digital forensic research report from the First Digital Forensic Research Workshop* (DFRWS). Utica, New York.

Paul, N. (2008). *Disk-level behavioral malware detection. Doctor of Philosophy*. University of Virginia.

Rathgeber, P., Ludovica, D., & Solis, V. (2009). *White paper: An intention based malware attack prevention system*. Ikona

RCFL. (2007). *Annual report for fiscal year 2007*. National program office annual report FY08.

RCFL. (2008). *Annual report for fiscal year 2008*. National program office annual report FY08.

Reith, M., Carr, C., & Gunsch, G. (2002). An examination of digital forensic models. *International Journal of Digital Evidence*, *1*(4), 1–12.

Riley, J., Dampier, D., & Vaughn, R. (2008). Time analysis of hard drive imaging tools. In Ray, I., & Shenoi, S. (Eds.), *IFIP International Federation for Information Processing* (*Vol. 285*, pp. 335–344). Boston, MA: Springer.

Rowlingson, R. (2004). A ten step process for forensic readiness. *International Journal of Digital Evidence*, *2*(3), 1–28.

RSA. (2011). *The current state of cybercrime and what to expect in 2011*. RSA 2011 cybercrime trends report.

Scanlon, M., & Kechadi, M.-T. (2010). Online acquisition of digital forensic evidence. In Goel, S. (Ed.), *Digital forensics and cyber crime* (*Vol. 31*, pp. 122–131). Berlin, Germany: Springer.

Schmidt, A.-D., & Albayrak, S. (2008). *Malicious software for smartphones*. Berlin, Germany: DAI-Labor der Technischen Universität Berlin.

Schmidt, A.-D., Schmidt, H.-G., Batyuk, L., Clausen, J. H., Camtepe, S. A., Albayrak, S., & Yildizli, C. (2009). *Smartphone malware evolution revisited: Android next target?* Paper presented at the Malicious and Unwanted Software (MAL-WARE), 2009 4th International Conference on Montreal, QC.

Shin, Y.-D. (2008, 2-4 Sep). *New digital forensics investigation procedure model*. Paper presented at the Networked Computing and Advanced Information Management, 2008. NCM '08. Fourth International Conference on Gyeongju

Skoudis, E., & Zeltser, L. (2003). *Malware: Fighting malicious code*. Prentice Hall PTR.

Stang, D. (2011). *Detection errors and scanner performance*. Retrieved 1 March, 2011, from http://www.upublish.info

Stolfo, S., Wang, K., & Li, W.-J. (2007). Towards stealthy malware detection. *Malware Detection, 27*, 231–249.

Symantec Enterprise Security. (2002). *W32.Appix. Worm Symantec security response threat writeups*.

Szor, P. (2005). *The art of computer virus research and defense*. Addison-Wesley Professional.

Tudor, A. (2006). *Worm/Letum.A – Worm*. Retrieved 3 June, 2011, from http://www.avira.ro/en/threats/section/details/id_vir/1990/worm_letum.a.html

Vacca, J. (2005). *Computer forensics: Computer crime scene investigation* (2nd ed.). Charles River Media.

Vassil, R. (2009). Hashing and data fingerprinting in digital forensics. *Computing in Science & Engineering, 7*, 49–55.

Venkatraman, S. (2009). *Autonomic context-dependent architecture for malware detection*. Paper presented at the e-Tech 2009, International Conference on e-Technology, Singapore.

Venkatraman, S. (2010). *Self-learning framework for intrusion detection*. Paper presented at the The International Congress on Computer Applications and Computational Science, Singapore.

Venkatraman, S. (2011). A framework for ICT security policy management. In Adomi, E. (Ed.), *Frameworks for ICT policy: Government, social and legal issues* (pp. 1–14). Hershey, PA: IGI Global.

ADDITIONAL READING

Attaluri, S., & McGhee, S. (2009). Profile hidden Markov models and metamorphic virus detection. *Journal in Computer Virology, 5*(2), 151–169.

Aycock, J. (2006). *Computer viruses and malware* (*Vol. 22*). Springer.

Bakshi, A., Dixit, V., & Mehta, K. (2010). Virus: A menace for information security. *Global Journal of Enterprise Information System, 2*(1), 58–70.

Balagani, K. S., & Phoha, V. V. (2010). On the feature selection criterion based on an approximation of multidimensional mutual information. *IEEE Transactions on Pattern Analysis and Machine Intelligence, 32*(7), 1342–1343.

Bilar, D. (2007). Opcodes as predictor for malware. *International Journal of Electronic Security and Digital Forensics, 1*(2), 156–168.

Blum, A. L., & Langley, P. (1997). Selection of relevant features and examples in machine learning. *Artificial Intelligence, 97*(1-2), 245–271.

Chan, K. Y., & Loh, W. Y. (2004). An algorithm for building accurate and comprehensible logistic regression trees. *Journal of Computational and Graphical Statistics, 13*(4).

Chandola, V., Banerjee, A., & Kumar, V. (2009). Anomaly detection: A survey. *ACM Computing Surveys, 41*(3), 1–58.

Choi, S., Park, H., Lim, H.-i., & Han, T. (2009). A static API birthmark for Windows binary executables. *Journal of Systems and Software, 82*(5), 862–873.

Christodorescu, M., & Jha, S. (2004). Testing malware detectors. *ACM SIGSOFT Software Engineering Notes, 29*(4), 34–44.

Cifuentes, C., & Gough, K. J. (1995). Decompilation of binary programs. *Software, Practice & Experience, 25*(7), 811–829.

Cohen, F. (1987). Computer viruses: Theory and experiments. *Computers & Security*, *6*(1), 22–35.

Cohen, F. (1994). *A short course on computer viruses*. New York, NY: John Wiley & Sons, Inc.

Dayhoff, J., & DeLeo, J. (2001). Artificial neural networks opening the Black Box. *Cancer Supplement*, *91*(8), 1615–1635.

Desai, P. (2010). A highly metamorphic virus generator. *International Journal of Multimedia Intelligence and Security*, *1*(4), 402–427.

Eilam, E. (2005). *Reversing: Secrets of reverse engineering* (1st ed.). Wiley.

Frawley, W., Piatetsky-Shapiro, G., & Matheus, C. (1992). Knowledge discovery in databases: An overview. *AI Magazine*, *13*(3), 213–228.

Hand, D. J., Mannila, H., & Smyth, P. (2001). *Principles of data mining*. The MIT press.

Hu, Q., Liu, J., & Yu, D. (2008). Mixed feature selection based on granulation and approximation. *Journal Knowledge-Based Systems*, *21*(4), 294–304.

Jacob, G., Debar, H., & Filiol, E. (2008). Behavioral detection of malware: From a survey towards an established taxonomy. *Journal in Computer Virology*, *4*(3), 251–266.

Jahankhani, H., & Al-Nemrat, A. (2010). Examination of cyber-criminal behaviour. *International Journal of Information Science and Management, Special Issue,* 41 - 48

Kenneally, E. E. (2004). Digital logs--Proof matters. *Digital Investigation*, *1*(2), 94–101.

Kohavi, R., & John, G. H. (1997). Wrappers for feature subset selection. *Artificial Intelligence - Special Issue on Relevance, 97*(1-2), 273-324.

Kolter, J. Z., & Maloof, M. A. (2006). Learning to detect and classify malicious executables in the wild. *Journal of Machine Learning Research, 7,* 2721–2744.

Kruse, W., & Heiser, J. (2001). *Computer forensics: Incident response essentials* (1st ed.). Addison-Wesley Professional.

Landwehr, C. E., Bull, A. R., McDermott, J. P., & Choi, W. S. (1994). A taxonomy of computer program security flaws. *ACM Computing Surveys*, *26*(3), 211–254.

Lawton, G. (2002). Virus wars: Fewer attacks, new threats. *IEEE Computer Society*, *35*(12), 22–24.

MacNamara, S., Cunningham, P., & Byrne, J. (1998). Neural networks for language identification: A comparative study. *Information Processing & Management*, *34*(4), 395–403.

Maria, T. A. (2011). The growing global threat of cyber-crime given the current economic crisis: A study regarding internet malicious activities in Romania. *Acta Universitatis Danubius, Œconomica*, *10*(1), 179–190.

McGraw, G., & Morrisett, G. (2000). Attacking malicious code: A report to the Infosec Research Council. *IEEE Software*, *17*(5), 33–41.

Patcha, A., & Park, J.-M. (2007). An overview of anomaly detection techniques: Existing solutions and latest technological trends. *Computer Networks*, *51*(12), 3448–3470.

Reed, C., & Angel, J. (2007). *Computer law: The law and regulation of information technology*. New York, NY: Oxford University Press, Inc.

Rogers, M., & Seigfried, K. (2004). The future of computer forensics: A needs analysis survey. *Computers & Security*, *23*(1), 12–16.

Sherman, L. W. (2002). Trust and confidence in criminal justice. *NIJ Journal*, March, 23-31.

Singh, N. (2007). Online frauds in banks with phishing. *Journal of Internet Banking and Commerce, 12*(2), 1–27.

Sommer, P. (1999). Intrusion detection systems as evidence. *Computer Networks, 31*(23-24), 2477–2487.

Tang, K., Zhou, M.-T., & Zuo, Z.-H. (2010). An enhanced automated signature generation algorithm for polymorphic malware detection. *Journal of Electronic Science and Technology, 8*(2), 114–121.

Townsend, K. (2010). Anti-virus: A technology update. *Infosecurity, 7*(6), 28–31.

Wang, X. G., Tang, Z., Tamura, H., Ishii, M., & Sun, W. D. (2004). An improved backpropagation algorithm to avoid the local minima problem. *Neurocomputing, 56*, 455–460.

Wong, W., & Stamp, M. (2006). Hunting for metamorphic engines. *Journal in Computer Virology, 2*(3), 211–229.

Xiao, J., Liu, B., & Wang, X. (2007). Exploiting word positional information in Ngram model for Chinese text input method. *Journal of Information and Computing Science, 2*(3), 215–222.

Yanfang, Y., Tao, L., Qingshan, J., & Youyu, W. (2010). CIMDS: Adapting postprocessing techniques of associative classification for malware detection. *IEEE Transactions on Systems, Man and Cybernetics. Part C, Applications and Reviews, 40*(3), 298–307.

KEY TERMS AND DEFINITIONS

Alternate Data Streams (ADS): Is a feature of NTFS file system supported by all versions of Windows started in Windows NT 3.1.through the current version, Windows 7. The NTFS file system the primary data stream called $DATA, each file has an associated $DATA attribute that describes the content of the file. ADS is more than one $DATA attribute that is associated with a file.

Code Obfuscation: Is an evasion method used to morph the program code in such a way as to make it hard to read and difficult to understand without changing the main goal of the program. Some of the common code obfuscation techniques used are polymorphism, metamorphism and packing.

Computer Forensic: Is the science of preserving, identifying, extracting, analysing and documenting evidence found in computing devices at crime scenes so that this evidence may be used in a court of law. It also answers questions and attempts to provide full descriptions of a digital crime scene investigation.

Cybercrime: Is an unlawful activity using computer, devices and the Internet to send or receive data for criminal purposes such as financial gains, identity theft, denial of service, etc.

Hidden Malware: Is a special type of malware that is stealthy and hides itself in the computer from being detected by any countermeasure such as antivirus engine.

Intrusion Detection: Is the process of identifying if an unknown party has gained illegal access to a computer without the permission of the authorised user of the computer.

Malware: Is a computer program designed to perform illegal activities that cause damage and affect the integrity and functionality of digital electronic devices. Malware (*Mal*icious Software) includes viruses, worms, Trojans, exploits, backdoors, keystroke loggers, rootkits, spyware, and spam. These terms are coined based on the functionality and behavior of the malware.

Master File Table (MFT): Is the cores of NTFS file system, it contains information details of every file and folder on the volume, this information takes the form of two attributes an attribute header and an attribute content to store information, detailed information about a file or directory such as the type, size, date/time of creation, date/time of most recent modification and author identity. MFT is 1 KB in size.

Portable Executable (PE): Is the standard executable format for all versions of the operating system. It consists of headers and data sections that help to figure out what are their dependents and tell the dynamic linker how to map the file into memory, such as EXE, NE, ELF, EFI and DLL.

Signature Based Detection: Is signature matching process used by traditional Anti-virus engines to scans the system in various locations for characteristic byte sequences or signature that match with the one in the database and declares existence of malware and subsequently blocking its access to the system.

Compilation of References

Abu-Musa, A. (2010). Information security governance in Saudi organizations: An empirical study. *Information Management & Computer Security*, *18*(4), 226–276.

Abu-Musa, A. A. (2008). Exploring information technology governance (ITG) in developing countries: An empirical study. *The International Journal of Digital Accounting Research*, *9*, 99–126.

Aggelis, V. G. (2005). *The bible of e-banking*. Athens, Greece: New Technologies Publications. (in Greek)

Akinci, S., Aksoy, S., & Atilgan, E. (2004). Adoption of Internet banking among sophisticated consumer segments in an advanced developing country. *International Journal of Bank Marketing*, *22*(3), 212–232.

Alazab, M., Layton, R., Venkatraman, S., & Watters, P. (2010). *Malware detection based on structural and behavioural features of API calls*. Paper presented at the 1st International Cyber Resilience Conference, Perth Western Australia.

Alazab, M., Venkatraman, S., & Watters, P. (2009b). Digital forensic techniques for static analysis of NTFS images. *Proceedings of International Conference on Information Technology* (ICIT2009), 3-5 June, Jordan. IEEE Computer Society.

Alazab, M., Venkatraman, S., & Watters, P. (2010). *Towards understanding malware behaviour by the extraction of API calls*. Paper presented at the Cybercrime and Trustworthy Computing, Workshop, Ballarat.

Alazab, M., Venkatraman, S., Watters, P., & Alazab, M. (2011). *Zero-day malware detection based on supervised learning algorithms of API call signatures*. Paper presented at the Ninth Australasian Data Mining Conference, Ballarat, VIC.

Alazab, M., Watters, P., Venkatraman, S., Alazab, A., & Alazab, M. (2011). *Cybercrime: Current trends of malware threats*. Paper presented at the International Conference in Global Security Safety and Sustainability / International Conference on e-Democracy, Thessaloniki, Greece.

Alazab, M., Venkatraman, S., & Watters, P. (2009a). Effective digital forensic analysis of the NTFS disk image. *Ubiquitous Computing and Communication Journal*, *4*(1), 551–558.

Allen, J. (2005). *Governing for enterprise security* (Tech. Rep.). Pittsburgh, PA: Carnegie Mellon University. (CMU/SEI-2005-TN-023)

Allen, J. (2007). *All characteristics of effective security governance*, 2007.

Allen, J. H., & Westby, J. R. (2007). *Governing for enterprise security implementation guide*. Software Engineering Institute - CERT.

Alperovitch, D. D. T., Greve, P., Kashyap, R., Marcus, D., Masiello, S., Paget, F., & Schmugar, C. (2011). *McAfee Labs - 2011 threats predictions*. McAfee, Inc.

Andermann, H. (2008). Microsoft v. Commission and the interoperability issue. *European Intellectual Property Review*, 395.

Angelakopoulos, G., & Mihiotis, A. (2011). E-banking: Challenges and opportunities in the Greek banking sector. *Electronic Commerce Research*, *11*, 1–23.

Aplin, T., & Davis, J. (2009). *Intellectual property law. Text, cases and materials*. Oxford, UK: Oxford University Press.

Arshad, N. H., May-Lin, Y., Mohamed, A., & Affandi, S. (2007). Inherent risks in ICT outsourcing project. *Proceeding of the 8th WSEAS Conference, 8*(4), 141 – 146. Retrieved July 20, 2011, from http://www.wseas.us/elibrary/transactions/economics/2007/24-107.pdf

Balz, S. D., & Hance, O. (1996). Privacy and the Internet: Intrusion, surveillance and personal data. *International Review of Law Computers & Technology, 10*(2), 219–230.

Baryamureeba, V., & Tushabe, F. (2006). The enhanced digital investigation process model. *Asian Journal of Information Technology, 5*(7), 790–794.

Basel Committee on Banking Supervision. (2003). *Risk management principles for electronic banking.* Retrieved July 20, 2011, from http://www.bis.org/publ/bcbs98.pdf

Basel Committee on Banking Supervision. (2005). *Outsourcing in financial services.* Retrieved July 20, 2011, from http://www.bis.org/publ/joint12.pdf

Baten, M. A., & Kamil, A. A. (2010). E-banking of economical prospects in Bangladesh. *Journal of Internet Banking and Commerce, 15*(2).

Berghel, H., & Brajkovska, N. (2004). Digital village: Wading into alternate data streams. *Communications of the ACM, 47*(4), 21–27.

Beunen, A. (2007). *Protection for databases: The European database directive and its effects in the Netherlands, France and the United Kingdom.* Nijmegen, The Netherlands: Wolf Legal Publishers.

Bignami, F. (2007A). *The US privacy act in corporative perspective,* (p. 7). Paper presented at the European Parliament Public seminar PNR/SWIFT/Safa Habour, Are Transatlantic Data Protected? Retrieved August 25, 2011, from http://europarl.europa.eu/hearings/20070326/libe/bignami_en.pdf

Bignami, F. (2007B). European versus American liberty: A comparative privacy analysis of antiterrorism data mining. *Boston College Law Review. Boston College. Law School, 48,* 609–698.

Biri, K., & Tentra, G. M. (2004). *Corporate information security governance in Swiss private banking.* Master's Thesis University of Zurich, Retrieved July 20, 2011, from http://www.isaca.ch/files/DO7_Diplomarbeiten/Diplom_CorporateInfSecGovernance_E.pdf

Bodeau, D. (1994). System-of-systems security engineering. In *Proceedings of 10th Annual Computer Security Applications Conference* (pp. 228–235). Los Alamitos, CA: IEEE Computer Society.

Bornkamm, J. (2000). *Time for a European copyright code.* Retrieved August 25, 2011, from www.europa.eu.int/comm/internal_market/copyright/docs/conference/2000-07-strasbourg-proceedings_en.pdf

Borst, W. N. (1997). *Construction of engineering ontologies for knowledge sharing and reuse.* Thesis, University of Twente.

Bowen, P. L., Cheung, M. D., & Rohde, F. H. (2007). Enhancing IT governance practices: A model and case study of an organization's efforts. *International Journal of Accounting Information Systems, 8*(3), 191–221.

Bowen, P., Chew, E., & Hash, J. (2007). *Information security guide for government executives.* National Institute of Standards and Technology.

Bowen, P., Hash, J., & Wilson, M. (2006). Information security governance. In *Information security handbook: A guide for managers.* National Institute of Standards and Technology.

Brachman, R. J., & Levesque, H. J. (2004). *Knowledge representation and reasoning.* San Francisco, CA: Morgan Kaufmann Publishers Inc.

Brotby, K. (2009). *Information security governance: A practical development and implementation approach.* Wiley.

Brown, W. (2006). *IT governance, architectural competency, and the Vasa.* Emerald Group Publishing Limited.

BSA. (2003). *Information security governance: Toward a framework for action.*

BSI-Std. BSI Standard 100-1. (2006). *Information security management systems.* Bonn, Germany: Bundesamt für Sicherheit in der Informationstechnik.

Bundesamt fr Sicherheit in der Informationstechnik (BSI). (n.d.). *IT baseline protection manual standard security safeguards.* Retrieved from http://www.bsi.bund.de

Business Software Alliance. (2003). *Eight annual BSA global software piracy study: Trends in software piracy 1994-2002.* Retrieved August 25, 2011, from http://www.bsa.org/country/Research%20and%20Statistics/~/media/Files/Research%20Papers/GlobalStudy/2003/IPR_GlobalStudy2003.ashx

Bygrave, L., & Koelman, K. (1998). *Privacy, data protection and copyright: Their interaction in the context of electronic copyright management systems.* IViR Publications. Retrieved August 25, 2011, from http://www.ivir.nl/publicaties/koelman/privreportdef.pdf

Cadbury, A. (1992). *The financial aspects of corporate governance.* London, UK: Gee.

Campbell, J. P. (1997). Speaker recognition: A tutorial. *Proceedings of the IEEE, 85*(9), 1437–1462.

Carrie, B. (2003). Defining digital forensic examination and analysis tools using abstraction layer. *International Journal of Digital Evidence, 1*(4), 1–12.

Carrier, B. (2005). *File system forensic analysis* (1st ed.). Addison-Wesley Professional.

Carrier, B. (2006). Risk of live digital forensic analysis. *Communications of the ACM, 49*(2), 56–61.

Carrier, B., & Spafford, E. (2003). Getting physical with the digital investigation process. *International Journal of Digital Evidence, 2*(2), 1–20.

Casey, E. (2004). *Digital evidence and computer crime: Forensic science, computers and the Internet* (2nd ed.). London, UK: Academic Press.

Cavoukian, A., & Tapscott, D. (1997). *Who knows: Safeguarding your privacy in a networked world.* New York, NY: McGraw-Hill.

Central Bank of Egypt. (2003). *Egyptian banking sector reform policy: Areas of future actions.* Retrieved September 4, 2010, from http://www.cbe.org.eg/public/Egyptian%20banking%20reform%20policy_WB.doc

Chander, A., Gelman, L., & Radin, M. J. (2008). *Securing privacy in the Internet age.* Stanford, CA: Stanford University Press.

Chen, X. (2009). The challenges and strategies of commercial bank in developing e-banking business. In *Proceedings of the International Conference ICHCC 2009-ICTMF 2009,* Sanya, Hainan Island, China, December 13-14, 2009, (pp. 68-74).

Chew, E., Swanson, M., Stine, K., Bartol, N., Brown, A., & Robinson, W. (2008). *Performance measurement guide for information security* (Tech. Rep.). Gaithersburg, MD: National Institute of Standards and Technology. (NIST Special Publication 800-55 Revision 1)

Cohen, J. E. (1996). A right to read anonymously: A closer look at copyright management in cyberspace. *Connecticut Law Review, 28,* 981–991.

Cohen, J. E. (2003). DRM and privacy. *Berkeley Technology Law Journal, 18,* 575–617. Retrieved August 25, 2011 from http://www.law.georgetown.edu/faculty/jec/drmandprivacy.pdf

Committee of Sponsoring Organizations of the Treadway Commission. (2004). *Enterprise risk management — Integrated framework.* Executive Summary, September. Retrieved July 20, 2011, from http://www.coso.org/documents/COSO_ERM_ExecutiveSummary.pdf

Conklin, A., & White, G. B. (2006). E-government and cyber security: The role of cyber security exercises. *Proceedings of the 39th Annual Hawaii International Conference on System Sciences.*

Corporate Governance Task Force (CGTF). (2004). Corporate governance task force report: Information security governance - A call to action. Retrieved July 20, 2011, from http://www.cyber.st.dhs.gov/docs/Information%20Security%20Governance-%20A%20Call%20to%20Action%20%282004%29.pdf

Corporate Governance Task Force. (2004). *Information security governance: A call to action.*

Corporate Information Security Working Group (CISWG). (2004). *Report of the best practices and metrics team.* Retrieved July 20, 2011, from http://net.educause.edu/ir/library/pdf/CSD3661.pdf

Crossroad. (2010). *Updated gap analysis report: A participative roadmap for ICT research in electronic governance and policy modelling.*

Da Veiga, A., & Eloff, J. H. P. (2007). An information security governance framework. *Information Systems Management, 24*(4), 361–372.

Dahlberg, T., & Kivijärvi, H. (2006). An integrated framework for IT governance and the development and validation of an assessment instrument. *Proceedings of the 39th Hawaii International Conference on System Sciences.*

Daniel, E. (1999). Provision of electronic banking in the UK and Republic of Ireland. *International Journal of Bank Marketing, 17*(2), 72–83.

Daoud, E. A., Jebril, I., & Zaqaibeh, B. (2008). Computer virus strategies and detection methods. *International Journal of Open Problems in Computer Science and Mathematics, 1*(2).

Daugman, J. (2004). How iris recognition works? *IEEE Transactions on Circuits and Systems for Video Technology, 14*(1), 21–30.

De Hert, P., & Bellanova, R. (2008). *Data protection from a transatlantic perspective: The EU and US towards an international data protection agreement?* Study requested by European Parliament, (PE 408.320). Retrieved August 25, 2011, from http://www.europarl.europa.eu/studies

De Hert, P., & Gutwirth, S. (2006). Privacy data protection and law enforcement. Opacity of the individual and transparency of power. In Claes, E., Duff, A., & Gutwirth, S. (Eds.), *Privacy and the criminal law* (pp. 61–104). Antwerp, Belgium: Intersentia.

de Oliveira Alves, G. A., Rust da Costa Carmo, L. F., & Ribeiro Dutra de Almeida, A. C. (2006). *Enterprise security governance: A practical guide to implement and control information security governance.* Business-Driven IT Management.

Debar, H., Kheir, N., Cuppens-Boulahia, N., & Cuppens, F. (2010). Service dependencies in information systems security. In *Proceedings of the 5th International Conference on Mathematical Methods, Models and Architectures for Computer Network Security (MMM-ACNS'10)* (pp. 1–20). Berlin, Germany: Springer-Verlag.

Dellit, C. (2002). Governance and the emerging salience of technology. *Software, October,* 19–24

Derclaye, E. (2008). *The legal protection of databases: A comparative analysis.* Cheltenham, UK: Edward Elgar Publishing.

Dewan, R., & Seidmann, A. (2001). Current issues in e-banking. *Communications of the ACM, 44*(6), 31–329.

Dreier, T., & Hugenholtz, P. B. (2006). *Concise European copyright law. Alphen aan den Rijn.* The Netherlands: Kluwer Law International.

Duran, L., Krieger, M. J., Maistry, U., Manasterski, A., Whetton, L., et al. (2008). *Technological measures to prevent the illegal uses of intellectual property rights.* MAS-IP Diploma Papers & Research Reports. Retrieved August 25, 2011, from http://e-collection.library.ethz.ch/eserv/eth:2193/eth-2193-01.pdf

Dusollier, S. (2005). Technological as an imperative for regulating copyright: From the public exploitation to the private use of the work. *European Intellectual Property Review, 27*(6), 201–205.

Egypt State Information Service. (2009). The banking sector in Egypt. Retrieved August 30, 2010, from http://www.sis.gov.eg/En/Economy/banking/bankingsector/050401000000000001.htm

Electronic Privacy Information Center – EPIC. (2007). *Privacy and human rights. An international survey of privacy laws and developments.* Washington, DC: Author. Retrieved August 25, 2011, from https://www.privacyinternational.org/article/phr2006-foreward

El-Morshedy, R. M. (2008). *Technology transfer of information systems auditing and control standards.* Unpublished thesis, Cairo University, Faculty of Computers & Information, Information Systems Department.

ENISA. (2006). *Risk management: Implementation principles and inventories for risk management/risk assessment method and tools.* European Network and information Security Agency - Technical Department Heraklion, Greece. Retrieved July 20, 2011, from http://www.enisa.europa.eu/rmra/files/D1_Inventory_of_Methods_Risk_Management_Final.pdf

Eriksson, A., & Wretling, P. (1997). How flexible is the human voice? A case study of mimicry. In *Proceedings of the European Conference on Speech Technology,* (pp. 1043–1046). Rhodes, 1997.

European Commission. (2003, May 15). *First report from the European Commission on the implementation of the Data Protection Directive*, (p. 15). Brussels, Belgium: Author. Retrieved August 25, 2011, from http://europa.eu/legislation_summaries/information_society/data_protection/l14012_en.htm

European Commission. DG Internal Market and Services. (2005). *First evaluation of directive 96/9/EC on the legal protection of databases.* Brussels, Belgium: Author. Retrieved August 25, 2011, from http://ec.europa.eu/internal_market/copyright/docs/databases/evaluation_report_en.pdf

European Patent Office. (2008). *Patents for software?* Retrieved August 25, 2011, from http://www.epo.org/news-issues/issues/computers/software.html

Fancourt, C. L., Bogoni, L., Hanna, J., Guo, Y., Wildes, R. P., Takahashi, N., & Jain, U. (2005). Iris recognition at a distance. In *Fifth International Conference on Audio- and Video-based Biometric Person Authentication* (AVBPA), (pp. 1–13). Rye Brook, USA, July 2005.

Farmer, D., & Venema, W. (2005). *Forensic discovery* (*Vol. 6*). Addison-Wesley Professional.

Federal Financial Institutions Examination Council (FFIEC). (2004). *Outsourcing technology services.* Retrieved July 20, 2011, from http://www.enpointe.com/assets/pdf/Outsourcing_Booklet.pdf

Federal Financial Institutions Examination Council (FFIEC). (2005). *Authentication in an Internet banking environment.* Retrieved July 20, 2011, from http://www.ffiec.gov/pdf/authentication_guidance.pdf

Federal Office for Information Security (BSI). (2007). *IT security guidelines.* Retrieved August 12, 2011, from https://www.bsi.bund.de

Felt, A. P., Finifter, M., Chin, E., Hanna, S., & Wagner, D. (2011). A survey of mobile malware in the wild. *Proceedings of the 1st ACM Workshop on Security and Privacy in Smartphones and Mobile Devices*, Chicago, Illinois, USA.

Financial Action Task Force (FATF). (1996). *The forty recommendations of the financial action task force on money laundering.* Retrieved July 20, 2011, from http://www.fincen.gov/news_room/rp/files/fatf_40_recommendations.pdf

Frankland, J. (2008). IT security metrics: Implementation and standards compliance. *Network Security, 6*, 6–9.

Gandhi, S., Gorod, A., & Sauser, B. (2011). A systemic approach to managing risks of SoS. In *Proceedings of 2011 IEEE International Systems Conference (SysCon'11)* (pp. 412–416). Piscataway, NJ: IEEE.

Ganley, P. (2002). Access to the individual: Digital rights management systems and the intersection of informational and decisional privacy interest. *Journal of Law and Information Technology, 10*(3), 241–293.

García-Teodoro, P., Díaz-Verdejo, J. E., Maciá-Fernández, G., & Vázquez, E. (2009). Anomaly-based network intrusion detection: Techniques, systems and challenges. *Computers & Security, 28*(1-2), 18–28.

Gaster, J. L. (2006). Das urheberrechtliche Territorialitätsprinzip aus Sicht des Europäischen Gemeinschaftsrechts. *Zietschrift für Urheber- und Medienrecht (ZUM), 1*, 8-14.

Gaster, J. L. (1999). *Der Rechtsschutz von Datenbanken: Kommentar zur Richtlinie 96/9/ EG: mit Erläuterungen zur Umsetzung in das deutsche und österreichische Recht.* Köln, Germany: Heymans Verlag.

Geiger, C. (2009). Intellectual property shall be protected!? Art. 17(2) of the charter of fundamental rights of the European Union: A mysterious provision with an unclear scope. *European Intellectual Property Preview, 31*, 113–117.

Generally Accepted Information Security Principles, Version 3.0 (GAISP). (2003). Retrieved July 20, 2011, from http://all.net/books/standards/GAISP-v30.pdf

Gervais, D. (2008). *The TRIPS agreement: Drafting history and analysis.* London, UK: Sweet & Maxwell.

Ghidini, G., & Arezzo, E. (2005). Patent and copyright paradigms vis-à-vis derivative innovation: The case of computer programs. *International Review of Intellectual Property and Competition Law, 36*, 159–170.

Ghosh, S., & Turrini, E. (2010). *Cybercrimes: A multi-disciplinary analysis.* Springer Verlag.

Gikandi, J. W., & Bloor, C. (2010). Adoption and effectiveness of electronic banking in Kenya. *Electronic Commerce Research and Applications, 9*, 277–282.

Ginsburg, J. (1999). Copyright legislation for the digital millennium. *VLA Journal of Law & the Arts, 23*, 137–143.

Golden, G., Richard, I., & Roussev, V. (2006). Next-generation digital forensics. *Communications of the ACM, 49*(2), 76–80.

Goldstein, P. (2001). *International copyright*. Oxford, UK: Oxford University Press.

Gotzen, F. (2007). *The industrial property right protection of the producer of a database. Some reflections in the future of European and Japanese protection schemes*. Tokyo, Japan: Institute for Intellectual Property.

Gotzen, F., & Minero, G. (2011). Comentario a la estrategia de la Comisión Europea para 2011-2014 en materia de propiedad intelectual, "Un mercado común para los derechos de propiedad intelectual. *Revista de Propiedad Intelectual, 38*, 115–126.

Gray, H. (2004). Is there a relationship between IT governance and corporate governance? Unpublished Master's thesis, UK.

Gregory, H. J. (2009). *Comparison of corporate governance guidelines and codes of best practice*. New York, NY: Weil, Gotshal & Manges.

Gruber, T. (1993). A translation approach to portable ontology specifications. *Knowledge Acquisition, 5*(2), 199–220.

Gruschke, B. (1998). Integrated event management: Event correlation using dependency graphs. In *Proceedings of Ninth Annual IFIP/IEEE International Workshop on Distributed Systems: Operations and Management (DSOM'98)*. Retrieved February 9, 2012, from http://www.nm.ifi.lmu.de/pub/ Publikationen/grus98a/PDF-Version/grus98a.pdf

Guldentops, E. (2002). Knowing the environment: top five IT issues. *Information Systems Control Journal, 4*, 15–16.

Hadden, L. B. (2002). *An investigation of the audit committee and its role in monitoring information technology risks*. D.B.A., Nova Southeastern University, AAT 3074875.

Halpern, S. W. (2009). *Copyright law. Protection of original expression*. Durham, NC: Carolina Academic Press.

Hamaker, S. (2003). Spotlight on governance. *Information Systems Control Journal, 1*, 15–19.

Hammond, A., Adriaanse, A., Rodenburg, E., Bryant, D., & Woodward, R. (1995). *Environmental indicators: A systematic approach to measuring and reporting on environmental policy performance in the context of sustainable development*. Washington, DC: World Resources Institute.

Hardy, G. (2006). Using IT governance and COBIT to deliver value with IT and respond to legal, regulatory and compliance challenges. *Information Security Technical Report, 11*, 55–61.

Harrison, W. R. (1981). *Suspect documents, their scientific examination*. Nelson-Hall Publishers.

Heschl, J. (2004). COBIT in relation to other international standards. *Journal of Information Systems Control, 4.*

Holmquist, E. (2008). *Which security governance framework is the best fit?* TechTarget ANZ Australia. Retrieved July 20, 2011, from http://searchcio.techtarget.com.au/ articles/24787-Whichsecuritygovernanceframework-is the-best-fit-.htm

Holvast, J., Madsen, W., & Roth, P. (2001). *The global encyclopedia of data protection regulation*. The Hague, The Netherlands: Kluwer Law International.

Hong, L., Jain, A. K., & Pankanti, S. (1999). Can multibiometrics improve performance? In *Proceedings of IEEE Workshop on Automatic Identification Advanced Technologies* (AutoID), (pp. 59–64). New Jersey, USA, October 1999.

Houmba, S. H., Franqueira, V. N. L., & Engum, E. A. (2010). Quantifying security risk level from CVSS estimates of frequency and impact. *Journal of Systems and Software, 83*, 1622–1634.

Hugenholtz, P. B. (2005). *The database right file*. IViR Publications. Retrieved August 25, 2011, from http://www.ivir.nl/files/database/index.html

Humphreys, E. (2008). Information security management standards: Compliance, governance and risk management. *Information Security Technical Report, 13.*

Hustinx, P. (2011A). *A citizen's agenda for fundamental rights*. Paper presented at the ETICA Conference on Ethics and Governance of Future and Emerging ICTs, European Parliament. Retrieved August 25, 2011, from http://www.edps.europa.eu/EDPSWEB/edps/cache/off/ EDPS/Publications/SpeechArticle/SA2011.

Hustinx, P. (2011B). *Data protection and privacy.* Paper presented at the International Data Protection Conference. Retrieved August 25, 2011, from http://www.edps.europa.eu/EDPSWEB/edps/cache/off/EDPS/Publications/SpeechArticle/SA2011.

Hustinx, P. (2011C). Data protection -A critical success factor for other important policy facts. *Engineering & Technology Magazine*, 35-38.

IFAC. (2004). *Enterprise governance: Getting the balance right.* International Federation of Accountants, Professional Accountants in Business Committee. Retrieved July 20, 2011, from www.ifac.org/Members/DownLoads/EnterpriseGovernance.pdf

Insley, R., Al-Abed, H., & Fleming, T. (2003). *What is the definition of e-banking?* Retrieved July 20, 2011, from http://www.bankersonline.com/technology/gurus_tech081803d.html

International Biometric Group. (2005). Independent testing of iris recognition technology: Final report. Retrieved from http://www.biometricgroup.com/reports/ public/ITIRT.html

International Organization for Standardization. (2005). *ISO17799:2005.* Retrieved from http://www.iso.org

International Standards Organization (ISO). (2005). *ISO/IEC 27001:2005 Information technology-security techniques- Information security management systems-Requirements.* Retrieved August 12, 2011, from www.iso.org

ISACA. (2009). An introduction to the business model for information security. Retrieved August 12, 2011, from www.isaca.org

ISO (International Organization for Standardization), & IEC (International Electrotechnical Commission). (2005). *ISO/IEC 17799:2005 Information technology – Security techniques – Code of practice for information security management.*

ISO 15489-1:2001. (2001). *International standard, information and documentation – Records management, part 1: General.* Retrieved July 20, 2011, from http://www.javeriana.edu.co/archivo/07_eventos/preservaciondigital/memorias/index_archivos/norma/iso_15489-1.pdf

ISO 15489-2:2001. (2001). *Technical report, information and documentation – Records management, part 2: Guidelines.* Retrieved July 20, 2011, from http://www.javeriana.edu.co/archivo/07_eventos/preservaciondigital/memorias/index_archivos/norma/iso_15489-2.pdf

ISO 17799 News. (2006). *ISO27000 newsletter, 14.* Retrieved August 12, 2011 from http://www.molemag.net/16.htm

ISO 27001 Security. (2011). *ISO27k FAQ quick links.* Retrieved August 12, 2011 from http://www.iso27001security.com/html/faq.html

ISO/IEC 20000-2:2005. (2005). *ISO/IEC.* Retrieved from www.iso.org

ISO/IEC 27000 doc_iso27000_all.pdf. (2011). *ISO International Organization for Standardization.* Retrieved from http://www.iso27000.es/download/doc_iso27000_all.pdf

ISO/IEC 27002:2005. (2005). *ISO International Organization for Standardization.*

ISO/IEC 27004:2009. (2009). *Introduction to ISO 27004.* The ISO 27000 Directory. Retrieved July 20, 2011, from http://www.27000.org/iso-27004.htm

ISO/IEC 27005:2011. (2011). *ISO International Organization for Standardization.* Retrieved from http://www.iso.org/iso/iso_catalogue/catalogue_tc/catalogue_detail.htm?csnumber=56742 ISO/IEC 27006:2011. (2011). *ISO/IEC 27006:2011. Information technology. Security techniques. Requirements for bodies providing audit and certification of information security management systems Edition: 2. JTC 1/SC 27 ICS: 35.040.*

ISO/IEC 38500:2008. (2008). International standard, corporate governance of information technology. Retrieved July 20, 2011, from http://webstore.iec.ch/preview/info_isoiec38500%7Bed1.0%7Den.pdf

ISO/IEC 38500:2008. (2011). *Corporate governance of information technology.* Retrieved from www.iso.org: www.iso.org

ISO/IEC. (2008). *ISO/IEC 38500:2008 Corporate governance of information technology.*

ISO/TC-Std. 31000:2008. (2008). *Risk management-Principles and guidelines on implementation* (draft). International Organization for Standardization (ISO), Switzerland, 2008.

ISO-Std. ISO/IEC 27001:2005(E). (2005). *Information technology - Security techniques - Information security management systems - Requirements.* International Organization for Standardization (ISO), Switzerland, 2005.

ISO-Std. ISO/IEC 27005:2008. (2008). *Information technology – Security techniques - Information security risk management.* International Organization for Standardization (ISO), Switzerland, 2008.

ISO-Std. ISO/IEC TR 13335-1. (1996). *Information technology - Guidelines for the management of IT security - Concepts and models for IT security.* International Organization for Standardization (ISO), Switzerland, 1996.

ISPL, Information Services Procurement Library. (2011). Retrieved from http://projekte.fast.de/ISPL/

IT Governance Institute (ITGI). (2000). *Board briefing on IT governance.* Retrieved from www.itgi.org

IT Governance Institute. (2005). *Control objectives for information and related technologies* (COBIT). Retrieved from http://www.isaca.org/KnowledgeCenter/COBIT/Pages/Overview.aspx

ITGI. (2006). *Information security governance: Guidance for boards of directors and executive management* (2nd ed.). Rolling Meadows, IL: IT Governance Institute.

ITGI. (2006a). *COBIT mapping to ISO/IEC 17799:2000 with COBIT.*

ITGI. (2006b). *Information security governance: Guidance for boards of directors and executive management* (2nd ed.).

ITGI. (2007). *COBIT 4.1 excerpt: Executive summary – Framework.* Retrieved July 20, 2011, from http://www.isaca.org/KnowledgeCenter/cobit/Documents/COBIT4.pdf

ITGI. (2007). *Control objectives for information and related technology (COBIT 4.1).*

ITGI. (2008a). *Governance of investments, the val IT framework 2.0.*

ITGI. (2008b). *Information security governance: Guidance for information security managers.*

ITGI. IT Governance Institute. (2007). *COBIT 4.1 en Español.* Retrieved from http://www.isaca.org/

Jain, A. K., Bolle, R., & Pankanti, S. (Eds.). (1999). *Biometrics: Personal identification in networked society* (pp. 87–102). London, UK: Kluwer Academic Publishers.

Jain, A. K., Flynn, P., & Ross, A. A. (2008). *Handbook of biometrics.* New York, NY: Springer.

Jain, A. K., & Ross, A. (2004). Multibiometric systems. *Communications of the ACM. Special Issue on Multimodal Interfaces, 47*(1), 34–40.

Jamshidi, M. (2008). System of systems engineering – New challenges for the 21st century. *IEEE Aerospace and Electronic Systems Magazine, 23*(5), 4–19.

Jansen, W. (2010). *Directions in security metrics research.* Darby, PA: DIANE Publishing Company.

Johnston, A. C., & Hale, R. (2009). Improved security through information security governance. *Communications of the ACM, 52,* 126–129.

Jones, K., Bejtlich, R., & Rose, C. (2005). *Real digital forensics: Computer security and incident response.* Addison-Wesley Professional.

Keane, A. (2008). *The modern law of evidence* (6th ed.). Oxford University Press.

Keizer, G. (2007). *Symantec false positive cripples thousands of Chinese PCs.* Retrieved 3 March, 2010, from http://www.computerworld.com/action/article.do?command=viewArticleBasic&articl-eId=9019958&intsrc=hm_list.

Kent, A. (2008). A business model for information security. *Information Systems Control Journal, 3.*

Khan, A., Wiil, U. K., & Memon, N. (2010, 20-20 May). *Digital forensics and crime investigation: Legal issues in prosecution at national level.* Paper presented at the Fifth IEEE International Workshop on Systematic Approaches to Digital Forensic Engineering.

Kirby, M. (1999). *International dimensions of cyberspace law.* Paris, France: United Nations Educational, Scientific and Cultural Organization (UNESCO).

Knapp, K. J., Morris, R. F., Marshall, T. E., & Byrd, T. A. (2009). Information security policy: An organizational-level process model. *Computers & Security, 28,* 493–508.

Koelman, K. J. (2001). *The protection of technological measures vs. the copyright limitations.* Paper presented at the ALAI Congress Adjuncts and Alternatives for Copyright, New York, NY. Retrieved August 25, 2011, from http://www.ivir.nl/publicaties/alaiNY.html

Koelman, K., & Helberger, N. (1998). *Protection of technological measures,* (pp. 8-12, 30). IViR Publications. Retrieved August 25, 2011, from http://www.ivir.nl/publicaties/koelman/technical-pdf

Kolondisky, J. M., Vermont, B., Hogarth, M. J., & Hilgert, M. A. (2004). The adoption of electronic banking technologies by US consumers. *International Journal of Bank Marketing, 22*(4), 238–259.

Kondabagil, J. (2007). *Risk management in electronic banking: Concepts and best practices.* Wiley Finance.

Kosutic, D. (2010). *Problems with defining the scope in ISO 27001.* Retrieved August 12, 2011, from http://blog.iso27001standard.com/2010/06/29/problems-with-defining-the-scope-in-iso-27001/

Kouns, J., & Minoli, D. (2010). *Information technology risk management in enterprise environments: A review of industry practices and a practical guide to risk management teams.* Wiley.

Kritzinger, E., & von Solms, S. H. (2006). E-learning: Incorporating information security governance. *Issues in Informing Science and Information Technology, 3,* 319–325.

Kruse, W., & Heiser, J. (2001). *Computer forensics: Incident response essentials* (1st ed.). Addison-Wesley Professional.

Lee, L., Berger, T., & Aviczer, E. (1996). Reliable on-line human signature verification systems. *IEEE Transactions on Pattern Analysis and Machine Intelligence, 18*(6), 643–647.

Ligaarden, O. S., Refsdal, A., & Stølen, K. (2012). *Using indicators to monitor security risk in systems of systems: How to capture and measure the impact of service dependencies on the security of provided services* (Tech. Rep.). Oslo, Norway: SINTEF. (SINTEF A22301)

Lipovatz, D., Stenos, F., & Vaka, A. (1999). Implementation of ISO 9000 quality systems in Greek enterprises. *International Journal of Quality & Reliability Management, 16*(6), 534–551.

Li, S. Z., & Jain, A. K. (Eds.). (2005). *Handbook of face recognition.* Springer-Verlag.

Lloyd, I. J. (2004). *Information technology law.* Oxford, UK: Oxford University Press.

Lomas, E. (2010). Information governance: Information security and access within a UK context. *Records Management Journal, 20*(2), 182–198.

Long, X., Qi, Y., & Qianmu, L. (2008). Information security risk assessment based on analytic hierarchy process and fuzzy comprehensive. In *Proceedings of the International Conference on Risk Management& Engineering Management,* (pp. 404-409).

Louwers, E. J., & Chow, S. T. (2009). *International computer law. A practical guide to international information technology law.* New York, NY: Bender.

Lund, M. S., Solhaug, B., & Stølen, K. (2010). *Model-driven risk analysis: The CORAS approach* (1st ed.). Berlin, Germany: Springer-Verlag.

Luo, L. (2005). *Legal protection of technological measures. A comparative study of US, European and Chinese anti-circumvention rules.* Hauser Global Law School Program, working paper 08/05. Retrieved August 25, 2011, from http://www.nyulawglobal.org

Luthy, D., & Forcht, K. (2006). Laws and regulations affecting information management and frameworks for assessing compliance. *Information Management & Computer Security, 14*(2), 155–166.

Lysemose, T., Mahler, T., Solhaug, B., Bing, J., Elgesem, D., & Stølen, K. (2007). *ENFORCE conceptual framework* (Tech. Rep.). Oslo, Norway: SINTEF. (SINTEF A1209)

Mahncke, R. J., McDermid, D. C., & Williams, P. A. H. (2009). Measuring information security governance within general medical practice. *Proceedings of the 7th Australian Information Security Management Conference.*

Maio, D., Maltoni, D., Cappelli, R., Wayman, J. L., & Jain, A. K. (2004). FVC2004: Third fingerprint verification competition. In *Proceedings of International Conference on Biometric Authentication (ICBA)*, (pp. 1–7). Hong Kong, China, July 2004.

Maltoni, D., Maoi, D., Jain, A. K., & Prabhakar, S. (2009). *Handbook of fingerprint recognition*. New York, NY: Springer.

Matsumoto, T., Matsumoto, H., Yamada, K., & Hoshino, S. (2002). Impact of artificial gummy fingers on fingerprint systems. In *Optical Security and Counterfeit Deterrence Techniques IV, Proceedings of SPIE*, volume 4677, (pp. 275–289). San Jose, USA, January 2002.

Mellado, D., Blanco, C., Sanchez, L. E., & Fernandez-Medina, E. (2010). A systematic review of security requirements engineering. *Computer Standards & Interfaces*, *32*, 153–165.

Minero, G. (2012). Reflexiones acerca de la protección jurídica de las páginas web y la posible aplicación de la tutela de las bases de datos. *Revista de Propiedad Intelectual, 39*.

Minero, G. (2011). Protección jurídica de las bases de datos: Estudio de la aplicación de la Directiva 96/9/CE tres lustros después de su aprobación y comentario a la primera evaluación realizada por la Comisión Europea en 2005. *Revista de Propiedad Intelectual, 37*, 13–101.

Monks, R. A. G., & Minow, N. (2004). *Corporate governance* (3rd ed.). Malden, MA: Blackwell.

Monrose, F., & Rubin, A. (1997). Authentication via keystroke dynamics. In *Proceedings of Fourth ACM Conference on Computer and Communications Security*, (pp. 48–56). Zurich, Switzerland, April 1997.

Moreira, E., Martimiano, L. A. F., Brandao, A. J., & Bernardes, M. C. (2008). Ontologies for information security management and governance. *Information Management & Computer Security*, *16*(2), 150–165.

Moulton, R., & Coles, R. S. (2003). Applying information security governance. *Computers & Security*, *22*(7), 580–584.

MSNBC. (2010). Massive bank security breach uncovered in New Jersey. Retrieved July 20, 2011, from http://www.msnbc.msn.com/id/3303539

Nalwa, V. S. (1997). Automatic on-line signature verification. *Proceedings of the IEEE*, *85*(2), 215–239.

National Institute of Standards and Technology (NIST). (2011). *Special publication 800-126 Rev. 1: The technical specification for the security content automation protocol (SCAP): SCAP Version 1.1*. February. Retrieved July 20, 2011, from http://csrc.nist.gov/publications/nistpubs/800-126-rev1/SP800-126r1.pdf/

Negin, M., Chmielewski, T. A., Salganicoff, M., Camus, T. A., Seelan, U. M. C., Venetianer, P. L., & Zhang, G. G. (2000). An iris biometric system for public and personal use. *IEEE Computer*, *33*(2), 70–75.

NIST Special Publication 800-39. (2011). *Managing information security risk organization, mission, and information system view*. Retrieved July 20, 2011, from http://csrc.nist.gov/publications/nistpubs/800-39/SP800-39-final.pdf

Nsouli, S. M., & Schaechter, A. (2002). Challenges of the E-banking revolution. *International Monetary Fund: Finance & Development*, *39*(3). Retrieved July 20, 2011, from http://www.imf.org/external/pubs/ft/fandd/2002/09/nsouli.htm

O'Gorman, L. (2002). Seven issues with human authentication technologies. In *Proceedings of Workshop on Automatic Identification Advanced Technologies* (AutoID), (pp. 185–186). Tarrytown, USA, March 2002.

OCTAVE. (2003). *Operationally critical threat, asset, and vulnerability evaluation*. Retrieved July 20, 2011, from http://www.cert.org/octave/approach_intro.pdf, Organization for Economic Co-operation (OECD). (2004). *Principles of corporate governance*. Retrieved July 20, 2011, from http://www.oecd.org/dataoecd/32/18/31557724.pdf

Office of the Under Secretary of Defense for Acquisition, Technology, and Logistics. (2002). *SoS and FoS FAQ*. Retrieved February 9, 2012, from http://www.acq.osd.mil/dpap/Docs/FAQs -- SoS & FoS.doc

OGC. (2006). *Service delivery: Best practice*. itSMF.

OGC. (2006). *Service Soport: Best practice*. itSMF.

OGC. (2007). *Continual service improvement. Office of Government Commerce*. TSO.

OGC. (2007). *ITIL: The official introduction to the ITIL service lifecycle.* London, UK: Office of Government Commerce, TSO.

OGC. (2007). *Service design. Office of Government Commerce.* TSO.

OGC. (2007). *Service Operation. Office of Government Commerce.* TSO.

OGC. (2007). *Service strategy. Office of Government Commerce.* TSO.

OGC. (2007). *Service transition. Office of Government Commerce.* TSO.

OGC. (2008). *Best management practice: ITIL V3 and ISO/IEC 20000. Office of Government Commerce.* TSO.

OGC. (2009). *English-ITIL V3 qualification scheme brochure.* Retrieved from http://www.itil-officialsite.com/nmsruntime/saveasdialog.aspx

OMG (Object Management Group). (2004). *Unified modeling language specification, Version 2.0.*

Ozkan, S., & Karabacak, B. (2010). Collaborative risk method for information security management practices: A case context within Turkey. *International Journal of Information Management, 30,* 567–572.

Palmer, G. (2001). *A road map for digital forensic research report from the First Digital Forensic Research Workshop* (DFRWS). Utica, New York.

Park, H., Kim, S., & Lee, H. J. (2006). General drawing of the integrated framework for security governance. *Lecture Notes in Computer Science, 4251,* 1234–1241.

Pasquinucci, A. (2007). Security, risk analysis and governance: A practical approach. *Computer Fraud & Security, 7,* 12–14.

Pathak, J. (2005). *Information technology auditing.* Berlin, Germany: Springer.

Paul, N. (2008). *Disk-level behavioral malware detection. Doctor of Philosophy.* University of Virginia.

PCI. (2010). *About the PCI data security standard* (PCI DSS). Retrieved July 20, 2011, from https://www.pcisecuritystandards.org/security_standards/pci_dss.shtml

Peltier, T. (2004). Risk analysis and risk management. *Information Systems Security, 13*(4), 44–56.

Phillips, P. J., Grother, P., Micheals, R. J., Blackburn, D. M., Tabassi, E., & Bone, J. M. (2003). *FRVT2002: Overview and SUMMARY.* Retrieved from http://www.frvt.org/FRVT2002

Poore, R. S. (2005). Information security governance. *EDPACS, 33*(5), 1–8.

Posthumus, S., & Solms, R. v. (2004). A framework for the governance of information security. *Computers & Security, 23,* 638–646.

Posthumus, S., & Solms, R. v. (2006). *A responsibility framework for information security.* International Federation for Information Processing.

Prabhakar, S., Pankanti, S., & Jain, A. K. (2003). Biometric recognition: Security and privacy concerns. *IEEE Security and Privacy Magazine, 1*(2), 33–42.

Pretorius, E., & Solms, B. (2004). Information security governance using ISO 17799 and COBIT. *Integrity and Internal Control in Information Systems, 6*(140), 107–113.

Privacy Working Group. (1995). *Information infrastructure task force, privacy and the national information infrastructure: Principles for providing and using personal information.* Retrieved August 25, 2011, from http://www.ntia.doc.gov/legacy/ntiahome/privwhitepaper.html

Przybocki, M., & Martin, A. (2004). NIST speaker recognition evaluation chronicles. In *Odyssey: The Speaker and Language Recognition Workshop,* (pp. 12–22). Toledo, Spain, May 2004.

Pulkkinen, M., & Hirvonen, A. P. (2005). Organizational processes in ICT management and evaluation. Experiences with large organizations. In D. Remenyi (Ed.), *Proceedings 12th European Conference on Information Technology Evaluation,* Turku, Finland, 29-30 September 2005, Trinity College Dublin, Ireland. ISBN: 1-905305-08-7

Putte, T., & Keuning, J. (2000). Biometrical fingerprint recognition: Don't get your fingers burned. In *Proceedings of IFIP TC8/WG8.8 Fourth Working Conference on Smart Card Research and Advanced Applications,* (pp. 289–303).

Rao, H. R., Gupta, M., & Upadhyaya, S. J. (2007). *Managing information assurance in financial services*. Hershey, PA: IGI Publishing.

Rastogi, R., & Solms, R. v. (2006). Information security governance - A re-definition. *International Federation for Information Processing, 193*, 223–236.

Rastogi, R., & Von Solms, R. (2006). *Information security governance a re-definition. International Federation for Information Processing, 193*. Boston, MA: Springer.

Ratha, N. K., Connell, J. H., & Bolle, R. M. (2001). An analysis of minutiae matching strength. In *Proceedings of Third International Conference on Audio- and Video-Based Biometric Person Authentication* (AVBPA), (pp. 223–228). Halmstad, Sweden, June 2001.

Rathgeber, P., Ludovica, D., & Solis, V. (2009). *White paper: An intention based malware attack prevention system*. Ikona

RCFL. (2007). *Annual report for fiscal year 2007*. National program office annual report FY08.

RCFL. (2008). *Annual report for fiscal year 2008*. National program office annual report FY08.

Refsdal, A., & Stølen, K. (2009). Employing key indicators to provide a dynamic risk picture with a notion of confidence. In *Proceedings of Third IFIP WG 11.11 International Conference (IFIPTM'09)* (pp. 215–233). Berlin, Germany: Springer-Verlag.

Reichman, J. H., & Samuelson, P. (1997). Intellectual property rights in data? *Vanderbilt Law Review, 50*, 132–134.

Reid, P. (2003). *Biometrics for network security*. Prentice Hall PTR.

Reinbothe, J. (1992). Der Schutz des Urheberrechts und der Leistungsschutzrechte im Abkommensentwurf GATT/TRIPS. *GRUR International, 1992*, 709.

Reith, M., Carr, C., & Gunsch, G. (2002). An examination of digital forensic models. *International Journal of Digital Evidence, 1*(4), 1–12.

Reserve Bank of India. (2011). *Working group on information security, electronic banking, technology risk management and cyber frauds*. Retrieved June 20, 2011, from http://www.rbi.org.in/scripts/PublicationReportDetails.aspx?UrlPage=&ID=609

Ridley, G., Young, J., & Carol, P. (2004). COBIT and its utilization: A framework from the literature. *Proceedings of the 37th Hawaii International Conference on System Sciences – 2004*. New York, NY: IEEE.

Riley, J., Dampier, D., & Vaughn, R. (2008). Time analysis of hard drive imaging tools. In Ray, I., & Shenoi, S. (Eds.), *IFIP International Federation for Information Processing* (Vol. 285, pp. 335–344). Boston, MA: Springer.

Rogers, E. M. (1962). *Diffusion of innovations*. New York, NY: The Free Press.

Ross, A. A., Nandakumar, K., & Jain, A. K. (2006). *Handbook of multibiometrics*. New York, NY: Springer.

Rowlingson, R. (2004). A ten step process for forensic readiness. *International Journal of Digital Evidence, 2*(3), 1–28.

RSA. (2011). *The current state of cybercrime and what to expect in 2011*. RSA 2011 cybercrime trends report.

Rugina, A., Kanoun, K., & Kaâniche, M. (2007). A system dependability modeling framework using AADL and GSPNs. In de Lemos, R., Gacek, C., & Romanovsky, A. (Eds.), *Architecting Dependable Systems IV* (pp. 14–38). Berlin, Germany: Springer-Verlag.

Sage, A. (2003). Conflict and risk management in complex system of systems issues. In *Proceedings of 2003 IEEE International Conference on Systems, Man and Cybernetics* (pp. 3296–3301). Piscataway, NJ: IEEE.

Saint-Gemain, R. (2005). Information security management best practice based on ISO/IEC 17799. *Information Management Journal, 39*(4), 60–65.

Samangooei, S., Nixon, M., & Guo, B. (2008). The use of semantic human description as a soft biometric. In *Proceedings of BTAS*, 2008.

Samuelson, P. (2003). Mapping the digital public domain: Treats and opportunities. *Law & Contemporary Problems, 66*, 147-172. Retrieved August 25, 2011, from http://www.law.berkeley.edu/phpprograms/faculty/facultyPubsPDF.php?facID=346&pubID=131

Samuelson, P. (2000). Privacy as intellectual property? *Stanford Law Review, 52*, 1125–1173.

SANS Institute. (2003). *Using a capability maturity model to derive security requirements*. Retrieved July 20, 2011, from http://www.sans.org/reading_room/whitepapers/bestprac/capability-maturity-model-derive-security-requirements_1005

Sarvanan, D., & Kohli, R. (2000). *The IT payoff: Measuring the business value of information technology investment*. New Jersey: Prentice Hall.

Scanlon, M., & Kechadi, M.-T. (2010). Online acquisition of digital forensic evidence. In Goel, S. (Ed.), *Digital forensics and cyber crime (Vol. 31*, pp. 122–131). Berlin, Germany: Springer.

Schmidt, A.-D., Schmidt, H.-G., Batyuk, L., Clausen, J. H., Camtepe, S. A., Albayrak, S., & Yildizli, C. (2009). *Smartphone malware evolution revisited: Android next target?* Paper presented at the Malicious and Unwanted Software (MALWARE), 2009 4th International Conference on Montreal, QC.

Schmidt, A.-D., & Albayrak, S. (2008). *Malicious software for smartphones*. Berlin, Germany: DAI-Labor der Technischen Universität Berlin.

SEI. (2009). *CMMI for services process area quick reference from CMMI-SVC, v1.2*. (SEI, Ed.) Retrieved from www.sei.cmu.edu/

SEI. (2010). *CMMI for services*, vol. 1.3. Retrieved from http://www.sei.cmu.edu/library/abstracts/reports/10tr034.cfm

Shah, M. H., & Siddiqui, F. A. (2006). Organisational critical success factors in adoption of e-banking at the Woolwich bank. *International Journal of Information Management, 26*, 442–456.

Shah, M., & Clarke, S. (2009). *E-banking management: Issues, solutions, and strategies*. Hershey, PA: IGI Publishing.

Shaw, T. J. (2011). *Information security and privacy: A practical guide for global executives, lawyers and technologists*. USA: American Bar Association, Section of Science & Technology.

Shin, Y.-D. (2008, 2-4 Sep). *New digital forensics investigation procedure model*. Paper presented at the Networked Computing and Advanced Information Management, 2008. NCM '08. Fourth International Conference on Gyeongju

Simonsson, M., & Johnson, P. (2006). Assessment of IT governance - A prioritization of COBIT. *Proceedings of the Conference on Systems Engineering Research*.

Singer, G., & Sundararajan, A. (2004). Are digital rights valuable? Theory and evidence from the e-book industry. In *Proceedings 25th International Conference on Information Systems*, Washington, DC, (pp. 533–545).

Skoudis, E., & Zeltser, L. (2003). *Malware: Fighting malicious code*. Prentice Hall PTR.

Smedinghoff, T. J. (2008A). *Information security law: The emerging standard for corporate compliance*. Ely, UK: IT Governance Publishing.

Smedinghoff, T. J. (2008B). Defining the legal standard for information security. In Chander, A., Gelman, L., & Radin, M. J. (Eds.), *Securing privacy in the internet age* (pp. 15–40). Stanford, CA: Stanford University Press.

Sohal, A. S., & Fitzpatrick, P. (2002). IT governance and management in large Australian organizations. *International Journal of Production Economics, 75*(1/2), 97–112.

Soliman, K. (2006). Managing information in the digital economy: Issues & solutions. In *Proceedings of the 6th International Business Information Management Association (IBIMA) Conference* 19-21 June 2006, Bonn, Germany, (pp. 227- 232).

Solms, B. v. (2005). Information security governance: COBIT or ISO 17799 or both? *Computers & Security, 24*, 99–104.

Solms, R. v., & Solms, S. H. B. v. (2006). Information security governance: A model based on the direct–control cycle. *Computers & Security, 25*, 408–412.

Solms, S. H., & von Solms, R. (2009). *Information security governance*. Springer.

Son, S., Weitzel, T., & Laurent, F. (2005). Designing a process-oriented framework for IT performance management systems. *The Electronic Journal Information Systems Evaluation, 8*(3), 219–228.

Southard, P. B., & Siau, K. (2004). A survey of online e-banking retail initiatives. *Communications of the ACM, 47*(10).

Stallings, W. (2010). *Network security essentials applications and standards* (4th ed.). Prentice Hall.

Stang, D. (2011). *Detection errors and scanner performance.* Retrieved 1 March, 2011, from http://www.upublish.info

Stapleton, J. (1999). DSDM: Dynamic systems development method. *TOOLS '99 Proceedings of the Technology of Object-Oriented Languages and Systems.* Washington, DC: IEEE Computer Society.

Stibbe, M. (2005). E-government security. *Infosecurity Today, 2*, 8–10.

Stolfo, S., Wang, K., & Li, W.-J. (2007). Towards stealthy malware detection. *Malware Detection, 27*, 231–249.

Street, P. A., & Fernie, J. M. (1993). Costs, drawbacks and benefits : BS 5750. *Training for Quality, 1*(1), 21–24.

Studer, R., Benjamins, V. R., & Fensel, D. (1998). Knowledge engineering: Principles and methods. *IEEE Transactions on Data and Knowledge Engineering, 25*, 161–197.

Svendsen, N. K. (2008). *Interdependencies in critical infrastructures: A qualitative approach to model physical, logical, and geographical interdependencies.* Doctoral dissertation, University of Oslo, Oslo. (In series of dissertations submitted to the Faculty of Mathematics and Natural Sciences, University of Oslo, No. 748)

Symantec Enterprise Security. (2002). *W32.Appix.Worm Symantec security response threat writeups.*

Szor, P. (2005). *The art of computer virus research and defense.* Addison-Wesley Professional.

Tan, T. C. C., Ruighaver, A. B., & Ahmad, A. (2010). Information security governance: When compliance becomes more important than security. In *Proceedings of the 25th IFIP TC 11 International Information Security Conference,* (pp. 55–67).

Tanampasidis, G. (2008). A comprehensive method for assessment of operational risk in e-banking. *Information Systems Control Journal, 4.*

Task Force on Financial Integrity and Economic Development. (2011). *Response to FATF consultation paper: Review of the standards.* Preparation for the 4th Round of Mutual Evaluations. Retrieved July 20, 2011, from http://www.financialtaskforce.org/wpcontent/uploads/2011/02/Task_Force_on_Financial_Integrity_and_Economic_Development_Response_to_FATF_Consultation_Paper.pdf.pdf

The Institute of Chartered Accountant of India. (n.d.). *Auditing.* Retrieved from www.icai.org

Trompeter, C. M., & Eloff, J. H. P. (2001). A framework for the implementation of socio-ethical controls in information security. *Computers & Security, 20*(5), 384–391.

Tsiotras, G., & Gotzamani, K. (1996). ISO 9000 as an entry key to TQM: The case of the Greek industry. *International Journal of Quality & Reliability Management, 13*(14), 64–76.

Tsoumas, V., & Tryfonas, T. (2004). From risk analysis to effective security management: Towards an automated approach. *Information Management & Computer Security, 12*(1), 91–101.

Tudor, A. (2006). *Worm/Letum.A – Worm.* Retrieved 3 June, 2011, from http://www.avira.ro/en/threats/section/details/id_vir/1990/worm_letum.a.html

Tudor, J. K. (2000). *Information security architecture—An integrated approach to security in an organization.* Boca Raton, FL: Auerbach.

Tuttle, B., & Vandervelde, S. D. (2007). An empirical examination of COBIT as an internal control framework for information technology. *International Journal of Accounting Information Systems, 8*(4), 240–263.

United Kingdom Information Commissioner Office. (2006). *A surveillance society report.* Retrieved August 25, 2011, from http://news.bbc.co.uk/1/hi/uk_politics/6260153.stm

US Department of Commerce. (2006). *NIST (Draft) SP 800-80: Guide for developing performance metrics for information security.*

US Department of Health and Human Services. (1996). *Health Insurance Portability and Accountability Act* (HIPAA), 1996. Retrieved from http://www.hhs.gov/ocr/privacy

US Securities Exchanges Commission. (2004). *Performance and accountability report*. Retrieved from www.sec.gov/about/secpar.shtml

US Security and Exchange Commission. (2007). *Spotlight on Sarbanes-Oxley rulemaking and reports*. Retrieved August 25, 2011, from http://www.sec.gov/spotlight/sarbanes-oxley.htm

Vacca, J. (2005). *Computer forensics: Computer crime scene investigation* (2nd ed.). Charles River Media.

Vachirapornpuk, S., & Broderick, A. J. (2002). Service quality in internet banking: The importance of customer role. *Marketing Intelligence & Planning, 20*(6), 327–335.

Van Compel, S., Guibault, L., Helberger, N., & Hugenholtz, P. B. (2009). *Harmonizing European copyright law. The challenges of better lawmaking. Alphen aan den Rijn*. The Netherlands: Kluwer Law International.

Van Der, P. (2009). *ASL 2: A framework for application management*. Zaltbommel, The Netherlands: Van Haren Publishing.

Van Grembergen, W. a. (2009). *Enterprise governance of IT: Achieving strategic alignment and value*. Springer.

Vassil, R. (2009). Hashing and data fingerprinting in digital forensics. *Computing in Science & Engineering, 7*, 49–55.

Venkatraman, S. (2009). *Autonomic context-dependent architecture for malware detection*. Paper presented at the e-Tech 2009, International Conference on e-Technology, Singapore.

Venkatraman, S. (2010). *Self-learning framework for intrusion detection*. Paper presented at the The International Congress on Computer Applications and Computational Science, Singapore.

Venkatraman, S. (2011). A framework for ICT security policy management. In Adomi, E. (Ed.), *Frameworks for ICT policy: Government, social and legal issues* (pp. 1–14). Hershey, PA: IGI Global.

Vijayan, J. (2010). *Five indicted in cybertheft of city's bank account*. Retrieved July 20, 2011, from http://www.computerworld.com/s/article/9177409/Five_indicted_in_cybertheft_of_city_s_bank_accounts

Villarroel, R., Fernandez-Medina, E., & Mellado, D. (2005). Secure information systems development – A survey and comparison. *Computers & Security, 24*, 308–321.

Von Lewinski, S. (2008). *International copyright law and policy*. Oxford, UK: Oxford University Press.

Von Solms, S. H. (2005). Information security governance. Compliance management vs operational management. *Computers & Security, 24*(6), 443–447.

Waller, A., & Craddock, R. (2011). Managing runtime re-engineering of a system-of-systems for cyber security. In *Proceedings of 6th International Conference on System of Systems Engineering (SoSE'11)* (pp. 13–18). Piscataway, NJ: IEEE.

Walter, M. M., & Von Lewinski, S. (Eds.). (2010). *European copyright law. A commentary*. Oxford, UK: Oxford University Press.

Wayman, J. L., Jain, A. K., Maltoni, D., & Maio, D. (Eds.). (2005). *Biometric systems: Technology, design and performance evaluation*. Springer.

Webb, P., Pollard, C., & Ridley, G. (2006). Attempting to define IT governance: Wisdom or folly? *Proceedings of the 39th Hawaii International Conference on System Sciences*.

Weill, P., & Ross, J. W. (2004). *IT governance: How top performers manage IT decision rights for superior results*. Boston, MA: Harvard Business School Press.

Westby, J. R. (Ed.). (2004A). *International Guide to Privacy*. American Bar Association, Section of Science & Technology.

Westby, J. R. (Ed.). (2004B). *International guide to cyber security*. American Bar Association, Section of Science & Technology.

Westby, J. R. (Ed.). (2005). *Roadmap to an enterprise security program*. American Bar Association, Section of Science & Technology.

Williams, P. (2006, September 19). A helping hand with IT governance. Computer Weekly, p. 26. Retrieved September 3, 2010, from http://www.computerweekly.com/Articles/2006/09/19/218517/a-helping-hand-with-it-governance.htm

Williams, P. (2001). Information security governance. *Information Security Technical Report, 6*(3), 60–70.

Wilson, C., Hicklin, A. R., Bone, M., Korves, H., Grother, P., & Ulery, B. … Watson, C. (2004). *Fingerprint vendor technology evaluation 2003: Summary of results and analysis report*. NIST Technical Report NISTIR 7123, National Institute of Standards and Technology, June 2004.

Wimmer, M., & Bredow, B. v. (2002). A holistic approach for providing security solutions in e-government. *Proceedings of the 35th Hawaii International Conference on System Sciences*.

Yip, F. (2006). *Corporate security compliance in a heterogeneous environment.*

Yip, F. (2011). *A framework for semantic enabled applications: A case study in regulatory compliance.* Ph D Thesis, School of Computer Science and Engineering, University of New South Wales, Sydney.

Zadeh, L. (1965). Fuzzy sets. *Information and Control, 8*, 338–353.

Zhang, I. X. (2005, February). *Economic consequences of the Sarbanes-Oxley Act of 2002.*

Zhang, D., Kong, A. W.-K., You, J., & Wong, M. (2003). Online palmprint identification. *IEEE Transactions on Pattern Analysis and Machine Intelligence, 25*(9), 1041–1050.

About the Contributors

Daniel Mellado holds a PhD and MSc in Computer Science from the Castilla- La Mancha University (Spain) and holds a degree in Computer Science from the Autonomous University of Madrid (Spain), and he is Certified Information System Auditor by ISACA (Information System Audit and Control Association). He is Assistant Professor of the Department of Information Technologies and Systems at the Rey Juan Carlos University (Spain). He participates at the GSyA research group of the Department of Information Technologies and Systems at the Castilla- La Mancha University. He is civil servant at the Spanish Tax Agency (in Madrid, Spain), where he works as IT Auditor Manager. His research activities are security governance, security requirements engineering, security in cloud computing, security in information systems, secure software process improvement and auditory, quality, and product lines. He has several dozens of papers in national and international conferences, journals, and magazines on these subjects and co-author of several chapter books. He belongs to various professional and research associations (ASIA, ISACA, ASTIC, ACTICA, etc.).

Luis Enrique Sánchez is PhD and MsC in Computer Science and is an Assistant Professor at the Escuela Superior de Informática of the Universidad de Castilla- La Mancha in Ciudad Real (Spain) (Computer Science Department, University of Castilla La Mancha, Ciudad Real, Spain), MSc in Information Systems Audit from the Polytechnic University of Madrid, and Certified Information System Auditor by ISACA. He is the Director of Professional Services and R&D departments of the company Sicaman Nuevas Tecnologías S.L. COIICLM board or committee member and responsible for the professional services committee. His research activities are management security system, security metrics, data mining, data cleaning, and business intelligence. He participates in the GSyA research group of the Department of Computer Science at the University of Castilla- LaMancha, in Ciudad Real (Spain). He belongs to various professional and research associations (COIICLM, ATI, ASIA, ISACA, eSEC, INTECO, etc.).

Eduardo Fernández-Medina is PhD and MSc in Computer Science. He is Associate Professor at the Escuela Superior de Informática of the Universidad de Castilla- La Mancha at Ciudad Real (Spain). His research activities are security requirements, security in databases, data warehouses, web services and information systems, and also in security metrics. He is the co-editor of several books and chapter books on these subjects, and has several dozens of papers in national and international conferences. He leads the GSyA research group of the Department of Information Technologies and Systems at the University of Castilla- La Mancha, in Ciudad Real (Spain). He belongs to various professional and research associations (ATI, AEC, AENOR, IFIP, WG11.3, etc.).

Mario Piattini is MSc and PhD in Computer Science from the Politechnical University of Madrid. He is certified information system auditor by ISACA (Information System Audit and Control Association). He is Associate Professor at the Escuela Superior de Informática of the Castilla- La Mancha University (Spain). He is author of several books and papers on databases, security, software engineering, and information systems. He leads the ALARCOS research group of the Department of Information Technologies and Systems at the University of Castilla- La Mancha, in Ciudad Real (Spain). His research interests are: advanced database design, database quality, software metrics, object-oriented metrics, and software maintenance.

* * *

Hisham M. Abdelsalam holds a Master of Science and a Ph.D. in Mechanical Engineering (Old Dominion University, Norfolk, Virginia, USA). He obtained his Bachelor degree with honors in Mechanical Engineering from Cairo University (Cairo, Egypt). Dr. Abdelsalam is an Associate Professor in the Operations Research and Decision Support Department, Faculty of Computers and Information, Cairo University. In 2009, Dr. Abdelsalam was appointed as the Director of the Decision Support and Future Studies Center in Cairo University. During the past four years, Dr. Abdelsalam has led several consultancy and research projects and published eight scholarly articles on e-government.

Moutaz Alazab is a PhD research student at the Deakin University in the school of Information technology, his PhD thesis title is "Prevention and Detection Mobile Malware Based on Behavioural Features." He received his Bachelor degree (Hons) in Computer Engineering from Al-Balqa Applied University in 2009. He worked as a System and Network Administrator for different firms in Jordan and Australia. His research interests are: mobile malware, computer malware, mobile digital forensic, reverse engineer, mobile ad-hoc network, and host and network intrusion detection. He published research papers in difference well-known international conference and journals

Mamoun Alazab is a Research Assistant (Cyber Security) at the Regulatory Institutions Network, Australian National University (ANU), College of Asia and the Pacific, in the ARC Centre of Excellence in Policing and Security (CEPS). He obtained his Doctor of Philosophy degree (PhD) from the School of Science, Information Technology and Engineering, University of Ballarat, Australia, with the thesis title "Forensic Identification and Detection of Hidden and Obfuscated Malware," while employed as a research assistant at the Internet Commerce Security Laboratory (ICSL). His Master thesis from Al-Balqa Applied University was in the area of Cyber Security and Networking titled "Cyber security Analysis Using Attack Countermeasure Trees for Information Assurance Analysis," and his higher diploma thesis was titled "Network Security Using Intelligent Packet Analysis." Alazab also earned his Bachelor's degree in Computer Science. He is a Computer Security Researcher & Practitioner, has industry and academic experience, teaching and researching in the areas of Computer Security. He has authored and co-authored more than 30 peer-reviewed papers in high prestigious journals and well known international conferences.

Magdalena Arcilla holds a PhD in Computer Science. She is Assistant Professor in the Languages & Computer Science Department of the UNED (Spanish Open University). She is teaching in the area of Software Engineering. She has also worked in the Computer Science Department of the Carlos III University of Madrid and she has 8 years of experience as software developer at CustomWare Company. She is author of several international papers related to the software engineering area. She is author of a book in the software engineering topics. She holds the ITIL® v2 and v3 Foundation certificates.

Chatzipoulidis Aristeidis holds a Bachelor's degree in Marketing from the Alexander Technological Educational Institute of Thessaloniki. He has a Master of Science degree in International Marketing from the University of Strathclyde, Scotland and he is currently a Doctoral candidate at the department of Applied Informatics, University of Macedonia. Aristeidis has published in several conference proceedings and main research interests include consumer behavior in electronic banking, international marketing, corporate social responsibility, IS risk management methods, and IS governance. He is currently an academic Teaching Assistant in the Marketing Department in Alexander Technological Educational Institute of Thessaloniki.

Jose A. Calvo-Manzano holds a PhD in Computer Science. He is an Assistant Professor in the Facultad de Informática at the Universidad Politécnica de Madrid. He is teaching in the area of Software Engineering, specifically in the area of software process management and improvement. He has participated in more than 20 research projects (European, Spanish Public Administration, as well as with private enterprises). He is author of more than 50 international papers. He is author of books related to software process improvement and software engineering topics also. He is the Head of the "Cátedra for Software Process Improvement for Spain and Latin American Region," where he has been a member of the team that has translated CMMI-DEV v1.2 and v1.3 to Spanish. He also holds the ITIL® v2 and v3 Foundation, and CMDB Certification.

Mercedes de la Cámara is a Professor in the School of Computer Science at the Universidad Politécnica de Madrid. She is teaching in the area of Languages and Information Systems, specifically in the area of IT services management, and quality and security in computing. She holds the ITIL® and CMDB Foundation certificates. She has participated in various ITSM events as a member of the organizing committee and presenting research papers. She has also participated in several European Social Fund projects teaching security and ITSM. She is member of the "Cátedra for Software Process Improvement for Spain and Latin American Region."

B.B.Chakrabarti (Ph. D in Economics, Jadavpur University, Kolkata, India, AICWA, Indian Institute of Cost and Works Accountants of India, MBA (specialization in Finance) Indian Institute of Management Calcutta, India) is a Professor in Finance and Control Group. He has over 20 years of industrial experience and had wide range of consulting experience in organizations like United Nations – World Food Programme, Centre for Development and Environment Policy, McNally Bharat Engineering Company Limited, National Test House, Ministry of Consumer Affairs, Govt. of India, Indian Institute of Legal Metrology, Ministry of Consumer Affairs, Govt. of India, Ministry of HRD, Govt. of India, Consolidated Energy Consultants Ltd., Confederation of Indian Industries, National Mineral Development Corporation, Esab India Ltd, Damodar Valley Corporation, Ordnance Factories Board, Indian Oil Corporation Ltd, APJ Securities Ltd., Warren Tea Ltd., India Knowledge Centre, Dubai, Gas Authority of India Ltd., SAIL, Investec Services, Colombo, L & T, National Thermal Power Corporation, DONER,HSBC, ICICI Bank,

Deustche Bank, Standard Chartered Bank, ONGC, Macmillan India Ltd., et cetera. He held the position of President in number of companies including NICCO, UCO Financial Services Ltd., Keventer Agro Ltd., et cetera. He also extensively published in number of reputed national and international journals.

Ioanna Dionysiou joined University of Nicosia in October 2006 as an Assistant Professor of Computer Science. Dionysiou received her PhD from Washington State University (2006), MSc and BSc degrees from Washington State University (2000 and 1997 respectively) and Diploma degree from Higher Technical Institute (1994). Dionysiou's research focuses on formal trust models and trust management in collaborative environments. Her PhD dissertation work investigated trust requirements and challenges for large-scale infrastructures, with an exemplary infrastructure being the US Electric Power Grid. Dionysiou's PhD research was supported by three USA national organizations: NIST (National Institute of Standards and Technology), NSF (National Science Foundation), and DOE (Department of Energy). In particular, HESTIA, a configurable trust management framework devised by Dionysiou, was part of the NSF-funded project Trustworthy Cyber Infrastructure for the Power Grid (TCIP). Dr. Dionysiou has several publications on trust management and security and served in various program committees.

Haitham S. Hamza received the B.S. (Hons.) and the M.S. degree in Electronics and Communication engineerIng from Cairo University, Cairo, Egypt, in 1998 and 2002, respectively. He received the M.S. and Ph.D. degree in Computer Science from the University of Nebraska-Lincoln in 2002 and 2006, respectively. Dr. Hamza is a Fling Fellow of the University of Nebraska-Lincoln. He is currently is an Assistant Professor of Information Technology at Cairo University. Dr. Hamza has more than 50 papers published in international journals and conferences such as *IEEE/ACM Transaction on Networking, IEEE/OSA Journal of Lightwave Technology, Journal of Photonic Network Communications, IEEE Globecom, IEEE ICC*, and *Broadnets*. He is the recipient of the Best Paper Award for the Optical Networking Track in Broadnets 2005. Dr. Hamza is the author of a new book entitled "Wavelength Exchanging Switching Networks" published in 2010. His research interests include wireless and cognitive radio networks, design and analyses of photonic switches, optical interconnect architectures, and WDM networks protection algorithms.

Thedosis P. Iacovou is currently working in the insurance sector where he is a Project Manager for an ERP company wide solution. He earned his B.Sc. in Management Information Systems in Florida Atlantic University in 2003. His also spent his last two years as a Teacher Assistant (the only undergraduate TA in his college). He then received his M.Sc. from Middlesex University in Business Information Technology, where his thesis "Reinventing the Internet" awarded the first degree. Just recently, earned his MBA from University of Nicosia. Theodosis P. Iacovou is also an A+, Network+, MCP, MCSA 2003, and MCSE 2003. He truly believes that the real prize is in the journey itself and studies the biography of Steven Paul Jobs.

Angelika Kokkinaki's research interests include inter-organizational IT systems and MIS. She is an Associate Professor at the University of Nicosia and she currently serves as Associate Dean at the School of Business. She has worked as Researcher and Lecturer in USA (Northeastern University and University of Louisiana at Lafayette) and in EU (Erasmus University, The Netherlands and De Montfort University, UK). She was involved in many research and development projects in Greece and EU. She has received her Ph.D. in Computer Science from University of Southwestern Louisiana (now University of Louisiana at Lafayette -ULL) at Lafayette, LA, USA in 1995, M.Sc. in Computer Science from Northeastern University, Boston, MA, USA in 1991 and a 5-year curriculum Diploma in Computer Engineering and Informatics from Patras University in 1987. She is a Chartered Engineer (Technical Chamber of Greece, 1987) and an accredited Project Manager (MIT Professional Programs, 1998).

Skevi Magirou has earned her BSc in Computer Science from University of Nicosia in 2010. She has extensive experience with conducting surveys and analyzing survey data.

Ambuj Mahanti, D.Sc, is a Professor at the MIS group in IIM Calcutta for about three decades. He has been a UN Fellow on number of occasions and taught several years in the University of Maryland at College Park, USA. He has published widely in noted international journals and guided numerous theses on management and technology. He has also widely consulted and conducted many high-level training programs. He has served as the Dean (planning and administration) at IIM Calcutta. His current interests include heuristics, business intelligence, cloud computing, social networking, and ontology based compliance systems.

Ahmed M. Marzouk holds a Master degree in Business Administration with globalization focus from Maastricht School of Management in Netherlands in 2009. Ahmed is a Senior Technical Sales Specialist for IBM Tivoli products, specialized in service and asset management domain from 2007 till now. He has an extensive experience in consulting and implementing service management in many enterprises and Egyptian banks. Ahmed started his career as a System Programmer in General Authority of Educational Buildings for system i-Series and then he moved to work for IBM Egypt in Global Technology Services department where he was responsible for implementing all IBM solutions on system i-Series and p-Series from 2001 till 2006. During this period, he gained an extensive experience in understanding banking environment.

Gemma Minero holds degrees in Law and LLM in European Law and Intellectual Property from the University Autónoma of Madrid. Prior to joining the University Autónoma of Madrid, she practiced in some national and international law firms both in Madrid and London. From 2009 to 2011, she was a PhD student and works as a Lecturer at the University Autónoma of Madrid. She also spent time as a visitor-researcher at the Max-Planck Institute for Intellectual Property and Competition Law (Munich) in 2011. Her main interests are intellectual property law, in particular databases and computer programs.

Mathew Nicho, MBA, MIS, CEH, SAP-SA, RWSP, Ph.D., is an Assistant Professor of Information Systems at the College of Information Technology of the University of Dubai. He did his Master's (CRM software) and Doctorate (COBIT measurement) from Auckland University of Technology and was teaching there before joining Dubai University. He has presented his research on ITG to numerous international conferences in US, New Zealand and Dubai. His articles on ITG and PCI DSS has appeared in international journals namely *International Journal of Information Security and Privacy, Information Systems Audit and Control Association Journal,* and the *Bulletin of Applied Computing and Information Technology*. He has presented professional seminars to ISACA chapters in Auckland and Dubai as well as delivered keynote presentation to the PCI DSS conference. He also conducts professional course on Ethical Hacking for IT professionals.

Nandan Parameswaran (Ph.D. Computer Science, Indian Institute of Science, Bangalore, India) is a Senior Lecturer at the School of Computer Science and Engineering, University of New South Wales, Sydney, Australia. His research interests include ontology development, design of intelligent systems and multi-agent systems, event modelling and event management systems, mobile devices programming, and policy modelling. He has more than 60 publications in reputed international journals and conferences. He is currently involved in the design and implementation of dialog based agents in enterprise applications using agent technology.

Pradeep Ray is a Senior Member of the Academic staff at the University of New South Wales, Australia. He is the founder of the Asia-Pacific Ubiquitous Healthcare Research Centre (APuHC) aimed at conducting research on achieving ubiquitous healthcare using emerging technologies, such as the mobile broadband communication technologies (see www.apuhc.unsw.edu.au). His research interest in business include e-Business security & management, collaborative systems and applications, semantic interoperability, policy-based systems and ontology based agents (see www.apuhc.org/pradeep). As an active member of the Institute of Electrical and Electronic Engineers (IEEE), he has been involved in organising a number of international conferences, such as IEEE Globecom Symposia, IFIP/IEEE DSOM, APNOMS, IEEE/IEC EntNet@SUPERCOMM. Prof Ray led the IEEE Technical Committee on Enterprise Networking from 2002-2004 and helped launch international business events, such as Healthcom and Financecom. He is the Chair of the IEEE Technical Committee on eHealth (eHealthTC) and the founder of IEEE Healthcom that is now the forum of discussions for the IEEE/ITU-D/WHO initiatives on e-Health and m-Health. He has been leading a number of collaborative research projects with reputed International Research Organisations in Europe, Americas, Asia-Pacific, and Australia/NZ. Prof Ray is also leading a number of international initiatives, such as the ITU-D/IEEE Mobile eHealth Initiative for Developing Countries and the Global Longitudinal Study on the Assessment of mHealth.

Oscar Rebollo holds a MSc in Computer Science from the Alcalá de Henares University (Spain) and a degree in Telecommunications from the Polytechnic University of Madrid (Spain). He participates at the GSyA research group of the Department of Information Technologies and Systems at the Castilla- La Mancha University. He is civil servant at the IT Department of the Spanish Social Security (in Madrid, Spain). His research activities are related to the security governance and security in cloud computing. He has several papers in national and international conferences and journals. He belongs to various professional associations (ASTIC, etc).

Atle Refsdal received his PhD in Computer Science from the University of Oslo in 2008. His research interests include formal specification and analysis, as well as model-based security risk and trust analysis. Currently he works as a Researcher in SINTEF Information and Communication Technology, where he is involved in international as well as national research projects. His previous experience includes working as a knowledge engineer in Computas AS and working with industrial automation as a project engineer in Bejer Electronics AS.

Javier Sáenz is a Professor in the School of Computer Science at the Universidad Politécnica de Madrid. He is teaching in the area of Languages and Information Systems, specifically in the area of IT services management, and quality and security in computing. He holds the ITIL® and CMDB Foundation certificates. He has participated in various ITSM events as a member of the organizing committee and presenting research papers. He has also participated in several European Social Fund projects teaching security and ITSM. He is member of the "Cátedra for Software Process Improvement for Spain and Latin American Region."

Partha Saha is a Ph. D. candidate in Management Information Systems from Indian Institute of Management Calcutta, India. He has over 14 years of experience in IT Industry. He is a first-class honours graduate in Electronics and Communication Engineering from National Institute of Technology, Calicut, Kerala, India and an M.B.A. from Indian Institute of Management Calcutta, India with specialization in Finance & MIS. His research interests include RDBMS, multi- agent systems modelling, simulation, ontology development, and compliance auditing. He has hands on experience in designing client-server infrastructure, business analysis, requirements gathering, application integration, and customization. He has extensive work experience in client interaction for system study, requirements gathering and analysis and workflow analysis as well as smooth implementation and testing of the application at client location.

Luis Sánchez is a Professor in the School of Computer Science at the Universidad Politécnica de Madrid. He is teaching in the area of Languages and Information Systems, specifically in the area of IT services management, and quality and security computer. He holds the ITIL® v2 and v3 Foundation certificates. He has participated in various ITSM events as a member of the organizing committee. He is member of the "Cátedra for Software Process Improvement for Spain and Latin American Region." He was Systems Operations Manager and currently is Director of an ICT company.

Sanjay K. Singh is Associate Professor in Department of Computer Engineering at Institute of Technology, Banaras Hindu University, India. He is a certified Novel Engineer and Novel administrator. His research has been funded by UGC and AICTE. He has over 30 publications in refereed journals, book chapters, and conferences. His research interests include computational intelligence, biometrics, video authentication, pattern recognition, and machine learning. Dr. Singh is a member of IET, IEEE, ISTE, and CSI.

Olav Skjelkvåle Ligaarden received his Master's degree in Computer Science from the University of Oslo in 2007. He is currently working on his PhD at the University of Oslo and at SINTEF Information and Communication Technology. His main field of interest is assessment of risk in system of systems. In particular, he focuses on how to capture and measure the impact of service dependencies on risk to quality of services provided by systems in the system of systems. Other research interests include risk analysis and monitoring, security indicators, and dependency modeling and analysis in system of systems, trust, and security.

Ketil Stølen is Chief Scientist and Group Leader at SINTEF. Since 1998 he is Professor in Computer Science at the University of Oslo. Stølen has broad experience from basic research (4 years at Manchester University; 5 years at Munich University of Technology; 12 years at the University of Oslo) as well as applied research (1 year at the Norwegian Defense Research Establishment; 3 years at the OECD Halden Reactor Project; 10 years at SINTEF). He did his PhD at Manchester University. At Munich University of Technology his research focused on the theory of refinement and rules for compositional and modular system development – in particular, together with Manfred Broy he designed the Focus method as documented in the Focus-book published in 2001. At the OECD Halden Reactor Project he led several research activities concerned with the modeling and dependability-analysis of safety-critical systems. From 2001-03 he was the technical manager of the EU-project CORAS which had 11 partners and a total budget of more than 5 million EURO. He has recently co-authored a book on the method originating from this project. He is currently managing several major Norwegian research projects focusing on issues related to modeling, security, risk analysis, and trust.

Kargidis Theodoros is an Associate Professor at the Technological Educational Institute (TEI) of Thessaloniki, at the Department of Marketing in Greece. He holds a bachelor degree in Economics from the Department of Economics of the Aristotle University of Thessaloniki. He has a Master of Science degree in Economics from Universite Paris I Pantheon Sorbonne and a PhD from the department of Applied Informatics, University of Macedonia in E-learning. His has a numerous publications in journals and conferences.

Tsiakis Theodosios is a Lecturer in the Department of Marketing, at School of Management and Economy, of TEITHE. He belongs in the Division of Organization and Management, expert in economics and specialized in Management of Information Systems. He graduated from the department of International and European Economic and Political Studies from the University of Macedonia and received his Ph.D. in Information Security Economics from the department of Applied Informatics, of the University of Macedonia. His research interests are security economics, e-business, risk management, trust and Information Systems Management. He has several publications in scientific journals and conference proceedings.

Shrikant Tiwari received his M.Tech. degree in Computer Science and Technology from University of Mysore, India, in 2009. He is currently working toward the PhD degree at the Institute of Technology, Banaras Hindu University, Varanasi, India. His research interests include biometrics, image processing, and pattern recognition.

Sitalakshmi Venkatraman is a Senior Lecturer at the School of Science, Information Technology and Engineering, University of Ballarat, Australia. She holds a Doctoral Fellowship (PhD) from NITIE, Bombay, with the thesis title, "Efficient Parallel Algorithms for Two-Dimensional Pattern Recognition." Her prior educational qualifications include B.Sc. Mathematics from University of Madras, M.Sc. Mathematics and M.Tech. Computer Science and Engineering from Indian Institute of Technology, Madras, and M.Ed. from University of Sheffield, UK. She has about 25 years of work experience - in industry, developing turnkey projects, and in academics, teaching and researching in the areas of Information Technology & Management. Her current research interests concentrate on e-commerce and internet security. She has published about 30 research papers in internationally well-known refereed journals that include *Information Sciences, Information Management & Computer Security,* and *Journal of Artificial Intelligence in Engineering.*

Paul Watters is currently the Research Director of the Internet Commerce Security Laboratory and Associate Professor in Information Security at the University of Ballarat. He was previously Head of Data Services at the Medical Research Council's National Survey of Health and Development, and an Honorary Senior Research Fellow at University College London. He has many years of software and systems R&D experience in security, working with partners such as Google, Village Roadshow, Boeing, IBM, and the Australian Federal Police on profiling, forensics, malware and identity crime. Since 2006, he has primarily worked with major financial institutions, such as the National Australia Bank and Westpac, to defeat cybercrime. He is a Fellow of the British Computer Society and a Member of the IEEE.

Frederick Yip is a Ph. D. candidate in the University of New South Wales, Sydney, Australia. He graduated from University of New South Wales as a first-class honours graduate in software engineering in 2005. He has over 12 years of industrial experience in the IT industry and extensive consulting experience with banking and financial organizations. He was selected as a member of the Worldwide Microsoft Partner Advisory Council (PAC). His current research interests are in IT governance, compliance management, ontology reasoning, and Semantic Web applications. He has published widely in the areas of compliance management and semantic web applications. His ontology-based robust production systems are one of the earliest where ontology mapping and fuzzy reasoning techniques were incorporated to achieve semantic-based approximated reasoning.

Index